D0460910

# Style and Music

Studies in the Criticism and Theory of Music

Janet M. Levy. *Beethoven's Compositional Choices: The Two Versions of Opus 18, No. 1, First Movement.* 1982

Robert O. Gjerdingen. *A Classic Turn of Phrase: Music and the Psychology of Convention.* 1988

Lee A. Rothfarb. *Ernst Kurth as Theorist and Analyst.* 1988

Leonard B. Meyer. *Style and Music: Theory, History, and Ideology.* 1989

# Style and Music

*Theory, History, and Ideology*

Leonard B. Meyer

University of Pennsylvania Press
Philadelphia

LC

Copyright © 1989 by the University of Pennsylvania Press
All rights reserved
Printed in the United States of America

Library of Congress Cataloging-in-Publication Data

Meyer, Leonard B.
  Style and music : theory, history, and ideology / Leonard B.
Meyer.
     p.   cm. — (Studies in the criticism and theory of music)
  Bibliography: p.
  Includes indexes.
  ISBN 0-8122-8178-0
  1. Style, Musical.   2. Music—19th century—Philosophy and
aesthetics.   3. Romanticism in music.   I. Title.   II. Series.
ML430.5.M5   1989
781—dc19                                        89-31354
                                                    CIP
                                                    MN

*For Janet*

# CONTENTS

# PREFACE

". . . and the last shall be first." So it also is with prefaces. Written last, they are usually read first (if at all). And before they are written, the manuscript is reviewed one more time. As I reviewed this one, I was sensible of the many debts that my work owes to others, and was distressed because in many cases I could not recall the source of a viewpoint, an idea, or a concept. This failure can be attributed to both the age of the author and the duration of the project.

Early in a career, experience is limited enough that provenance is not as a rule problematic. Influences can readily be traced to parents, a few friends, two or three extraordinary teachers, a countable contingent of colleagues, and a modest number of memorable books and articles. Late in a career, however, it is often impossible to identify sources. Beliefs, attitudes, cognitive proclivities, and even information come from countless encounters with students and colleagues, with papers heard and conversations overheard, with books studied or scanned and periodicals read or perused. The names of many of those who have influenced my work appear in what follows, but many others do not. Omissions occur because influences may be negative (ideas are formed in opposition to what is conceptually uncongenial) or may be catalytic (the stimulus that suggests the idea figures nowhere in the end result).

Provenance is also a problem because work on this book dates back close to twenty years when I was planning a study to be called "Music as a Model for History." Though vestiges are apparent in Part II of this book, that study was never finished because my ideas about the nature of style change kept changing. (Most importantly, I came to favor a mixed, but significantly externalist, account of style change rather than an internalist one.) At the time I read extensively in the philosophy of history and in the literature concerned with the nature of style and style history. Once again, owing to temporal distance and sheer quantity, I have doubtless forgotten to acknowledge important indebtedness. My gratitude must, therefore, be general, though not on that account any less sincere. It is extended to scholars such as R. G. Collingwood from whose writings I benefited enormously, though he does not happen to be mentioned in my book; and it goes to students and colleagues, past and present, who in discussion and at times intense dispute have helped, indeed forced, me to formulate and refine concepts, hypotheses, and arguments.

Acknowledging influence and indebtedness is problematic for less personal reasons as well. These merit mention because they relate to matters considered in my study. First, a culture's beliefs and attitudes—its ideology—often lead to consensus about concepts. As a result, ideas and hypotheses proudly cherished as brilliantly original turn out to have been proposed independently by others. Second, the relevant literature—about style, about history, and about Romanticism—is so vast that, although I have read widely, I have undoubtedly missed studies that should have been consulted. Put differently, post-Renaissance culture has led to such abundance and diversity that, as art critic Harold Rosenberg observed, in the twentieth century a work of art ( = idea, hypothesis, etc.) "does not have to be actually new, it only has to be new to somebody." Last, as I shall argue later, the provenance of ideas, hypotheses, and so on, is less interesting for theory than the nature of their interrelationships, and less important for history than the reasons for their replication.

Since this is a book about style, it seems appropriate to say something about the cognitive style of the author and the conceptual style of the text. I am not one who yearns for "oneness." Rather I delight in distinction and difference, in contrast and comparison, and especially in paradox and the discomfiting of received opinion. Yet I also relish discerning connections, especially between seemingly disparate ideas or behavior—for instance, the parallels, suggested in Chapter 6, between the humble passion of romantic love and the patrician austerities of aesthetic formalism. For me, then, scholarship is playfully inquiring, yet intensely serious, speculation.

Though I have tried to make my book coherent in thought and consistent in argument, it presents neither an axiomatic account of the nature of style nor a philosophical theory of style change. Rather, its method is modestly empirical. What is observed—the data—is the culturally qualified behavior of human beings in specific historical/cultural circumstances. From this point of view, my disciplinary outlook is akin to that of cultural anthropology or social psychology. What I hope to understand and explain are the compositional choices made by individual men and women who are members of some culture. These choices create what we call musical styles, and it is from changes in choice that we construct music histories.

Broadly speaking, the first two parts of this book deal with the nature of style and style history. They are replete with definitions and distinctions, inferences and hypotheses. These do not constitute a formal system, but a network of interrelated, complementary concepts. The last part of the book is an attempt to show how the concepts developed earlier might be used to explain as specifically and concretely as possible the ways in which the ideological beliefs of an epoch—in this case, the nineteenth century—were translated into musical constraints and thereby affected the choices made by composers. What was to have been a brief, illustrative "sketch-history," however, became considerably more extensive than envisaged. And it may seem to some that the tail came to wag the dog. But in order for the tail to wag at all, there must be a dog—however strangely proportioned—to do the wagging.

Though my book is about style in *music,* I hope that it will be of interest to scholars in other fields: art, literary, and cultural historians; critics and aestheticians;

and perhaps cultural anthropologists. I also believe that laymen with some knowledge of music theory will find the book intelligible. For while it is conceptually intricate, it is neither technically abstruse nor metaphysically abstract. I have tried to make ideas precise, hypotheses explicit, analyses accessible, and lines of argument evident. As a result my work is open—indeed, vulnerable—to debate and criticism. This is as it should be. For concepts, hypotheses, analyses, and so on, are seldom unconditionally true. Here Vilfredo Pareto's declaration seems pertinent: "Give me fruitful error anytime, full of seeds, bursting with its own correction. You can keep your sterile truths for yourself." And in order for correction to occur, evidence must be manifest and argument apparent.

Correction need not, however, entail rejection. For as mentioned earlier, I have not constructed a deductive system, but have tried to weave data and hypotheses together to create a coherent tapestry picturing the relationships among nature and nurture, choice and constraint, style structure and style change. Consequently, my work should not fail even though one or two strands of the fabric prove to be faulty.

Recalling remote sources and distant indebtedness is difficult, but acknowledging concrete encouragement and specific help is not. My work on this book was supported by a number of institutions. The first chapter was written for and presented at a Summer Institute in Aesthetics (Boulder, Colorado) organized by Berel Lang, who subsequently included most of my lecture in *The Concept of Style*. Much of Chapter 3, taken from the unfinished manuscript of "Music as a Model for History," was begun when I was a Guggenheim Fellow. The first draft of Chapter 6 was written during a wonderful month at the Rockefeller Foundation's Bellagio Study Center, and parts of Chapters 7 and 8 formed the basis for the Tanner Lectures in Human Values which were given at Stanford University. Finally, the University of Pennsylvania helped not only with research funds but, most importantly, with a light teaching load. To each, my warm thanks.

Even more important than institutions were people. My manuscript was read, criticized, and edited by a number of people: Stephen Fisher, Richard Freedman, Catherine Gjerdingen, Eugene Narmour, and Ruth A. Solie. Peter Hoyt was the devoted research assistant during the tedious revising of this book. All of them made suggestions that have improved this book, and I am most grateful. My colleagues at Penn have contributed by talking with me about a number of matters considered in what follows. They, too, have my thanks. But how shall I thank my wife, Janet Levy? She not only read, criticized, and helped me revise the entire manuscript, but she was also the source, both directly and through frequently fervent discussions, of many of the ideas and distinctions that I have used. Without her help, conceptual as well as editorial, my work would have been less discerning, cogent, and clear.

# PART I

Theory

# CHAPTER 1

# Toward a Theory of Style

## A DEFINITION OF STYLE

I begin, perhaps somewhat unceremoniously, with a definition: *Style is a replication of patterning, whether in human behavior or in the artifacts produced by human behavior, that results from a series of choices made within some set of constraints.*[1] An individual's style of speaking or writing, for instance, results in large part from lexical, grammatical, and syntactic choices made within the constraints of the language and dialect he has learned to use but does not himself create. And so it is in music, painting, and the other arts. More generally, few of the constraints that limit choice are newly invented or devised by those who employ them. Rather they are learned and adopted as part of the historical/cultural circumstances of individuals or groups. Since constraints allow for a variety of realizations, patterns need not be alike in *all* respects in order to be shared replications, but only in those respects that define the pattern-relationships in question. For instance, though they differ in many important ways, the melodies given in Examples 1.1*a* and *b* replicate a pattern of pitches (8–7/2–1; see graphs 1 and 2) frequently chosen by composers of the Classic period.

*a.*

EXAMPLE 1.1. (*a*) Haydn, Symphony No. 46 in B Major, ii

1. Somewhat similar definitions have been proposed by other scholars: for instance, Jan LaRue (*Guidelines for Style Analysis,* p. ix) and Charles E. Osgood ("Some Effects of Motivation," p. 293). Only shortened references will be given in the notes; full documentation is given in the bibliography.

EXAMPLE 1.1. (*b*) Mozart, Piano Quartet in G Minor (K. 478), i

The implications of, and reasons for, this definition of style will, I hope, become clear in the course of what follows. But even thus baldly stated, the formulation should not be problematic, except perhaps for the reference to choice. The presence of choice is stipulated because there are replicated patternings in the world—even in what might be considered aspects of human behavior—that would not normally be thought of as being "stylistic": for example, the structure of crystals, the flowering of plants, the behavior of social insects, and even human physiological processes. Thus it would, I think, be abnormal usage to speak of the style of someone's breathing, even though such breathing involved regular replication, and even though the particular patterning could be differentiated from the breathing of other individuals. Similarly it would seem strange to speak of the style of an oak tree versus that of an elm, or of the style of watercress versus that of spinach. But as soon as human choice plays a part in the resulting patterning, style is possible; thus it seems entirely proper to speak of the style of eighteenth-century versus nineteenth-century landscaping, or of French versus Italian cuisine.

The word *choice* tends to suggest conscious awareness and deliberate intent. Yet only a minute fraction of the choices we make are of this sort. For the most part human behavior consists of an almost uninterrupted succession of habitual and virtually automatic actions: getting out of bed in the morning, washing, dressing, preparing breakfast, reading the mail, driving to work, conversing with colleagues, playing the violin, and so on. Were each act dependent upon conscious choice, an inordinate amount of time and psychic energy would be expended in considering alternatives, envisaging their possible outcomes, and deciding among such possibilities. We could scarcely survive, let alone compose music, write books—or fight wars. By far the largest part of behavior is a result of the interaction between innate modes of cognition and patterning on the one hand, and ingrained, learned habits of discrimination and response on the other. Most of the time this symbiotic relationship between nature and nurture chooses for us. Having learned to speak, play the violin, or drive a car, we are seldom conscious of selecting particular words or grammatical constructions, of deciding when and where to put our fingers down on the fiddle, of thinking about braking or shifting gears.[2]

But even when behavior is not deliberate, human actions are for the most part considered to be the result of choice—or so, at least, our culture has taught us to believe. And since such beliefs are themselves ingrained habits in terms of which we perceive and pattern the world, they affect our understanding of and response to human behavior, including works of art. As a result, it would surely seem peculiar—at odds with our ordinary way of understanding human behavior—to contend that speaking, playing the violin, or driving a car were unintentional or involuntary or whatever the antonym of choice may be.[3]

To take an example from music: Mozart evidently composed with such astonishing facility that only a small portion of his choices could have involved a deliberate decision among possible alternatives. But it would seem strange to suggest that he did not *choose* the relationships in the Overture to *Don Giovanni,* even though, according to legend, that work was written in less than twenty-four hours. Looked at the other way around, if Bartók and Schoenberg composed fewer works than Mozart, it was not necessarily because they were less gifted than he, but because the styles they employed required them to make many more conscious, time-consuming decisions. Mozart could compose with astonishing facility partly because the set of constraints he inherited (and which he partly modified), the so-called Classic style, was especially coherent, stable, and well established. As a result, Mozart had to make relatively few deliberate choices among alternatives. And so it is with human behavior generally: styles of behavior in all realms—in the arts and sciences, business and technology, religion and military tactics—involve choosing within some set of constraints. But only a small proportion of such style-defining choices involve

2. Deliberate, conscious choice does take place when we are acquiring some skill: learning to talk, play the violin, or drive a car. Then (particularly if we are learning the skill at an advanced age) we are aware of our own behavior—of the act of choosing. Once such skills become ingrained as habits of mental/motor behavior, choice becomes conscious only when the situation seems problematic in some way. Problems of this sort may arise for a host of different reasons: for example, (a) when important issues hang on subtle distinctions (as in the writing of a law, which requires that we choose our words carefully, consider alternatives, envisage possible interpretations by others, and so on); (b) when the called-for behavior is out of the ordinary (in performing a particularly difficult passage from a violin sonata, we think about alternative fingerings and bowings); or (c) when possible alternatives have different advantages (as when one route to a destination is scenic but long and tortuous, while the other involves taking a shorter but tedious superhighway). In such situations we will probably weigh the relative merits of the alternatives and our choice will be conscious and reasoned).

The problems of choice may also be related to the simplification of means, which seems characteristic of the late styles of a number of composers—for instance, Beethoven, Verdi, and Bartók. For such simplification may occur not only because the composer has reached a point at which ego and bravura are superfluous, but because old age is accompanied by physiological slowing down and a concomitant need to conserve energy—to reduce the number of deliberate compositional choices made. Both simplification and the use of familiar constraints serve this purpose. Hanslick seems to have this phenomenon in mind when he remarks that Verdi's "*Falstaff* certainly exhibits an invaluable method for composers of genius who have experience and technique of many years, but no longer the burgeoning imagination of youth" (quoted in Conati, *Interviews and Encounters with Verdi,* p. 246).

3. The scarcity of true antonyms for *choice* in the thesaurus and dictionary may be a symptom (and perhaps evidence) of our cultural belief that behavior is almost always the result of choice.

conscious consideration of alternatives. In the midst of battle, Napoleon, like Mozart, must often have let his ingrained habits of discrimination choose for him.[4]

Frequently, of course, one alternative is so obvious or probable in a particular situation that others are not even thought of, let alone made the subject of deliberation. But if alternatives exist at all, a choice has been made.[5] For instance, though it may never have occurred to him to do so, Mozart might have written the Overture to *Don Giovanni* in the "learned" style of late Baroque music. The option was available to him.[6] And in this sense he chose not to employ the style. But he did not choose not to write the Overture in the style of, say, Wagner because that option was simply not available to him.[7] These matters are important because, as we shall see, works of art are understood and appreciated not only in terms of what actually occurs, but in terms of *what might have happened* given the constraints of the style and the particular context in which choice was made.

The concept of choice may also be problematic because of its connection with views about the nature of style that are different from those adopted in this essay. Style has frequently been equated with the *manner* in which something is expressed, as distinguished from the *matter* being presented. When this view is adopted—when style is taken to be the domain of *how* things are stated, as distinct from *what* is

---

4. Behavior is at times unintentional in the sense that had a deliberate choice been made, the resulting action would have been different. Such unintentional actions take place: (*a*) when habits have not become sufficiently ingrained—for example, when a violinist plays out of tune or produces a poor tone; (*b*) when ingrained habits are brought into play where they are inappropriate—for example, if having driven on the right-hand side of the road all of our lives, we unwittingly do so when driving in England; and (*c*) when a disposition is so strong that conventionally governed conscious choice is overpowered—as when a slip of the tongue reveals what we really think. (That such slips are considered significant is further evidence of our culture's belief that even unconscious acts are the result of choice.)

Yet in each of these cases of unintentional behavior, the individual involved would be considered responsible for his act. The presumption of responsibility implies the existence of alternatives; the existence of alternatives, in turn, entails the possibility of choice. The violinist could have (should have) played in tune, the driver could have stayed to the left, and our real thoughts should have been different.

Responsibility and, hence, choice are related to context. For example, were the violinist a beginner still acquiring skills, he would probably be absolved from responsibility for his mistakes. Given the context, his lack of competence is understandable. But if the performance were in a public concert, the player would be held responsible for his errors because we have reason to expect considerable competence. In blaming such a performer, we imply that he had other options: playing well, or perhaps not at all. It might, say, be urged that he should have practiced more. Thus, though his mistakes are unintentional, his antecedent behavior (not practicing diligently enough) is considered the choice responsible for his poor performance.

5. Even coercion and compulsion do not as a rule negate the possibility of choice. For instance, the probability of being arrested or of having a serious accident are high if I drive on the left-hand side of the road in the United States, but it is possible to do so. Driving on the left does, of course, occur when passing a car on a two-lane highway. And in such a case, the choice may well be deliberate: noting the disadvantages of alternatives (staying behind a slow car or risking the possibility of a car coming in the opposite direction), envisaging possible outcomes (being late for an appointment or having an accident), and judging between them. And these will be the basis for conscious choice. In this very real sense, I choose to drive on the right. Even in an extreme case, when my life is threatened in a holdup, options are available: attempting to escape, resisting physically, or handing over my wallet. And observe that in both of these instances my style will be defined and characterized partly by the kinds of choices I tend to make—for example, it is a risk-taking, a cautious, or a cowardly style. Only when overwhelming force is actually applied is choice precluded.

6. He did in fact choose to employ this style extensively when he wrote the Overture to *The Magic Flute*.

7. This point is borrowed from E. H. Gombrich. See his "Criteria of Periodization," p. 124.

being asserted—choice tends to be understood as a decision between alternative ways of "saying" the same things. In this way style is taken to be dependent upon the possibility of synonymity. Since these matters have been effectively dealt with by Nelson Goodman,[8] I will consider them only briefly.

What is presented in, say, a Crucifixion painting by Crivelli is at once the same as, yet different from, what is presented in a Crucifixion by Rubens. From this point of view it is tempting to equate variability in manner of representation with style. But this is, in my view, questionable. On a high stylistic level, replicated subject matter links the two paintings, making both part of the style of Western painting from the Middle Ages to the present and, on that level, distinguishing the broad style of Western painting from that of, say, Indonesia. On a lower level, differences in manner distinguish the styles of the two painters. Put in terms of the definition given at the beginning of this essay: to the extent that any *what* (i.e., subject matter, plot, pattern, concept) is replicated in the work of an artist, a movement, an epoch, or even a culture, it must be considered to have been chosen by the artist from a set of constraints, just as much as any *how* is chosen. And for that reason it constitutes an aspect of that artist's style, as well as of the style of the movement, epoch, or culture.[9]

It seems clear that were style dependent upon synonymity, then nonsemantic arts such as music, architecture, and abstract design could not be thought to be in identifiable, describable styles—as they obviously are.[10] For in the absence of some sort of external reference with respect to which they are understood to be the same, it is difficult to imagine how two stimuli or patterns could be synonymous.[11]

The position just described is connected with one that accounts for the essence of any style in terms of those features of patterning deviating from some standard practice. This view, and the preceding ones, are mistaken and misleading because they equate the style of a work or group of works primarily with those features that make identification and classification possible. But the characteristic manners, choice of synonyms, and deviations that make recognition possible may be but the trappings and the suits of a style—symptoms of more fundamental connections among the elements of some work or group of works. In short, as I will argue in Chapter 2, all of these positions confuse the *recognition* and classification of a style, which admittedly are often facilitated by characteristic deviations and differences in manner, with an *explanation* or *analysis* of the structural and functional relationships within the style, in which *all* recurrent features (standard as well as deviant ones) are related to one another according to some hypothesis about their interactions.

Choosing among alternatives does not, then, depend upon "what" versus

8. "The Status of Style."

9. It is not, as Goodman seems to suggest (ibid., p. 807), merely that matter is *occasionally* an element of style. Unless the thing represented is unique and nonrecurring, what is represented is always an aspect of style.

10. According to Goodman (ibid., pp. 800–801), it is doubtful that there are genuine synonyms even in representational arts such as painting and literature. Also see Westergaard, "On the Notion of Style," p. 72.

11. In music, for instance, are two tones of 440 Hz played by different instruments synonymous? or two authentic cadences at the close of different phrases? or two melodies belonging to the same class (see Example 1.1)?

"how" differences, upon the possibility of synonyms, or upon the presence of deviation. Rather it depends upon the existence of a set of constraints that establishes a repertory of alternatives from which to choose, given some specific compositional context. A discussion of the nature of such constraints forms the core of this chapter, and it is to this that we now turn.

## CONSTRAINTS IN GENERAL

Human behavior is subject to the constraints of the physical, biological, and psychological worlds, as well as to those of the realm of culture.[12] The constraints of the physical world—gravity and the rotation of the earth, the chemicals present on earth and the ways they combine, the earth's geography and climate—affect the way we move, our schedules of work and rest, where and how we live, the kinds of shelters we need and build, and even such matters as the size and construction of musical instruments and the architecture of concert halls and theaters. Biological constraints—the principles of molecular biology and vertebrate physiology, the nature of human development, the need for food, rest, and protection, and so on— affect the maintenance of health and the length of life, the care and education of the young, the ways in which food is gathered and cultivated, the time available for work and rest, and even the range of sounds employed in communication.[13] Psychological constraints—the nature of human perceptual capacities and cognitive processes, the nature of human learning, the need for communication, companionship, and psychic security—influence the ways in which the phenomenal world is conceptualized and patterned, events are comprehended and remembered, goals are established and pursued: in short, the ways in which human beings understand, respond to, and manipulate their environments. Because they directly affect the organization and processes of works of art, psychological constraints will be considered when the nature of musical style is discussed.[14]

Though the constraints of the physical and biological worlds tend to encourage modes of living, patterns of social organization, kinds of technology, and so on, they do not determine human behavior. Human beings respond to particular environments (to climate and prevalent natural resources, the character of the terrain, etc.) in quite variable ways. Similarly, they fulfill biological needs (for food and rest, shelter and

12. Though there is, of course, continual and intimate interaction both within and among these worlds and realms, there are important distinctions between them.

13. Thus in some respects music is directly affected by both physical and biological constraints. But when such constraints permit no choice whatsoever, they are not relevant for discussions of style.

14. The high-level effects of physical and biological constraints can for the most part be ignored because, as Mario Bunge has observed, "*every system and every event can be accounted for (described, explained or predicted, as the case may be) primarily in terms of its own levels and the adjoining levels. . . .* For example, most historical events can be accounted for without resorting to physics and chemistry, but they cannot be properly understood without some behavioral science." See his "Metaphysics, Epistemology and Methodology of Levels," p. 24. A comparable statement can, in my view, be made about the explanation of stylistic constraints: they cannot be understood without recourse to some behavioral science—and preeminently, psychology.

security, etc.) in different manners. Generally speaking, however, such constraints do not affect works of art directly. Rather they affect the larger organization and processes of a culture: that is, the highest levels of cultural style.[15] The relation of such high-level cultural choices to the constraints of the natural world is the province of anthropology. My study, however, is primarily concerned with those constraints that affect styles of patterning more directly—that is, with psychological and cultural constraints.

Cultures can be analyzed—divided and subdivided—in many different ways. The specific divisions employed in the analysis of a particular culture (or part of a culture) depend on: (*a*) the structures and processes of the culture itself, as evidenced by the behavior of individuals and groups—including their ideologies (beliefs, attitudes, and explicit theories), their institutions (kinship systems, governments, means of commerce and education), their technologies (notational systems, transportation, production of goods and services), and their semiologies (lexicons, grammars, gestures, and other means of communication); (*b*) the analyst's ideas (whether consciously considered or unconsciously employed) about the nature of human culture, which are, as a rule, based on the beliefs characteristic of his or her *own* culture; and, related to both of these, (*c*) the kinds of relationships the analyst seeks to illuminate and explain.

In this book, cultures are analyzed as comprising different areas of human activity—different parameters—according to categories that are largely customary in Western culture. That is, cultures are divided into fields such as politics and economics, commerce and religion, social organization and the sciences, and games, sports, and the several arts. These areas not only overlap and complement one another in various ways, but within each  further divisions may be discerned. But whatever the divisions may be, they are made possible because the parameters distinguished are understood to be governed by somewhat different constraints. To put the matter the other way around (and more accurately): when two spheres of human activity—or of relationships in the natural world—are found to be governed by somewhat different constraints, they tend to be distinguished as being different parameters.

When two parameters are thus distinguished, one is understood as being external to the other. This is important because to conceive of one parameter as influencing another entails the notion of externality—of relative independence.[16] How the various parameters of Western culture have interacted with music and influenced the

15. These in turn often affect styles of art.

16. Once again, it should be emphasized that distinctions among parameters, and our notions about how they interact, depend not only on the observed behavior of the culture, but on the analyst's hypotheses about the nature of human behavior, cultural interactions, historical change, and the like.

It is important to emphasize that, as I am using the word, a parameter is any facet of the world that is conceptualized as being governed by a distinguishable set of constraints. One consequence of this usage is that few parameters are simple, pure, or monolithic. Thus political behavior is a parameter even though it is a composite resulting from beliefs, laws, conventions; similarly, in music rhythm is considered a parameter even though it is dependent upon duration, pitch relationships, dynamics, and so on. External parameters must be considered if the *history* of a style is to be explained, but they are not required for an *analytic* account of the structure and process of a style. Thus the external/internal distinction is introduced here largely for the sake of matters to be considered in later chapters.

history of musical styles will be considered later. But it should be noted that external parameters—political and economic circumstances, religious beliefs and intellectual currents, and the like—have continually impinged upon the theory and practice of music and have, at times, significantly affected the course of style history. Our present concern, however, is with the nature of the constraints internal to musical styles.

The constraints of a style are *learned* by composers and performers, critics and listeners.[17] Usually such learning is largely the result of experience in performing and listening rather than of explicit formal instruction in music theory, history, or composition.[18] In other words, knowledge of style is usually "tacit":[19] that is, a matter of habits properly acquired (internalized) and appropriately brought into play. Even when a composer invents a new rule or, more commonly, discovers a novel strategy for realizing some existing rule, the invention or discovery may be largely tacit. He or she finds a relationship that works but may be unable to explain *why* it does so—how it is related to other features and other constraints of the style.

It is the goal of music theorists and style analysts to explain what the composer, performer, and listener know in this tacit way. To do so, they must make explicit the nature of the constraints governing the style in question, devising and testing hypotheses about the function of these constraints and their relationships to one another. This can be done only by making inferences from observable data—the replicated patternings present in works of art—to general principles.[20]

Style analysis must, of course, begin with description and classification, that is, with an account of the features replicated in some work or repertory of works.[21]

17. Even those constraints that might be thought of as being innate because they result from the operation of universal psychological principles (the *transcultural* laws discussed below) are learned. For not only are the natural proclivities of the human mind invariably strengthened or weakened by learning, but whatever universal, cross-cultural principles exist are always actualized through more restricted rules and strategies, which are culturally specific.

18. Textbooks dealing with harmony, counterpoint, form, and so on, are *not*, despite customary usage, theoretical treatises explaining the bases for the constraints employed in some style. Rather they are practical manuals of how-to-do-it rules. They bear the same relationship to the theory of music as an instruction book for radio repairing bears to the theory of radio transmission; or, more to the point, they bear the same relationship to the theory and analysis of music as an English grammar of the eighteenth century bears to the style of, say, the poetry of William Blake.

During the twentieth century a new kind of theory has become prevalent—a prescriptive theorizing that is concerned with the devising of new constraints (or the systematic modification of existing constraints) for the composition of music. As a result, the conceptualization of constraints precedes, rather than follows, compositional practice. Thus, the theoretical ambiance of, say, Fux is quite different from that of Babbitt (for instance in his "Twelve-Tone Invariants"): though both are concerned with constraints, the former describes an already existing practice, while the latter prescribes a practice yet to be realized.

19. See Polanyi, *Personal Knowledge*, pt. 2.

20. The delineation of any style is a construct, but so is all knowledge—even tacit knowledge. A style construct based on theory and hypothesis is no more unreal or arbitrary than the theory of gravity or any other principle formulated on the basis of observed data and tested empirically.

21. In actual practice what inquiries begin with is not naïve, ignorant observation "pure and simple," but a mixture of observation guided and qualified by often vague and inchoate hypotheses—hunches based on prevalent cultural beliefs and attitudes about the nature of relationships in the world: about natural causation, human purposes,

But it cannot stop there. Description—lists of traits and frequency counts—can only provide what John R. Searle calls "brute facts." An intelligible analysis of a musical style, however, requires what Searle calls "institutional facts"—facts (essentially hypotheses) about the constraints that guide and limit the brute facts observed and in terms of which the brute facts are understood and interpreted. Searle illustrates the inadequacy of attempting to account for institutional facts in terms of brute facts with the following example:

> Let us imagine a group of highly trained observers describing an American football game in statements only of brute facts. What could they say by way of description? Well, within certain areas a good deal could be said, and using statistical techniques certain "laws" could even be formulated. For example, we can imagine that after a time our observer would discover the law of periodic clustering: at statistically regular intervals organisms in like colored shirts cluster together in a roughly circular fashion (the huddle). Furthermore, at equally regular intervals, circular clustering is followed by linear clustering (the teams line up for the play), and linear clustering is followed by the phenomenon of linear interpenetration. Such laws would be statistical in character, and none the worse for that. But no matter how much data of this sort we imagine our observers to collect and no matter how many inductive generalizations we imagine them to make from the data, they still have not described American football. What is missing from their description? What is missing are all those concepts which are backed by constitutive rules, concepts such as touchdown, offside, game, points, first down, time out, etc., and consequently what is missing are all the true statements one can make about a football game using those concepts. The missing statements are precisely what describe the phenomenon on the field *as a game of football*. The other descriptions, the descriptions of the brute facts, can be explained in terms of institutional facts. But the institutional facts can only be explained in terms of the constitutive rules which underlie them.[22]

The same can be said of musical phenomena—the replicated patternings that make up a style of music. One can list and count traits—say, the frequency of *sforzandi* in Beethoven's music or the number of deceptive cadences in Wagner's

---

and connections between observed phenomena. Indeed the very fact that we choose to study a particular set of phenomena, rather than some other, indicates that we have hypothesized that its components are related. Of course, our initial hypotheses may well be mistaken, and it may be necessary to make a number of guesses about what the constraints are and how they are related to one another before we hit upon one that provides an adequate explanation for the functioning of the characteristics of some style. The goal, then, is to refine preliminary hypotheses by testing them against the data discerned in works of art, ultimately relating separate hypotheses to one another in order to create a coherent theory.

22. Searle, *Speech Acts,* p. 52.

operas—till the end of time; but if nothing is known about their functions (structural, processive, expressive, and so on), it will be impossible to explain why they are there, how their presence is related to other features observed, or why their frequency changes over time. Such traits may even serve as reasonably reliable "identifiers" of Beethoven's or Wagner's style, yet contribute nothing to our understanding of how the style functions. Put in another way: all the traits (characteristic of some work or set of works) that can be described and counted are essentially symptoms of the presence of a set of interrelated constraints. What the theorist and analyst want to know about are the constraints of the style in terms of which the replicated patternings observed can be related to one another and to the experience of works of art.

But we are not in precisely the same position as Searle's observers. They can find knowledgeable informants in the grandstand or on the playing field who can tell them what the rules are; indeed the rules of football are written down and can be studied. In the arts, however, the constraints governing the choices made are seldom explicitly recorded or consciously conceptualized, even by those most accomplished in their use. As we have seen, they are usually known tacitly. As a result the theorist/ style analyst must infer the nature of the constraints—the rules of the game—from the play of the game itself. In this respect he or she is comparable to the natural scientist who attempts to infer the constraints governing natural phenomena from observed regularities. But there is a crucial difference between the constraints governing relationships in the natural world and those governing the world of human behavior. Many of the former are evidently invariable over time and space (for instance, such things as the speed of light, the nature of chemical reactions, and the character of biological processes are the same whenever and wherever they occur), while most of the latter change with time and place (for instance, the constraints of music are not the same today as they were in the sixteenth century, and are not the same in Indonesia as they are in Western culture).

This raises what seems a fundamental issue in the epistemology of the arts: whether we can ever have satisfactory knowledge of the constraints of a style— whether we can successfully infer the rules of the game from the behavior of the players. I believe that we can, at least in principle. But to do so, we must be able to describe, analyze, and interpret the variable behavior exhibited by works in diverse styles in terms of invariable laws of human perception and cognition. The difficulty with this enterprise is that until a coherent and viable theory relates cognition to neurophysiology—connecting conceptualization to biochemistry—cognitive psychology, too, must infer invariable laws from variable human behavior, including that manifest in works of art.[23] And this study is only in its beginning stages.[24] Neverthe-

23. Because works of art provide perhaps the most coherent and precisely documented evidence of complex human cognition, they should, I believe, be among the most important data for formulating and testing psychological theories of perception and cognition.

24. The central problem in cognitive psychology is, as I see it, that of experimental design: how to get at the rules governing highly complex perceptual/cognitive processes empirically. For neither introspection nor interviews yields reliable data because in both cases the subject's responses are filtered through the biased lenses of language and culture. In other words, there is distortion because the responses are made in terms of the conceptual framework

less, present theories, though they are necessarily provisional and speculative, may still provide illuminating and heuristically useful ways of looking at the nature of style.

## THE HIERARCHY OF CONSTRAINTS

Styles, and the constraints governing them, are related to one another in hierarchic fashion. This fact is responsible for considerable confusion in discussions of the nature of style. For the term *style* has been used to refer to quite disparate hierarchic levels: levels running from the constraints of a whole culture (as when anthropologists speak of the style of a culture), through those of some epoch (e.g., the Baroque) or movement (e.g., impressionism), to that of the *oeuvre* of a single composer, and even to the constraints characteristic of a single work of art (as the term is often used in literary criticism).[25] In what follows, I have sought to order this hierarchy by dividing it, according to the nature of the constraints involved, into three large classes: *laws, rules,* and *strategies.*

### *Laws*

Laws are transcultural constraints—universals, if you will. Such constraints may be physical or physiological. But for present purposes the most important ones are psychological. Specifically, they are the principles governing the perception and cognition of musical patterns. The following are examples of such laws: proximity between stimuli or events tends to produce connection, disjunction usually creates segregation; once begun, a regular process generally implies continuation to a point of relative stability; a return to patterns previously presented tends to enhance closure; regular patterns are, as a rule, more readily comprehended and remembered than irregular ones; because of the requirements of memory, musical structures usually involve considerable repetition, and are frequently hierarchic. The discovery, formulation, and testing of such laws, as well as the analysis of relationships among

---

prevalent in the subject's culture. The probability of such distortion is especially high in the case of complex, long-range relationships such as are found in works of art. For an example of the kinds of complexities possible in even a seemingly simple piece, see my article "Grammatical Simplicity and Relational Richness."

25. It is interesting in this connection to observe that the notion of style favored by literary critics is different from that usually employed by art historians and musicologists. The latter connect the concept of style with those features that are *common* to (replicated in) a work, the *oeuvre* of an artist, a movement or period, or even a whole culture. What most literary historians and critics seem to mean by style—or at least "stylistic"—is those features that are *peculiar* to a particular poem, play, or novel. Partly for this reason, art and music historians have tended to emphasize the importance of *shared* conventions and norms, while literary critics have not infrequently connected style with *deviation* from such conventions and norms. It is obvious from the definition and discussion at the beginning of this chapter that I agree with the position of the music and art historians. Even deviations must be replicated (shared within the work in question) if they are to be considered traits of the style of the work. A single deviation cannot define a style.

them, are the province of music theory. Because their differentiation is a consequence of lawlike, perceptual cognitive constraints, it is appropriate at this point to distinguish between two large classes of musical parameters.

### PRIMARY AND SECONDARY PARAMETERS.

To understand the basis for differentiating between the primary and the secondary parameters of music, we must briefly consider both the necessary conditions for the existence of syntax and the nature of the different parameters of music. In order for syntax to exist (and syntax usually differs from one culture and one period to another), successive stimuli must be related to one another in such a way that specific criteria for mobility and closure are established. Such criteria can be established only if the elements of the parameter can be segmented into discrete, nonuniform relationships so that the similarities and differences between them are definable, constant, and proportional. A series of exactly equivalent elements (e.g., a succession of half steps or whole steps, of quarter-notes or, on a higher level, dotted rhythms), a series of entirely disparate stimuli (as occurs at times in random music), or a gradually graded continuum (e.g., a *crescendo* or *accelerando*) cannot establish criteria for closure. Each can stop at any point, at any time. But because no stability/instability relationships establish preferential points of articulation, none can close.

Because of the nature of the perceptual/cognitive capacities of the human nervous system, some of the material means of music can be readily segmented in constant, nonuniform, proportional ways. In most musics of the world, this is the case with those parameters that result from the organization of, and interaction between, pitches and durations: melody, rhythm, and harmony. When the relationships within such a parameter are governed by syntactic constraints, the parameter will be called *primary*.[26]

The material means of other parameters cannot be readily segmented into proportional relationships. There is, for instance, no relationship in the realm of dynamics that corresponds to a minor third or a dotted rhythm. And the same is true of tempo, sonority, timbre. In short, dynamics may become louder or softer, tempi may be faster or slower, sonorities thicker or thinner, timbres brighter or duller. But because they cannot be segmented into perceptually proportional relationships, there are no specific closural states for such *secondary* parameters. It is, then, the presence of syntactic constraints that distinguishes primary from secondary parameters.[27]

26. The terms *primary* and *secondary* are value-neutral and imply nothing about the importance of any parameter in the shaping of a particular musical/aesthetic experience. As indicated in the preceding paragraph, pitches may be organized uniformly (as in a chromatic scale or an augmented triad) or in an unarticulated continuum (as in a glissando), and durations may be exactly equivalent (as in the ticks of a clock) or unarticulated (as in tremolo). In none of these cases, however, are the resulting relationships syntactic.

27. It follows from this discussion that a parameter which is syntactic in one style may not be so in another. For instance, as will be argued shortly, harmony is not a fully syntactic parameter in Renaissance music; it becomes so in the music of the tonal period, but it is totally without syntax in contemporary serial music. In other words, while harmony was a primary parameter in the eighteenth century, it is a secondary parameter in many twentieth-century styles.

Syntax also makes possible the existence of complex hierarchic structures. Thus the melodic, rhythmic, and harmonic relationships that shape the opening of the slow movement of Haydn's "Military" Symphony (Example 1.5) establish mobile processes and closural articulations that define motives as entities and relate them to one another to form phrases; and, on a higher level, phrases are defined and related to one another to create a complex rounded binary form. In general, the possibility of hierarchic organization depends on the existence of different kinds and strengths of closure created by syntax.[28]

Secondary parameters tend to be described in terms of amounts rather than in terms of classlike relationships (antecedent-consequent melody, authentic cadence, or anapest rhythm) as the primary parameters are. That is, dynamic levels, rates of activity, and sonorities are characterized as being more or less, greater and smaller, and the like. In fact they can be measured and quantified in ways that melodic, rhythmic, and harmonic syntax cannot. Thus, if the primary parameters are said to be *syntactic,* the secondary ones might be labeled *statistical.*

Though not governed by syntactic constraints, secondary parameters may give rise to processive relationships. They do so because, once established, a particular mode of activity tends to persist, usually until the primary parameters create some sort of articulation. Such modes of activity may be ones of constancy, as in an established *forte* dynamic level, an *allegro* tempo, a homophonic texture, or the timbre of a string section; ones of gradual change, as in a *crescendo,* a *ritardando,* or an increase in the number of voices or rate of activity; or one of regular alternation, as in an antiphonal statement and response or a repeated contrast in register.[29] In other words, a mode of activity implies its own continuation, and such implication is understood as being processive. Lacking syntax, however, such processes cannot specify definite points of termination.[30] As noted earlier, they may cease, but they cannot close.

In emphasizing the importance of syntactic constraints for the specification of closure, I do not wish to imply that the secondary parameters do not have preferred closural states.[31] They do. For example, gradual lowering of dynamic level, slowing of tempo, reduction of overall rate of activity, simplification of texture, use of less discordant intervals, and, in nontonal music, descending pitch contours all are signs

---

28. This in no way denies that nonsyntactic parameters may contribute to the definition of the closure created by the primary parameters.

29. The role of texture is problematic, particularly since it partly results from the activity of the primary parameters. But because texture does not establish specific criteria for closure, serving instead to intensify or mitigate the mobility and closure created by the primary parameters, it has been grouped with the secondary parameters.

30. Points of closure specified by the syntactic parameters may, of course, be temporarily delayed or even abrogated altogether. But the competent listener is aware of how the music "should have gone"—e.g., what the cadence should have been. It is clear, for instance, that a $ii^6 - v^7$ progression is *not* closed, and there are no relationships in dynamics, timbre, register, or texture comparable to such nonclosure.

31. For a discussion of the ways in which secondary parameters foster closure, see Hopkins, "Secondary Parameters and Closure."

of impending closure. But because such suggestions of "dying away" are parts of continua, no specific criteria for closure are stipulated. Put the other way around, it is precisely because of the existence of syntactic constraints that pieces (or parts of pieces) in the style of tonal music can close with rising inflections, complex textures, high rates of activity, and *forte* dynamics.

One consequence of this view, which may at first seem surprising, is that secondary, statistical parameters function as *natural* signs of closure, while primary, syntactic ones are *conventional*.[32] This may help to account for the increased use at points of closure of *ritardandos, diminuendos,* textural simplifications, descending pitch contours, and the like, in the music of the past one hundred years. For as the rejection of convention led to a weakening of syntax (somewhat during the last half of the nineteenth century, and often radically in the twentieth), secondary parameters became more and more important for the generation of musical processes and the articulation of closure.[33]

Even in a style that is primarily governed by syntactic constraints, however, secondary parameters often play important roles, reinforcing or undermining the processes generated by the primary parameters. In tonal music, *crescendos, accelerandos,* shifts to higher registers, and so on, frequently accompany and intensify the goal-directed processes shaped by the primary parameters. This sort of reinforcement occurs, for instance, at the end of the slow introduction of the first movement of Schumann's "Spring" Symphony (mm. 25–39). Or, consider the more interesting case in which secondary parameters act to deny goals established by primary ones. Because, as noted earlier, a mode of activity tends to persist to a point of articulation defined by primary parameters, the *forte* dynamics and tutti orchestration of measures 174–77 from the second movement of Haydn's "Military" Symphony (see Example 1.4) should continue to the accent that creates cadential closure. The abrupt *piano* on the first beat of measure 178, together with the change to a concertino-like orchestration, denies the clear closure created by the primary parameters. That is, the secondary parameters signal that this is not the *real* point of arrival. Fully satisfactory arrival occurs at measure 182. There, together with the harmonic and melodic relationships of the earlier cadence, the previously denied dynamics and orchestration are resumed.

Although the division of parameters into primary and secondary is governed by the lawlike constraints of human perception and cognition, both the nature of any musical syntax and the further differentiation of parameters are largely a matter of rules.

32. Of course, what is *conventional* is not necessarily *arbitrary.* As observed earlier, since syntactic constraints are subservient to transcultural laws, they cannot be matters of mere whimsy or caprice.

33. See Chapters 7 and 8.

## *Rules*

Rules are intracultural, not universal. They constitute the highest, most encompassing level of stylistic constraints. Differences in rules are what distinguish large periods such as Medieval, Renaissance, and Baroque from one another; and it is the commonality of rules that links Classic and Romantic musics together. Rules specify the permissible material means of a musical style: for example, its repertory of possible pitches, durational divisions, amplitudes, timbres, and modes of attack. Rules also establish the relational possibilities and probabilities among such means. For instance, as observed earlier, the laws of perception and cognition govern which parameters can be primary ones. But whether a parameter actually becomes primary depends on the existence of syntactic constraints, and these arise on the level of rules. The most familiar examples of such rules are surely those of counterpoint and harmony—rules having to do with voice leading and dissonance treatment, chord formation and harmonic progression.

A comprehensive account of the rules of a particular style is a formidable task, one that continually confronts music theorists, style analysts, and historians. Fortunately it is beyond the scope of this study. Nevertheless, in attempting to formulate a theory of style, it is important to distinguish among different kinds of rules, of which there appear to be three: *dependency* rules, *contextual* rules, and *syntactic* rules.[34] To exemplify the differences among them, I propose the following hypothesis: *On the highest level of style change, the history of harmony can be understood as involving ever-greater autonomy and eventual syntactification.*

Harmony is not a parameter in the style of Gregorian chant. With the advent of organum, however, the sounding of simultaneous pitches creates intervallic relationships that are, at the very least, protoharmonies. But even in the elaborate organum of the Notre Dame school, the relationships between such protoharmonies are governed not by their own independent constraints—that is, by rules governing possible and probable successions of verticalities—but by the rules of melodic voice leading and intervallic concord and discord.[35] And to the extent that certain intervals, notably the octave and fifth, accompany closure, they do so because concords are

---

34. These do not constitute a separate level of constraints. That is, they are not what will presently be distinguished as *strategies*.

35. The terms *concord* and *discord* will be used to designate the psychoacoustic tensional quality of vertical combinations when harmony is a secondary (nonsyntactic) parameter; the terms *consonance* and *dissonance* will designate tensional relationships when harmony is a primary (syntactic) parameter. This distinction makes it possible to characterize discords that are understood to require no resolution as being consonant (as is not infreqently the case in, say, the music of Debussy), and some concords as being dissonances (e.g., in the opening movement of Beethoven's String Quartet in B♭ Major, Opus 130, the first beat of measure 5 is a concord which, because it is understood as an appoggiatura, functions as a dissonance). Of course, in tonal music dissonances are usually also discords, and consonances are usually also concords.

cognitively more stable than discords and hence create preferred closural states. Because the succession of vertical events in organum is determined by the constraints of modal melody, together with the states of concord and discord, harmony is a secondary parameter governed by *dependency rules*. That is, its organization is dependent upon the syntactic rules of another parameter.

The nature of this dependency is made clear in David Hughes's discussion of the relationship of the organal voice to the chant. According to Hughes,

> it is quite likely that by the eleventh century a good deal of the Gregorian and post-Gregorian chant of the greater feasts was sung polyphonically. Despite the various advances in technique, however, polyphony remained essentially a manner of performance of the chant: an organum was not so much a new composition as an embellishment of a given melody. Toward the end of the eleventh century, three developments took place that finally raised organum to the rank of original composition.[36]

It seems implicit in this description that as an "embellishment" the organal voice was initially a dependent parameter and that it subsequently gained sufficient independence that each newly devised organal voice gave rise to a new composition.

During the later Middle Ages, a number of harmonic successions become more or less standardized. This is the case in, say, the music of Machaut. But such successions occur only at particular points in a piece, usually at cadences. That is, their use is governed by *contextual rules*. Since the progressions between cadences are still governed by the constraints of modal melody and contrapuntal voice leading, harmony is not fully syntactic.[37] Even when cadential formulae are acoustically similar to the dominant-tonic progression characteristic of later tonal music, harmony remains presyntactic. Subsequently, "the infiltration of cadential progressions into the interior of the phrase is also more common than in earlier music; but Josquin, like other composers of the period, still employs a wide variety of internal chord progressions: sixteenth-century music is by no means 'tonal' in the later sense of the word."[38]

---

36. *History of European Music*, p. 49. A parameter within music may be dependent upon a parameter outside of music. It seems probable, for instance, that the rhythm of earliest chant was determined by the rules (and perhaps the strategies) of text declamation. And a bit later, the medieval lyric "may well have been one of the sources of the rhythmic modes. . . ." (ibid., p. 67).

37. In general, secondary parameters are governed by contextual rules. This is true of the dynamic contrasts typical of the Baroque concerto grosso, of *crescendos* that often accompany retransitions in Classic sonata-form movements, and of the articulation of closure in much twentieth-century music.

38. Hughes, *History of European Music*, p. 133. Even at the end of the Renaissance, harmony is not fully syntactic. As Susan McClary observes, modal harmony "does not functionally indicate the final through a consistent leading-tone. The sense of progression and the structural functions are linear. . . . [T]he harmonic collections are generated by and derive their meanings from the melodic line. The chord is not an independent functional entity" ("Transition from Modal to Tonal Organization," pp. 79, 80).

Toward the beginning of the seventeenth century, all harmonic successions come to be governed by an independent set of constraints in which root motion by fifths and the subdominant-to-dominant progression play a central role. The result is a repertory of possible progressions capable of denying as well as fulfilling implications, defining—instead of being subservient to—contexts, and forming hierarchic tonal structures. In short, harmony becomes a primary parameter governed by full *syntactic rules*.[39]

Syntactic rules establish sets of *possible* functional relationships within parameters. In addition, because of the rules, some simultaneities and some successions tend to be more *probable* than others. In tonal harmony, for instance, it is more likely that a chord built on the second degree of the scale (II) will be followed by one built on the fifth (V) than by one built on the third (III) or the tonic (I). But neither of the latter progressions is impossible. Though such probabilities are consequences of syntax (in this case, of the central importance of the fifth relationship in harmonic progression), they are not in themselves rules. Rather they are aspects of strategy.[40]

Before considering strategic constraints, however, it should be noticed that the frequency with which a particular strategy is employed does not change the rules that govern its use and significance. For instance, though the frequent use of deceptive cadences in late nineteenth-century music changes the listener's sense of the probability of their occurrence (and consequently of the occurrence of authentic cadences as well), his or her understanding of the syntactic function of such progressions does *not* change. To take an example discussed in *Emotion and Meaning in Music:*[41] although the authentic cadence just before rehearsal number 77 in the score of Strauss's *Ein Heldenleben* is somewhat surprising because the ubiquity of deceptive cadences in that work (and others in the same style) leads the listener to suspect that one will occur here, the ii–I$^6_4$–V–I progression is understood as authentic. That is, we know it is more closed than a perhaps more probable deceptive cadence would have been. The "moral" of this seems to be that strategies, however prevalent they may be, do not change rules.

---

39. The change to full syntactification may not have been a process of incremental accretion, as some scholars have suggested; rather it may have occurred all of a sudden, though earlier changes undoubtedly established necessary conditions. Once harmonic syntax existed, important modifications took place in the constraints of other parameters. But these were changes in strategy, not in rules.

40. Since rules establish what is permitted in a style, the question arises as to whether, according to the definition given at the beginning of this chapter, they can be considered as properly "stylistic." The answer is that, since they are variable over time and locale (as laws are not), rules are consequences of human choice. Sometimes when new rules are invented—as with the creation of serialism—the fact of choice is obvious. But when the initial instance of some rule cannot be identified (and that is usually the case), the presence of choice is obscured, though choice must have occurred.

41. P. 66.

## *Strategies*

Strategies are compositional choices made within the possibilities established by the rules of the style.[42] For any specific style there is a finite number of rules, but there is an indefinite number of possible strategies for realizing or instantiating such rules. And for any set of rules there are probably innumerable strategies that have never been instantiated. For this reason it seems doubtful that styles are ever literally exhausted, as they are sometimes said to be.[43] Though style change is more carefully considered in Chapters 4 and 5, it should be mentioned here that most changes in the history of Western music have involved the devising of new strategies for the realization of existing rules, rather than the invention of new rules. Rule changes, as suggested earlier, occur only on the highest level of the history of Western music—that is, the level designating epochs such as the Middle Ages, the Renaissance, the Age of Tonality (ca. 1600–1918), and the "Age of Modernity." *Within* these epochs what changed was strategic constraints.

The relationship between rules and strategies is enormously complex because it involves not only the interactions among the constraints governing the various musical parameters of a style, but the influence of parameters external to music as well. For the strategic constraints of various styles have at times been significantly affected by other parameters of culture, most directly and notably by ideology, social history, and conditions of performance. How such external parameters have influenced the history of musical styles is considered in the second part of this book. Here only the interactions among the parameters of music will be discussed, and only in a cursory way.

Generally speaking, a change in the rules of one parameter of a style—e.g., the syntactification of harmony discussed above—requires some adjustment in the strategic constraints governing the other parameters of the style. It may, in addition, permit certain strategies not previously possible. In music of the Renaissance, for example, the relationships among simultaneously sounding voices were governed by the melodic/intervallic rules of counterpoint. Fourth-species counterpoint was one strategy for the realization of those rules. With the syntactification of harmony, however, fourth-species progressions had to be modified to accommodate harmonic mo-

---

42. The concept of strategy may seem problematic, particularly in light of the game analogy in Searle's account. For strategies suggest goals. In games we know what the goal is: it is winning. But what is the goal of a compositional strategy? Answering that question is, as I see it, the ultimate goal of the game of music scholarship—of theory and history, analysis and criticism. For, as I argue in Chapter 5, the choices of composers (past and present) can be understood and explained only in the light of their goals—goals that are largely set by the ideology of the culture.

It is possible, too, that some styles of art may be more like sports than like games, if a sport is defined as a rule-governed activity in which there is no such thing as winning. Like bicycle riding or swimming, such works of art would be enjoyed as activities, perhaps for the sense of well-being they engender.

43. That is, styles do not change because no strategic possibilities remain. Rather, because they change, we *infer* (on the basis of certain culturally derived hypotheses) their exhaustion.

tion by fifths. What changed was not the rules of counterpoint, however, but their strategic realization. Rule changes may also make new formal structures possible, and such structures may in turn call for new strategies. Tonal harmony, for instance, makes antecedent-consequent periods possible. And when a melodic motion from the fifth down to the tonic is coordinate with such periods, the descending line must be so constructed that it reaches a tone of the dominant triad (frequently the second degree of the scale) at the close of the first phrase; then the second phrase repeats the descent with modifications that allow the cadence to occur on a note of the tonic triad.

Not only do changes in the constraints governing one parameter often produce changes in others; they may also lead to shifts in the relative importance of the several parameters constituting stylistic means. From this point of view, styles can in part be characterized and defined by what might be called *dominance* of parameters.[44] For example, timbre scarcely serves even to qualify process and structure in the music of the Renaissance, and it is clearly less important than texture. In the music of the Baroque and Classic styles, the role of timbre is more important: it contributes to the definition of form and may, as observed earlier, even act to deny goals articulated by the primary parameters. In some twentieth-century music, the dominance relationships prevalent in the Baroque and Classic styles are reversed. Harmony, which was a dominant (primary) parameter in the earlier styles, no longer functions syntactically but is little more than a byproduct of the coincidence of simultaneous pitches resulting (for instance) from the manipulations of a tone row; at the same time, an attempt is made to employ secondary parameters such as timbre and dynamics syntactically for the articulation of form and the shaping of process.[45]

In any given epoch some strategies are especially prevalent. In Renaissance music, for instance, certain bass patterns occur again and again, and some rhythms are particularly characteristic; in the Classic style, some melodic patterns, cadential progressions, and phrase structures are ubiquitous. Once such patterns or procedures become established as stylistic norms, they may serve as the basis for *strategic play*.

---

44. The dominance of parameters characterizes styles on other levels as well. Just as melody, harmony, timbre, and so on, are parameters within music, so music (together with politics, economics, technology, philosophy, etc.) is a parameter within culture. And just as parameters within a culture are distinguished from one another because they are governed by somewhat different constraints, so it is with the parameters of music: melody, harmony, timbre, etc., are more or less independent variables. Moreover, just as some parameters are primary shaping forces within music while others are secondary (in that they complement and qualify the primary shaping forces), so in a culture some parameters are primary shaping forces (in our culture, for example, social, political, economic, and technological processes) while others are secondary (in our culture, for example, music). In other words, like musical styles, cultural styles are partly characterized and defined by the dominance relationships among the parameters present. And it follows from this that the history of musical style or of cultural styles is partly the history of dominance relationships among parameters.

45. It is, I think, generally agreed that this attempt has failed. It has done so because, as noted earlier, not all perceptual dimensions are capable of being segmented—a requirement for the existence of syntactic relationships. And this may serve to illustrate the relationship between rules and laws: though rules are conventional, they are not arbitrary. They must conform to the constraints prevalent on the level of laws.

For example, the Trio of Mozart's String Quartet in G Major (K. 387) begins with what promises to be an antecedent-consequent period, a typical schema in the style of Classic music. But instead of cadencing on the tonic, as a proper consequent phrase should, the second phrase-group ends (m. 114) in the relative major (B♭). Only near the end of the Trio is the proper consequent phrase-ending presented. In short, because the antecedent-consequent relationship is well established, it can (almost paradoxically) function as the basis for a strategy that significantly delays its own realization.

Strategic play may also involve the manipulation of *contextual probabilities*. In Classic music, for instance, deceptive cadences are important strategies for delaying closure. As a result they most often occur toward the end of periods or sections. Beginning a movement with a deceptive cadence—as Beethoven does in the Piano Sonata in E♭ Major, Opus 81a ("Les adieux")—is, therefore, contextually improbable. This opening gambit is intimately connected with Beethoven's strategic choices throughout the remainder of the movement.[46]

Though my concern thus far has been with the strategic use of primary parameters, secondary parameters can also be the basis for strategies that become highly characteristic of a particular style. In the Baroque concerto grosso, for example, more or less regular contrasts in dynamics, instrumentation, and texture become shared strategies for reinforcing the articulation of process and structure. And, as we have seen, dynamics and instrumentation can be used strategically to deny the closure created by the primary parameters. Or to take a well-known case: what is unusual about the famous *fortissimo* chord in the slow movement of Haydn's "Surprise" Symphony is not its dynamic level per se. The *fortissimo* is surprising, even shocking, because the syntactic simplicity and regularity of the folklike theme establish a context in which continuation, not forceful disturbance, seems appropriate and probable.[47]

Why some strategies rather than others become prevalent, given a particular set of rules, is a question of paramount importance for the history of music. The situation, which can only be briefly dealt with here,[48] seems to be somewhat as follows. Novel strategies are continually being devised, though the rate of such devising varies, depending on stylistic and cultural circumstances as well as on the personality of individual composers. But only a small fraction of such innovations become part of the ongoing, traditional practice of the style. Those strategies that do survive—that are replicated—must possess properties such as symmetry and coherence, stability, and a degree of redundancy. Because they are especially memorable and their fundamental structure can be readily replicated, such patterns can be significantly ex-

---

46. Some of the consequences of this opening are discussed in my *Explaining Music,* chap. 8.

47. Searle's illustration of the football game still seems apt. It is improbable that a team in possession of the ball deep in its own territory will elect to pass on a fourth down. But there is nothing in the rules that prevents such a play, and to achieve surprise, the team may decide that a "contextually improbable" long pass is its best strategy.

48. These matters are discussed in greater detail in Chapter 5.

tended and elaborated without losing their identity and the ability to shape musical experience.

But even stable, memorable patterns may fail to become part of the common stylistic practice of a period. In order for them to become part of common practice, patterns must, I suspect, be consonant with prevailing musical strategies on the one hand, and with the style of the larger culture—its ideals and institutions—on the other.[49] In addition, some strategies receive such forceful embodiments that they can scarcely fail to become exemplars for later composers. One thinks, for instance, of Beethoven's Ninth Symphony, of Wagner's *Tristan,* and of Stravinsky's *Le sacre du printemps.*

## PREVALENT CONSTRAINTS AND PARTICULAR PATTERNS

### Dialect, Idiom, and Intraopus Style

A rule or strategy may serve as a constraint in the repertory of a group of composers, in the *oeuvre* of a single composer, or in a specific composition. Thus, just as stylistic constraints can be ordered hierarchically, so compositional choices can be grouped according to their prevalence. Three levels will be distinguished: dialect, idiom, and intraopus style.

DIALECT.

Dialects are substyles that are differentiated because a number of composers—usually, but not necessarily, contemporaries and geographical neighbors—employ (choose) the same or similar rules and strategies. Depending partly on what they seek to illuminate, analysts or historians divide a repertory according to somewhat different criteria. Dialects can, for example, be subdivided in terms of geographical area, nationality, or movements: northern versus southern Renaissance music, Venetian versus Roman opera, impressionism versus expressionism. Or a dialect may be defined by social class or cultural function: folk music versus art music, military music versus dance music. But most often dialects are distinguished historically. For instance, though their music is, in my view, governed by the same set of rules as that of Bach and Handel, Haydn and Mozart choose strikingly different possibilities within those rules: that is, they employ, and at times devise, quite different strategic

---

49. Since both of these may change over time, strategies not at first perpetuated as shared conventions may do so subsequently. For instance, Beethoven's late string quartets were not influential in the nineteenth century, perhaps because their expression derives from textural, tonal, and motivic contrasts, which were not entirely congenial to the aesthetic ideals of Romanticism. But their influence in the twentieth century has been considerable. In Joseph Kerman's words, "twentieth-century consciousness has been able to respond very directly to something in the expressive content of the late quartets—something overreaching and pure and characteristically indefinable" (*The Beethoven Quartets,* pp. 192–93).

constraints. And within the larger dialects of the Baroque and Classic styles, sub-dialects may be distinguished. These, too, may be historical. For example, the early Classic style of Sammartini and Wagenseil employs somewhat different strategies from the high Classic style of Haydn and Mozart. Within the high Classic style further distinctions may be drawn: the constraints that Haydn and Mozart use in their sacred music differ somewhat from those used in their secular music. Most often, of course, several criteria are used to distinguish a given dialect: for example, French versus Italian opera in the first half of the eighteenth century.

IDIOM.

Within any dialect, individual composers tend to employ some constraints rather than others; indeed, they may themselves have devised new constraints. Those that a composer repeatedly selects from the larger repertory of the dialect define his or her individual idiom. Thus, though Bach and Handel use essentially the same dialect, they tend to choose somewhat different strategic constraints and hence have somewhat different idioms.[50] Like dialects, idioms may be subdivided in various ways— according to genre or function, for instance. But, as in the case of dialects, the most common division made by historians and analysts is historical. That is, when the strategies chosen by a composer change over time, his or her idiom may be divided into periods such as early, middle, and late. This is the case with Beethoven, Verdi, and Stravinsky.

INTRAOPUS STYLE.

While dialect has to do with what is common to works by different composers, and idiom has to do with what is common to different works by the same composer, intraopus style is concerned with what is replicated within a single work. What is replicated may be a foreground relationship such as a motive or harmonic progression, a texture or a dynamic ordering; or replication may occur on a more extended hierarchic level. In a sonata-form movement, for example, the organization of the exposition may function as a constraint ordering not only the events of the recapitulation, but those of the development section as well.[51] Or the key scheme of a slow introduction may serve as a constraint governing the succession of keys through the remainder of the movement. And some forms—theme and variations and chaconne are notable examples—are, of course, specifically based on the principle of replication on the level of intraopus style.

---

50. It might be urged that Bach and Handel employ the same constraints but in different *manners*. Manners, however, are simply subtle replications that result from ingrained predilections to choose some relationships rather than others. And below the level of rules, all constraints are basically strategic.

51. For instance, Janet M. Levy has shown that when Beethoven revised the first movement of his String Quartet in F Major, Opus 18 No. 1 he made the relationship between the exposition and the development sections more patent; that is, the exposition section became a more explicit constraint for the succession of events in the development. See her *Beethoven's Compositional Choices*, pp. 39–40.

EXAMPLE 1.2. (*a*) Beethoven, Symphony No. 5 in C Minor, Opus 67, i; (*b*) Folk tune; (*c*) Mozart, Clarinet Quintet in A Major (K. 581), iv

Even though a pattern replicated as part of the intraopus style of some composition occurs in other works—as a feature of the dialect of the period or of the composer's idiom—it functions as a specific constraint within the particular composition in which it occurs. For instance, despite its forceful individuality, the motto that begins Beethoven's Fifth Symphony (Example 1.2*a*) is a transformation, most importantly through change of mode and rhythm, of a melodic pattern characteristic of the tonal period (Examples 1.2*b* and 1.2*c*). Many years later the same motto, somewhat varied, occurs in Charles Ives's Concord Sonata. Though borrowed by Ives, the motto nonetheless serves as one of the constraints defining the intraopus style of his sonata. In Beethoven's symphony, the motto acts as a constraint within the first movement, affecting, for example, the texture of the first key area, the beginning of the second key area, the materials used in the development section, and, through the replication of the fermata, the articulation of important divisions in formal structure. The motto is also replicated in the third and fourth movements of the Fifth Symphony where it again serves to define the intraopus style of the work.

## Intraopus Style and Intraopus Structure

The intraopus style of a work must be distinguished from what I will call its *intraopus structure*.[52] When a pattern is viewed as an aspect of the intraopus style of a work it is understood as a replicated, classlike event. But every pattern within a work also enters into nonrecurrent relationships with each and every other event or pattern in that work. Thus understood as nonrecurrent and unique, the pattern is an aspect of the work's intraopus structure. For instance, if we are primarily concerned with the similarities among statements of the motto of Beethoven's Fifth Symphony, we are directing attention to the work's intraopus style; when we attend to the individuality of each presentation of the motto, and with the peculiarity of its pervasive presence, we are concerned to understand the intraopus structure of the symphony. Even when the exposition section of the first movement of the symphony is repeated (as it ought to be), the structural significance of the second playing is not the same as that of the first, because the very fact of its being a repetition changes relationships.

---

52. Though I am using different terminology, this distinction was first made clear to me by Eugene Narmour, who uses the word *idiolect* for what I am calling intraopus structure. See his *Beyond Schenkerism*, chap. 11.

This distinction helps, I think, to clarify some issues in the areas of style analysis and criticism. For it suggests that, though they are complementary disciplines, criticism is not merely a more meticulous, refined stage (and perhaps one touching on values as well) of style analysis. Rather the disciplines are significantly, albeit subtly, different. Though criticism depends on the generalizations of style analysis, it uses these to illuminate what is unique about particular compositions. Style analysis, on the other hand, is not concerned with what is nonrecurrent. Instead, individual works serve as the basis for generalizations about the nature of the constraints (the rules and strategies) that guided the choices made by some composer or group of composers.

Since the distinction between intraopus style and intraopus structure is both intricate and important, let us consider an example. The second movement of Haydn's Symphony No. 100 in G Major ("Military") begins with a familiar, indeed a stock, figure in which a turn embellishing the second degree of the scale over dominant harmony on the weak part of the meter resolves to tonic harmony on the accented part of the next measure (Example 1.3a). Both from the rule-governed melodic, harmonic, and metric relationships and from repeated encounters with this specific figure, the competent listener knows (though perhaps tacitly) this is a pattern that customarily closes a phrase, section, or movement. It does so, for instance, in the trios of Haydn's String Quartet in Bb Major, Opus 64 No. 3 (Example 1.3b), and Mozart's Symphony No. 40 in G Minor (K. 550) (Example 1.3c).[53]

EXAMPLE 1.3. (a) Haydn, Symphony No. 100 in G Major, "Military," ii; (b) Haydn, String
    Quartet in Bb Major, Opus 64 No. 3, iii; (c) Mozart, Symphony No. 40 in G Minor (K.
    550), iii

The essential relationships of the figure, which are replicated in a number of different dialects, are constrained by the rules of tonal music. The figure itself (including even the grace note) is a feature of the dialect of the high Classic style: it occurs again and again in the works of many different composers. And the use of an unmistakable cadential formula at the beginning of a movement is a strategy of which Haydn was especially fond. In other words, this sort of usage is a characteristic of Haydn's idiom, both in the specific sense that Haydn often begins with a closing

53. What precedes the figure, of course, affects the kind of continuation expected. Because Examples 1.3b and 1.3c form part of a descending melodic motion, they are more closed than Example 1.3a.

figure and in the broader sense that he was prone to employ, in playful and at times seemingly capricious ways, the forms and procedures established by the dialect.[54]

When a pattern, no matter how conventional and familiar, is presented in a particular work and a specific context, it is an aspect not only of its dialect and idiom, but of its intraopus style, since it acts as a constraint peculiar to the work in which it occurs. Thus the figure that opens the second movement of Haydn's "Military" Symphony functions as an aspect of both intraopus style and intraopus structure.

As an aspect of intraopus style, the figure is ubiquitous. For instance, it is employed in varied form in measures 3 and 4 (Example 1.4a); because what had been a grace note (marked 0 over the figure) is now treated as an appoggiatura, the pattern is displaced with respect to the meter so that its fourth note (4) is an accent and fifth note (5) is transformed into a mobile weak beat. The middle section of the movement begins (m. 57) like the first, but in the minor mode (Example 1.4b). After rising to the G in measure 61, the rhythm of the pattern recurs, though the direction of motion is descending instead of ascending. Even here, melodic relationships suggest replication; for the eighth-notes are a kind of retrograde inversion of the original

EXAMPLE 1.4. Haydn, Symphony No. 100 in G Major, "Military," ii

54. Haydn's Trio in G Major for Flute, Cello, and Piano (No. 15), first movement, is another example of beginning with a closing gesture, one that in this case also closes the movement. Clearly the enormous advantage of conventions and formulae is the subtle strategic play they make possible. This kind of strategic play was, of course, used by other Classic composers as well. See Ratner, "Ars Combinatoria," pp. 358–60.

turn figure. Not surprisingly, since it is a *closing* pattern, the figure plays an important role in the coda, both before and after the important cadence at measures
176–78 (Example 1.4c).

The figure also plays an important role in the intraopus structure of the movement.[55] Its aberrant statement at the beginning of a phrase implies its normal occurrence as a close. This implication is strengthened by the cadence at the end of the
first phrase (Example 1.5, mm. 7–8). There, continuing the descending motion begun in measure 5 (Example 1.5, graph 4), the repeated D's are followed by the conventional turn figure, which moves to a half cadence that defines the close of the
antecedent phrase (Example 1.5, graph 3a). Though the cadence at the end of the
antecedent confirms, even reinforces, our sense of its closing function, the figure has
yet to be presented in its proper context.

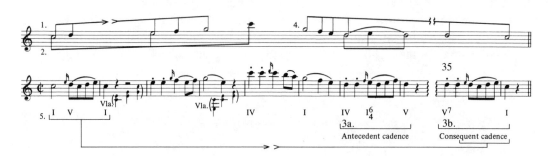

EXAMPLE 1.5.  Haydn: Symphony No. 100 in G Major, "Military," ii

It is presented properly at the end of the consequent phrase (Example 1.5, mm.
35–36, graph 3b). But instead of following the antecedent directly, as it might have
done, the consequent arrives only after a twelve-measure prolongation of dominant
harmony (not shown in the example), during which motivic relationships previously
presented are somewhat varied. This "prolonging interpolation" is another instance
of strategic play, a means, common in the Classic style, of delaying closure and
heightening the tension of goal-directed motion.[56] The two strategies discussed complement one another. Used at the beginning of a movement, the cadential figure implies its use as a close; and this implication is made more intense—the strategy is
made more effective—because interpolation delays realization.

To discuss fully the significance of the formulaic figure that begins the second
movement of Haydn's "Military" Symphony, then, would require a long and de-

55. The following discussion owes a considerable debt to Janet M. Levy's analysis of the strategic use of a
closing figure at the beginning of a movement—specifically, the first movement of Haydn's String Quartet in B♭
Major, Opus 50 No. 1. See her "Gesture, Form and Syntax."

56. Though such strategic play occurs (is replicated) in many compositions of the Classic period, each instance is unique and hence an aspect of intraopus structure.

tailed critical essay. For the significance of the pattern is defined by *all* the relationships of which it forms a part: not only its connections and interactions with all the patternings within the movement itself and, to the extent that they are illuminating, its connections with other movements of the symphony, but the salient, yet unrealized, potential relationships that might have occurred given the rules and strategies of the style—that is, its *implied structure*.[57] This task is clearly beyond the purview of this chapter. But a few such relationships will be mentioned by way of illustration.

a. The figure is related to the exposition section of the first movement of the symphony, whose first period (mm. 38–39) closes with the same cadential pattern (Example 1.6a), and, through this, to a pattern present in the tune of the second key area (Example 1.6b, m. 96).

b. The figure is defined by its immediate context. It occurs at the beginning of the movement, a position that at once contradicts and implies its conventional function. As a result of context, the figure generates implications, instead of realizing them as it normally does. The cadential figure usually occurs at the end of a descending melodic line. For instance, it does so in the Trio of Haydn's String Quartet in B♭ Major, Opus 64 No. 3 (Example 1.6c). As a result, the motion from tonic to super-

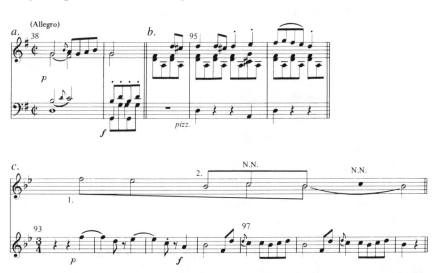

EXAMPLE 1.6. Haydn: (*a,b*) Symphony No. 100 in G Major, "Military," i; (*c*) String Quartet in B♭ Major, Opus 64 No. 3, iii

---

57. For this term I am indebted to Narmour's *Beyond Schenkerism*, p. 212. It is partly because the full significance of a work depends on an understanding of its implied structures that style analysis is indispensable for criticism (see below, sections b and c of the Commentary). Since texts and titles are integral parts of compositions, implied structure need not be solely a matter of "purely musical" relationships. For instance, the style and significance of the third movement of Stravinsky's *Symphony of Psalms* are in part defined by the fact that text reference to musical instruments (e.g., "Praise him with the sound of trumpets") is *not* accompanied by a trumpetlike fanfare. And for a competent listener (one who knows, albeit tacitly, the tradition of text setting in Western music since the Renaissance) this omission enhances, rather than diminishes, the power of both text and music.

tonic and back (B♭–C–B♭; mm. 96–98 in Example 1.6c) is subsumed within the overall descending motion (graph 1).[58]

Because no descending motion precedes the cadential figure that begins the second movement of the "Military" Symphony, the rising motion from C to D—the first motion of the movement—is understood as a generative melodic process implying linear continuation to a point of relative stability (see Example 1.5, graph 1). The linear motion is continued as the melody moves through E and F (m. 3) to G (m. 4), a point of relative stability.

Once the E is presented and the figure is repeated in varied form, a higher structural level of triadic motion—C to E, implying G—is generated, and continuation to octave completion on a high C is probable (Example 1.5, graph 2). The sense of triadic patterning is enhanced by the explicit, foreground triads played by the violas in measures 2 and 4. The stable G (over tonic harmony) is reached in measure 4, at the end of the half phrase. But the high C at the beginning of measure 5 counts only as a *provisional* realization of the implied triadic continuation because, instead of being harmonized by the tonic, it forms part of a subdominant chord. A satisfactory realization of the high C—accompanied by tonic harmony, played by the violins (which generated the pattern in the first place), and occurring on an accent—does not take place until the last four measures of the movement, where the motion from G to C is insistently reiterated.

c. The fact that the final measures do *not* realize the possibility latent in the opening figure of the movement focuses attention on the role of implied structure. That is, even though the realization of the high C (as tonic) implied in the opening phrase (and in its subsequent repetitions) may serve to explain why the movement ends as it does, the denial of latent possibility—namely, that the figure might have closed the movement—affects our retrospective understanding not only of the beginning figure but of the movement as a whole.[59] Implied structure, then, is an aspect of intraopus structure. But its existence depends on the prevalence of the strategic constraints of the dialect of Classic music.

Finally, it is important to recognize that the style of a work is not only a matter of intraopus constraints but of constraints prevalent on the levels of idiom and, most significantly, dialect. For instance, the antecedent-consequent period discussed earlier is an instance of a constraint on the level of dialect, while the strategic play evident in beginning with a closing gesture is an aspect of Haydn's idiom.

---

58. Notice that the larger descending pattern (Example 1.6c, graph 1) itself creates a familiar cadential motion.

59. That this unrealized alternative was a real possibility is shown by the fact that this movement of Haydn's "Military" Symphony was based almost in its entirety on the slow movement of his Concerto No. 5 in G Major for Two Hurdy Gurdies and Orchestra. But in that work the possibilities merely implied in the symphony are actually realized; that is, the movement does *end* with the closing formula with which it began.

COMMENTARY

In this final section, I wish to consider some of the ramifications of the preceding discussion of the nature of style.

a. The distinction between rules and strategies helps, I think, to clarify the concept of originality, as well as its correlative, creativity. For it suggests that two somewhat different sorts of originality need to be recognized. The first involves the invention of new rules. Whoever invented the limerick was original and creative in this sense, and Schoenberg's invention of the twelve-tone method also involved this sort of originality. The second sort of originality, on the level of strategy, does not involve changing the rules but discerning new strategies for realizing the rules.[60] A Bach or Haydn, devising new ways of moving within established rules—or an Indian sitar player improvising according to existing canons on an age-old *rag*—is original and creative in this way.[61] "It is surprising to note," observes Josephine Miles,

> that the so-called great poets as we recognize them are not really the innovators; but if you stop to think about it, they shouldn't be. Rather they are the sustainers, the most deeply immersed in tradition, the most fully capable of making use of the current language available to them. When they do innovate, it is within a change begun by others, already taking place.[62]

And the same seems true in music. For though some composers have both invented new rules and devised new means for their realization—Schoenberg is surely the exemplary instance—most of the acknowledged great masters (Bach and Handel, Haydn and Mozart, and even Beethoven) have been incomparable strategists.

b. A knowledge of style is indispensable for criticism because, as observed earlier, to appreciate fully what something *is*—to comprehend its significance—is to have some notion (however informal or unformulated) about what it *might have been*. The special savor of a brilliantly sunny winter snowscape, the inventiveness of a strategy for testing some scientific hypothesis, the involvement of the United States in the Vietnam conflict—all are understood partly, but nonetheless importantly, in terms of our knowledge of the alternatives possible and probable in the specific

---

60. The conditions for the success of new strategies were touched on earlier. I am not sure why rules survive and become part of a common practice. It seems plausible, however, that no constraint that contravenes the laws of human perception and cognition can become a prevalent rule. This may in part explain the failure of Vicentino's experiments and some of the forays into microtonal intervals and novel scales in twentieth-century music. Constraints that might become rules must probably also be consonant with whatever rules are already in force—unless, of course, the whole system is being scrapped. That is, the harmonic syntax developed near the beginning of the seventeenth century became the rule because existing melodic, rhythmic, and contrapuntal constraints could be accommodated to it.

61. Obviously this is also true in the case of jazz improvisation.

62. "Values in Language," p. 11.

situation. The road actually taken is invariably understood partly in terms of those not taken.

And so it is with works of art. We understand and appreciate a work not only in terms of the possibilities and probabilities actually realized, but in terms of our sense of what might have occurred in a specific compositional context: that is, in terms of the work's implied structure. This is perhaps especially clear in music. A cadence is called deceptive precisely because the competent listener is aware of what might have been (indeed, of what was probable): namely, that the progression might have closed on the tonic. Often such understanding is retrospective. That is, we are aware of what might have been only when the possible realization actually takes place. This is particularly true with long-range relationships.[63] But possibility does not depend on actualization. Even though it never occurs, a possibility may be implied, as is the case with the possibility that the opening figure of the second movement of Haydn's "Military" Symphony will function as its close. Indeed, the relationship of implication to realization may itself be a stylistic trait. For instance, one difference between the dialect of Classic music and that of Romantic music is that in the former style implied structure is usually actualized, though often after considerable delay, while in the latter style the implied structure frequently remains unrealized: implicative possibilities transcend closure. An understanding of implied structure, as well as of actualized structure, clearly depends on knowledge of both the rules and the strategies that establish the alternatives available to the composer.

c. Not only is understanding dependent upon stylistic knowledge, but so is evaluation. For the patterns that result from a composer's actual choices are judged, as well as understood, in terms of the options known to have been available given the constraints of the style he employed. This view is confirmed by most explicit evaluations. For example, when Charles Rosen writes that the beginning of Haydn's Keyboard Divertimento in A♭ Major (XVI:46) "shows the same limping tonic cadences, which enforce nothing beyond themselves . . . and the same unprepared animation, convincing only if one does not put too high a price upon one's convictions,"[64] he must have some idea, however vague or general, about what more effective, nonlimping cadences and more adequately prepared animation would be like.[65] And Rosen can have such ideas only because his intimate acquaintance with the style of Classic music suggests more felicitous alternatives that Haydn might have chosen, given the constraints employed.[66]

More generally, conceiving of style as a hierarchy of constraints may help to illuminate some problems of value. To the extent that universal laws (especially

63. See, for instance, the discussion of the third movement of Mahler's Fourth Symphony in Chapter 7 of this book.

64. *The Classical Style*, pp. 150–51.

65. As E. H. Gombrich has observed, "the evaluation of expressiveness will largely depend on a knowledge of choice situations" ("Style," p. 358).

66. I hasten to add that this in no way suggests that Rosen should be able to compose such cadences or such a preparation. One may have to be a composer to lay an egg, but for a critic it suffices to know that better eggs (alternatives) were available.

those of human perception and cognition) govern whatever stylistic constraints a culture develops, patterns that are entirely incompatible with these laws must be without musical value. For instance, a composition with pitches so high as to be inaudible would be valueless, and so, I believe, would be a work that so overloaded the cognitive capacity of the listener that no patterns whatsoever could be discerned.[67] On the level of rules, values are cultural in the broadest sense; that is, rules establish the criteria for "winning" the "game" of music. In our culture, since the Renaissance at least, that game has generally been considered to be aesthetic. And strategies have been concerned with realizing aesthetic goals. The musics of other cultures (e.g., Indonesia) or subcultures (e.g., religious groups) may have other goals (and hence other strategies) that establish criteria for value in a piece of music.

Given the goal of aesthetic enjoyment, value is significantly related to what I have called *relational richness*.[68] Since richness arises from implied structure as well as from actualized structure, works whose constraints are unknown or incomprehensible necessarily lack this aspect of aesthetic value. This is true, for instance, of aleatory music[69] and perhaps of totally statistical music also.[70]

d. The relationship between evaluation and choice may explain what is meant by the concept of *inevitability,* which is so often said to be a crucial criterion for judging works of art.[71] For in terms of the analysis presented here, to contend that X was inevitable seems not only to mean that the critic was unable to imagine any alternative that was preferable to the one actually chosen but suggests that the composer's choice was optimal, while to say that Y was not inevitable may merely be a way of suggesting that more felicitous alternatives might be imagined. Thus the sense of inevitability, too, is dependent upon a knowledge of the style of the work being discussed, since only if the critic knows the style well enough to be aware of possible alternatives can one of them be judged to be preferable to others. One cannot sense inevitability in a work whose style is unfamiliar.

The concept of inevitability is closely related to the idea that musical relationships can be conceived of as being *logical.* But in order for the notion of logic to be more than a misleading metaphor, the constraints governing the relationships in question must be fully known, whether tacitly or conceptually. Consider the case of a game such as chess, which can, in some sense, be thought of as being logical. The constraints governing the choices made by the players can be fully known because

---

67. In this connection, see my *Music, the Arts, and Ideas,* pp. 290–93.

68. "Grammatical Simplicity and Relational Richness."

69. As Cage recognizes; see below, section f.

70. But in other contexts (e.g., as a cultural or historical phenomenon) such styles may be seen as significant and, in some sense, valuable.

71. The notion that musical relationships are, or should be, inevitable has a pernicious effect on analysis and criticism. This is the case because the valuing of inevitability directs attention almost exclusively to those possibilities that *are* actualized. But, as argued here, a full appreciation of a relationship involves an understanding of its implied structure as well. The tacit line of argument would seem to run somewhat as follows: the best relationships are necessary (inevitable) ones; hence the best compositions exhibit a high degree of inevitability. Since we customarily study and criticize excellent compositions, what happens in them must be inevitable, and for this reason, we need not trouble ourselves with unrealized possibilities.

they are finite and stable over time. But this is scarcely true of the "game of music." To mention only two differences (albeit major ones): (1) The choices of a chess player are made in relation to a single goal (checkmating the opponent), while the choices of composers are almost invariably the result of compromise among a number of competing, and often incompatible, goals (from the wholly aesthetic, to pleasing patrons, to fulfilling what are taken to be the imperatives of history). (2) While the constraints of chess have remained stable over time and are accessible partly for this reason, those of music have changed and have seldom been fully known even by the most accomplished "grand masters."

e. If evaluation depends on knowing what a composer might have chosen, as well as what he actually chose, then it is scarcely surprising that critics (including knowledgeable listeners) have occasionally misjudged works in an unfamiliar style. For until the rules and strategies of a style have been internalized as habits of perception and cognition—or, at a later stage, conceptualized—the alternatives actually chosen by a composer cannot be understood in relation to those available. Rather, what is surprising is that, over the course of history, the evaluation of new works has been as perceptive and prescient as it has. One reason, perhaps, why there have been relatively few significant misevaluations is that most style changes have involved the use of novel strategies rather than novel rules. Listeners familiar with an existing set of rules evidently have relatively little difficulty in adjusting to and comprehending shifts in strategy.

f. It follows from the theory sketched in this chapter that the evaluation of truly aleatory music is not merely problematic in practice; it is impossible in principle. For since successive sounds (pitches, durations, timbres, and so on), whether notated or recorded, are by definition unrelated to one another, what *is* cannot be distinguished from what *might have been*.[72] The notions of alternatives, choices, and hence evaluations are irrelevant. As Cage himself astutely observes, "value judgements are not in the nature of this work. . . . A 'mistake' is beside the point, for once anything happens it authentically is."[73] The second sentence of Cage's statement reminds us that, since the specific sound successions generated by random means are not consequences of human choice, they are not, according to the definition given at the beginning of this chapter, stylistic. Rather, like phenomena in the natural world, they simply exist.[74]

Human choices are involved in the making of aleatory music. First, the possibility of choosing to write aleatory music is a feature of twentieth-century cultural

72. Since the specific succession of sounds in a piece of aleatory music has no implied structure, relational richness is restricted to what actually occurs. For this reason a recorded performance of aleatory music tends to be impoverished by rehearing, while that of style-generated music tends to be enriched by rehearing, up to a point. See my *Music, the Arts, and Ideas*, chap. 3.

73. *Silence*, p. 59.

74. The fact that Cage's compositions can be distinguished from one another and from those of other composers—even other aleatory composers—is not evidence that his works have style. For we can easily differentiate phenomena that would scarcely be characterized as stylistic: e.g., between kinds of rocks or insects. This contention is entirely consonant with Cage's own belief that his music should be understood as nature is.

style, as well as an aspect of the style behavior of the individual. And second, a table of random numbers or the throwing of dice to generate a series of pitches, durations, and so on, is chosen as a constraint. This choice, however, is not among compositional alternatives but among cultural ones. Aleatory composers make choices, then, not on the level of successive sound-relationships within works, but on the level of precompositional constraints: rules (that the work be aleatory) and strategies (that randomness be generated by means such as throwing dice). As a result, it seems reasonable to argue that though style plays no role in the listener's understanding and experience of such pieces, the composer's behavior has style[75] and can for this reason be evaluated.[76]

g. The viewpoint adopted here suggests that the relevance for criticism of preliminary sketches and drafts is at once different and more complicated than is generally supposed. First, it should be observed that it is not the sketches that illuminate compositions, but the compositions that illuminate sketches. Without the finished work, it would, as a rule, be impossible to know how to interpret the sketches. Second, despite considerable opinion to the contrary, sketches and drafts cannot reveal relationships in a completed work that could not have been discovered without them. Either a relationship is present in a score or recording, in which case it can *in principle* be discerned without reference to sketches, or it is not present, in which case, there is nothing for sketches to reveal.[77]

Rather, according to the present analysis, sketches and drafts are significant because they affect our understanding of what the completed work actually *is* by making us aware of particular alternative versions of what it *might have been*. That is, knowledge of alternatives explicitly considered and rejected imparts a kind of specificity to our evaluation of what a composer actually chose for his work.[78] For example, had Haydn composed another version of the Keyboard Divertimento in A♭ Major—one such as Rosen indicates might be imagined, in which tonic cadences did not limp and animation was adequately prepared—it would in part have been

75. Clearly Cage's style is defined not simply by his decision to write aleatory music, but by his choice of randomizing means: the *I Ching,* maps of the heavens, and so on.

76. In some cases evaluation may be impossible, not because randomness makes choice irrelevant, but because choice is prohibited by the culture, as it sometimes is when the arts are inseparable from religious rituals. And this prohibition of choice may in part explain the absence of aesthetic/evaluative terms in such cultures. Even in cases where choice is possible, it may be regarded as being primarily religious, and the terms used to describe it may not suggest aesthetic judgments. In like manner, masks from New Guinea or the music of African puberty rites are transformed into artworks (aesthetic objects) because our cultural community has come to regard them as such.

77. This is not to deny that sketches may make us notice especially subtle and intricate relationships sooner rather than later. But to be relevant for criticism, the relationship must be in the work, not only in the sketches. Nor does this position deny that the study of sketches may illuminate the composer's creative process (his compositional style), a subject of great interest in its own right. But to confuse the genesis of a relationship with its structure is to commit a serious error. A number of scholars have discussed the relationship between sketches and finished compositions. See, for instance, Gossett, "Beethoven's Sixth Symphony"; Johnson, "Beethoven Scholars and Beethoven's Sketches," pp. 13ff.; and Levy, *Beethoven's Compositional Choices,* pp. 2–4.

78. It is perhaps worth noting that there is no necessary relationship between the number and extent of sketches for a particular passage and the aesthetic significance of that passage. As anyone who has written anything (music or language) knows, one can get stuck on an essentially trivial problem—e.g., a minor connection or a single word-choice.

understood and appreciated in terms of the changes made from the existing version.

But even in this procedure there are dangers, though they are psychological rather than logical. For the possibilities actually sketched represent only a minute fraction of the stylistically conceivable alternatives that were not chosen, and there is no compelling reason to suppose that such sketched options have privileged status. "Any expression," in John Ellis's words,

> derives its meaning from the choice of that expression rather than others which contrast with it in a variety of different ways. From a linguistic standpoint, then, to contrast a variant with a literary text is to limit the range of meaning of an expression by limiting the possible meaningful contrasts it involves, and to give one particular contrast a special status for which there is no conceivable justification. . . . Instead of seeing one particular contrast as a clue to meaning, therefore, we must think of all possible contrasts as parts of the meaning of a piece of language.[79]

In other words, sketches and preliminary drafts may be illuminating, but their significance should not be exaggerated. For if they are allowed to obscure the wider range of alternatives possible given the constraints of the style, they will limit, and thereby distort, the meaning and evaluation of the composition being studied.

h. Last, a few further, but important, remarks about choice. The concept of choice not only presupposes the presence of alternative possibilities, but entails the existence of intentions (though such intentions need not be consciously conceptualized). Furthermore, the existence of intentions in turn entails the existence of goals. As I will argue in Chapters 3 and 5, the choices of composers (whether on the level of dialect, idiom, or intraopus style) can be understood and explained only in light of the intentions generated by goals—goals that are implicit in the constraints of the style and are largely set by the ideology of the culture. From this point of view (to revert to the game analogy), the whole history of music aesthetics/theory may be seen as a succession of attempts to determine what constitutes winning in the game of art—or put differently, what makes a winning work of art.

A sense of style is, then, the foundation on which the understanding, appreciation, and evaluation of works of art must rest.[80] For the composer, performer, and

---

79. *Theory of Literary Criticism*, pp. 122–23.

80. And this is true of their performance as well. Perhaps one of the differences between a profound and revealing interpretation of a work and an accurate but routine one is that in the former case the performer is able to suggest something about the work's implied structure, even as he or she presents and illuminates its intraopus structure.

listener such knowledge may be, and often is, tacit. But not for the critic, and not for the historian. If the choices made by composers, either within a work or between successive works, are to be explained, then the constraints governing such choices must be made explicit.[81] Making such constraints explicit and developing hypotheses about their interrelationships is the central task of style analysis.

81. It is important to recognize that explaining the choices made by a composer does not mean knowing what actually went on in the composer's mind during the act of choosing (neither we nor the composer can probably ever know that with precision); rather it is a matter of understanding the psycho-logic of the alternatives open to the composer, given a set of stylistic/compositional and cultural circumstances.

# CHAPTER 2

# Style Analysis

It is the goal of style analysis to describe the patternings replicated in some group of works, to discover and formulate the rules and strategies that are the basis for such patternings, and to explain in the light of these constraints how the characteristics described are related to one another.[1] The works in a group, or repertory, which are treated as a set, will always have shared characteristics, but the basis for selection may be quite varied. For instance, the set may consist of

a. The works of a single composer (divided into periods or taken as a whole).
b. Works by a group of composers, usually, but not necessarily, written during a given time period and in the same culture (for example, the repertory of the Parisian chanson, of Viennese Classicism, of impressionism—whether French, English, or American).
c. Works written in the same geographical area or national tradition (the style of Russian, as differentiated from German, music regardless of historical period; South Indian, as distinguished from North Indian, music).
d. Works written in a particular genre (opera, *lied,* chamber music, tone poems).
e. Works written for some socially defined segment of a culture, perhaps transcending cultural or geographical boundaries (folk music, popular music).
f. Works written for some utilitarian purpose (liturgical music, military music, music for factories).
g. Works written over a considerable period of time in the same extended cultural area (in the West, music of the Renaissance, Baroque).
h. The music of a whole civilization or some segment thereof (music of the cultures of the South Pacific, American Indian music, Western music since the Renaissance).

---

1. Style analysis may also aim to account for relationships on the level of intraopus structure—i.e., for the patterns replicated within a particular composition. However, this level of analysis will not be a central concern in what follows.

The possible divisions and subdivisions are innumerable. As in any discipline, the ways in which entities are grouped depend on the interests of the investigator. If a painter, a cartographer, an ecologist, an urban planner, a geologist, and a politician were asked to pattern the same geographical area, each would probably segment it somewhat differently according to his or her particular viewpoint and (perhaps informal or even unformulated) hypotheses about the connection among entities being considered. But it does not follow from such differences that the several segmentations or patternings are arbitrary or fictitious. The similarities and differences, proximities and disjunctions on which groupings are based are discovered in the data. But the possibility of alternative groupings does not mean that all are equally fruitful. For instance, one might decide to examine the set of all pieces of Western music that are less than fifteen measures long or all those that contain a part for flute. But in both cases the constraint involved—size and instrument—makes it seem doubtful that musical/stylistic relationships will be significantly illuminated.

## CLASSIFICATION, HISTORY, AND ANALYSIS

### *Classification*

Style analysis begins with classification—that is, with the recognition that in some repertory particular relationships and traits may be replicated on one or more levels of structure. To study such replicated relationships and traits, works and parts of works are taken out of time and are treated as isolable entities. Such an entity—be it an interval, a rhythmic pattern, a harmonic progression, a textural arrangement, or a formal schema—is related to other entities, not because it forms part of a larger temporal process, but because similarity leads us to group the entities together as members of some class of events.[2] For instance, the motives presented in Example 1.3 can be classed together because of their melodic, rhythmic, and harmonic similarity;[3] and on a higher level the melodies given in Example 1.1 are similar and can be classed as changing-note melodies.[4] Even within a single work, where motives (or other entities) might be understood as being processively connected, such patterns can be taken out of time and related to one another because similarities make it

2. Depending on the interests of the analyst, such classes may be limited or expanded in various ways. For instance, the class of triads may be limited to major triads (and further to those in root position), or it may be extended to include any set of three different pitches. Similarly, the class of sonata-form movements may be limited to those that are tonal or extended to include those that are not.

3. The identity and integrity of each motive is, of course, defined by the closure created by internal melodic, rhythmic, and harmonic processes. But the motives are not themselves processively related. This is *not* because they come from different compositions, however. For the motives might be understood as being processively related on the level of style history. Rather it is because they are being analyzed as members of a class that is synchronic, not diachronic.

4. It is important to recognize that any specific pattern may be a member of several different conformant classes, even with respect to a single parameter. Thus the melody given in Example 1.1*b* belongs not only to the class of changing-note patterns (graph 2), but to the class of what I have called "Adeste Fidelis" tunes (graph 3) and to the class of foreground gap-fill patterns (graph 4).

possible to understand them as being members of the same class. Thus the opening measures of the slow movement of Haydn's "Military" Symphony can be understood in terms of motivic similarity (Example 1.4a, graph 1) as well as processive motion (Example 1.5, graph 1).

Class membership may occur on the same or on different hierarchic levels, either within or between compositions. For instance, linear melodic patterns that descend from the fifth of the scale to the tonic (5–4–3–2–1) may occur on the foreground, note-to-note level or on levels encompassing whole sections; comparable rhythmic groupings—for example, end-accented anapests—may occur on low or high structural levels; duple meters may occur on the levels of the beat, the measure, or even the phrase; and formal types—for example, rounded binary structures—may be the basis for relatively brief themes or for whole movements.[5] Finally, it should be observed that similar kinds of expression and representation—for instance, demonic or celestial, passionate or restrained, pastoral or heroic—may also be the basis of a classification.[6]

Because they are connected by no process, the members of a class are not related to one another *in* a hierarchy. This is so despite the fact that, as observed earlier, members of the same class may occur *on* different hierarchic levels.[7] Even when similar patterns are processively related within a composition—for instance, when the patterns of the first key area of a sonata-form movement return in the recapitulation—they are hierarchically connected not primarily by virtue of their similarity, but by virtue of their participation in the higher-level syntactic process of the whole movement.[8]

---

5. This analysis helps to clarify the difference between understanding a work as *being a form* and as *having form*. (See my *Explaining Music*, pp. 91–92). When one understands a pattern as *being* an antecedent-consequent phrase, a rounded-binary period, a ritornello organization, or a fugal texture, one is considering it in terms of its similarity to comparable patterns of the same class. On the other hand, when one speaks of a particular composition as *having* form, one is considering the peculiar processive relationships that make its structure unique. One is referring, that is, to its intraopus structure.

6. Although many—perhaps most— class relationships result from the prevalence of rules and strategies, some arise as the result of constraints on the level of laws. Thus the classification of pitches (as C s, C♯ s, etc.) is evidently a consequence of innate perceptual/cognitive principles that produce the sense of octave identity; the presence of gap-fill melodies in the musics of many different cultures may be traced to the cross-cultural psychological need for completion; and the ways in which certain affects are delineated and subjects represented (e.g., agitation or winter) may be ascribed in part to synesthesia.

7. This is not to deny that similarity may function as an aspect of process, as, for instance, when the return of a melody heard earlier serves to enhance closure.

8. Rather than a hierarchy, what similarity relationships create is a continuum that extends from those relationships resulting from the operation of laws, through those arising from the presence of rules, to those dependent upon the existence of shared strategies. Thus the psychological law of completeness gives rise to the class of gap-fill melodies, the rules of tonality stipulate what constitutes a satisfactory fill, and the particular manner of filling may depend on the kinds of strategies favored by a particular composer or group of composers. Since such classes form a continuum, there is *in principle* no way of definitively separating those features of the style of a work that result from the presence of laws and rules from those that result from the idiosyncratic realization of a strategy. For this reason, once a composer has adopted some set of constraints, every instance of replication must be considered part of his style, even though many of the patterns he employs occur in the works of other composers.

Class relationships, then, are essentially synchronic rather than diachronic. Even though two similar entities occur in a specific chronological order in the same work (or in different works), or in the same style period (or different style periods), that order is irrelevant for purposes of classification. An octave is an octave regardless of when or where it occurs, and the same is true of triadic melodies, imitative textures, deceptive cadences, ternary forms, the representation of winter, and so on. Consequently it makes no difference, methodologically, in what order a class is formed or analyzed. For instance, in forming the class of "*Tristan* motive," one can in principle begin anywhere in Wagner's opera; indeed, one might even begin with the occurrence of the motive in Berg's Lyric Suite. This is true of all such analyses, including those of Rudolph Reti and his followers as well as the set-theory analyses of serial compositions.[9]

## Classification and History

If classification is synchronic, then history would seem irrelevant for style analysis. But the relationship between history and style analysis is considerably more complex and problematic. For if, as proposed in Chapter 1, a style is defined as a result of the choices made among possible alternatives, then its characterization depends not only on objective, actualized traits, but on our knowledge of the unrealized alternatives available to the composer—knowledge, that is, of the full range of possibilities from which the specific traits in some work(s) were chosen. The dilemma is plain. Consider what would happen if a symphony believed to have been written by, say, Dittersdorf were discovered to have been written by a twentieth-century composer. In terms of taxonomic traits, it would still seem to belong to the corpus of Classic compositions; in terms of comprehension and appreciation, however, its style would be significantly different.[10] I do not know how to resolve this dilemma

9. Similarity relationships per se cannot give rise to hierarchic structures because such relationships do not involve functional differentiation. Rather they might be thought of as a kind of secondary parameter, since similarity is a matter of degree. Perhaps this is why it has proved impossible to devise a syntax governing the succession of motives. For instance, one of the perplexing problems that serial theorists and composers are concerned to solve is that of the higher-level orderings of conformant relationships (i.e., of the various versions of the tone row). Their efforts have not, as far as I can see, been notably successful.

An equally important problem has to do with the aesthetic significance of similarity relationships. The question is whether such relationships create the unity presumed by those theorists—tonal as well as serial—who emphasize their importance. In my view (see *Explaining Music*, pp. 57–60), membership in some class per se creates only a *weak* kind of unity, like the unity of a coral colony. *Strong* unity, as Meyer Schapiro has observed (in personal conversation), comes not from similarity of pattern but from differentiation of function.

10. Functioning heuristically, however, historical knowledge may affect the classification of compositions. Knowledge that the symphony was written by a twentieth-century composer may well lead to a search for, and perhaps the discovery of, traits that preclude its membership in the class of Classic music. That is, once we know who wrote the piece, we cannot resist asking, "How successful was the imitation? What 'modernisms' have unwittingly found their way into it?" and so on. And such inquiries may lead to the formation of a special class—e.g., the class of contemporary imitations of past styles.

except to suggest that style analysis necessarily transcends classification.[11]

A related problem concerns the significance of statements that characterize styles by remarking on the absence of some trait or even parameter. How, for example, is one to understand a statement such as "Gregorian chant is without harmony"? For, according to the definition of style being used in this study, the absence of harmony cannot be a feature of the style of Gregorian chant, since harmony was not an available option. To refer again to Gombrich's observation about the relationship between option and choice: Prokofiev's style is partly defined by the presence of harmonic syntax, and Boulez's style is partly defined by its absence. But just as Julius Caesar was not a nonsmoker, so chant composers were not nonharmonists.[12] Nevertheless, styles *are* frequently described in this negative way: Medieval painting is said to be without linear perspective, American Indian culture is characterized as being without the wheel, and so on.

Though such negative descriptions are not analytically useful, they may be heuristically helpful. Stating that chant is without harmony seems to be a way of characterizing it in order to establish a class—that is, in order to identify it by distinguishing it from another style (in this case probably that of tonal music) which, because of its familiarity, is taken to be a norm or standard. But to classify chant in this way is not to explain how it "works"—how its replicated patterns result from the constraints that govern relationships within and between the parameters *actually* present—any more than saying that lichens are "without chlorophyll" accounts for their biological processes and structures. This is not to deny the need for classification, but only to insist, once again, that it is different from explanatory analysis.

Classification does, however, affect both style analysis and history. It affects style analysis because, even though it tells us nothing about the constraints governing the class distinguished, it does tell us what features occur together and leads us to ask why they do so. From this point of view, to say that chant is without harmony (or lichens are without chlorophyll) is to suggest that we inquire about how the functioning of some less familiar class is affected by the absence of a parameter present in some class that is more familiar and better understood.

The relationship between classification and history is quite intricate. When an earlier class of events is related to a later one historically, the former tends to be understood not only in terms of its own process and structure, and in terms of what is thought to have led to it, but also in terms of the events or relationships believed to have followed from it. In other words, our comprehension of temporal events— whether within compositions or, on a higher level, between compositions (or classes of compositions)—is both prospective and retrospective. Viewed prospectively,

---

11. Comparable problems arise in biology because taxonomy is not invariably linked to genesis. According to the biologist David Wake, "for many years evolutionary biologists have equated morphological similarity with close genetic relationship. This is clearly not necessarily the case" (quoted in Lewin, "Seeds of Change," p. 43). The problems broached here are considered again in Chapter 5 in connection with a discussion of miming, choice, and replication.

12. See Chapter 1, at note 7.

without benefit of hindsight, the concept of harmony is irrelevant for the understanding and analysis of chant. Retrospective views are more problematic.

Though retrospective understanding (e.g., that chant is without harmony) may be heuristically fruitful, there is considerable danger that it will result in a teleological view of history—one in which earlier events are thought to be directed toward some goal (in this case, toward the style of tonal harmony). But as James S. Ackerman has put it: "What is called 'evolution' in the arts should not be described as a succession of steps toward a solution to a given problem, but as a succession of steps away from one or more original statements of a problem. . . . The pattern of style change, then, is not determined by any destiny nor by a common goal, but by a succession of complex decisions as numerous as the works by which we have defined the style." [13]

From a retrospective point of view, the statement that chant is without harmony must be interpreted as referring not to alternatives *within* a style, but to a diachronic relationship *between* styles. But if such a relationship is to be credible and illuminating (more than a descriptive truism asserting that chant was eventually followed by styles in which harmony was a parameter), it must be informed by a hypothesis about the historical process of Western music—a hypothesis such as that suggested in Chapter 1 in which the constraints governing chant were related to those governing tonal music.

## Classification and Style Analysis

Classification is essentially a descriptive discipline. It tells us what traits go together and with what frequencies they occur, but not why they do so. Style analysis is more ambitious. It seeks to formulate and test hypotheses explaining why the traits found to be characteristic of some repertory—its replicated melodic patterns, rhythmic groupings, harmonic progressions, textures, timbres, and so on—fit together, complementing one another. [14] As René Wellek and Austin Warren observe:

> Stylistic analysis seems most profitable to literary study when it can establish some unifying principle, some general aesthetic aim pervasive of a

13. "A Theory of Style," p. 232. Similarly, Herbert A. Simon has observed that "complex forms can arise from the simple ones by purely random processes. . . . Direction is provided to the scheme by the stability of the complex forms, once these come into existence" ("The Architecture of Complexity," p. 471). Also see Burgers, "Causality and Anticipation." As far as I can see, the change need not necessarily be one from simple to complex forms. It might be from simple to simple, or from complex to simple. It is also important to note that the persistence of forms—their tendency to endure through replication—is not solely a matter of their stability, but depends, as I argue below, on their compatibility with other constraints prevalent in the cultural environment.

14. Even on the level of description, however, hypotheses—usually unconscious or unformulated ones— are involved. If we describe and count some traits (for instance, as mentioned earlier, the presence of *sforzandi* in Beethoven's music), it is because we have reason to suppose, or have been taught to believe, that they are significant attributes of the style in question.

whole work. If we take, for example, an eighteenth-century descriptive poet such as James Thomson, we should be able to show how his stylistic traits interlock. The Miltonic blank verse puts certain denials and demands on the choice of vocabulary. The vocabulary requires periphrasis, and periphrasis implies a tension between word and thing: the object is not named but its qualities are enumerated. . . . Such a procedure . . . must not, of course, be misunderstood to mean a process of ascribing priority, either logical or chronological, to any of these elements. Ideally, we should be able to start at any given point and should arrive at the same results.[15]

Stylistic traits, then, occur in clusters comparable to what biologists refer to as coadapted gene complexes. For instance, just as "mutually suitable teeth, claws, guts, and sense organs evolved in carnivore gene pools,"[16] so the traits characteristic of Wagner's music are interdependent ("mutually suitable"). To relate such traits to one another, we must begin by inferring from particular instances the kinds of constraints and strategies employed and then interpret the constraints in the light of a theory or hypotheses about their connections. Perhaps I can make the sort of account I have in mind clear by providing a short analysis.

## A Sketch-Analysis

In histories of Western music, the following are frequently cited as salient features of Richard Wagner's mature style:[17]

a. Leitmotifs with distinctive delineation.
b. Sequential organization both within and between phrases.
c. Chromaticism, both melodic and harmonic.
d. Modulation—frequent, and often to remote keys.
e. Deceptive cadences.
f. Rhythms with feminine endings: for example, ⌐ ᵕ    ⌐ ᵕ - ᵕ
g. Elisions between phrases.
h. Contrapuntal textures.
i. Rejection of stock accompaniment figures.
j. Bar-form phrase structure—that is, A A′ B or 1 + 1 + 2.

---

15. *Theory of Literature*, p. 182. Edward T. Cone's description of a "complete style" can also serve as the ideal for style analysis, "one that interrelates in an all-embracing unity every aspect of musical composition: tempo, meter, rhythm, melody, harmony, form." See his *Musical Form and Musical Performance*, p. 58.
16. Dawkins, *The Selfish Gene*, p. 212.
17. See, for instance, Crocker, *History of Musical Style*, pp. 457–65; Grout, *History of Western Music*,

But, of course, Wagner's style is far more than a mere compendium of these attributes. And what one wants to know is how they imply, complement, reinforce, and are otherwise connected with one another. In short, *why* do the traits described "go together"? To explain this, it is necessary to relate the strategies employed both to one another and to the rules of the style, including in particular the ways in which the several parameters interact.

In what follows, I will suggest some ways—and others are certainly possible—in which the attributes listed above might be related to one another. Though I will begin by discussing the relationship of the leitmotif to other traits, this should not be taken to indicate that the leitmotif or any other trait is considered to be "prior" or "privileged" either logically or chronologically. Rather, the several traits are conceived of as coexisting and as constituting an atemporal relational set. In other words, the account is not diachronic but synchronic.[18]

Because such relational sets are understood as being synchronic, style analysis need not consider parameters external to music—ideology, political and social circumstances, and so on. Even style traits that might readily be related to their cultural context or their past are not so. For instance, though the verse forms and prosody that Wagner chooses can be connected with his aesthetic/ideological stance, in a "pure" style analysis they would be directly related to musical period structure without benefit of cultural context.[19] But the history of style cannot, in my view, be explained without reference to aspects of culture external to music.[20]

Leitmotif technique was a strategy for relating musical patterns to a dramatic action. It was derived, one surmises, from the use of referential themes in program music (e.g., Berlioz's *Symphonie fantastique*) and opera (e.g., Weber's *Euryanthe* or Wagner's *Flying Dutchman*). In these works the themes, though patently profiled, were relatively long. But when Wagner extended musical reference to include a much larger number of characters and concepts, actions, and objects, the length of patterns tended to become shorter; that is, themes became motives. And as the length of a pattern becomes shorter, its sound and substance need to be especially striking if it is to be readily recognized. The delineation of profile was also important because a leitmotif had to be identifiable in a wide variety of musical/dramatic con-

---

pp. 561–67; and Hughes, *History of European Music*, pp. 417–25. Other traits mentioned as characteristic of Wagner's style—his orchestration, the declamatory nature of his vocal lines, and so on—will not be considered in the following sketch. Naturally, the list of attributes is scarcely exhaustive. Some additional attributes might include, among others, plots, melodic structure, and "statistical form." Concerning these in particular, see Chapters 6, 7, and 8.

18. It should be emphasized that the following analysis ought not be taken to imply that Wagner thought in this way about the relationships discussed. Analysis is concerned, not with the psychology of the composer, but with an explanation of the relationships among the strategies employed by a particular composer given the prevailing laws, rules, and precedents that may have had an influence on his work.

19. See Carl Dahlhaus's discussion in *Richard Wagner's Music Dramas*, pp. 104–7.

20. My reasons for espousing an externalist view of style change, and rejecting internalist ones, will be considered in the chapters following this one.

texts. Thus, although motives were in some cases related to one another musically, they were for the most part powerfully individualized in rhythm, melody, harmony, instrumentation, register, and tempo. Observe that if identity and reference are to be preserved, variation—especially variation of the primary parameters—must be modest. One means for achieving variety and motion while preserving identity is the sequence. Sequence also allows referential motives to persist, thereby enabling them to comment on and characterize the dramatic situation.[21]

Sequential organization—particularly when motives are intervallically fixed or when harmonization is a characteristic feature of the motive—easily leads to chromaticism and, through this, to modulation. That is, if harmony, mode, and intervals are kept constant and a motive is changed in pitch level, then tonal center tends to change. This is because harmonies built on adjacent scale steps (e.g., tonic to supertonic, mediant to subdominant) or those separated by thirds (tonic to mediant, mediant to dominant) lead to changes in mode and interval if tonality remains constant. As Wagner's strategies make evident, openness and mobility are important goals of his style. For this reason his leitmotifs seldom involve cadential progression, and their sequential succession is often coupled with chromaticism, whose uniformity tends to weaken closure.[22]

Modulation is also facilitated, and perhaps encouraged, by the frequent use of deceptive cadences. For in Wagner's music such cadences often serve not to delay closure, as they usually do in the music of the eighteenth century, but to deflect and prevent it. That is, a resolution to, say, the submediant is treated not as the provisional realization of a progression that ultimately reaches the tonic, but as a more or less permanent change in which the chord of deceptive resolution serves as part of a new tonal center.[23] The fact that deceptive cadences both enhance continuity by weakening closure and facilitate modulatory mobility might alone explain their frequent use. But there are, I suspect, other reasons for the frequency of deceptive cadences in Wagner's mature style.

To understand these reasons, it must be recognized that difference, as well as similarity, among constituent elements is a necessary condition for pattern formation. Thus, if a pitch/duration element is repeated without significant variation in dynamics, timbre, or any other parameter (x . . . x . . . x . . . ), motivic patterning is impossible. Similarly, if a motive is repeated quite exactly (m . . . m' . . . m'' . . .), no structure will arise on the higher level of phrase or period because there will be no basis for comprehending closure. This will tend to be the case even with sequential repetition, especially if tonal syntax is attenuated and the sequence is uniform. The

21. See, for instance, Examples 7.36 and 8.23.

22. The tendency of nineteenth-century composers to choose strategies that fostered mobility and open forms can be related to the aesthetics of Romanticism—specifically, to the value of "Becoming." Concerning this, see Chapter 6.

23. The cadence in measure 17 of the Prelude to *Tristan and Isolde* is a familiar example. These matters are considered in Chapter 8, in the section "Changes in Usage."

motive itself may (and probably will) be patently patterned in several parameters, but on the level of its repetition there must be some sort of fairly clear differentiation if motives are to form phrases, and phrases periods—that is, if closure is to be established. Put differently, a fundamental problem—even dilemma—confronting Wagner was how to maximize mobility and continuity yet create higher-level structures that could take shape only if there was closure.

One solution favored by Wagner was, as Alfred Lorenz and many others have observed, the bar form: a phrase or period made up of a motive, a first repetition (often in sequence), and a second repetition so extended in length that this differentiation creates closure. The basic plan, subject to considerable variation through extension and interpolation, results in phrases or periods with the proportions 1(m) + 1(m') + 2(m''). The difficulty is that the plan produces closed, end-accented phrase-rhythms: ‿◡◡‿ . One function of the deceptive cadence is, then, to undermine the closural stability created by bar-form patterns.

Other strategies listed at the beginning of this section do so as well. Motives and phrases with feminine endings—i.e., rhythmic groups terminating with a weak beat—enhance mobility and weaken closure. Closure is also undermined by elisions in which the end of one phrase is the beginning of the next, and by overlappings in which a new phrase (usually based on a different motive) begins before the previous one has ended. Such overlappings are clearly related to—and probably encourage—the use of contrapuntal textures. And such textures themselves obviously foster continuity and mobility. But the use of counterpoint is more than a convenient way of promoting continuity. Given other features of the style, it is an almost necessary strategy. To understand why this is so, let us return to a consideration of the nature of the leitmotif.

One hallmark of the leitmotif is, as we have seen, its individuality. Marked individuality cannot easily be joined with stock accompaniment patterns such as those that support much eighteenth-century homophony—Alberti basses, repeated-note figures, triad embellishments. For example, the changing-note melody that begins the Trio of Mozart's Symphony No. 39 in E♭ Major (K. 543) (Example 2.1a and graph 1) is accompanied by two such patterns (Example 2.1b). One can scarcely imagine using either to accompany any of the motives from the *Ring*, unless what was wanted was a kind of comic incongruity.[24]

Observe that to preclude such figures is, to a considerable extent, to preclude homophonic texture. For a homophonic texture is one that is divided into figure (melody) and ground (accompaniment), and to be perceived as being a ground, the

---

24. Schumann made comparable remarks about Berlioz's powerful melodic profiling. He observed that Berlioz's "melodies are distinguished by such intensity of almost every individual tone that . . . they often defy ordinary harmonization and would lose sonority if subjected to it." See "A Symphony by Berlioz," in Cone's edition of Berlioz's *Fantastic Symphony*, p. 243.

Needless to say, the same problem arises with eighteenth-century melodies that are powerfully profiled. For instance, when Mozart instantiates the same changing-note pattern as that found in Example 2.1 at the beginning of the slow movement of the "Jupiter" Symphony, no stock figure accompanies the melody.

EXAMPLE 2.1. Mozart, Symphony No. 39 in E♭ Major (K. 543), iii

pattern must have a kind of uniformity—a repeatable, neutral regularity. In short, Wagner's choice of unison, homorhythmic, and contrapuntal textures, rather than homophonic ones, was partly a consequence of leitmotif technique.

The important point about this sketch-analysis of some features of Wagner's style is not whether it provides the best explanation possible, or even whether the relationships posited are correct. Rather the analysis was introduced to exemplify the *kind* of argument that would, in my view, illuminate any style of whatever composer, culture, epoch, or hierarchic level. It should be emphasized that in each case the relationship drawn between traits was grounded on a hypothesis, whether one derived from a transcultural law (for instance, that the existence of patterning is dependent on the presence of difference as well as similarity), a stylistic rule (for instance, that motion to the submediant weakens closure), or an informal, common-sense reason (for instance, that idiosyncratic motives cannot easily be coupled with stock accompaniment patterns).

## DEVISING HYPOTHESES

Tenable hypotheses must, of course, be based on reliable data. But the fact that there are many true statements about the world that are not relational (for instance, statements such as "The first pitch of Beethoven's C♯-Minor Quartet is G♯," or, "This symphony was written by Carl Stamitz") makes it clear that reliability is only a necessary condition for explanation. Moreover, some relational statements are primarily descriptive or classificatory (for instance, "The first interval of Beethoven's C♯-

Minor Quartet is a major third," or, "The first movement of this symphony by Stamitz is in what is called sonata form"). Such relationships might, following Searle, be called brute relationships.[25]

But facts and relationships are seldom really as "brute" as this discussion might seem to suggest. For most human perceptual/cognitive acts are informed by hypotheses (however inchoate or unconscious) about the orderliness of nature, the prevalence of human purpose, and so on. And though we may not know the rules of American football or the grammar and syntax of gamelan music, we assume that they exist and that those who participate in the activity, whether as players or audience, understand what is going on. In short, though not in themselves illuminating or intelligible, repeated clustering and recurrent correlations call for explanation—for hypotheses. As Robert R. Sokal observes, "Classifications that describe relationships among objects in nature should generate hypotheses. In fact the principle scientific justification for establishing classifications is that they are heuristic . . . and that they lead to the stating of a hypothesis which can then be tested."[26]

There appears to be a significant difference between the ability of the natural sciences to formulate viable hypotheses and the ability of the human sciences to do so. One reason for this difference is that, generally speaking, the constraints governing natural relationships remain invariant over time and space. The ways in which celestial bodies act upon one another or the ways in which chemicals combine are the same today as they were millions of years ago, and are the same in Bengal as in Boston. In the realms of human behavior, on the other hand, there is obviously much greater variability. The constraints guiding the choices of composers or affecting the decisions of politicians are not constant over time and space. This variability, as I argued elsewhere, is due in part to the fact that in the human world, unlike the natural world, there is feedback from conceptual theory to practice.[27] Without denying this difference, I now want to suggest that it occurs primarily because in the realms of human behavior one is for the most part concerned to explain patterns and relationships on the levels of rules and strategies rather than on the level of universal laws. And on the levels of rules and strategies, the natural sciences tend to exhibit comparable sorts of variability—variability that is also the result of feedback, if not from the conceptual environment, at least from the biophysical environment. Thus what might be comparable to the analysis of a musical style on the level of strategies would be the analysis of complex ecological systems.[28]

Hypotheses invariably guide observation, and in so doing, they affect the differentiation and grouping of traits in a classification. It is also apparent that observation may lead to the modification or change of hypotheses and hence to a revision of classifications. But the effect of observation on hypothesis and classification depends

25. Searle, *Speech Acts,* pp. 50–51.
26. "Classification," p. 1117.
27. "Concerning the Sciences," pp. 194–96.
28. In this connection, see ibid., pp. 205–6.

on hierarchic level. Though it clearly affects hypotheses about specific, low-level relationships, observation evidently has much less influence on high-level cultural beliefs—hypotheses about the nature of time and causation, about human needs and wants, and so on. This is so not only because we do not abandon one set of cultural beliefs until another is at hand,[29] but because high-level theories do not determine lower-level hypotheses. For instance, hypotheses of either gradual or sudden speciation are compatible with the theory of natural selection (though that of natural selection is incompatible with that of special creation). More generally, a number of alternative hypotheses may be compatible with a particular high-level theory, just as a number of alternative compositional strategies are compatible with a set of high-level stylistic rules.

Though new means for the observation and identification of traits are certainly welcome,[30] a time-honored, familiar method is at hand: that of keeping some feature(s) of a pattern constant and noting how others vary between different, usually closely related, styles. This comparative method has been fruitful in calling attention to characteristic traits in those parameters for which viable taxonomies exist: for instance, formal organizations and tonal harmonic progressions. What are needed are comparable constants for other parameters: melody, rhythm, texture, dynamics, and so on. Three ways of creating constants—illustrated in connection with melodic patterns—are suggested in what follows.

## Schema Instantiation

It has frequently been observed that we tend to comprehend the world in terms of relatively stable and enduring schemata. This is as true of aesthetic experience as of ordinary experience.[31] In literature, for instance, narrative plots can be grouped into readily recognizable types: "boy-meets-girl" stories, "who-done-it" mysteries, or "quest-trial" plots. Of course, such schemata need not be consciously conceptualized in order to function as frames for organizing experience. For example, although quest-trial plots are familiar to all of us—in attempting to reach some goal, often a physical or spiritual home, the protagonist undergoes a succession of trials—

29. See the section "The Axiom of Constancy" in Chapter 3.

30. For instance, electronic devices such as computers and melographs. Though these will undoubtedly help to refine observation, they do so largely on a "microscopic" level. But what are most urgently needed are more cogent theories and precise observations on the level of macroscopic patternings.

31. See, for instance, Gombrich, *Art and Illusion;* Frye, *Anatomy of Criticism;* Treitler, "Methods, Style, Analysis"; Gjerdingen, *A Classic Turn of Phrase;* and many references in the psychological literature from which only two will be given here: Bartlett, *Remembering;* and Rumelhart, "Schemata."

I have discussed the nature and function of musical schemata in *Explaining Music,* pp. 213–26; "Exploiting Limits," and (with Burton S. Rosner) "Melodic Processes." In these studies I usually referred to such stable, replicated patterns as *archetypes.* I prefer the term *schema,* however, not only because it is the term commonly used in cognitive psychology, but because there is a possible confusion with Jungian psychology, which uses *archetype* to refer to presumably innate universals. But as far as I can see, the schemata of, say, tonal music are significantly a matter of learning; that is, they arise on the levels of style rules, not cognitive universals.

we do not think about the nature of the schema as we attend to, say, Homer's *Odyssey*, Mozart's *Magic Flute,* or Frank Baum's *Wizard of Oz.* In music, formal schemata such as theme and variations, rondo, da capo arias, and sonata form are very familiar. And the histories of some of these have been described in considerable detail.

Schemata are patterns that, because they are congruent both with human perceptual/cognitive capacities and with prevalent stylistic (musical and extramusical) constraints, are memorable, tend to remain stable over time, and are therefore replicated with particular frequency. Consequently, they are useful constants in terms of which style differences, between contemporaries and over time, can be observed, identified, and classified. Consider the melodies given in Example 2.2. All are members of a class that I call the "Adeste Fidelis" schema.[32] Though it can be instantiated in a variety of ways, the schema is defined by: an opening motive (A) that either skips down from the tonic to the fifth of the scale or skips up from the fifth to the tonic; a varied repetition (A') of the initial motive, skipping down from the second of the scale to the fifth or skipping up from the fifth to the second; a somewhat different patterning (B), usually as long as A and A' combined, that moves (frequently by a skip) to the third of the scale and often beyond, and subsequently descends by more or less conjunct motion normally ending with a full or half cadence. Structurally, then, the schema is generally instantiated as a bar form, A A' B, with the proportions 1 + 1 + 2.

The advantages of using a schema such as this for purposes of comparison are obvious. For despite a basic kinship, the stylistic differences between the melodies in Example 2.2 are striking. Indeed, any reasonably experienced listener can recognize that the first three instantiations of the schema are Baroque and the next ones are Classic.[33] The question then is: What specific traits produce these differences and how are such traits, once identified, related to one another and to the traits characteristic of parameters other than melody?

One might begin by noticing that the Classic instantiations begin with a brief anacrusis and skip up from fifth to tonic, while the Baroque instantiations begin on

---

From this point of view, Schenker's *Ursatz* is not a universal on the level of laws, but rather one among a number of schemata for the instantiation of the rules of tonal music—albeit an especially prevalent one. Moreover, it seems that, like other melodic/harmonic schemata, it is essentially a middle-ground patterning rather than a background one. That is, like many theorists (myself included in the last part of *The Rhythmic Structure of Music*), Schenker extended his unquestionably important discovery beyond the hierarchic level of its normal occurrence.

32. For other more or less typical instantiations of the schema, see J. S. Bach, Sonata for Violin and Clavier in B Minor, BWV 1014, iv; Handel, Sonata for Recorder and Continuo in A Minor, Opus 1 No. 4, iv; Haydn, String Quartet in E♭ Major, Opus 50 No. 3, i, and String Quartet in G Major, Opus 54 No. 1, ii; Mozart, Concerto in E♭ Major for Horn and Orchestra (K. 447), iii, and Symphony No. 41 in C Major (K. 551), ii.

A schema need not, of course, be melodic. Schemata may arise in connection with any parameter. For instance, the pattern of tutti and solo in a concerto grosso is a schema. Other schemata are discussed toward the end of the book in Chapter 7. One of the important tasks of style analysis is, as I see it, to identify and classify the schemata for all parameters in a particular repertory.

33. The last example (2.2g) is stylistically a bit more problematic, for reasons considered below.

the accent and skip down from tonic to fifth.[34] This observation, coupled with a modicum of theory, indicates that in the Classic style rhythmic groupings tend to be end- or middle-accented, while Baroque rhythms tend to be beginning-accented. Often such groupings are emphasized by the patterning of the accompaniment. For instance, the durational relationships of the Handel Sonata in G Minor for Two Violins and Continuo, Opus 2 No. 2, fourth movement, and the Mozart Sinfonia concertante in E♭ Major (K. 297b), third movement, are quite similar, but the accompaniment of the Handel sonata (Example 2.2c) supports beginning-accented groups, while that of the Mozart sinfonia (Example 2.2d) reinforces end-accented groupings.[35] Consequently, in the Classic instantiation the pattern of rising pitches (1–2–3) overpowers whatever patterning might be created by the reiterated upbeats on the fifth of the scale. This effect occurs because an anacrusis (especially a relatively short one) strongly emphasizes the accent to which it moves, and because, even when not otherwise stressed, notes reached by a skip tend to be marked for consciousness. Put succinctly: in the Classic instantiation of the Adeste Fidelis schema, the lower fifth acts as a subordinate, ancillary event that makes the primacy of the upper rising pattern patent.

In Baroque versions of the schema, on the other hand, the fifth of the scale is much more important. This is most obvious in the first and second melodies. In Handel's Sonata in G Major for Flute and Continuo, Opus 1 No. 5 (Example 2.2a), the fifth (D) is strongly marked not only because it is skipped to, but because its relative duration and the presence of the trill call attention to it. In Bach's Clavier Concerto (2.2b), the prominence of the fifth (F♯) results not only from its threefold repetition and from the fact that it is skipped to, but from the initial figure's rhythmic closure ( ♫♩ ), which makes the F♯ seem like the beginning of a relatively independent pattern. This analysis indicates that Baroque instantiations of the Adeste Fidelis schema generally give rise to bilinear melodies, while Classic ones tend to be monolinear. The slurs from fifth to tonic in the Classic instantiations seem to reflect this difference. That is, the slurs make it clear that fifth and tonic are part of a single event. For this reason the skip functions more as a gap to be filled than it does in the Baroque instances.[36]

The last instantiation of the schema (Example 2.2g), the beginning of the theme of the second movement of Beethoven's Piano Sonata in C Minor, Opus 111,

---

34. As always, statistics—the nature of the sample (see below)—are crucial. There are Baroque instantiations of the Adeste Fidelis schema that begin with the rising anacruses—for instance, Handel, Sonata in F Major for Violin and Continuo, Opus 1 No. 12, ii and iv; and Bach's Brandenburg Concerto No. 1 in F. Major, v. Conversely, there are Classic instantiations of the schema that begin on the downbeat with a descending skip—for instance, the aria "Voi che sapete" from Mozart's *Marriage of Figaro* or the opening of the Piano Quartet in G Minor (K. 478) in which the Adeste Fidelis schema is combined with a changing-note schema (as shown in Example 1.1b). Nevertheless, an admittedly unsystematic sampling of the repertories involved argues for the validity of the generalizations being made.

35. The patterns of the accompaniments are shown beneath the music.

36. These observations suggest that the rhythmic character of Baroque music, including the use of ornaments, is related to the tendency to value bilinear melodic structures.

EXAMPLE 2.2. (*a*) Handel, Sonata in G Major for Flute and Continuo, Opus 1 No. 5, v;
(*b*) Bach, Clavier Concerto No. 3 in D Major (BWV 1054), ii; (*c*) Handel, Sonata in G
Minor for Two Violins and Continuo, Opus 2 No. 2, iv; (*d*) Mozart, Sinfonia concertante
in E♭ Major (K. 297*b*; KV⁶: Anh. C14.01), iii; (*e*) Mozart, Piano Concerto in E♭ Major
(K. 482), iii; (*f*) Beethoven, Trio in B♭ Major for Clarinet, Cello, and Piano, Opus 11, ii;
(*g*) Beethoven, Piano Sonata in C Minor, Opus 111, ii

merits brief comment. In contrast to Beethoven's early trio (Example 2.2*f*), which is
wholly Classic in instantiation,[37] the theme of the second movement of Opus 111
combines the descending skip characteristic of Baroque instantiations with the ana-

37. Notice, too, that Beethoven's theme (Example 2.2*f*), like the melody of Mozart's Piano Quartet in G
Minor (see Example 1.1*b*), combines the Adeste Fidelis schema with a changing-note schema: 1–7/2–1.

crustic rhythmic grouping typical of Classic ones.[38] Not only is this instantiation very different from that of Beethoven's trio, but it is quite similar to the theme of another late work, the Diabelli Variations.[39] In short, the use of the Adeste Fidelis schema as a constant can help to define some of the traits characteristic of Beethoven's late style that may result from his interest in the music of Handel and Bach.

At times, surface disparities obscure the presence of a shared schema. For instance, it is surprising to discover that the opening melody of Mahler's Fourth Symphony (Example 2.3a) and the chorus "and He shall reign for ever and ever" from Handel's *Messiah* (Example 2.3b) belong to the same family. But only a modest bit of analysis makes it apparent that Mahler's melody, like Handel's, instantiates a schema of linked triads (Example 2.3c).[40]

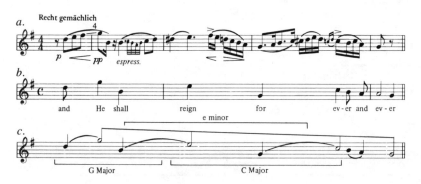

EXAMPLE 2.3.  (a) Mahler, Symphony No. 4, i; (b) Handel, *Messiah*, Hallelujah Chorus

It can be illuminating not only to compare different instantiations of a schema, but to ask why, after thriving for several generations, a particular schema ceases to be chosen by the compositional community. For instance, the Adeste Fidelis schema, often encountered in the music of the Baroque and Classic periods (and whose replication is a feature of those styles), occurs very infrequently in the music of the nineteenth century. This "nonoccurrence" can, as we shall see, tell us something about the style of Romantic music. Even more revealing than such nonoccurrences, however, are the changes that take place in the ways in which a schema is instantiated. Discerning the nature of such changes and relating them to other characteristics of a dialect or idiom is one of the chief goals of style analysis; explaining why the changes occurred is a central concern of music history.

38. Though the score indicates that the first three sixteenth-notes of the theme are an anacrusis, in performance the function of these notes is somewhat ambiguous. The grouping perceived depends significantly on the pianist's interpretation. There are Baroque instances of this "mixed" configuration—cf. "Qui sedes ad dextram patris" from Bach's B-Minor Mass.

39. If it is observed that, after all, the theme was written by Diabelli, one can respond that Beethoven *chose* to use it for a major composition.

40. For the sake of comparison, Handel's melody is given in G rather than D. Both melodies, and the process of linked triads (see the brackets in the analytic graph) which they share, are discussed in my *Explaining Music*, pp. 165–66.

## Paraphrase, Modeling, and Borrowing

The fundamental habits and disposition of an individual (or a group)—those modes of perceiving and responding to the world that are so ingrained that they cannot be denied—are often strikingly revealed when an attempt is made to adopt an alien manner or style, as, for example, when a bumpkin poses as a sophisticate, or a foreigner pretends to be a native. Similarly, the fundamental stylistic proclivities of a composer may be revealed when he or she seeks to employ alien stylistic means or orchestrate a work by another composer who wrote in a style remote in time or place.[41]

Paraphrase, modeling, and borrowing of the sort that I have in mind have been prevalent in all periods, though perhaps especially so in the twentieth century. One thinks perhaps of Handel's extensive borrowings from the works of Telemann and Keiser or of Mozart's Overture in the Style of Handel from the Suite in C Major (K. 399), of Schubert's use of Beethoven's works as models and sources, of Schoenberg's orchestration of Brahms's Piano Quartet in G Minor, and of the many parodies and borrowings of twentieth-century composers: Prokofiev being "Classical"; Stravinsky being "Baroque," "Classic," and "Gothic," or using Gesualdo and Pergolesi; Bartók using folk materials;[42] and various composers being "Balinese," "Japanese," and so on. In cases such as these, the peculiarities of both the earlier and the later composers' ways of musical thought and conception can be illuminated through a close examination of differences between works being compared.

To take but one obvious example, the Finale of Haydn's String Quartet in F minor, Opus 20 No. 5, is a fugue on essentially the same subject as two Baroque fugues in the same key: Bach's Fugue in F Minor from Book II of the *Well-Tempered Clavier* and Handel's chorus "And with His stripes we are healed" from *Messiah* (Example 2.4). Despite patent similarities in genre and texture, melody and har-

EXAMPLE 2.4. (*a*) Haydn, String Quartet in F Minor, Opus 20 No. 5, iv; (*b*) Bach, Fugue in F Minor (BWV 881), from the *Well-Tempered Clavier*, Book II; (*c*) Handel, *Messiah*, "And with His stripes"

41. A related observation is frequently made in the discussion of forgeries, when it is suggested that forgers cannot avoid seeing and hence painting with the conceptual proclivities of their own milieu and that therefore, while they can deceive their contemporaries, they cannot fool later generations. See Friedländer, *On Art and Connoisseurship*, pp. 259–62.

42. See Roberts, "Handel's Borrowings from Telemann" and "Handel's Borrowings from Keiser"; Cone, "Schubert's Beethoven"; Webster, "Schubert's Sonata Form"; and Arauco, "Bartók's Romanian Christmas Carols."

monic syntax, Haydn's fugue sounds unmistakably Classic. By attempting to define precisely how Haydn's fugue differs from those of Bach and Handel—asking, for instance, about the significance of the fact that Haydn's fugue is characterized by frequent dovetailing of the head of the subject in sequence but relatively few overlappings of the entrance of the subject (as occurs in both Baroque fugues), or why the second subject of Haydn's fugue (marked $X$) does not sound Baroque as do seemingly comparable repeated-note patterns in Bach or Handel—the style analyst may be led to formulate hypotheses about the nature of the constraints governing Haydn's compositional choices.

## Transformation

Transformation is a kind of do-it-yourself paraphrase in which the analyst modifies a passage composed in one style in such a way that it resembles some other style—usually one that differs only in dialect. Insofar as possible the basic structure of the original pattern—for example, its harmonic processes, melodic structural tones, phrase lengths—should be maintained while other parametric relationships (usually foreground ones) are changed to produce the stylistic transformation. In Example 2.5 b, for instance, I have rewritten—transformed—the first eight measures of the Menuet from Bach's Orchestral Suite in C Major, keeping as much as possible constant, in order to make a melody that seems more Classic. The success of such

EXAMPLE 2.5. (a) Bach, Orchestral Suite No. 1 in C Major (BWV 1066), Menuet I

a transformation might be tested by asking competent listeners to judge, when the paraphrase is presented with a group of genuine Classic and Baroque minuet melodies, which style it should be grouped with.[43]

By asking questions about how the change of style was effected—about changes in melody, rhythm, and so forth, from the original to the transformation—it may be possible to devise hypotheses about the general nature of the stylistic differences. In addition, it seems probable that some aspects of patterning resist transformation; it

---

43. It should be emphasized that the changes made may well be the result of trial and error in which the final result depends on the analyst's sense of style—which he or she might not be able to explain.

would surely be interesting to know which ones they are and to speculate about why this is the case. In short, in the act of "making over" one hopes to learn something about the characteristics of both the original patterning and the transformed variant.

In the end, of course, whatever hypotheses are generated by these or other strategies must be tested against a much larger sample of the repertories being studied. And such tests must, whether we like it or not, be statistical.

## STATISTICS

The classification of dialects, genres, idioms, and the like, is based on observed correlations and repeated concatenations of traits—that is, on statistical samplings. Thus far scholarly samplings have, for the most part, been ad hoc, informal, and unsystematic. And though I am convinced that more sophisticated and carefully controlled methods are indispensable for the further refinement of style-analytic formulations, the use of statistics poses a number of problems. Many of these are obvious, and most have been considered by others. Nevertheless, the subject is so important that some discussion is warranted, if only by way of review.

### Character of the Sample

The distinctions among classes of artworks, whatever the basis for the groupings, tend to lack precise boundaries because the stylistic differences that most concern the analyst and historian result from differences in strategic rather than rule constraints. And such differences are for the most part ones of degree rather than kind. As a result, classes tend to overlap. For this reason, one of the central problems in the statistical analysis of style is that of establishing the limits of the sample. Clearly the most unambiguously defined sample, and hence the one most often used, is that of the *oeuvre* of a single composer. Yet such samples may not always be the most illuminating or useful, since style traits often transcend such limits.

Equally problematic is the question of what will count as a trait for purposes of statistics and classification. It makes little sense, for instance, to count all the A s (440 cps) lasting a quarter-note in Mozart's music. For in this music the significance of a pitch depends on its syntactic function in the specific work and context in which it occurs. The A might be a tonic, a dominant, a leading tone, a nonharmonic tone, and so on. But there may be styles in which the relative frequency of some pitch-class or sonority establishes a sense of tonal center; then such counting might be appropriate.[44]

More generally, what is to be included in a sample—what is thought to be significant—depends on our prior knowledge and understanding of the constraints gov-

---

44. Such counting is not uncommon in the analysis of twentieth-century and ethnic musics.

erning the repertory being considered. As suggested earlier, our knowledge of a style, whether it be explicitly formulated or experienced tacitly, is antecedent to and determines the relational traits we regard as significant and choose to include in our analysis. Particularly when computerization forces us to define traits with precision, statistics can help us to refine our discriminations among classes and styles. But in the absence of hypotheses about syntactic rules and strategic goals, raw statistical data may lead to meaningless or plainly foolish results. As Ernest Nagel has pointed out, "if nothing is known concerning the mechanism of a situation under investigation, the relative frequencies obtained from samples may be poor guides to the character of the indefinitely large population from which they are drawn." [45] Just how silly correlations can be, if the constraints governing the distribution of traits within a population is ignored, is clear from the following excerpt from Willard R. Espy's *Almanac of Words at Play:*

> "As his name is, so is he," says I Samuel, and there is something to that. I am lucky to have a surname beginning in E. If my name began with M, says the Council for Alcoholism, I should be eight times more prone to alcoholism than the average drunk. If my name began with any letter from S through Z (this according to the British Medical Association), I should have twice the usual susceptibility to ulcers, and be three times as subject to heart attacks. [46]

Obviously these correlations result from the distribution of the beginning letters of surnames in the English language, not from any real causal connection.

But what is a "real" causal connection? As Norwood Hanson has observed, "The notions behind 'the cause $x$' and 'the effect $y$' are intelligible only against a pattern of theory, namely one which puts guarantees on inferences from $x$ to $y$." [47] For this reason even correlations not based on special distribution in the population are credible only insofar as they are warranted by our theories, whether explicit or tacit, about how the world works. For example, after the election of 1960, *The Scientific American* predicted that President Kennedy would die in office on the basis of this statistical correlation: that every president since Lincoln who was elected in a year ending in zero had done so. Yet we regard this correlation as accidental because our theories provide for no such numerological causes.

The traits with which statistical studies deal are, then, relational. And often the most important relationships are to be found in levels other than that of the "facts" notated in a score. This presents the formidable methodological problem of developing objective and rigorous rules for defining and differentiating patterns above the level of the foreground—the note-to-note level. What are needed are rules for distin-

---

45. *Theory of Probability,* p. 59.
46. P. 153.
47. *Patterns of Discovery,* p. 64.

guishing structural tones, harmonies, accents, and so on, from ornamental ones on all hierarchic levels. Though I doubt that such rules can ever be perfected, the situation is not hopeless. For if statistical studies deal with large enough samples, it may not be necessary to worry about those cases in which the structural tone selected (say, according to a computer program) does not seem intuitively "right," since the "error" will be absorbed into the data-mass, which will itself be correct. In this process it may be useful to work by trial and error, beginning with a computer program that seems reasonable and then adjusting it so that its results conform to stylistic experience. After adjustments produce musical results that seem right, the program itself can be studied—used as a heuristic device—in order to develop theories about the relationships that underlie the program. But in using statistics and computers, it must never be forgotten that programs must be devised and samples selected with some sort of hypotheses about how the style works. Otherwise, collecting, counting, and computing are exercises in futility.

## Size of the Sample

The nature of our theories affects not only the character of a sample—what is counted—but the size of the sample necessary for making valid inferences and connections. In general, the more powerful the theory connecting phenomena, the fewer the number of instances required to confirm it; conversely, the weaker the theoretical framework organizing some body of data, the greater the number of instances needed to support any hypothesis suggested by it. Theories in the natural sciences tend to be powerful because, as noted earlier, the laws governing relationships studied in sciences such as physics, chemistry, or molecular biology are evidently invariant. As a result, such theories can generally make do with relatively few data. A single experiment, meticulously designed and executed, may suffice to support or refute some hypothesis. Moreover, when a network of interconnected theories supports a given hypothesis, discrepant data may be fudged or provisionally disregarded because the coherence of the paradigm warrants the belief that discrepancies can be accounted for with minor qualifications of existing theories.

Particularly in those realms of human activity where attention is directed to rules and even more to strategies—and style theory and analysis is one of these—powerful theories are difficult to discover and formulate. Consequently, rather large samples are needed to confirm or disconfirm hypotheses. But even in these areas, two considerations mitigate the uncertainties of style analysis. First, statistics is concerned with relative frequencies—that is, with probabilities. For this reason, one or two counterexamples need not invalidate statistical generalizations. The observation, made earlier, that in Wagner's music deceptive cadences usually serve to establish new tonal areas would not be invalidated by a few instances in which such cadences served merely to delay closure, any more than the statistical claim that women live longer than men is falsified by the fact that some women die before the age of thirty. Moreover, as Eugene Narmour has pointed out, "the higher [the style analyst] ascends in the epistemological hierarchy—from the study of the works of one composer to the study of a genre or a period—the more he must generalize";[48] and hence the smaller effect, whether pro or con, any particular instance will have on the analyst's hypothesis.

Second, as in other fields, hypotheses about style gain credibility through their "fit" with other facets of theory—for instance, with hypotheses about the constraints of related parameters. And, as has often been remarked in connection with scientific theories, discrepant data are often disregarded for the sake of an elegant hypothesis with broad explanatory capability. "The noblest scientific laws," as Nelson Goodman has observed, "are seldom quite true. Minor discrepancies are overridden in the interest of breadth or power or simplicity. Science denies its data as the statesman denies his constituents—within the limits of prudence."[49] The seemingly insatiable urge in the humanities to accumulate data is, then, perhaps not-so-mute testimony to a lack of satisfactory theory.[50]

One danger of employing statistics is the temptation *merely* to count—for example, the number of six-four chords in Bach's chorales or the number of triplets in early Haydn minuets. The problem with mere counts is that they produce averages or means. What we really need to know, however, is the relation of the average to some norm or ideal type. Only in this way can the characteristic features of the specific style be recognized.

The difference between an average and a norm might be crudely illustrated thus: If the colors of all American cars were averaged by mixing all their various colors together in statistically proper proportions, the result would probably be some sort of nondescript gray. Yet we know perfectly well that most cars have a definite color and that relatively few are in fact gray. More accurately, what I have in mind is something like what physicians mean when they speak of a normal heart. What is meant is not an average heart, for most hearts are faulty or at least peculiar in some respect. Rather, the term *normal* means that the components of the heart function properly with respect to one another and to the circulatory system of which they form a part. And physicians know how the heart should function because they have a theory about the relationships among the constraints that govern its behavior.

So, too, it is in music. Thus, despite recent fashion that has tended to emphasize what is peculiar about compositions, to depreciate the notion of norms—ideal types of sonata form, fugue, and so on—I do not see how style analysis can do with-

---

48. *Beyond Schenkerism*, p. 176.

49. *Languages of Art*, p. 263. In this connection, also see Westfall, "Newton and the Fudge Factor."

50. In theorizing it is important to recognize that one need not be able to explain *everything* about a phenomenon in order to account for some of its attributes, and that theories should be valued for what they *do* explain, not for what they fail to account for. As facts accumulate, it will become more and more difficult to know what there is to be known: the amount of information will be beyond the processing capabilities of individuals. As this happens, theory will become an increasingly important area of musicology. For theories are what enable us to comprehend and control the prolixity and diversity of the world.

out such constructs (for that is obviously what they are).[51] Of course, no particular sonata-form movement is an exemplar of such an ideal type, any more than any particular heart is so. But constructs are indispensable because without them the peculiarities of the specific work would be unknowable and the averages gleaned through statistical analysis would be unilluminating. For we can interpret general changes in the handling of some strategy or form only in the light of some concept of its normal operation.

Related to the distinction between average and norm is the difference between statistical probability and subjective probability. The probability relationships that are involved in understanding a piece of music, as they are sensed by a competent listener, are not solely a matter of frequency, but depend upon the nature of human cognitive processes (including the ways in which memory modifies perceived patterns), upon the nature of the style of the work (for instance, whether it is strongly syntactic),[52] and upon the breadth of the sample on which probability estimates are based.

## Markers and Authentication

In *Style and Language,* Roger Brown writes:

> In many ways the fingerprint is a good concretization of the notion of style. We can make a definition of the superordinate class of phenomena as the markings on the ends of the fingers that can be registered by an ink pressing. The resulting data have two important properties. The values for an individual are constant through time—they are an enduring characteristic. . . . In the second place the fingerprint data yield unique values for every living person.[53]

This view (particularly prevalent in literary studies), which tends to equate style with the intraopus structure of a specific work, is in my opinion both mistaken and misleading. It is mistaken because, except perhaps within works, styles do not remain constant over time as fingerprints do.[54] Even for a single individual, stylistic behavior is variable, both contextually and chronologically. Contextually, as Charles E. Osgood has pointed out,[55] our linguistic (or musical or graphic) styles may change

51. Human beings evidently have an uncanny ability and a strong inclination to abstract "ideal types" or norms from the perception of a number of different individual instantiations. See, for instance, Posner and Keele, "Genesis of Abstract Ideas."

52. If the style of a piece arises out of a coherent set of syntactic constraints, the listener's sense of its probable behavior will be less affected by statistical frequency than if syntactic relationships are weak or absent altogether.

53. Pp. 378–79.

54. Moreover, given the definition of style adopted in this study, fingerprints cannot be analogous to styles. This is so because fingerprints are not *chosen* and, correlatively, because no alternative possibilities are available. And it would surely be strange to speak of the style of someone's fingerprints.

55. "Some Effects of Motivation," p. 293.

significantly depending on what we are doing—talking on the telephone, giving a lecture, or writing a novel; composing a Broadway musical or a symphony; painting a mural or illustrating a book. Depending on the roles we are taking, we assume different guises. Chronologically, styles—of composers, of aesthetic movements, and so on—change in various ways. Without historical information, it would probably be impossible to guess that the Symphony in C Major of 1831 was written by the same man who composed *Tristan and Isolde* in 1859.

The view is misleading because it fosters a search for *markers* or *identifiers* that serve as convenient clues to classification. Though such markers may differentiate styles from one another with precision and consistency, they tell us virtually nothing about other traits of the style that are more important in defining its inner structure, or about the relationships among the traits.[56] For instance, the number of horns or the presence of tubas in a symphony orchestra is probably a reasonably reliable marker for distinguishing German symphonies of the late Romantic period from Classic symphonies. But per se (as brute facts), they are trivial traits.[57] They tell us little more about the differences between the way each style works than the fingerprint of Stalin tells us about his behavior as distinguished from that of Gandhi.

Though style analysis has too often been confined to the discovery and description of such markers, I do not wish to suggest that the traits used as markers may not be significant.[58] But they become significant only when they are related to other features of the style. For instance, it might be possible to distinguish Wagner's operas from Verdi's in terms of the relative frequency of deceptive cadences. But unless one can explain how the frequency of deceptive cadences is related to other features of Wagner's style the trait will be no more than a marker.

Again, the situation is more equivocal than this discussion implies. On the one hand, William Thomson is probably right that "the notion that musical experience is primarily . . . an act of stylistic identification can lead [to] . . . slovenly listening habits."[59] On the other hand, identification *is* important for criticism and appreciation. It is so for criticism because, as observed earlier, understanding and evaluation depend on knowing the stylistic alternatives available to the composer. For the listener, identification is important because enjoyment depends on bringing appropriate perceptual and cognitive sets into play. That is, because sensitive musical responses depend on knowing (usually tacitly) the kinds of events that are likely to occur in a

56. In this connection, see Thomson, "Style Analysis," pp. 201–2.

57. Notice, however, that unexplained (and hence initially trivial) style traits may be significant because they lead to a search for hypotheses about the relationships among traits. And such hypotheses, too, are heuristic, fostering the search for other traits and other relationships.

58. Conversely, traits that are not markers are not for that reason to be ignored, as Jan LaRue seems to suggest when he observes that what needs to be noticed is the exceptional rather than the normal: "To take a simple example, the progression $V^7$–I occurs so rarely in the fourteenth century that it should immediately draw our attention; yet to comment upon this cadence in a piece written about 1750 would be completely superfluous" (*Guidelines for Style Analysis*, p. 4).

59. "Style Analysis," p. 201.

composition, and knowing what is likely to occur depends in turn on style identification, markers often facilitate listening.[60]

Because music history must be based on a correct chronology of compositions, it too depends on identification. And it is sometimes urged that were style analysis sufficiently rigorous and refined, works could be attributed to their proper composers; genuine works could be authenticated, spurious ones rejected. But while style analysis may make attributions more or less probable, it is impossible in principle to authenticate a work solely on stylistic grounds. This is so because our conception of a style assumes that the set of compositions constituting it is complete. If the work to be authenticated were genuine, however, then the nature of the set would be both different and incomplete and, for that reason, could not be used to establish authenticity.

Suppose, for instance, that a composition attributed to Mozart were discovered in some archive and that stylistically the work was obviously anomalous—perhaps it was the Overture in the Style of Handel mentioned earlier. It could not be authenticated on stylistic grounds because, if it were genuine, the canon of Mozart's *oeuvre*— the set of compositions on which an analysis of his style had been based—would have changed. E. H. Gombrich cites a comparable case in which "an essay published under Diderot's name was deleted from the author's canon on stylistic grounds but had to be restored to it when the original draft in his hand was found."[61]

Nor, for similar reasons, can an authenticated work be assuredly assigned a chronological position in a composer's *oeuvre* on the basis of style alone. For our account of a composer's stylistic development also assumes that the subsets characteristic of the stages differentiated are complete. If the work in question belongs to one of them, then that subset was incomplete prior to its inclusion. For instance, writing of Beethoven's *An die ferne Geliebte,* Joseph Kerman suggests that even if the work could be attributed to Beethoven on stylistic grounds, its position in Beethoven's stylistic development might be misconstrued:

> Power, complexity, overwhelming feats of construction and development, motivic unity, high drama—these, rather than artless strains, were qualities associated then (as now) with the composer of the *Eroica Symphony.* His contemporaries can be forgiven, too, if they viewed the turn toward simplicity in this song cycle as a sport in the composer's output. He did not continue writing such songs, and the great sensation of the next opuses . . . was a turn toward fugue of a particularly gritty kind.[62]

60. Observe, too, that recognition (identification per se) is a powerful pleasure because it is connected with our sense of control and power—with our ability to make intelligent choices. In this connection, see the section "The Axiom of Constancy" in Chapter 3.

61. "Style," p. 360.

62. "An die ferne Geliebte," p. 135. These observations make it clear that criticism is dependent on history. For instance, our understanding and evaluation of Beethoven's song cycle is qualified both by our knowledge of the idiom employed and by our awareness of alternatives *not* chosen.

The problems of statistical method have been considered, perhaps at undue length, not to cast doubt on their propriety. Quite the opposite. Since all classification and all generalization about stylistic traits are based on some estimate of relative frequency, statistics are inescapable.[63] This being so, it seems prudent to gather, analyze, and interpret statistical data according to some coherent, even systematic, plan. That is, instead of employing informal impressions of the relative frequencies of casually defined traits (in the case of Wagner's music, for instance, what actually is the relative frequency of deceptive cadences? in what ways is their occurrence correlated with that of bar forms? how exactly is chromaticism to be defined? and so on), it would appear desirable to define as rigorously as possible what is to count as a given trait, to gather data about such traits systematically, and to collate and analyze it consistently and scrupulously—in short, to employ the highly refined methods and theories developed in the discipline of mathematical statistics and sampling theory. I should add that I have no doubt about the value of employing computers in such studies, not merely because they can save enormous amounts of time but, equally important, because their use will force us to define terms and traits, classes and relationships with precision—something most of us seldom do.

Though the data produced by statistics call for explanation, and though relative frequencies of traits may contribute to the confirmation of hypotheses, statistics per se are not a source for the concepts used to relate style traits to one another. This is so because theories about the nature of the relationships governing phenomena come not from the phenomena themselves, but either from concepts developed in disciplines such as psychology and philosophy or from cultural ideology.[64] Thus, behind the concepts of set theory and ideas about motivic unity lie beliefs about the importance and naturalness of similarity relationships; hypotheses about the importance of psychoacoustic phenomena in shaping organic musical processes constitute the background of Schenker's theories; and the implication/realization model relies heavily on concepts gleaned from cognitive psychology. The primacy of such beliefs, hypotheses, and concepts (in relation to musical data) is shown in the fact that essentially the same set of stylistic traits may be explained by a succession of different theories.[65] This being so, it would seem at once the height of folly and the depth of formalism to contend, as far too many scholars have, that works of art provide the bases for their own analysis.[66] One cannot analyze or criticize a piece of music "in its own terms" because such terms do not reside in works of art. Indeed, without prior concepts (adapted from ideology, related disciplines, or existing music theory) about the way the world (including music) works, not only would it be impossible to

63. I have occasionally heard humanist-scholars scoff at statistical studies. Their contempt is unwittingly misguided; for they continually traffic in relative frequencies (statistics), albeit in casual, if not sloppy, ways.

64. This is not to contend that data plays no role in hypothesis formulation. But it seems that, generally speaking, paradigms take precedence over particulars.

65. In this connection, see Balthazar, "Intellectual History and Concepts of the Concerto."

66. The nature of formalism is discussed in Chapter 6.

know what and how to analyze, but the very notions of "style" and "analysis" would not exist.[67]

Style analysis is, as we have seen, concerned to identify the traits characteristic of some work or group of works, and to relate such traits to one another. It is not primarily concerned with why the traits observed were chosen by a composer or group of composers. Such explanation is the province of history—the subject of the next part of this book.

67. The ideas presented above suggest that a viable history of music theory will depend more on intellectual/ideological history than on the history of musical practice. This does not mean, however, that musical practice was unaffected by music theory. Clearly, the formulation of concepts such as *triad* or *sonata-form* or *sets* has had a significant influence on the thinking, and hence the practice, of composers.

# PART II

History, Innovation, and Choice

CHAPTER 3

# Thoughts About History

Why particular traits are chosen and how the choices of composers change over time are the concerns of music history. This chapter will urge that a chronological arrangement of style traits will not give rise to a history of style unless hypotheses relate the traits not only to one another, but also to the reasons why the traits were chosen. Before considering the problems peculiar to writing the history of an art such as music, however, some observations about history in general will serve to make the viewpoint of this study clear. Few of the observations that follow are new or surprising; most have been made by other scholars.

## History in General

*Knowledge of the Past*

Let us begin with W. H. Walsh's statement: "The word 'history' is itself ambiguous. It covers (a) the totality of past human actions, and (b) the narrative or account we construct of them now." [1] It is obvious, however, that we do not and cannot know "the totality of past human actions." For we can know only what has been preserved in documents, artifacts, and the like. And despite the vast quantity—indeed the overabundance—of documented data from the past, what is preserved is but a minute fraction of the countless events that must have occurred. In this respect the remote past and recent past are alike. "Even the events of the past few hours," writes George Kubler, "are sparsely documented. . . . Though finite, the total number of historical signals greatly exceeds the capacity of any individual or group to interpret all the signals in all their meanings." [2] For the most part unrecorded and forever lost,

---

1. *Philosophy of History*, p. 14. By "now" Walsh means the historian's present—whenever the account was written. As we shall see, not all histories are diachronic narratives about the past. Some are essentially synchronic accounts, analogous to style analyses.

2. *The Shape of Time*, pp. 22–23. One can go even further. It would seem to be impossible *in principle* to know the totality of past human events. For such knowledge would involve an infinite regress. That is, a document

"the short and simple annals of the poor" are, then, largely a subject for poetic conjecture rather than historical construction.

The past is only partially preserved, not primarily because documents that once existed have been lost, however, but because it was selectively recorded at the time. It was so first of all because human beings are not passive, neutral receivers of what William James called the "booming, buzzing confusion" that everywhere surrounds and impinges upon us. Both by nature and by nurture our finely tuned cognitive circuits filter and separate, connect and organize this haphazard input into understandable patterns and coherent processes. Even when events are part of some present, they are not experienced and comprehended in some miraculously direct way. They are always mediated by the patterning proclivities of the human mind—by the cognitive laws discussed in the first chapter. And these laws are in turn constrained and realized through the concepts and classes, categories and hypotheses established by the stylistic rules and dialectic strategies of a particular culture, as well as by the idiomatic interests, cognitive habits, and prejudices of individual observers. What are recorded and documented, then, are those events that, for cultural and individual reasons, someone believes to be significant and, consequently, notices. Victor F. Weisskopf cites an especially striking instance of this process of selection:

> One of these explosions occurred in the year A.D. 1054 and left behind the famous Crab Nebula, in which we see the expanding remnants of the explosion with a pulsar in the center. This explosion must have been a very conspicuous phenomenon, in its first days surpassing the planet Venus in brightness. So different from today's attitudes was the mental attitude in Europe at that time that nobody found this phenomenon worth recording. No records whatsoever are found in contemporary European chronicles, whereas the Chinese have left us meticulous quantitative descriptions of the apparition and its steady decline. What a telling demonstration of the tremendous change in European thinking that took place in the Renaissance![3]

More important still, even if, by some miracle, accurate and complete information about some segment of the past were available, such information would not be history. For as innumerable scholars have emphasized, history is not merely a collection of data chronologically arranged. It invariably entails relating documented events and actions to one another in such a way that an intelligible pattern emerges. HISTORY (the totality of past events) is to history (a patterning, whether perceived or written, of some of those events) as NATURE (all of creation) is to natural history

---

or artifact from the past is itself the result of some human action which must itself have been recorded if we are to know history in Walsh's first sense. But such a record was also the result of a human action which must, in its turn, have been documented, and so on ad infinitum.

  3. "Physics in the Twentieth Century," p. 930.

or science (our patterning of some events in the natural world). Both may be comprehended by God, or may be known in some mystical way by genuine gurus. But for most of us HISTORY ("as it really happened") is unknowable.

*Interpretation*

These observations suggest that there are no such things as uninterpreted events, actions, or artifacts. To understand the world at all, to know that something *is* an event or object—that is, to segment and select, classify and relate—is to interpret experience.[4] In this sense, all of us are historians. We may be more or less competent. But like Socrates or Caesar, St. Francis or Leonardo, Newton or Beethoven, we pattern our present, which of course includes not only the immediate and remote past but the envisaged future as well. Thus there is an important aspect of history missing from Walsh's classification: every individual's cognition of his own time and past, as he knows it, is a kind of historical understanding. And when the term *history* is used in this study, it will designate not HISTORY but either an explicitly constructed account (usually written) or some patterning of events as interpreted by a more or less competent observer.

It should be mentioned in this connection that many, perhaps most, interpretations are based not only on documents but on prior interpretations. Here an analogy between musical and historical interpretation may be helpful. Except perhaps for a première, most musical performances are partly derived from, or are reactions against, interpretations that the performer has heard or has learned from teachers. Similarly, most criticisms of compositions or their performance—and these, too, are results of interpretation—are influenced by earlier criticism; this is particularly obvious when a later interpretation is a reaction against an earlier one. Furthermore, every interpretation, whether the first or the most recent, is dependent upon a tradition of interpretation that is in itself influenced by changes not only in musical style and in the theory of music, but in the ideological beliefs of some culture. During the second quarter of the twentieth century, for instance, interpretations of Beethoven's "Pathétique" Sonata were affected by a shift in emphasis such that formal and processive relationships became more important than they had been previously relative to affective or programmatic ones.

The same is true of historical interpretations. Most are modifications of, or reactions against, existing interpretations. And all are influenced by traditions of interpretation that are themselves affected both by changes in cultural outlook and by

---

4. Even Searle's brute facts are not uninterpreted. Searle's observer does not "see" in some direct, unmediated way, but "perceives" organisms in colored shirts moving in particular ways. And he understands what is perceived in the light of informal classes and beliefs—for example, that the organisms are behaving purposefully. All these involve interpretation. Searle's facts are brute, not because they are uninterpreted, but because the available hypotheses cannot satisfactorily account for observed relationships.

changes in theories about the nature of historical change. Again during the second quarter of the twentieth century, interpretations of the American Revolution were affected by a turning away from the "great man" approach to history and by an emphasis on economic theories, which were themselves partly responsible for the change in viewpoint.

Interpretations are never definitive in the sense of being infallible or final. This is not primarily because new documents ("facts") may be discovered. In the case of past music, the discovery of a new work or a more authoritative source (say, the composer's autograph) is becoming more and more unlikely, though such an event might call for changes in interpretation. In the case of history (including the history of music), as the amount of data from the past increases, it becomes less and less likely that the basic facts will change significantly. Rather interpretations will change for two main reasons. First, because theories about the nature of relatedness in all realms (physical and biological, psychological and ideological, political and economic) will change, our interpretations based on such theories will do so as well. Second, as will be considered presently, our understanding, and hence our interpretation, of an event depends not only on its contextual present, but on the implications that the event is thought to have had for subsequent events. Because the future is open, interpretations cannot be definitive. As Arthur Danto points out, "our knowledge of the past is significantly limited by our ignorance of the future. . . . [A] complete account of the past would presuppose a complete account of the future."[5]

Though the implications of the past tend to reverberate in the future, for historians of a particular time some past events may seem largely closed out. For instance, according to J. H. Hexter,

> the history of the Treaty of Versailles of 1919 may indeed need to be written over a number of times in the next few generations as its consequences more completely unfold. But this is not true of the Treaty of Madrid of 1527. Its consequences for better or worse pretty well finished their unfolding a good while back.[6]

Moreover, though consequences may *seem* closed, it is impossible to be certain until history is over. And this is especially true in the arts, where reinterpretations of past works and styles have been quite common.

It does not follow from this variability that any interpretation is possible or that all are equally good. Though documents do not determine interpretations, they do establish objective limiting conditions—the facts; and though hypotheses may differ, they must be consonant with our general experience of the world. Interpretations must be *accurate* in the sense that they represent the documents faithfully and fully.

---

5. *Analytic Philosophy of History*, pp. 16, 17.
6. *Reappraisals in History*, p. 12. As just observed, however, the history of the Treaty of Madrid might be reinterpreted because theories about the nature and basis of historical change are modified.

An interpretation that distorts or omits relevant data is obviously faulty.[7] An interpretation should also be "objective" in the sense that, once documentation is established, hypotheses about relevant relationships are equitably and consistently employed. Objectivity in the humanities, like justice in the law, consists in the evenhanded application of posited principles.

An accurate interpretation may be valid but unilluminating. This is very clear in the case of music. A performance that is merely accurate is usually characterized as being pedestrian: "X played the notes but missed the music." And a merely accurate criticism (usually descriptive) is said to be pedantic or routine. A good interpretation illuminates what is documented even as it presents what is specified. It does so by explicating, either in sound or in words, the relationships—processive, formal, and ethetic—latent in the document, the composer's score. Similarly, a history may be merely accurate. Everything is faithfully presented, but somehow the connections and patterns discerned do not account for the essential relationships latent in the documents: "X presented the facts but failed to reveal their significance."[8]

Finally, it is relevant to mention that the language normally used in speaking about music suggests that the terms *true* and *false* are not applicable to interpretations. For we do not say that a performance, or even a criticism, of the "Pathétique" Sonata is true or false, but that it is accurate or full of mistakes, consistent or capricious, exciting or dull, illuminating or pedestrian. This is, I suspect, because truth or falsity is, strictly speaking, an attribute of general propositions that can at least in principle be confirmed or disconfirmed.[9] But interpretations are not general propositions. They are re-presentations (in the case of performances) or explications of the peculiar relationships discerned in the score that documents a specific composition. And so it is with histories. An account of the American Revolution or the history of Romanticism may be accurate or may contain factual errors; it may be consistent or biased, interesting or tedious, original or run-of-the-mill. But it is no more true or false than a performance or criticism of a piece of music. For histories, too, are re-presentations and explications of peculiar relationships discerned in some set of documents.

---

7. This is less of a problem in music than in history. For the performer or critic will presumably take into account whatever is documented in the composer's score. And what is notated there is usually limited as well as authoritative. But what is relevant documentation *is* a problem in historical interpretation if only because the historian must select from among myriad potentially relevant sources.

8. The comparison between music and history helps to explain an interesting difference between the interpretations of the critic and those of the historian—namely, that historians, narrating events in realms of human action, seek to recreate a sense of the experience being recounted more often than critics do. This is perhaps because critics usually presume that the work being interpreted has previously been experienced by the reader. That is, the critic need not be a "performer." But the documents interpreted, and the events recounted, by the historian will not, as a rule, have been previously experienced by the reader. As a result, historians often combine the roles of critic and "performer." They not only function as critical interpreters explaining the documented events, but present what might be thought of as an interpretive performance of those events, designed to enable the reader partly to share the experience of the events.

9. Thus a hypothesis about musical relationships might be true or false; but even though an interpretation based on a false hypothesis might be mistaken or misguided, we would not, I think, normally say that it was false. In this connection see my essay "Concerning the Sciences," pp. 182–85.

## *Historical Explanations: General Considerations*

Toward the close of Chapter 1 it was observed that what something *is*—its meaning for us—involves understanding realized alternatives in terms of those that might have occurred. And so it is in history. As Morris R. Cohen has pointed out: "We can understand the significance of what did happen only if we contrast it with what might have happened. . . . Indeed we could not grasp the full significance of what has happened, even though the facts of history were completely revealed to us, unless we had some idea of what the situation would have been otherwise." [10] Put in the terms being used in this study, understanding historical relationships, like understanding musical ones, involves an awareness of implied structure.

Cohen's assertion is amply borne out by the behavior of historians. Counterfactual conditionals—statements about what might have been—are by no means uncommon in their writings. This is scarcely surprising. For counterfactuals are, as far as I can see, essentially rhetorical devices that serve to dramatize the significance of what actually occurred by calling attention to alternatives. [11] In so doing, they emphasize both the pervasive presence of chance in the world ("but for a nail") *and* the centrality of choice—the choices made by protagonists (composers, commanders, priests, and politicians)—in human history. The following instance is especially

---

10. *The Meaning of Human History,* pp. 80–81. The same point has been made by many others, and from quite different points of view. In a review of Wendell R. Garner's book *The Processing of Information and Structure,* Ray Hyman writes that "Garner repeatedly emphasizes that the lesson of information theory is that the information is carried not by what the stimulus is but by what it could have been. . . . All the combinations of values generated by the dimensions define the *total set* of stimuli of which the particular stimulus is an instance. The informational properties of the stimulus can be determined only in relation to its total set" (p. 731).

Recall, moreover, that the *full* significance of any event, whether past or present, depends not only on an understanding of the alternatives not actualized, but on the event's implications for the future. Consequently, the significance of an event cannot be known until history is over, unless one adopts an eschatology—whether a Last Judgment or the final stage of a dialectical process—that posits the end of everything. From this point of view, the function of an envisaged end for history is not primarily to predict the future, but to interpret and understand the significance of both the present and the past.

These observations call attention to one of the many fascinating inconsistencies in nineteenth-century thought. On the one hand, the pervasive sense of change, which made understanding the present problematic, fostered a search for eschatologies that posited a point of historical closure. On the other hand, the ideology of Romanticism especially valued openness and the potentiality of Becoming. In this connection, see Chapter 8.

11. Here there is an interesting difference between criticism and history. Because composers can quite precisely imagine and virtually control the consequences of their choices, and because the documented choices (scores) selected for criticism are for the most part by composers considered accomplished, critics do not as a rule speculate about alternatives not taken, but direct their attention almost entirely to the choices the composer actually made. Only in those rare cases where the critic finds a passage wanting—as Rosen did with Haydn's sonata (see Chapter 1 at note 64)—are alternatives not employed considered. The position of the historian is, however, significantly different. Because he or she must consider the choices made by all the protagonists who played a part in some succession of events, the intelligence and propriety of those choices can scarcely be taken for granted; and because even the wisest and most powerful protagonists frequently have only partial control over the consequences of their choices, historians are usually aware that the choices of protagonists frequently have unforeseen and unwanted consequences. For both these reasons—and especially when a choice is believed to have had undesirable and unanticipated consequences—historians are prone to speculate about alternatives available to a protagonist in a given set of circumstances, and about what would have ensued had one or another alternative been chosen. In short, as a perusal of the respective literatures indicates, counterfactuals are much more common in historical than in critical writing.

striking and unusual because a long series of counterfactuals, stressing the possibility of alternatives in parameters such as politics and religion, is used to highlight the overriding importance of another parameter, economics:

> Had King Charles I and Archbishop Laud not tried to impose a prayer book and strengthen the episcopacy in Scotland, the Long Parliament need not have been called when it was; and if the Scottish Covenanters, thus provoked, had not invaded England successfully, Pym and his friends would never have been able to strike down Strafford and fasten their will on the King. Had it not been for the ill-treatment of the native Catholics in Ireland . . . the screw might not have been turned on the royal prerogatives to such a point that King Charles was presented with the alternatives of attacking the Commons in the citadel of their privileges or forfeiting his throne as he had inherited it. Finally, if Laud had not pushed through a policy of ritualistic reform in the Church of England . . . Parliament would not have found a body of supporters in the country ready to follow their leadership against a ruler to whom all the glorious traditions of the English monarchy still clung. Yet when all that is said, it still has to be recognized that it was a real shifting of economic power within the community that made the civil war possible.[12]

"Since men who act in history must calculate the possible consequences of various alternatives," write Lee Benson and Cushing Strout, "the historian in trying to understand them is lead to do the same. Questions of what would have happened can be answered, of course, only by judgments of probability based on knowledge of the actual situation."[13] Understanding the "actual situation" depends, as we have seen, on an intimate familiarity with, and sensitivity to, the musical or cultural style in question. An awareness of the alternatives possible and probable in some style, whether of an individual or a group, is the result of long experience, devoted attention, and fecund but controlled imagination. Such tacit skill may suffice for understanding. To *explain* events—those that occurred as well as those that might have been—however, requires not only sensitive understanding, but an ability to reconstruct how the composer or the protagonist interpreted the events he or she was involved in shaping: for example, what alternatives were possible given the stylistic situation, which ones were probably discerned, how their outcomes were envisaged, and why he or she might have chosen this alternative rather than some other.[14]

---

12. Ashley, *England in the Seventeenth Century*, p. 80. Notice that all the counterfactuals could have been stated in positive form. For instance, the first could have been put thus: "The Long Parliament was called when it was, because Charles I and Archbishop Laud tried to impose a new prayer book on the Scots and to strengthen the episcopacy."

13. "Causation and the American Civil War," pp. 90–91.

14. As pointed out in Chapter 1, such reconstructions are rational rather than psychological. For since neither the critic nor the historian can know with certainty what actually went on in the mind of a composer or protagonist (nor as a rule do composers or protagonists have such knowledge), what is reconstructed and explained is

In order to explain and to reconstruct, at least two assumptions must be made. The first is that human nature itself is fundamentally invariable, though the ways in which it is manifested are variable, depending on particular stylistic/cultural constraints (rules and strategies). Theories of behavior may, of course, change, and such changes will result in different explanations and reconstructions.[15] But the basic principles constraining human behavior—the laws considered in Chapter 1—have remained constant over time. Needs for air, food, and shelter, for repose, security, and companionship, for understanding, order, and stimulation were the same five thousand years ago as they are today. Without some such assumption, the behavior of our contemporaries as well as that of past composers and protagonists would be inexplicable.[16]

The second assumption, which complements and qualifies the first, is this: Unless shown to be otherwise, human behavior is the result of intelligent and purposeful—though not necessarily deliberate, fully-informed, or even judicious—choice. Without this assumption, which connects human choices to one another and to the circumstances in which they are made, it would be impossible to relate the particular events preserved in a musical score or historical document to the physiological and psychological needs that generated them. Thus the first assumption posits the existence of certain universal human needs which, it should be emphasized, are invariably specified by some set of stylistic/cultural rules; these needs generate, and establish the goals of, human behavior. The second assumption makes it possible to relate the particular choices made in some specific musical or historical situation to such needs and goals.

To put the matter in another way, what we know, based on documented evidence, is not what Beethoven or Caesar actually felt, believed, or understood, but their behavioral choices. To understand and explain these choices, we must reconstruct the total situation in which behavior occurred. This includes knowledge—based on all available sources—about the general needs and dispositions of humankind, about the habits and predilections of the particular composer or protagonist (his or her idiom), and about the alternatives available given the constraints present in the stylistic/cultural context. From such a reconstruction the critic or historian infers goals, motives, and reasons. Beethoven's aesthetic/affective purposes in writing a deceptive cadence at the beginning of the "Les adieux" Sonata or Caesar's political/personal goals in crossing the Rubicon do not come to us explicitly classi-

---

not the empirical "history" of choice, but the rational relationships among alternatives possible, the stylistic/cultural constraints operative in the specific circumstances, and the particular goals in view.

15. An account of a Bach partita in terms of the eighteenth-century doctrine of affections will be different from one based on twentieth-century concepts of Schenkerian *Ursatz,* and an explanation of Caesar's behavior in terms of the seventeenth-century theory of humors will be different from one based on Freudian psychology. I hasten to add that there is no warrant for supposing that theories formulated at the time some choices were made are necessarily preferable to those formulated subsequently. In this connection, see note 17 below.

16. As Ruth Solie has pointed out to me (personal communication), psychological needs tend to be more variable (in intensity) and more malleable (culturally) than physiological ones. However, though the need for, say, companionship may vary from one individual to another and subculture (hermit) to another (comedienne), some psychological needs—for instance, the need for cognitive stimulation—seem both powerful and inescapable.

fied and labeled, as in some how-to-do-it manual.[17] Rather, based on a reconstruction of the total situation (together with hypotheses, however informal, about human behavior), the critic or historian infers motives and reasons, needs and goals from specific documented choices. Such inferences are possible only if it is assumed that behavior is intelligent and purposeful. Without this assumption Beethoven's choices would be as perplexing as a table of random numbers, and Caesar's actions as inscrutable as those of a raving maniac.

## HYPOTHESES AND EXPLANATION

### Hypotheses in Histories of Music

Just as a synchronic analysis of style is more than a listing of traits, so a diachronic history of style is more than a chronological ordering of such analyses. It is a relating of successive style-frames to one another in terms of some hypothesis that accounts for their succession—that is, explains the process of change.

Any conjecture that patterns some set of observed data can serve as an explanatory hypothesis. What a hypothesis does is to transform data (Searle's brute facts) into a relational pattern (Searle's institutional fact). Because our understanding of the world is hierarchic, this process of transformation is so as well. That is, lower hierarchic levels consist of brute facts—of "mere" data—until those facts or events are related to one another according to some hypothesis in terms of which they are understood to be connected on the next higher level. Atoms or words, pitches or political statements are brute until they are related to one another in terms of physical or linguistic theories, or musical or political principles. On the next level, molecules or sentences, musical phrases or political conventions are similarly brute until they have been connected to one another in terms of some hypothesis. Thus, to use Searle's example once again, if we know the rules of football—have "institutional hypotheses" about how the game works—we can relate the observed brute facts to one another. But on the next higher level—that of a series of completed games for a national championship, or that of football as a cultural phenomenon—the individual game is itself a brute fact until it is related, according to some principle, to other games in the series or to features of American culture (its geography, economics, communications technology, and so on). In the same way, each stylistic configura-

---

17. It should be emphasized that statements by composers or protagonists about their motives, needs, and goals are *not* especially privileged sources. Such information must always be evaluated in the light of the actual evidence—their behavior. Caesar's contention that he was acting for the good of the Roman Republic, like any other piece of evidence, must be tested according to what is known. If his behavior indicates that he was personally ambitious, that trait will be imputed to him despite his claims to the contrary.

Erwin N. Hiebert, reviewing an essay by Heilbron and Kuhn in *Historical Studies in the Physical Sciences* about Niels Bohr's discovery of quantum mechanics, writes, "Here our historians of science have reconstructed, with unique documents in hand, one of the great accomplishments of physics; but in doing so they have provided an answer at variance (in some essential points) with the recollections of the man who did the actual work. In this case, the historians have set the discoverer straight—historically speaking—where tricks of the memory and certain retrospective overemphases are suspected" (p. 736).

tion, however exquisitely analyzed, remains a brute fact in the history of music until it has been related to either preceding or following styles, or to other features of its culture, in terms of some hypothesis about the connection between such styles or features.

The problem of devising viable hypotheses to explain style change in the arts is especially pressing. This is so because neither musical/cultural goals nor the relationships of such goals to specific compositional means have been subjects of common concern in our culture. Therefore, if style change is to be explained, explicit hypotheses must be devised about the nature of musical/cultural goals and about how these may be connected with specific compositional choices. Put the other way around: as one reads, say, political, social, or intellectual history, what often seems little more than a chronological narrative is actually understood as a reasoned explanation because the text or report is interpreted by competent readers in the light of unstated hypotheses about human motivation and goals, causal processes, and so on—hypotheses that are drawn from a shared repertory of reasons accepted by our culture. For instance, the following excerpt from *The Columbia History of the World* makes no mention of causes, principles, or hypotheses:

> Internal weakness and dissension, sharpened by the economic and so-cial injustices perpetrated under their rule, finally led to the downfall of the Umayyads. Large groups among the *mawālī* and Arabs, disenchanted with Umayyad policies and jealous of Umayyad dominance, joined anti-Umayyad parties. . . .[18]

Nevertheless, as we read the passage, we draw upon a repertory of culturally sanctioned reasons—ones having to do with political rivalries, social grievances, economic privation, and so on—in such a way that the narrative account functions as an explanation. We understand *why* the Umayyads were overthrown.

The situation in music history is, however, very different. True, a host of culturally consecrated hypotheses—for instance, ones positing the primacy of purely aesthetic goals, the prevalence of organic development, the power of influence (suggesting genetic succession), and causal connections between cultural changes and musical ones—make it seem that music histories are like other narratives. But the tacit, unexamined hypotheses are so general and vague that narrative-like accounts cannot *explain,* cannot, that is, become histories. For instance, the following account of the changes in the harmonic style of Renaissance music remains a chronicle—a description—because it is unclear *why* the changes described took place.

> Exploited in many devious ways, the traditional [intervallic] progres-sions assumed fantastic shapes between 1450 and 1500. The sounds of

---

18. Garraty and Gay, eds., p. 272. An excerpt about a remote, unfamiliar culture was chosen here because, had the account been from, say, European history, it might be thought that the description was relationally intelligible as a result of prior knowledge of the events and circumstances recounted.

music became richer, while the shapes lost their clarity and direction. The two-part framework, still for a time the basis of musical composition, was treated in such a way as to become almost unrecognizable, for composers now used the old principles and techniques in the most oblique, noncommittal ways they could find. Variety, not clarity, became the distinguishing feature of polyphony.[19]

(It should be pointed out that the need for explicit hypotheses is not confined to the arts. Whenever shared cultural beliefs fail to furnish "satisfactory" relational connections, explicit hypotheses will be required if change is to be explained. For instance, our culture furnishes no repertory of reasons to account for high-level political, social, or economic changes. To explain such changes, explicitly formulated hypotheses are required, such as those of Vico or Hegel, Pirenne or Turner, Marx or Spengler. The reason for this seems to be that, though we frequently understand the goals of human beings in specific contexts—for instance, as husband, wife, tennis player, politician—we seldom conceptualize the "goals" of larger historical processes. More generally, whenever the goal of some activity in some parameter is not part of our set of cultural beliefs, explicit explanatory hypotheses must be devised.)

Before considering some of the reasons for this difference between the writing of music history and other kinds of history, something needs to be said about the nature of explanatory hypotheses in general. As observed earlier, in my view any hypothesis that relates entities or events to one another can function as a basis for explanation. Except for ad hoc ones, hypotheses take the form of general principles. The most familiar case, that of causal explanation (for instance, Mary Queen of Scots was condemned to death *because* she plotted against Queen Elizabeth), will not be discussed here.[20] But there are other kinds of explanation, ones that are not causal. These may be divided into two main types: nontemporal and temporal.

## Nontemporal Explanations

SYNCHRONIC HISTORIES.

As distinguished from diachronic accounts, in which events are related to one another successively (through time), synchronic histories take a relatively closed segment of the past—often a considerable time span such as the Renaissance or the

---

19. Crocker, *History of Musical Style,* p. 155. Though it contains moments of "explanatory narrative," as well as of explicit explanation, the excerpt is, I think, reasonably representative; and it surely illustrates that, in the absence of explicit hypotheses, accounts of successive stages in a musical style fail to function as explanations of historical style change.

20. Rigorous causal accounts seem to me fraught with problems. Since what is to be explained is an event in all its peculiarities, it is virtually impossible to isolate a single variable as *the* cause, while keeping all others constant. Because possible causes "come not single spies, but in battalions," most historical events are overdetermined. Consequently, an unequivocal weighing of parameters is especially needed in causal accounts. And perhaps it is for this reason that most explicitly causal theories of history posit the primacy of a single kind of cause: the means of production, economic scarcity, political power, the supernatural, and so forth.

Enlightenment—and analyze it as a cross section or style-frame in which all manifestations of the culture are considered to coexist. Since temporal succession is in principle excluded, synchronic histories are of necessity noncausal. Instead of tracing changes and differences, such histories are concerned to show that the myriad seemingly diverse cultural phenomena—political, social, and economic; philosophic, scientific, and artistic—can be comprehended as a coherent, intelligible pattern of relationships. J. H. Hexter, following Spengler, makes the same distinction, calling diachronic accounts "file" histories, and synchronic accounts "rank" histories:

> 'File' history is concerned with what Spengler called the *nacheinanderung,* the 'after-one-anotherness,' of events. It deals with events in temporal sequence. It gives us our political histories of this place, and constitutional histories of that place. 'Rank' history is concerned with what Spengler calls the *nebeneinanderung* of events. It deals with the relation of more or less simultaneous events as manifestations of the temper of an age, or, as the anthropologists would have it, the pattern of culture. It gives our era histories—the Renaissance, the Age of Enlightenment.[21]

Explaining such a pattern, like solving a mathematical puzzle or deciphering a code, involves discovering the single principle that underlies the perplexing diversity of concepts, conditions, and events. Fredric Jameson describes the synchronic mode of analysis as aiming at "reducing the individual events to various manifestations of some basic idea . . . and ultimately reducing those ideas to some central notion of which they are all partial articulations, so that what at first seemed a series of events in time at length turns out to be a single timeless concept in the process of self-articulation."[22] For instance, one of the most famous synchronic histories, Jacob Burkhardt's *Civilization of the Renaissance in Italy,* relates the many disparate phenomena of the Renaissance to one another by demonstrating that all are manifestations of a single fundamental idea: the awakening spirit of the individual. As with most puzzles, temporal order is unimportant. From an analytical point of view, everything in the system of cultural relationships coexists in a kind of undifferentiated time. Thus, according to Siegfried Kracauer, both Burkhardt's classic and his *Age of Constantine the Great*

> testify to the same unconcern for the dynamics of the historical process. In both works Burkhardt brings time to a standstill and . . . dwells on the cross-section of immobilized phenomena which they present for his scrutiny. His account of them is a morphological description, not a chronological narrative.[23]

21. *Reappraisals in History,* p. 22.
22. *Prison-House of Language,* p. 70.
23. "Time and History," pp. 70–71.

Peter Gay's book *The Enlightenment: An Interpretation* is also in the synchronic mode, though it is concerned with only one aspect of the period, intellectual history. Toward the beginning of the book, Gay explicitly remarks not only on its atemporality and its difference from a possible sequential, diachronic account, but on one of the hallmarks of such histories, the emphasis on resemblances and correspondences. "In drawing this collective portrait," he writes, "I have indiscriminately taken evidence from the entire eighteenth century, from Montesquieu to Kant. This procedure has its advantages: it underlines the family resemblance among the little flock. But it may obscure the fact that the Enlightenment had a history." [24]

But there is a decisive difference between solving a puzzle and discovering intelligible synchronic relationships in the tangled skein of history. For since puzzles are designed to be solved, there are good grounds for believing that some common principle underlies surface disparity. But unless one believes that some supernatural force ordains the events of human history, there seems little warrant for assuming that a single principle will make historical events coherent and intelligible. History may be only partly coherent, and some of its diversity may be irreducible.

Perhaps the need to believe that there must be a simple solution, as in the case of puzzles, explains why the art-reflects-the-culture-out-of-which-it-arises thesis is so often stated as a canon calling for compliance rather than as a hypothesis to be tested.

> The art of a civilization, rightly interpreted, is a very precise reflection of the society which produced it. This is an *iron law* concerning man and all his artifacts. [25]

> *We must believe* that a connection exists . . . in all eras between music and the other creative activities of man; that the music produced in any age must reflect, in terms appropriate to its own nature, the same conceptions and tendencies that are expressed in other arts contemporary with it. [26]

Faith in the existence of an underlying principle of cultural coherence leads to, and often seems to compel, a search for similarities among apparently diverse phenomena. Or the historian may "search for a center, or for a cluster of interrelated foci, from which the totality can be understood and presented as a unified whole." [27] But it is dangerous to suppose that cultures are, or can be understood as, unified wholes, informed by a single common principle. [28]

---

24. *The Enlightenment: An Interpretation* 1 : 16–17.
25. Jordan, *Concise History of Western Architecture,* p. 6; emphasis added.
26. Grout, *History of Western Music,* p. 294; emphasis added.
27. Weintraub, *Visions of Culture,* pp. 6–7.
28. It is worth noting that synchronic histories are an invention of the nineteenth century. For the belief in national identity, coupled with the rapidity of technological, social, and ideological change, made the nature of cultural coherence seem problematic. And, as we shall see in Chapters 6 and 8, it is typical of nineteenth-century thought that the unity discovered turned out to be based on similarity relationships.

One problem is that, since the phenomena being compared are similar in some respects but not in others, correspondences are only partial. This is the case even within a single parameter, especially when the patterns being compared occur on different hierarchic levels. For since constraints always vary somewhat from one hierarchic level to another, seemingly similar patterns arise out of different constraints (are analogical) rather than from the same set of constraints (are homological). The danger of confusing analogical with homological patternings is even more acute when different parameters, and hence significantly different constraints, are involved. What are needed are, as suggested below, explicit and consistent translation codes that enable the historian to show that patterns, whether seemingly similar or dissimilar, are actualizations of some shared group of constraints.

It is relevant, finally, to note that there is a marked tendency to reify whatever principle is found to underlie and unite the various realms of culture. To a considerable extent, this tendency is probably a result of the proclivity of our culture to make all relationships *causal*.[29] That is, because the common principle is inferred from coexisting phenomena, it cannot be antecedent to and consequently cannot have "caused" the relationships discerned by the historian. But when reified—that is, when transformed in imagination into a concrete force whose existence is somehow independent of the particular cultural phenomena from which it was abstracted—the common principle seems theoretically prior to its particular manifestations in the various parameters of culture. Once reification certifies causality, the unity of culture and the significance of correspondences and correlations are, as it were, guaranteed. In addition, by providing temporal differentiation, reification somewhat mitigates the radical incompatibility between the timelessness of the synchronic mode and the changes characteristic of the diachronic.[30]

IDENTIFICATION.

The basis for another kind of atemporal, noncausal explanation is identification. To assert *what* something is—for example, that a set of political events is a convention or that a succession of musical events is a development section—is to identify it both by relating it to other members of the class and by contrasting it with phenomena that are not members, and, in so doing, to call attention to characteristic features of, and relationships within, such a *what*.[31] Obviously such identification is explanatory only if it is made within the context of institutional knowledge of some sort. If nam-

29. As discussed in Chapter 5, the concept of influence, too, tends to be formulated and understood as being causal.

30. Diachronic cultural histories must assume that the parameters of culture are noncongruent. For only if they are out of phase with one another (so that changes in some parameters precede changes in others) can there be interaction, influence, and historical process. The noncongruence of parameters is discussed in Chapter 5.

31. In this connection see Dray, " 'Explaining What' in History," p. 405.

ing is to be illuminating, that is, the general characteristics of political conventions or development sections must be known. Thus, to say that a particular phenomenon is a huddle or a lateral pass is explanatory only if we know the relational rules—the institutional facts—of football. In some sense, then, we can explain by saying *what* something is. But to name the class of something is neither to say what caused it or what caused the relationships that make it what it is. Rather it is to explain by saying how it works—how its characteristics function with respect to one another and in relation to the larger context of which it forms a part.

There are also statements that, though purely factual, play a role in explanation because they establish the style-context in which some phenomenon occurs. They tell us, that is, which sets of constraints from our learned repertory are relevant for what will follow. For instance, on reading in a concert program that the next work to be performed will be "a newly discovered theme and variations by Mozart," an experienced listener brings into play the stylistically appropriate habit responses (different from those that would have been appropriate for, say, a fugue by Bach) that make sensitive understanding possible. Similarly, in history, when we read that "Martin Luther was the son of a fairly prosperous Thuringian miner, who wanted his son to become a lawyer . . . In 1501 he entered the University of Erfurt . . . Then, following his father's wishes, he began to study law, but unexpectedly entered the local Augustinian monastery . . ."[32] our knowledge of the prevalent cultural/stylistic constraints establishes the context in which what is subsequently recounted will be understood and interpreted. Were time and place significantly different, quite comparable events would be understood in another way. In short, statements that establish context are cues: just as they tell us how to listen to music, so they tell us how to read a history.

## Temporal Explanations

LAWLIKE RELATIONSHIPS.
Changes over time, too, may be explained in terms of noncausal hypotheses. For instance, one of the laws of motion asserts that the state of motion of a body remains constant unless acted on by some outside force—for instance, gravity. But this law of motion, as well as the others, asserts nothing about causation. Thus, if someone asked why a satellite followed a particular trajectory at a given speed, it would be wrong to suggest that the laws of motion caused its trajectory and speed. And though gravity is commonly referred to as a *force*, suggesting notions of causation, properly speaking it is not a cause. As Henry Margenau writes, "Newton's law of gravitation . . . sets up a relation between an observation on the rate of change of the radial velocity between two masses on the one hand, and the distance between them

32. *The New Grove Dictionary*, Vol. 11, p. 365.

on the other. But it contains no criterion to determine the causal status of these observations." [33]

Nor, despite the frequent use of more or less causal language, is the theory of evolution strictly speaking a causal explanation. Though changes in the environment evidently *caused* the extinction of species, making ecological niches available for others, it would seem strange to suggest that the environment caused survival. [34] And, as far as I can see, the same holds for the survival of mutations and other changes in genotype: they can be explained retrospectively but not causally. Rather than suggesting, perhaps surreptitiously, that the environment caused the survival of various species, it might be preferable to anthropomorphize a bit and propose that from the plethora of alternative possibilities the environment *chose* certain species for survival.

IMPLICATION (NONBINDING).

There is another way of explaining temporal relationships, in which earlier events are understood to *imply* later ones. An implicative relationship is one in which an event or situation (a political convention, technological innovation, declaration of war, musical motive, or harmonic progression) is patterned in such a way that reasonable inferences, based on innate cognitive constraints and learned stylistic ones, can be made both about its connections with preceding events and about how the event or situation might itself be continued and perhaps reach relative closure and stability. By "reasonable inferences" I mean those that a competent, experienced observer/interpreter—one familiar with and sensitive to the constraints of a cultural or musical style—might make.

Though implicative accounts involve tacit or explicit awareness of if-then relationships, they are not causal but probabilistic. [35] To illustrate the difference between implication and causation, let us consider a musical example discussed in Chapter 1. The concept of implication was employed to account for connections within the opening melody of the second movement of Haydn's "Military" Symphony: "the rising motion from C to D—the first motion of the movement—is understood as a generative melodic process implying linear continuation to a point of relative stability. . . . The linear motion is continued as the melody moves through E and F

33. "Meaning and Scientific Status of Causality," p. 437. In a note on page 462 of Arthur Danto and Sidney Morgenbesser, eds., *Philosophy of Science,* is the following quotation from the conclusion of Newton's *Principia:* "I have not been able to discover the cause of these properties of gravity . . . it is enough that gravity does really exist, and act according to the laws we have explained."

34. To argue that species survived because they were fit (making fitness some sort of cause) is patently circular. For fitness is attributed to a species because we know that it survived.

35. Causality is a kind of implication in which an earlier event prescribes and determines a later one. But, as used here, the term *implication* is taken to be nonbinding because alternative continuations are considered to be possible.

(m. 3) to G (m. 4), a point of relative stability."[36] However, though the linear pattern from C to D may be said to imply continuation to E (given certain hypotheses about melodic relationships—i.e., that once an orderly pattern is begun, continuation to a point of relative stability is implied), it would surely be strange to suggest that the motion from C to D *caused* the following E. Nor would one want to say that a harmonic progression from the subdominant to the dominant caused the following tonic, though it certainly would have *implied* the tonic.

Similarly in historical accounts, earlier events or situations are understood (often only in retrospect) to imply later ones: "Never had the Churches seemed stronger than in the opening decades of the seventeenth century. Yet a single generation was to witness their deposition from political dominance. *The collapse was implicit in the situation of 1618.*"[37] Implicative relationships are not always as explicitly stated as this. Given our culture's penchant for construing earlier events as harbingers of later ones, implication may be suggested through concepts such as anticipation and even a phrase such as "paved the way for": "Renaissance Platonists such as Cusanus and Picino brought the notion of innate ideas back into prominence and thus paved the way for the later rationalistic position adopted by such thinkers as Descartes, Malebranche, Leibniz, and Kant."[38]

An implicative process may be deflected or delayed (through the interposition of other patterns) and then subsequently resumed. Such resumptions occur in both music and history. Let us take a musical example first. The last movement of Haydn's String Quartet in E♭ Major, Opus 50 No. 3, begins with a clearly profiled melody that rises by step every second measure.[39] But the implied continuation of this melodic pattern is broken by an essentially static "parenthesis" (mm. 5–8) after which the rising line is resumed and continued to a point of relative stability and closure.[40] Similarly in history, implications may be realized remotely. A clear example of delayed realization can be found in the history of the civil rights of blacks in the United States. The enfranchisement of blacks begun in the nineteenth century was broken off after the Civil Rights Act of 1875 and then resumed with the Civil Rights Act of 1975.[41]

It seems more difficult to identify unequivocal instances of remote realization

---

36. See Chapter 1, Example 1.5 (graph 1).

37. Wedgwood, "Futile and Meaningless War," pp. 10–11; emphasis added.

38. Kristeller, "Renaissance Platonism," p. 114.

39. This passage is discussed in my *Explaining Music*, pp. 240–41. Other instances abound in the music of the Classic period, but perhaps the most familiar case is that in which a process implying closure is broken and delayed by a cadenza.

40. Also see the Trio of Mozart's String Quartet in G Major (K. 387) and Beethoven's "Les adieux" Sonata mentioned in Chapter 1. A large-scale instance of remote realization, occurring in the third movement of Mahler's Fourth Symphony, is discussed in Chapter 7.

41. At times technological or scientific discoveries may, at least in retrospect, seem to be remote realizations. William Bevan, for instance, observes that "100 years separated Babbage's idea of a computing engine and the modern electronic computer . . . [and forty years] elapsed between Einstein's paper on stimulated emission and the first laser" ("Welfare of Science," p. 990).

in the history of music. One reason for this is, I think, that the notion of implication involves some sense of goals and hence of values as well. Thus, while we regard the achievement of individual human rights as a goal of society, the goals of music history seem obscure and elusive. For instance, despite metaphors of historical development (implying goals), it is a mistake to suggest that the mature Classic symphony was the goal of the early symphony (and before that of the concerto, opera overture, and so on). And for this reason, it seems wrong to say that the symphonies of Sammartini and Wagenseil *implied* those of Haydn and Mozart. Nor would one want to argue that the *ars combinatoria* of the eighteenth century implied the kinds of combinatoriality prevalent in the twentieth.[42]

## The Past: Importance and Manifestation

IMPORTANCE.
The past is, as noted earlier, replete with documented events, situations, artifacts, and so on. From these, historians choose to concern themselves with the very few that they believe to be significant. And to a considerable extent, significance is a function of implicative connection. As William Dray remarks, events "are judged important because of what they lead to."[43] For instance, the assassination of Caesar was an important historical event, not because Caesar's life was more valuable than the lives of countless minor Roman officials who were murdered, but because of the implications (largely known in retrospect) that the assassination had for later events. Notice that it is the importance of such "all-or-nothing" events that can most effectively be dramatized through the use of counterfactuals and that the counterfactuals would be pointless were it not for the possibility of making implicative inferences, inferences necessarily based on hypotheses of some sort about the constraints operative in the particular circumstances.[44]

Dray goes on to ask whether an event cannot be important because it is "judged

---

42. It is important to recognize that, as opposed to *actions* such as battles, political campaigns, or revolutions, artifacts such as works of art may be proximate (for instance, as influences) even though they were created in the remote past. Though created thirty thousand years ago, the cave paintings of Lascaux can be just as much a proximate stimulus as a painting made yesterday. Similarly, Aristotle's *Poetics* is just as much part of the present for a young philosopher as Nelson Goodman's *Languages of Art*. And so it is with music: the Machaut Mass, Mozart's *Magic Flute*, and Rameau's *Traité* are just as much part of the present as the most recent composition by Xenakis or the latest article on set theory.

43. *Philosophy of History*, p. 32. It is important to notice that even if a great, or perhaps revolutionary, discovery should in the long run prove to have been mistaken, it may yet have been a momentous event in intellectual history. Thus Isaiah Berlin, writing of the work of Karl Marx, contends: "Even if all its specific conclusions were proved false, its importance in creating a wholly new attitude to social and historical questions, and so opening new avenues of human knowledge, would be unimpaired" (quoted in Kracauer, *History*, p. 101). And so it is with the discoveries of Newton and Darwin, Freud and Einstein, and the theories of Rameau and of Heinrich Schenker. Their greatness lies not necessarily in their truth, but in their heuristic and mind-opening power—*and*, by no means least, in their implications for future understanding and action.

44. In this connection, see Murphy, "On Counterfactual Propositions," p. 32 and passim.

*intrinsically* interesting."[45] To answer, it is necessary to distinguish two kinds of intrinsic interest. The first involves history, and especially implicative relationships. For attending to implicative interactions and connections is among the most important and deep-seated human/cognitive dispositions. By nurture as well as by nature we delight in making inferences and comprehending implications. This is why we read histories that are not relevant to our immediate interests, as well as why we enjoy novels and detective stories. And it explains why a narrative such as Gibbon's *Decline and Fall of the Roman Empire* can be read as literature as well as history.[46]

MANIFESTATION.

A past event can be considered intrinsically interesting, however, for reasons that have nothing to do with history. For history, as I have been arguing, seeks to explain synchronic or diachronic patternings that have occurred in the past. But the past may also be fascinating because it offers what might be called "signal manifestations." That is, by recounting the extraordinary, especially in the realms of human behavior, the tales of the past show us "how the world is." The evil of Hitler or the sainthood of Gandhi, the catastrophe of the Lisbon earthquake or the flight of Halley's comet, may be of interest not only because they changed the course of events in some way, but because they significantly affect our conception of what is humanly or physically probable. (In a comparable way, we may be interested in an exemplary work of art not only because it was influential, but because it seems to establish some sort of limit or standard for the understanding and classification of the art. John Cage's *4'33"* is surely such a work.) Moreover, there are past events that, though they had little effect on the larger history of civilization, are nevertheless engrossing: for instance, the crimes of Heliogabalus. Notice that our interest in the past as manifestation is explicitly *non*historical. That is to say, it is not our understanding of *changing* historical events and circumstances that is affected, but our comprehension of what we take to be the *enduring* constraints of the world.

Looked at from another point of view, however, the past as manifestation is an enormous and variegated compendium of more or less outlandish gossip. And as with ordinary gossip—about the affairs and foibles of movie stars, politicians, preachers, and colleagues—we are intrigued because, by changing our sense of the probabilities of human behavior and natural phenomena (if only ever so slightly), such knowledge of the past enhances our ability to envisage and hence our ability to choose intelligently and successfully.

Delight in the gossip about the great protagonists of the past seems innocuous enough. Yet at times it may not be so. For the kind of information considered appropriate for a particular genre of history is largely prescribed by convention. And the

45. Dray, *Philosophy of History*, p. 33.
46. In this connection, see Ellis, *Theory of Literary Criticism*, p. 48.

mere inclusion (in a putatively serious study) of information that deviates markedly in kind or amount from common historical norms will be taken by readers as testimony to its significance and will raise questions as to the reasons for its presence. And unless the relationship between such information and the choices of protagonists is made explicit or can be gleaned from the repertory of culturally sanctioned reasons, conscientious readers will feel obliged to devise their own hypotheses. For instance, by recounting a trivial incident (say, seeing a runaway horse) or mentioning that the protagonist was afraid of snakes, a biographer/historian virtually compels readers to formulate hypotheses connecting information with behavior (otherwise why should the information have been included at all?)—hypotheses for which the author refuses in effect to assume any responsibility.

### The Axiom of Constancy and the Centrality of Choice—A Parenthesis

Our interest in the past as manifestation is related to our need to stabilize the world, and oddly enough, this is also true of our concern with temporal change. When we think about the history of anything—the cosmos, the earth, the realms of biology, mankind, a dramatic action, or a musical pattern—we tend to direct our attention to evident changes.[47] To direct attention to change is tacitly to assume that change (especially when it seems anomalous) is what calls for explanation and, correlatively, to take for granted that persistence is the norm of existence. Thus an *axiom of constancy* underlies not only historical interpretation but almost all forms of human comprehension.[48] The axiom asserts that, other things being equal, a patterning— that is, any relatively stable structure or established process of change—will tend to persist unless deflected by some external impingement. This is not to contend that there are no real disjunctions in the world. There are genuine discontinuities, as the possibility of surprise makes evident. But this very possibility confirms, as it were, the axiom of constancy; for we can be surprised only because we take continuity for granted.

The axiom of constancy can be related to an idea that has become almost a leitmotif in this study, the centrality of choice in human experience. The centrality of choice may itself be a consequence of the fact that only a minute fraction of human behavior seems to be genetically specified.

> While in lower organisms, behavior is strictly determined by the genetic program, in complex metazoa the genetic program becomes less constraining, more "open" as Ernst Mayr puts it, in the sense that it does not

47. That this proclivity transcends cultural constraints is evident in the fact that the neural/perceptive/cognitive organization of higher animals seems designed to attend to and respond to change.

48. It needs to be emphasized that the axiom has to do with how human beings understand and respond to the world, *not* with the way the world actually *is,* though there must be some correspondence, else the species would have long since become extinct.

lay down behavioral instructions in great detail but rather permits some choice and allows for a certain freedom of response. Instead of imposing rigid prescriptions, it provides the organism with potentialities and capacities. This openness of the genetic program increases with evolution and culminates in mankind.[49]

But the price of freedom is the imperative of choice. Intelligent, successful choices are possible only if alternative courses of action can be imagined and their consequences envisaged with reasonable accuracy.

Such envisaging must be based on the assumption that, once established, structures and processes tend to persist—to be reliably and recognizably alike from one time to another. It is the axiom of constancy, then, that enables us to relate the past to the present and the present to the future. Without it, the past would be irrelevant, and the future would literally be inconceivable. Learning would be pointless because experience would cease to be a reasonable guide to behavior.

The need to envisage leads us to search for orderly, predictable patterns in the world. This is the goal of all our theorizing. When such patterns are found, as they frequently are, the axiom of constancy tells us to attribute changes in patterning to the impingement of external forces. Or persistence may be sought through high-level theories: in science, for example, the theory of evolution; in economics, Gresham's Law; in music, the Schenkerian *Ursatz;* in history, recurrent cycles and dialectic processes. Each of these theories dispels the patent disjunctions and irregularities of perceived patterns by subsuming them within a higher-level order in which persistence prevails. And persistence makes envisaging possible. Even the sciences, seeming models of the desirability of "progressive" development, have changed not for the sake of change but in order to produce the most stable world possible. (After all, the experimenter hopes to refine or confirm a hypothesis.) Paradigms and theories are not easily abandoned. Significant counterevidence will not lead to rejection until a viable alternative theory is at hand. The axiom of constancy neatly accounts for this behavior; one does not give up the security of one basis for envisaging and choosing—one theory of how things work, however inadequate it may be—until another is available. Paradoxically, then, we attend to change in order to annul it, to control it by subsuming it within a constancy of some sort.[50]

---

49. Jacob, *The Possible and the Actual*, p. 61. Choosing—or, conversely, not choosing—seems directly related to the complexity of the animal nervous system. A simple nervous system cannot allow for many alternative behavioral possibilities or for much feedback. Few neurons = a small range of options. Thus the growth of the human brain "added enough neural connections to convert an inflexible and rather rigidly programmed device into a labile organ, endowed with sufficient logic and memory *to substitute non-programmed learning for direct specification* as the ground for social behavior" (Gould, *Ever Since Darwin*, p. 257; emphasis added).

50. Emphasis on the importance of constancy should not obscure the role of change. Some degree of change (variation or novelty) is evidently necessary for the successful functioning of all animals. More to the point here, there can be patterning (in music or in history) only if there is change. History vanishes when there is no change whatsoever, just as vision is impossible without eye movement.

But even the most prescient envisaging may be for naught. To make envisaging count—to transform preferred alternatives into actual choices—one must have power. Conversely, power depends on the ability to envisage accurately and hence to choose intelligently. Knowledge, as the saying goes, is power, because vision, which depends on knowledge, is indispensable for successful choice.

Vision and power: these, then, are the bases for choice and consequently for survival. Their centrality in human affairs is everywhere evident in literature. Thus the essence of tragedy, as I see it, concerns the terrifying trauma of failed choice. Such failure may occur because of external circumstances (fate, political conditions, and so on) that deprive the protagonist of power and thereby preclude fruitful choice, because of an almost irrational compulsion that overpowers the protagonist's judgment and clouds his vision (the frequent play on sightless vision versus visionless sight in so many tragedies is surely more than coincidental), or because of some combination of lack of power and want of vision. The broad appeal of *Hamlet* stems in part, I suspect, from the fact that problems of both vision and power are coupled with an explicit concern with the poignant tensions of human choice.

Choice is also the focus of dramatic action in both comedy and melodrama. These genres are not, however, concerned with the failure of choice, as tragedy is, but with its correction. In "classical" comedy, the ignorant, unreasonable, or foolish choices of the protagonist (who is usually upper-class and hence powerful) are corrected through a salutary change in his or her understanding of the implications of possible alternatives. As a result, the credibility of the social order is preserved.[51] In melodrama, conversely, the malevolent, destructive possibilities (alternative "choices") of an established social order are thwarted and corrected— often by a benign, external agent (*deus ex machina*) who is needed to counteract the power of some misguided agent of society—and the threatened protagonist is saved.[52]

## *Implication: Prospective and Retrospective Understanding*

Understanding implicative relationships, though involving enormously complex cognitive processes, is something that all of us do much of the time: in reading novels or histories, in listening to music, in observing nature, or in comprehending human behavior. The rumble of distant thunder and the piling up of dark clouds suggest that it will rain. Denied a sweet, a child pouts and his eyes water; we surmise that

51. Comedy criticizes the foibles and fashions of members of the establishment in order to improve the social order. Consequently, it is almost invariably politically conservative. (Real radicals seldom write comedies, and when they do, the results are usually sadly lacking in good humor.) Aristophanes, Plautus, Molière, W. S. Gilbert, Shaw, and Wilde suggest no revolutions, propose no serious reforms.

52. Seen thus, the plot of Beethoven's *Fidelio* suggests a conservative, not a revolutionary, political stance. Beethoven's political views seem to support this suggestion. According to Martin Cooper, Beethoven had no objection to the hierarchic order of the ancien régime and "was an admirer of a benevolent despotism like that of Joseph II rather than a republican" (*Beethoven: The Last Decade*, pp. 88–89).

tears will soon follow. The end of a phrase moves toward the cadence, and the competent listener senses that closure will follow. None of these implications may be realized. The clouds may blow away, the child hold back his tears, and the cadence prove to be deceptive. But this does not mean that the presumed consequents were not implied, only that the implication inferred was not in fact realized.

These examples call attention to the fact that our understanding of temporal events—our conception and characterization of them—is both prospective and retrospective. And, as we have seen in the section "Historical Explanations," it includes both an awareness of what might have happened and our knowledge, after the fact, of what actually did occur. "What is meant by historical sense," as Isaiah Berlin observes,

> is the knowledge not of what happened, but of what did not happen. When an historian, in attempting to decide what occurred and why, rejects all the infinity of logically open possibilities, the vast majority of which are obviously absurd, and . . . investigates only those possibilities which have at least some initial plausibility, it is this sense of what is plausible . . . that constitutes the sense of coherence within the patterns of life. . . .[53]

The implicative inferences, in other words, affect our understanding of both the antecedent and the consequent events, whether the consequent was the one thought to be implied or not. If stormy conditions do not actually lead to rain, then that fact is included in our retrospective understanding of those antecedent conditions: they implied but were not followed by rain. And our comprehension of the consequent is similarly qualified: the pleasant day is one that had been threatened by rain and is in that respect different from fair days not so threatened. And the same kind of qualification takes place if the implied consequent does occur: in retrospect, the stormy conditions are understood not only to have implied but to have been followed by rain, and the consequent rain is not something that came out of the blue, an unexpected squall, but a possibility implied by antecedent conditions.

Both prospective and retrospective points of view are necessary for the understanding and explanation of temporal events. Just as the interpreter of a piece of music (whether composer, performer, or critic) must comprehend the pattern of musical events in all the ambiguity and uncertainty of their unfolding *and* as they are understood in retrospect after implications have been realized, so the historian must comprehend and explain the past both as seen from the perspective of the protagonists whose vision was necessarily limited and whose knowledge was partial *and* as viewed from the historian's vantage point in which many of the implications of the past are known.

---

53. "Concept of Scientific History," pp. 48–49.

According to C. V. Wedgwood:

> There is . . . an antagonism between two ways of looking at history, both interesting, both legitimate, but devoted to quite different ends. It is a valuable study, for instance, to trace the growth of the party system in English Parliamentary government. We can distinguish and map its origins in the earlier half of the seventeenth century and note the increasing tension between crown officials, courtiers and court nominees on the one hand, and those who were outside the Court Circle. In the present state of our knowledge the growth of the two parties, Court and Country, Tory and Whig, can be more or less clearly traced and demonstrated. But such a demonstration is relevant to the present rather than to the past. It is interesting because of what has happened *since* in English Parliamentary life, but too much emphasis on it inevitably colours, and falsely colours, our attitude to what was actually happening in Parliament at the time.[54]

Such a dual perspective may be difficult to achieve and hard to sustain. But the viewpoints are not antagonistic, at least not in the sense of being incompatible or mutually exclusive. Rather they are complementary. For the documented past becomes history only through its connections with other events, whether past or future, proximate or remote. That this is so seems evident from Wedgwood's own sketch of the Parliamentary situation in England during the reign of Charles I.

> In the autumn of 1641, when the war between King Charles I and Parliament was rapidly approaching, and the House of Commons was very bitterly divided between the supporters of John Pym and his opponents, Dr. William Chillingworth was sent to the Tower for having incautiously referred, in a private conversation, to the existence of two sides in the House of Commons. This was denounced as a highly dangerous and subversive statement because the House of Commons was, they most strenuously believed, a single and united body. . . . Of course, every sensible Parliament man in the autumn of 1641 could see quite plainly that there *were* two sides in the House; but not one of them had the additional advantage of knowing that this was the beginning of the famous two-party system, a useful political invention of which their descendants would justly boast. On the contrary they thought it disastrous; they saw it as contrary to all that they believed about the function of Parliament, and they pretended that it had not happened.
>
> It is easier to understand the ultimate development of Parliamentary government in England by tracing the party system to its origins; but we shall understand the Civil War and the Long Parliament better if we real-

---

54. Wedgwood, *Truth and Opinion*, p. 38.

ize, not merely objectively, as a quaint oddity, but with full intellectual sympathy, how repugnant this idea of a divided Parliament was to the men of the time.[55]

The historian must certainly appreciate the protagonists' viewpoint "with full intellectual sympathy." For only by understanding the alternatives available and by imagining how they interpreted them and envisaged their consequences can the historian explain why they chose as they did. But it is equally clear that our appreciation of the significance of those choices depends in part on what the historian takes to be their consequences. The events of 1641 merit recounting not primarily because of their intrinsic interest but because of the implications they are found to have for the subsequent history of English political institutions.[56] As Benson and Strout have pointed out, historians discover "the relevant antecedents retrospectively with the help of the illumination of the consequences, which call out for a past."[57] Moreover, "those who come after an event can, with the help of emotional distance, awareness of consequences, and wider perspective, know more about it than any participants."[58] And from this point of view we know more, historically speaking, about the "Eroica" Symphony than Beethoven did. Indeed, Beethoven himself would have known more about its implications in 1825 than he did in 1803.

As Wedgwood's discussion makes evident, to comprehend the past from the protagonists' point of view is neither to accept their professed beliefs unquestioningly nor to recount their behavior uncritically. Rather, interpreting each in the light of the other, the historian attempts to reconstruct what happened—and why. Thus the asserted belief that the House of Commons was a united body is interpreted in the light of the fact that the House was plainly divided. The historian's account, then, is a reconstruction of what, following Berlin, it is plausible to suppose, given (a) the action itself, (b) surrounding events and circumstances, including what was said about the choice by the protagonist and others, and (c) the historian's knowledge of the stylistic context and the "laws" of human behavior. To construct such an account, to transform documents into history, is to understand and explain the choices made by protagonists, whether they be politicians, soldiers, or composers.

In her biography of Mary Queen of Scots, Antonia Fraser explains why Mary wrote the letter to Babington that was to lead to her trial and execution.[59] The explanation consists of a description and analysis of the situation at the time: Mary's character, her prolonged isolation from the world of affairs, the events about which she

---

55. Ibid., pp. 38–39.
56. Note the change from prospective to retrospective understanding. For members of the House in 1641, the idea of a divided Parliament was "disastrous" because of what seemed (prospectively) to be its implications; viewed retrospectively, however, this division is understood to have been the beginning of the "famous two-party system."
57. "Causation and the American Civil War," p. 88.
58. Ibid., p. 91.
59. *Mary Queen of Scots*, pp. 480–81.

heard (such as James's treaty with England), and her health. Contemporary evidence—Mary's letters, Nau's memoirs, and so on—is, of course, the basis for Fraser's interpretation. But the explanation is not empirical in the sense that Fraser really knows what went on in Mary's mind. Indeed, even if Mary had written her own psychological account, this would not be accepted as incontrovertible evidence. Its validity would, like that of all the other evidence, be scrutinized for its reliability and its relationship to the total patterning of events. All that Fraser, or any historian, can tell us about the basis for Mary's choice is what, given the structure of the situation as she construes it, it is plausible to believe might have gone on in Mary's mind. Consider a tangential necessary condition suggested as one reason why the fatal letter was written: Fraser observes that Mary's health had improved, and "with renewed health came greater energy to escape." [60] Now had some intrepid journalist of the sixteenth century asked Mary (probably as she ascended to the execution platform) why she had written the letter, it is doubtful that Mary would have replied, "Why? Because my health had improved and my desire to escape was renewed." And had she been interviewed at greater length (perhaps for something analogous to the oral histories currently fashionable in the arts), her reasons for writing the incriminating letter would probably have been very different from those suggested by Fraser. These observations apply with equal force to the testimony of creative artists, theorists, and even critics. They are no more reliable witnesses to their own motives—the basis for their choices—than are other protagonists of history.

## History and Historical Fictions—A Digression

Here I take the liberty of indulging in a brief digression. The difference between a historian's account of events and that which might be given by a protagonist suggests that the distinction between a history and a historical fiction is not fundamentally one of accuracy of fact or vividness of representation. A history can be vivid and compelling, and a carefully documented fiction can be accurate. Nor does the distinction lie in the freedom of the novelist or playwright to select, as Wedgwood suggests: "the writer is free to use and reject what he wants, to present a heightened or simplified picture; he is not subservient to the facts he has accumulated or the observations he has made." [61]

But a history is a relational, selected patterning of data. And though the relationships discovered by the historian must be warranted by the evidence, they are not self-evident in the facts alone. Like the writer of a fiction, the historian constructs. On the other hand, writers are less free than Wedgwood allows. Once their generative premises—situation, character, initial incidents—have been established in conformance with the documented data they have accumulated, writers (like historians)

60. Ibid., p. 490.
61. *Truth and Opinion*, p. 93.

must develop and sustain a pattern in which situation and character, incident and implication are related to one another in a coherent and credible way. While the historian may have greater difficulty creating coherence, the writer has greater difficulty establishing credibility. For the unexpected and the coincidental are familiar attributes of experience. When they occur in a history, their truth is, as it were, guaranteed by their context. We believe that the historian did not invent the Lisbon earthquake to heighten our anxiety, or the storm that destroyed the Spanish Armada in order to provide the English with a happy ending. But the writer of fiction must struggle to prevent the unexpected from seeming incredible, and the coincidental from seeming implausible.

Nor is the difference between a history and a historical fiction primarily one of imaginative identification, of empathy. In neither a history nor a historical fiction is the audience called upon to believe and feel as the protagonists did; rather the reader is asked to comprehend their represented feelings and beliefs as an understandable basis for their behavior. When Caesar hesitates about whether to go to the Senate on the fateful day in 44 B.C., Shakespeare is not asking us to feel as Caesar felt; rather, based on our knowledge of the total situation, including the behavior of all the characters (their speeches, gestures, choices), we make plausible inferences that enable us to *understand* Caesar's uncertainty.

If the difference between history and historical fiction were a matter of degree of accuracy, vividness of representation, selectivity, or affective identification, then there would be an unbroken continuum from one to the other. But this is not the case. The distinction is more decisive. It depends on *whose* hypotheses are taken to be the basis for explanation. In historical fiction, it is the hypotheses of the protagonists that the audience uses to explain the choices made and the behavior recounted. It is in terms of the protagonists' understanding of their own and others' motives and circumstances, beliefs and actions that the series of events is comprehended.[62] In history, on the other hand, the protagonists' hypotheses are part of the data, but the theory that relates these to observed behavior—that explains why people chose as they did, why they entertained the hypotheses they did, and why events happened as they did—is that of the historian.

In the following account, historian David Ogg interprets and explains the behavior of the protagonist, Gustavus Adolphus, by relating his choices to his beliefs, motives, and goals:

> Gustavus Adolphus was influenced by two motives—anxiety for Protestantism, which seemed about to succumb before the onslaughts of the Hapsburgs; and desire for territorial recompense in Germany, by which the impoverished Swedish exchequer would benefit. Modern opinion

---

62. Once again the critic (and members of an audience always function as more or less competent critics) is comparable to the historian. For it is the critic who interprets the patterning presented in a historical fiction, just as it is the historian who interprets the documented actions of the past.

would dissociate such motives: to Gustavus and seventeenth-century opinion they were inseparable, for religious security could be maintained only
by landed possession.[63]

Had the account been a historical fiction, the protagonist's motives and goals would
have been embodied in the narrative, and the reader would have interpreted his
choices in such terms as cultural constraints, motives, and goals. In short, though
the historian must sympathetically understand how protagonists experienced, comprehended, and responded to the events in which they participated, explanation—the
implicative relationships discovered and the hierarchic or similarity patterns discerned—is in terms of the historian's interpretive hypotheses, not the protagonist's.


## Implication and Probability

The possibility of alternative consequences and, consequently, of the retrospective
revision of understanding may help to account for the difference between implication
and causation. For though both involve if-then relationships, causation is a special
case—one in which, because the antecedent (cause) is a sufficient condition for the
consequent (effect), there can be no alternatives. This difference in our understanding of the two concepts is reflected in ordinary language. Though it seems entirely
proper to assert that "X **implied** Y, but Y did not occur," it would seem incongruous
to assert that "X **caused** Y, but Y did not occur."

Because alternatives are possible, the relationship between an implicative event
and its realization is probabilistic.[64] Such probabilities are not, however, solely matters of statistical frequency. Rather, as we have seen, the sense of implicative probability (in history as in music) is in considerable part a result of the internalization of
style forms—the norms and schemata that arise from interaction between the constraints of human cognition and those of the particular style. These constraints not
only establish and limit the possible alternatives, forming a network of strategies,
but define the probabilities of the several alternatives possible.

The style of tonal music, for instance, provides for less probable deceptive cadences as well as for more probable authentic ones, and these syntactic probabilities
are themselves dependent upon compositional context: a deceptive cadence is more
probable toward the end of a phrase, where goals are patently established, than toward the beginning of one. Finally, it is important to recall that, though frequency
may at times alter our sense of the likelihood of some progression, it does not change
our understanding of the rules—the basic structural principles—of a style.

63. *Europe in the Seventeenth Century,* p. 152.
64. When it is said that "X probably caused Y," what is meant is either that the theory guaranteeing the
connection between X and Y has yet to be adequately confirmed or that the data are not fully known—as, for instance, when in answer to the question "Why did he fail his exam?" we answer, "Probably because he didn't study
hard enough," but we are not certain that was in fact the case.

Just as in music we can know what happened yet assert that a particular succession was not the most probable one, so in history, what actually occurred may seem improbable not only to those who participated in and shaped events, but even to those coming afterward. For instance, according to C. V. Wedgwood, religious compromise and peace seemed probable at the beginning of the seventeenth century:

> Such arrangements made it look as though, after a long period of struggle, diversity of religion and coexistence would be henceforth accepted.
>
> But what in fact happened in the seventeenth century—that century which we see, in the perspective of time, as the beginning of the modern world: the scientific age, the century of Galileo and Newton? *Contrary to what might have been expected,* religious passions blazed up afresh.[65]

As these examples suggest, constraints are parametric in both music and history, and the probabilities of implied continuations are so as well. This does not mean, however, that a realization—what actually happens to one of the parameters in music or history—is not affected by the impingements of other parameters. In the last movement of Mozart's Symphony No. 39 in E♭ Major (K. 543), for instance, the most probable continuation of the theme of the second key area is deflected by harmony, after which a combination of parameters creates a temporary digression, albeit one that has significant consequences in the development section.[66] When the probable cadential pattern occurs some fifteen measures later, its significance is changed; the closure it creates is passing, because it has been embodied within an ongoing, processive passage.

The effects of the impingement of parameters on one another are quite variable.[67] For instance, the interaction between politics and economics is quite intimate and readily comprehended. But the effects of parameters such as politics and economics on musical/aesthetic choices tend to be much more problematic. The following account of the effect of economic changes on political events in France before the revolution of 1830 seems self-explanatory:

> The aristocrats led by Charles X had voted themselves a large indemnity for the loss of their estates suffered in the 1790's. To pay the indemnity,

---

65. "The Division Hardens," p. 108; emphasis added.

66. The passage is briefly discussed in my *Explaining Music*, pp. 10–13.

67. Some parameters seem to be naturally interdependent: in music, melody and rhythm; in history, economic and social arrangements. Other relationships bewteen parameters are largely the result of stylistic/cultural constraints: in music, the relationship between melody and instrumentation; in history, between politics and religion.

Moreover, just as a musical style is characterized in terms of the parameters differentiated and their dominance relationships, so cultural styles are characterized by parametric differentiation and dominance relationships. And just as the history of musical style is in part a history of changes in parametric differentiation and dominance, so a history of cultural style involves tracing the changes in the parameters differentiated and their dominance relationships. If this has merit, it follows that the weighing of parameters cannot be fixed axiomatically but must be inferred from the study of each particular culture and epoch.

the state lowered the interest rate on the national debt, that is, took the money out of the pocket of the bondholders, mostly well-to-do bourgeois. The elections of 1827 brought into the Chamber a bourgeois majority, which the King disregarded. He appointed as minister an émigré of the old days . . . and when the conflict between Chamber and minister grew tense, Charles issued ordinances against the press and the chamber and called for new elections.

The ordinances did not last a day: journalists and publicists at once called for a general insurrection in the name of popular sovereignty, and in three days' fighting forced the abdication of Charles.[68]

But what was the effect of these events on Berlioz's choices as he wrote the *Symphonie fantastique* (1830)? Or on Corot's painting of Chartres Cathedral (also 1830)?

## Explanation in Music History

The problem, as stated above, is that our culture does not provide satisfactory hypotheses relating the constraints of parameters external to music to the choices made by composers. Perhaps this is because of the humble position that music occupies in the hierarchic ordering of cultural parameters.[69] But there are, as I see it, other reasons as well.

a. In the realms of social action—politics, economics, diplomacy, warfare, religious ritual, and so on—choice-realization space seems linearly limited and temporally exclusive. There could be only one Peace of Westphalia resolving the conflicts that preceded it, only one Catholic Emancipation Act, one attack on Pearl Harbor. Though protagonists envisage the consequences of possible alternatives in such cases, once a choice has been made, it occupies an exclusive time/space slot in the succession of events that constitute the history of the parameter in question. Given a culturally sanctioned account of individual and collective goals, such linear succession allows for the formulation of common-sense hypotheses connecting earlier and later events and choices. And given the proclivities of Western culture, it is scarcely surprising that such successions tend to be interpreted causally.

Because time/space slots seem less exclusive in the arts, linear successions are more difficult to discern and define. A host of different, but comparable, symphonies, string quartets, and the like, coexisted (as alternative realizations) in a single time and space during the second half of the eighteenth century. And it is difficult to

---

68. Garraty and Gay, eds., *Columbia History of the World*, p. 877.
69. The centrality of causality in the thinking of Western cultures seems evident once again. For the hierarchy of parameters—their relative importance and weighting—is directly related to what is believed to be their causal efficacy. When God is believed to be an important cause, religion and theology are influential cultural constraints; when economics is considered the prime mover, the means of production and manufacturing resources rise in the hierarchy and things religious are dethroned.

show that an earlier set of choices (a particular composition) was the necessary—let alone sufficient—condition for some subsequent set of choices. For instance, the choices resulting in Mozart's "Jupiter" Symphony do not seem to have depended on specific antecedent choices (whether in music or in parameters external to music) in the same way that the fall of the Bastille did one year later.

This discussion may help to explain why the most frequently recounted successions in the arts are those that restrict the variety of time/space slots by considering the changes occurring within the *oeuvre* of a single artist. Once linearity is assured, then the concept of "artistic development" provides a culturally sanctioned model in terms of which changing choices can be explained. Perhaps the need for linearity also accounts for the tendency of an art to be formulated in terms of intraparametric influences. This point of view suggests that the appeal of the idea of influence in art lies in the fact that it provides a kind of linearity, implying the possibility of development. The history of an art, then, like the continuity of bloodlines in thoroughbred racehorses, becomes a matter of "genetic" connection: for example, the structure of Haydn's sonata-form movements "out of" those of Wagenseil and Sammartini; Beethoven's *Fidelio* "out of" operas by Gluck, Cherubini, and Mozart.

b. Parameters external to music may, and often do, affect the choices made by composers and thereby the history of music. The problem in this case is understanding how the constraints governing the choices made in one parameter influence constraints governing choices in another. How, for instance, do particular political beliefs, circumstances, and events constrain the pitch and rhythmic patterns, harmonic progressions, and formal designs chosen by a composer or a group of composers? What is required is a code that *translates* the constraints of one parameter into those of another. In general, the less intimately interrelated the parameters are, the greater the need to make the translation code explicit. Just as our culture enables us to interpret accounts of political and social choices as explanations but fails to do so for musical ones, so it enables us to understand the interaction of closely related parameters such as politics and economics but provides no codes for directly connecting political choices with musical ones. This is why we readily understand the interaction between the economic and political choices that led to the French revolution of 1830, but are uncertain, save in a broad and imprecise way, about how to connect what occurred in these realms with artistic choices—whether contemporary or somewhat later.

This is not to deny that particular circumstances—e.g., explicit political control of compositional choices (the case of Shostakovich) or specific economic constraints (the situation with Stravinsky's *Histoire du soldat*)—may on occasion directly affect musical choices.[70] But most often and most importantly the effects of the parameters of action (politics, economics, social arrangements) reach music through

---

70. It is important to notice that, generally speaking, when particular political, economic, or social constraints affect music directly, their influence is transient. The choices affected, usually on the level of intraopus style, are not replicated and are therefore inconsequential for music history.

the mediation of ideology. That is, the constraints of the parameters of action are translated into the concepts, beliefs, and attitudes that constitute the ideology of the culture (or subculture), and these are in turn translated into the constraints that govern musical choices.[71] Because rules and strategies arise out of specific material means, which vary from one parameter to another, translation codes do so as well. What get changed, then, are means rather than ends. That is, the values and goals established by the dominant parameters are translated into the strategies (and much less frequently, the rules) appropriate to those parameters being influenced—in our case, music. But the nature of such values and goals and their relationship to strategic choices seem more difficult to understand in music than in the realms of action.

c. In a broad but important sense we know about goals in the realms of action and concept: in politics the goal is power, in finance it is wealth, in the sciences confirmed theories. And because in our culture strategies are generally regarded merely as means that are subservient to goals, we can readily understand the choices made by protagonists in these realms. We can do so not only because we have made comparable decisions in our everyday lives and have observed others doing the same, but because we are familiar with goals through our reading of history and literature. As a result, there is nothing enigmatic or strange about the statement that "Caesar crossed the Rubicon and returned to Rome because he was ambitious and sought political power."

In music, on the other hand, the whys and wherefores of the choices made by composers—and, hence, the changing succession of choices that constitutes music history—are difficult to comprehend and account for.[72] This is not primarily because few of us have had experience in composing. Even accomplished composers are often at a loss to explain why they chose as they did. Rather, compositional choices are difficult to explain because, from a historical point of view at least, the most important goals of composers are established to a significant extent by the often unconscious and unconceptualized beliefs and attitudes of the larger culture—above all, by ideology.[73] Though the problems are indeed formidable, it seems to me inescapable that to transform brute facts (scores, events recounted, theories of music) into history, it is necessary to understand and explain the musical choices made by composers;[74] and to understand and explain their choices requires an account of *the*

---

71. Because ideologies endure despite local fads and fashions in all realms of culture, their influence does so as well. The result is the conjoining of replication and variation that becomes music history. Once they have occurred, changes in ideology influence the parameters of action as well as other parameters in the culture. The view of ideology employed in this study is presented at the end of Chapter 5.

72. It does *not*, I hasten to add, follow from this that the music itself is difficult to understand. In this connection, see my *Explaining Music*, pp. 14–16.

73. Especially when ideology encourages the belief that the essential meaning and value of art is purely aesthetic (as in our culture), with the result that means and ends become indistinguishable in principle, the relationship between strategies and goals becomes problematic. In a sense, that is, the strategy becomes the goal.

74. Of course, composers have other roles to play: roles in the realms of action (in dealing with family, patrons, or publishers) or of concept (e.g., as theorists or teachers). What is striking is that their worldly choices are

*goals in terms of which those choices were made.* In the absence of hypotheses about the goals that guided compositional choice, together with some theory of human psychology relating strategic choices to goals, the reconstructed past is at best a collection of style analyses strung on the slender thread of chronology.[75]

d. Indeed, most "histories" of music consist of a series of synchronic style-frames ordered chronologically on some hierarchic level. On the highest level, for instance, the history of Western music is presented as a succession of relatively independent sets of constraints: Medieval, Renaissance, Baroque, and so on, up to the present. Usually such large frames are subdivided, often into early, middle, and late style-frames. And these frames are customarily understood to be composed of the styles characteristic of the music of individual composers. In every case, on each level of the style-frame hierarchy, common characteristics (of form, harmony, texture, etc.) are described. But no matter what the hierarchic level, there is seldom an attempt to account for why the constraints of the style changed.

The absence of hypotheses illuminating style change is seldom noticed or questioned, however. Textbooks consisting of chronological successions of more or less thoughtful style-analytic frames, routinely foisted on innocent students, become models of what a history is supposed to be. Passive acceptance is possible because, as suggested earlier, lurking behind such chronologies, linking successive style-frames to one another, are unexamined axioms and unacknowledged models.

The main unexamined axiom is that changes in music are a result of—or a "reflection of"—changes in culture. What is unexamined is precisely how cultural/social change affects the choices made by composers. The model lending a kind of sub rosa coherence is that of organic development with its attendant metaphors and corollaries: like individual men and women, styles are "born, mature, grow old, and die"; composers "exhaust" the possibilities of some form, schema, or strategy (which then becomes a lifeless mechanical device or mold). This model is problematic because in both nature and culture different hierarchic levels tend to be characterized by different patterns of change. For instance, though the model of such developmental change may be applicable to individual organisms, it cannot account for higher-level changes such as genetic drift or evolution.

e. Similarly in the history of musical style, the nature of change tends to differ from one hierarchic level to another. The developmental model (youth, maturity, and final refinement) seems to provide a plausible account of the changes that generally, but not invariably, take place within the idiom of individual composers, though it tends to slight the impingement of external circumstances. But when the model is

---

usually readily understood because, as in the case of political/social history, their goals seem evident. As the biography of almost any composer makes manifest, "business" choices are more easily explained than musical ones.

75. As we shall see, choices are often hard to explain because they frequently involve the reconciliation or weighing of competing but incompatible claims (goals)—for instance, pleasing a patron or accommodating a performer versus achieving the "purely" aesthetic.

transposed to the hierarchic level of dialect, the phases of stylistic development (for instance, archaic, classic, mannerist) often seem forced and distortion tends to occur, especially when a succession of necessary and inherent cycles is posited.[76]

The level of dialect, then, is characterized not by inherent development but by what I have called *trended change*. Such changes are statistical both in the sense that they are matters of amount, degree, or frequency and in the sense that, as observed in Chapter 2, no individual instance can either confirm or disconfirm a hypothesized trend. Since the changes I analyze in the last part of this book are trended, a few general remarks seem appropriate. First, trended changes, which are probably the most common kind of change in history, occur at the levels of both dialect and strategy. Second, since high-level rule changes are not involved, trends are reversible in either the short or the long run. Third, most trends are, I suspect, significantly shaped by parameters external to music.

Once a trend has been initiated, there is a tendency for it to continue until in some instances it conflicts with the constraints of other musical parameters or with those of parameters external to music (e.g., patronage, politics, ideology). Given the relative independence of parameters, the longer any trend continues, the more likely such conflict is. For instance, the trend (from, say, 1780) in which symphonic movements became longer ended quite abruptly in the first decades of the twentieth century, partly because the weakening of tonal syntax and the coordinate attenuation of hierarchic structure made both the composition and the comprehension of very long works problematic, partly because the limits of human aural memory were approached, and partly because sheer magnitude became a less important cultural value.

Not all changes are trended—matters of degree. Differences in kind also occur. Such changes have been called *mutational*.[77] Mutational changes generally occur on the level of rules. For instance, the changes described in Chapter 1 from the constraints of modal counterpoint to those of tonal harmony involved innovation on the level of rules.

The term mutation calls attention to another model of change: the theory of evolution. Since that theory has occasionally been used—often loosely, sometimes improperly—to account for the history of art (or even culture as a whole), it is important to distinguish it from the developmental models mentioned above. The difference is fundamental. What cyclic or dialectic models of change posit is an invariable pattern of stages determined by some *inherent* process whose mechanism is unknown. Evolution, on the other hand, posits neither an inherent process nor an invariable pattern. Rather what is posited is a mechanism (natural selection) ac-

---

76. Explicit theories of inherent "laws" of style change have frequently been formulated by art historians (cf. Schapiro, "Style," pp. 287–303). Music historians, as noted above, have generally been content to let prevalent and powerful metaphors and models bear the burden of explanation.

77. Nisbet, *Social Change and History,* p. 100. George Kubler also uses the term *mutation* in connection with his theory of art history (see *The Shape of Time,* pp. 40–41), and according to Fredric Jameson (*Prison-House of Language,* p. 20), Roman Jakobson does so as well.

counting for the changes that have taken place over the long history of living things. For this reason, the explanations of evolution are necessarily retrospective.

More generally, the classification of change—whether developmental, trended, or mutational—is usually retrospective. Revision is not merely possible; it is often imperative. For later events may force historians to comprehend earlier compositional choices in new ways because the implications of the past may be apparent only when their consequences are known. What seemed part of the development of a particular composer's idiom may prove to have been part of a trended change in dialect, or perhaps even an instance of mutational change. Conversely, what may at the time have seemed a major mutation may subsequently be understood to have been part of a trend, even to have been a historical dead end.

The preceding discussion calls attention to one of the crucial questions for any theory of style change: that of the nature of the interaction between trended changes and mutational changes. Though I am inclined to agree with Robert Nisbet's contention (about history in general) that *"there is no historical evidence that macro-changes in time are the cumulative results of small-scale, linear micro-changes,"* [78] it seems likely that at times cumulative trended changes result in a situation in which a mutational change will endure.[79] For instance, the continued weakening of the constraints of tonal syntax not only made it very difficult to create large-scale hierarchic structures in the early decades of the twentieth century, but also resulted in a need for musical constraints in terms of which intelligent musical choices could be made. As observed in the last part of this book, the proliferation of musical styles during the first half of the twentieth century was a clear consequence of this need—a need that was in important ways a result of trended changes that took place during the nineteenth century. And it remains to be seen which, if any, of the mutations will survive.[80]

78. Robert Nisbet, *Social Change and History*, p. 288; emphasis in the original.

79. It does not follow, however, that the trend *caused* the mutational change, only that the stylistic/cultural situation created by the trend made it possible for the mutation to endure—be replicated.

80. This is not to assert, as is often done, that the abandonment of tonality was a *necessary consequence* of the weakening of tonal syntax, of the "forces of history," and so on. Nor is it supposed that if a stylistic consensus takes place, the new rules (mutations) will be a result of prior trends or strategies. It is possible, perhaps even likely, that major style changes are to some extent fortuitous and hence only partly explicable.

# CHAPTER 4

## Innovation—Reasons and Sources

### INTRODUCTION: INNOVATION, REPLICATION, AND HIERARCHY

Since the history of music is the result of choices made by individual men and women in specific compositional/cultural circumstances,[1] an understanding both of how composers devise or invent novel means and of why they choose some means rather than others must be central to any account of the nature of music history. The distinction between devising and choosing is necessary because, as we shall see, composers usually have at their disposal many more alternatives than can be used in a particular work. The distinction is important because considerable confusion ensues when the side of creativity that involves the devising of novelty is emphasized at the expense of the side that entails choice.

The term *choice* refers both to the use of newly devised means and to the replication of existing ones. The distinction between devising and replication calls attention to the question of what should count as an innovation. For instance, any performance of a piece of music that does not slavishly parrot an earlier one involves what might be called *interpretive innovation*. This is why performers are considered creative artists. Within the constraints of the performance traditions of a musical culture, they devise novel realizations (interpretations), and they choose among the possibilities devised. On the level of performance, then, there is innovation. But on the level of the "work," there is replication: although performances may vary, the identity of the composition is not in question. Whether the piece being played is interpreted by Klemperer, Reiner, or Toscanini, we have no difficulty in recognizing it as, say, Beethoven's "Eroica" Symphony.[2]

---

1. From this point of view, the history of music is no different from the histories of other cultural parameters, all of which attempt to explain the choices made by protagonists: politicians and generals, priests and scientists, philosophers and novelists.

2. The situation is more problematic when there is no notation. In the case of a jazz performance or that of an Indian sitar player, it is sometimes doubtful whether one is hearing a new interpretation of a traditional work or a new composition. For interpretation and composition often constitute a single indivisible act.

Because most music is hierarchically structured, what is novel on one level may not be so on another. For instance, on the level of foreground patterning (pitch and time relationships, dynamics and tempo, and so forth), the melodies given in Example 1.1 are patently different. Yet on the next level, both melodies are realizations of the same changing-note schema (as graphs 1 and 2 of the example show). Novelty on a lower level becomes replication on a higher one.

But the converse is also possible: higher-level novelty may arise out of lower-level replication. For instance, the patterns given in Example 1.3 all replicate an archetypal closing figure whose devising lies buried somewhere in the early history of tonality. On a foreground level, then, there is no innovation. But since the figure functions somewhat differently in each of the phrases, there is novelty on the next level. The differences are obvious. For instance, Example 1.3a is the beginning of an ascending melodic line, while Example 1.3c is the close of a descending one.[3]

Although the replication of foreground patterning may be the basis for higher-level novelty, the occurrence of innovation is essentially coordinate with the hierarchic structuring of style described in Chapter 1. That is, unchanging constraints on high levels support the invention and selection of novelties on lower ones. Thus, enduring laws form the basis for novel rules; stable rules may give rise to innovative strategies; replicated strategies may be realized as original intraopus structures; and, finally, the same intraopus structure (composition) may be newly interpreted in a particular performance.

In what follows, I will be mainly concerned with innovations that arise on the middle levels of this hierarchy—that is, with the devising of new strategies and novel realizations. It is important to realize that there is a significant difference between these kinds of innovation. For a strategy is a general principle which can serve as the basis for innumerable individual and novel realizations. Thus, schemata such as those given in Examples 1.2, 2.2, and 2.3 can be actualized in quite diverse dialects and in markedly different and novel ways; the same is true of formal principles (such as da capo form, variation form, or rounded binary form) and of genres (such as *opera buffa,* oratorio, or tone poem).

Though new strategies and novel instantiations of existing strategies may be readily distinguished in principle, they are less so in practice. The reason is that composers do not compose strategies. They compose individual compositions. These are made of particular patternings, of which some may realize prevalent constraints, some may subsequently prove to be the basis for generalization, and some may (as we shall see) be so idiosyncratic that no classlike relationships can be discerned in them. It is the second possibility that is of interest here. Namely, patterns at first understood to be simply novel realizations of existing constraints may subsequently be found (whether by the original composer, by other composers, or by music theorists) to be the basis for innovative strategies. Because style history occurs when, so

---

3. On a still higher level, however, the figure of Example 1.3a, together with what immediately follows, forms part of a familiar triadic schema (see Example 1.5, graph 2) and in that respect is not novel.

to speak, no one is attending, unequivocal instances of this kind of change are, admittedly, hard to come by. But the sort of thing I have in mind is quite clearly described in David Hughes's account of the textural changes that occurred in Dufay's style:

> The number of voices was increased to four; the old disjunct contratenor was, as it were, split into two separate voices—the contratenor altus . . . and the contratenor bassus. . . .
>
> *While such a scheme may also be found in the fourteenth century, Dufay's use of it was new.* He took intense interest in certain successions of sonorities, especially at the ends of phrases. These were possible only when the lowest sounding part had a specific, rather disjunct shape. Since a preexistent melody . . . would be unlikely to have such a shape, the placement of the contratenor bassus below the tenor permitted Dufay to employ both the cantus-firmus principle and his preferred successions of sonorities.[4]

And Dufay's innovation subsequently became common compositional practice.

The present chapter will be concerned both with the *reasons for innovation* (that is, why novelties are devised at all, since the axiom of constancy posits persistence) and with the *sources of novelty*. Chapter 5 will be concerned with choosing (that is, why particular possibilities are chosen—or rejected). In most instances, choice is affected by constraints both internal and external to music. Generally speaking, those reasons or sources that can be explained in terms of prevalent musical constraints and specific compositional problems will be considered internal. External constraints—those arising from political and social conditions, economic, intellectual, or technological circumstances—always impinge upon and sometimes influence both the invention of novelty and its selection.

## REASONS FOR INNOVATION

### *Internal Constraints*

THE COMPOSER.

Whether the reasons why composers innovate should be considered internal or external to the parameter of music is, oddly enough, problematic. This is so because it is through the choices made by composers that both internally generated style changes and externally influenced ones are actualized as musical relationships. But for present purposes the composer's temperament and ingrained habits of mind, however formed, as well as native talent, as refined by early learning, will be considered internal to the parameter of music. Though these attributes are undoubtedly affected by cultural milieu, composers are the conduits through which the traditions of music

---

4. *History of European Music,* p. 113; emphasis added.

are transmitted, and only when a composer's nature has been ascertained can the influence of external impingement be discerned at all.

Only individuals compose.[5] This being so, it seems reasonable to suppose that the character or temperament of the particular composer whose *oeuvre* is being considered may be a reason for innovation. That is, because of the combined effects of native talent and training (nonmusical as well as musical), some individuals are prone to be innovators, while others tend to be elaborators. And within the group of innovators two types should probably be distinguished: those who devise novel strategies for solving problems they have inherited from their predecessors (Haydn would seem to fall into this class), and those who both pose new problems and devise strategies for dealing with them (the early Classic composers, such as Sammartini, would seem to belong to this class).

Though evidently of great importance, the relationship of temperament to innovation is, for a number of reasons, enormously difficult to analyze adequately. First, we cannot know about an individual's native talent directly.[6] Nor are early training and environment usually adequately documented—and even if they were, their effect on the composer's temperament and character would be virtually impossible to ascertain. As a result, an individual's temperament must be inferred from his or her behavior. Such inferences might be a basis for characterization if it could be assumed, as it often is, that human beings are coherent, homogeneous "wholes."[7] For then it would be possible to use nonmusical as well as musical choices as evidence for personality and temperament.

But as far as I can see, there is little warrant for believing in the consistency and homogeneity—the psychic unity—of human beings generally.[8] Some individu-

---

5. At times, of course, an improvising group may do so. But for present purposes such collectivities can be treated in the same way as individual composers.

6. In this connection, it is pertinent to question the notion that musical talent is special in that it is genetically specified. Musical ability is genetic in the sense that it is a native endowment—e.g., having a retentive memory for pitch, superior motor coordination, etc. But there is no evidence that musicality per se is biologically inherited, any more than a talent for politics or business is so. Particularly before the nineteenth century, the profession did, of course, run in families: the Scarlattis, the Couperins, the Bachs, and so on. But the basis for this phenomenon was sociological, not biological. Crafts—indeed, occupations in general—ran in families. Even in fields like politics and banking this kind of continuity was not uncommon; one thinks perhaps of the Adams family in the United States or the Rothschilds in Europe. But continuities such as these are not explained in terms of biological inheritance. And how can one account for the fact that when the craft system ended, the phenomenon of successive generations of composers did so as well? That Wagner's son or Stravinsky's became a musician is surely no more remarkable than that the sons or daughters of doctors often become physicians, the children of lawyers often become lawyers, and so on.

7. I would guess, though I have not tried to verify it, that most studies that use personality to explain artists' choices make some such assumption.

8. Significant personality differences have been identified in children, but these persist throughout life only in extreme cases. See Kagan, Reznick, and Snidman, "Biological Bases of Childhood Shyness."

Normal individuals do, of course, possess a sense of identity, what Anthony Storr described as a continuous sense of entity or sameness. But the sense that we are the same entity at sixty that we were at six does not preclude psychological disparity. That is, a particular individual may be, and usually is, a mixture of often incompatible tastes, beliefs, values, and sensibilities. See Storr, "Kafka's Sense of Identity," p. 1.

als may be entirely homogeneous, but many more are clearly not so. (Perhaps, contrary to generally held opinion, the great creators have been precisely those who were psychically *least* homogeneous and uniform.) Ordinary observation of humankind indicates that someone may be a tyrant at home and a Caspar Milquetoast at the office, or decisive in choosing in one sphere of behavior but indecisive in some other. An individual may be conservative in religion and politics but devise revolutionary compositional strategies and rules—Schoenberg would be a clear example; or a person may be radical in politics but not especially innovative as an artist—perhaps the case with Jacques Louis David. Since individuals are seldom psychically homogeneous, then, there is as a rule little warrant for using behavior in one realm to explain choices made in some other. As a result, one is in the difficult position of inferring the composer's compositional temperament from his compositional choices and then using such inferences to explain his innovative (or noninnovative) behavior. The danger of such circularity is, I think, very real.

There is a semantic-logical danger as well. In order to compare or contrast the idioms of composers, it is often useful to characterize them in quite general terms such as classic, romantic, and mannerist, or conservative and innovative. It is, then, but a small step—one perhaps suggested by the phrase "style is the man"—to assume that such characteristics are a direct result of the composer's temperament and personality. Stylistic circumstances and cultural conditions also affect a composer's idiom, however, and these constraints may either discourage or encourage innovation. Palestrina's style is usually characterized as conservative. But,. given the outlook of the Counter-Reformation, the edicts of the Council of Trent, and the traditions of Roman music, all of which favored a conservative stylistic stance, any inferences from Palestrina's compositional choices to his "naturally" conservative temperament must seem somewhat suspect. All that can reasonably be inferred is that, considering his productivity and the history of his choices, Palestrina's temperament was probably not incompatible with a conservative stance. How he would have chosen in other circumstances—had he been born, say, fifty years later—is impossible to judge. Conversely, in our own time, which has until very recently strongly encouraged innovation, it seems doubtful whether one can legitimately make inferences about Stockhausen's native temperament from his radical compositional choices.

Because the variables of temperament, stylistic conditions, and cultural circumstance have a degree of independence, there may be cases in which it is possible—perhaps even necessary—to attribute the kinds of choices a composer makes to temperament. What I have in mind are those cases in which the range of choices generally made by a particular composer are noticeably different from those made by most members of the musical community in which he finds himself. For instance, if a composer regularly innovates in a cultural-compositional situation where others are primarily concerned with the elaboration of existing means and manners, then it seems reasonable to suppose that temperament played a significant role in his compositional choices. Charles Ives, who composed in a community in which the dialect of late Romanticism was ubiquitous, would seem a clear instance. Conversely, a composer who tends to employ prevailing means, while the larger community is for the most part posing new problems or devising novel strategies, might legitimately be considered temperamentally conservative. In both these kinds of cases, however, one must be aware of all the variables involved. Clearly, one cannot make valid inferences about Shostakovich's temperament, even though he wrote relatively conservative music during a period characterized by experimentalism and innovation, because we know on other grounds that his choices were influenced by political pressures.

Categorically innovative or unequivocally conservative temperaments are probably very rare. Even if a few are "born" innovators, most people—whether politicians or generals, scientists or artists—achieve innovation or have it thrust upon them. And when a composer's choices are comparable in their general range of novelty to those made by other members of the musical community, I see no way of isolating temperament as a variable and explicitly attributing to it whatever novel problems are posed or strategies devised for their solution. The most that can be safely inferred in most instances is that, if a composer was productive, then his temperament was probably not incompatible with the stylistic circumstances and the cultural conditions in which he found himself.

STYLISTIC CIRCUMSTANCES AND COMPOSITIONAL PROBLEMS.
When the rules and strategies of a style are inconsistent either with one another or with the laws of human cognition, or when the resulting music is no longer compatible with the ideological/aesthetic values of the culture, then there will be a search, often by trial and error, for greater stability—for more coherent, consistent, and compatible constraints. Such a search will almost always result in innovation. Our century provides a particularly striking instance of this sort of innovation-producing search. Indeed, most of the stylistic movements broached during the past seventy years—serialism, neoclassicism, aleatory music, statistical music, and so on—can be regarded as attempts to devise viable stylistic constraints not merely on the level of strategies, but on the level of rules. Because choosing becomes problematic in such circumstances, one of the symptoms of stylistic instability is, as noted earlier, a noticeable decline in the productivity of composers.[9]

Conversely, when the stylistic constraints inherited by composers are coherent and well established, as well as compatible with prevalent aesthetic/cultural ideals, innovation will tend to be quite modest, taking the form of the elaboration and refinement of existing strategies. In a broad sense, this was the situation in which J. S.

9. In some cases choosing seems to have become so onerous that composers found it desirable to share their burden with the performers, requiring them to do some of the choosing; in the case of aleatory music, listeners are required to do so as well.

Bach and Mozart found themselves. Stylistic stability facilitates choosing because possibilities and alternatives are clearly understood and coherently interrelated; as a result, periods of stability are usually characterized by high rates of productivity.[10]

But there is another, intermediate possibility: a situation in which the fundamental principles of a style—its basic rules and strategies—have already been established, but significant compositional possibilities remain to be realized. In such situations, innovation involves the devising of new strategies and schemata. Haydn's development of some of the possibilities latent in the dramatic principle of sonata form were strategic innovations of this kind. Here the general stylistic situation merges with specifically compositional problems.

Every composition, even the most conventional and routine, is an actualization of possibilities latent in the constraints of a style. And in this sense, every composition is the solution of a problem: that of choosing musical materials and discerning how their implications might be realized, given the alternatives possible in the style. Often, of course, composers choose quite ordinary means and develop them in more or less routine ways. But because the implicative possibilities of any musical pattern are manifold, the composer may create musically rich relationships out of entirely conventional means. And such relationships may in turn lead to the modification and extension of existing means or, more radically, to the devising of novel means.[11] Haydn and Dittersdorf used comparable harmonic, melodic, and rhythmic means. But Haydn discerned in them processive and formal possibilities that were not perceived by, or did not interest, Dittersdorf. And to realize such possibilities, Haydn at times modified existing strategies or used new ones. The choice of unusual melodic, rhythmic, or harmonic means may also call for appropriately modified or novel strategies. For instance, Wagner's development of the music drama involved the invention of strategies reconciling the claims of verbal narrative and dramatic action with those of musical syntax and formal structure.

But few problems are formulated in such general, conceptual terms. Most arise out of the immediate act of compositional choice. What possibilities are latent in this particular pattern, and how can the pattern be modified so as to enhance its richness and potential? What kind of retransition will be most effective in this sonata-form movement? What countersubject is most felicitous and effective given this fugue subject? and so on. Moreover, once any choice has been made, whether deliberately or unconsciously, further alternatives are generated. In this process, some composers seem more prone than others to discern novel possibilities. The question is *why*. Why, for instance, did Haydn discern and develop more of the potential latent in the Classic style than Dittersdorf?

---

10. Such stability and instability are not explicitly documented or directly observed. Rather, historians infer these conditions from the behavior of composers. In other words, the analysis presented should properly be put the other way around: stylistic diversity, experimentation, and declining rates of productivity are symptoms of stylistic instability, while stylistic coherence, continuity, and high rates of productivity are symptoms of stability.

11. What I take to be some of the difficulties of the problem-solving model are discussed in Chapter 5.

Thus we are brought back, willy-nilly, to the composer's temperament. For though the peculiar cultural circumstances in which Haydn flourished were undoubtedly important for the development of his style, his creative proclivities—his ingrained habits of mind as well as his native musical intelligence—must have been of crucial importance in his tendency to innovate. One is, in short, brought face to face with that mystery of mysteries, the nature of creativity. And since in this area of inquiry the evidence is scant and impressionistic, one can only speculate. Native talent is obviously a necessary condition, and so, probably, is an ability to tolerate ambiguity. But talent, even genius, may be content with continuity—with the elegant and skillful use of constraints already established. One discerns new possibilities only if one is, in some way, ready to do so because one is, consciously or unconsciously, receptive to novelty. For instance, the composer may for reasons of temperament simply enjoy the excitement of choosing beyond the bounds of the tried and true, of playing the game boldly.

Even with respect to what seems to be a single trait such as the proclivity to innovate, the behavioral temperament of composers is not usually monolithic. That is, they are not usually innovative in all aspects of their art. A composer may be more innovative in one kind of music than another (e.g., Haydn's instrumental music versus his sacred music), or with respect to one parameter but not another (e.g., Brahms's rhythmic-metric invention versus his orchestration), and so on. Such *selective* innovation is partly a function of the state of the style: at a particular point in the history of a style some features are ripe for change while others are not. But selective innovation also depends in part on the composer's sensitivity to and command of a particular facet of his art. For it seems clear that one composer may be especially responsive to and competent in, say, the structuring of harmonic process (as Chopin was), while another is so with respect to formal-dramatic relationships (as Rossini was). It seems reasonable to suppose that such differences come about because the level of aesthetic aspiration is high in those aspects of music to which the composer is especially sensitive and because the risks of innovation are generally taken in those areas in which one feels confident command.[12]

## External Constraints

Strategic innovation may be either encouraged or discouraged by the cultural circumstances in which compositional choices are made. Such circumstances may be broad and encompassing, having to do with the culture's general attitude toward change per se, or they may be quite specific, having to do with the function of music

---

12. Some of the disagreements among listeners and among critics probably arise because selective sensitivity leads to different levels of aesthetic aspiration for different aspects of music, one listener or critic being especially sensitive to harmonic process, another to formal structure, and so on. Put differently, taste is partly a function of selective sensitivity.

in the culture, political and economic conditions, particular currents in intellectual history, and so on.


GENERAL CULTURAL CONDITIONS.
Some cultures have been particularly receptive to change, others especially resistant. A culture's stance toward innovation is, to a considerable extent, dependent upon its beliefs about how the cosmos functions and, consequently, about man's relationship to the totality of creation—past, present, and future. Cultures in which the order of the cosmos is believed to have been divinely established tend to be inimical to innovation. Conservative adherence to traditional constraints—often an almost ritual replication of cultural patterning—is valued and cultivated. Such conservation and persistence have been notable in a number of cultures, for instance, those of Japan, India, and ancient Egypt.

The signal example of a culture that has welcomed innovation, valuing it virtually for its own sake, is, of course, Western civilization since the Renaissance. Western culture has done so because its beliefs posited that beneficent laws of nature and the nature of mankind provided for progressive betterment in all realms of human existence. Change was equated with improvement. Hence the more innovation, the sooner the arrival at a golden age of peace and plenty. The tendency toward change received additional impetus from the idea, developed toward the end·of the eighteenth century, that changes in parameters external to the arts would necessarily generate changes within the arts. This idea (that every epoch developed a style of art peculiarly appropriate to it) tended to make the occurrence of innovation a self-confirming prophecy.

There is another, more general condition that seems to encourage change, one that may be partly responsible for the West's belief in the primacy of innovation. Change is promulgated when there is a discrepancy between the constraints of different parameters within a culture. What I want to suggest is that when the constraints governing the parameters of a culture are not compatible or congruent with one another, there is a kind of cognitive/cultural dissonance whose resolution requires adjustment and change. In this connection it is important to distinguish between the *kinds* of changes that may occur and the *rate* at which change takes place. The specific kinds of change that occur in the constraints of some style depend both on particular musical/stylistic and cultural circumstances and, as we shall see, on the hierarchic level of the changes being considered. The rate of change, however, seems to depend not only on the culture's beliefs about the desirability of change, but also on the presence and degree of congruence, or noncongruence, among the parameters of the culture.

Parametric noncongruence has been remarked upon by scholars in a number of different fields. George Kubler, for instance, doubts that "the poets and artists of one place and time are the joint bearers of a central pattern of sensibility from which their various efforts all flow like radial expressions. . . . [T]he cross-section of the instant, taken across the full face of the moment in a given place, resembles a mosaic of pieces in different developmental states, and of different ages, rather than a radial design conferring its meaning upon all the pieces." [13] C. E. Labrousse attributes the economic crisis that preceded the French Revolution partly to the disparity between the growth rate of agricultural production and the rate of population increase: "Advances in production . . . were still made very slowly. With its great dependence on hand labor, agricultural production with its traditional inelasticity stood in striking contrast to the sudden elasticity of the population." [14] More generally, Charles P. Kindleberger has argued that the realms of "economics and society are in a state of tension. In the short run, the pressure of economic change on society may have to be filtered or diluted to keep the speed of social change tolerable." [15]

Here we must pause to consider the nature of parametric differentiation. To begin with, it seems clear that if some phenomenal realm is to be distinguished as a parameter, its patterning must be understood as being somewhat different from that of other realms. Indeed, without such discrepancy it would be impossible to know that there was anything to be distinguished. Suppose, for instance, that in the monophonic singing of some culture there was a constant correspondence between dynamic level and pitch; then, other things being equal, dynamics could not be perceived as a separate parameter in the music of that culture. And indeed many traditional cultures do not distinguish between religion and science, the aesthetic and the practical, the natural world and that of human activity. According to Stencel, Gifford, and Morón, for example, "it is not surprising that Angkor Wat integrates astronomy, the calendar, and religion since the priest-architects who constructed the temple conceived of all three as a unity. To the ancient Khmers, astronomy was known as the sacred science." [16] Similarly David P. McAllester observes that in American Indian culture "most of the music is religious. This is a corollary of the integrated quality of American Indian life in which art, theater, medicine, and religion are not separated into different categories but overlap each other to such an extent that there are often no separate terms for them in the native languages." [17] In such cultures, realms we differentiate as separate parameters seem to move "in unison," as when a string orchestra plays a single melodic line. Only when some incongruity or disparity is noticed—when the sections of the orchestra are, as it were, perceived to be playing somewhat different melodic lines—will parameters be distinguished from one another. Then the shaman's role will be divided into priest and natural philosopher, the

13. *The Shape of Time*, pp. 27–28. In this connection, see also my *Music, the Arts, and Ideas*, pp. 112–14.
14. "Crisis in the French Economy," p. 63.
15. Review of Karl Polanyi's *Great Transformation*, p. 51.
16. Stencel, Gifford, and Morón, "Astronomy and Cosmology," p. 281. From the present point of view, the authors have stated the process backwards: that is, the culture of Angkor Wat did not "integrate" anything since the parameters had not previously been separated; rather they did not differentiate, since they evidently perceived no discrepancy among the phenomena involved.
17. "Indian Music in the Southwest," p. 216.

sacred into astronomy and architecture or music and medicine, the philosopher into natural and social scientists.

Though of signal importance for the understanding of history, parametric autonomy is neither absolute nor uniform. Within music, for instance, it is often possible to explain melodic relationships without reference to orchestration, but it would not be possible to explain melodic relationships without referring to rhythmic structure. Similarly, on a higher cultural level, it is evidently possible to write a history of genetic theory in the twentieth century without mentioning either the Great Depression or the musical revolution proposed by Schoenberg,[18] and it is possible to write a political history of the United States during the same period without discussing the research of T. H. Morgan or the music of Aaron Copland. But it would not be possible to account for the political changes of the period without considering economic events—for example, the Great Depression, technological changes, immigration, and the First World War. This variability of connection occurs because, though all the parameters of a culture may be inextricably interrelated, it by no means follows that they are equally interdependent.

For most historians, the highest degree of interdependence occurs within parameters. An earlier political event is more likely to influence a later political event than it is to influence technology, military strategy, the history of genetic theory, or musical style. As Siegfried Kracauer observed:

> Successive events in one and the same area obviously stand a better chance of being meaningfully interrelated than those scattered over multiple areas: a genuine idea invariably gives rise to a host of ideas dependent on it, while, for instance, the effects of social arrangements on cultural trends are rather opaque. To simplify matters, it may be assumed that the events in each single area follow each other according to a sort of immanent logic. They form an intelligible sequence.[19]

Such an internalist viewpoint seems plausible and attractive. Because parameters tend to be differentiated according to material means (melodic versus harmonic relationships; political versus economic processes), connections by "lineage" within parameters are more easily understood than those between parameters. And lineage relationships are often simplified because of the tendency (mistaken in my view) to assume that within any parameter all events, whatever the hierarchic level, are governed by the same set of constraints. In music, for instance, it is frequently assumed that the constraints governing foreground harmonic progressions are the same as those governing high-level tonal relationships; similarly, in economics it is sometimes suggested that federal and family finances are (or should be) governed by the same constraints.

Learning, too, supports the tendency toward internalism. Because to do other-

---

18. See Jacob, *Logic of Life*, and Stent, *Coming of the Golden Age*.
19. *History*, pp. 145–46.

wise would involve insuperable complexity, human beings learn the constraints of their cultures in terms of more or less distinct parametric traditions. In Western culture, for instance, we learn to understand and make choices in realms such as language, social behavior, politics, philosophy, economics, and music. Moreover, our theories about the world tend themselves to be parameter-specific. And such theories (about political, social, musical, and psychological patterns and processes) not only affect our understanding by emphasizing the autonomy of parameters; they feed back to and influence the behavioral practice from which they were originally derived.

Behavioral and conceptual differentiation at once leads to and is reinforced by social separation. Politicians tend to associate with politicians, philosophers with philosophers, musicians with musicians, and so on. As a rule the members of such occupational or recreational "tribes" have had similar educational experiences, read a common literature, and have comparable goals and aspirations.[20] Such differentiation often occurs even in such closely related fields as science and technology. As J. D. Bernal writes:

> Each field, the technical as much as the scientific, has its own inner co-
> herence, not only in the logical unfolding of new discoveries on the basis
> of older researches and in the making of new inventions drawing on older
> technical advances, but also in their being in the hands of two largely dis-
> tinct sets of men, the scientists and the engineers.[21]

That the constraints governing different parameters, whether natural or cultural, often have considerable autonomy seems evident in the practice of historians. For though some diachronic histories may occasionally consider the influence of external parameters, most are primarily concerned to describe and explain changes *within* a single parameter—e.g., politics, philosophy, physics, music, military tactics.[22] Were all the parameters of a culture inextricably interdependent, such disciplinary histories would not be possible. On the other hand, it is worth remarking that the tendency to write diachronic histories in terms of single parameters is itself reinforced by the educational system (itself a cultural parameter), which institutes programs and grants degrees in such disciplines.

20. It is important to recognize that most individuals belong to a number of such tribes. For instance, a politician may belong to the subcultures of bridge playing, wine tasting, jazz appreciation, and Anglican theology. And in each case the individual will learn the constraints of the subculture's parameters and behave accordingly. This diversity of parametric learning suggests one reason why, as noted earlier, individuals are seldom homogeneous wholes whose choices are consistent and constant from one realm to another.

It does not seem implausible to suggest that the high level of tension in twentieth-century existence results in part from the fact that individuals learn and are guided by a large number of different, noncongruent constraint sets. As a result, goals tend to be incompatible and choices conflicting. The relation between proliferation of parameters and rate of cultural change is discussed below.

21. *Science and Industry*, p. 10.

22. As a rule, of course, these broad parametric designations are further delimited, perhaps by national boundaries or periods, subcultures or substyles. The result may be, for example, a history of politics during the reign of Louis XIV or a history of jazz.

But the preponderance of continuity within parameters does not preclude significant interaction between them. Consequently the view, espoused by both Kracauer and Bernal, that the history even of a single parameter exhibits a "logical" development, undisturbed by the impingements of external constraints, seems very unlikely to be correct. Even the dominant parameters of a culture invariably interact to some extent, however small, with less influential ones. In addition, all are subject to the vicissitudes of chance; for instance, political and intellectual histories were significantly affected by the catastrophic Lisbon earthquake of 1755.

Though the autonomy of cultural parameters is never absolute, some parameters seem less susceptible to external impingement than others. For instance, because physical and biological phenomena are not as a rule affected by the theories devised to explain them, histories of the discoveries of the laws governing them tend to exhibit a more coherent internal pattern of change than do the histories of those cultural parameters whose rules and strategies are not infrequently influenced by feedback from conceptualization to behavior. The susceptibility of human activities to external impingement may itself be minimized when such activities are governed by a strongly integrated set of constraints; one thinks, for instance, of the history of mathematics or of the game of chess. Extending this line of thought still further, it seems reasonable to suppose that whenever a parameter is governed by an especially coherent and well-integrated set of constraints, it will tend to resist the impingement of parameters external to it.

PARAMETRIC DIFFERENTIATION AND CULTURAL CHANGE.
Broadly speaking, the histories of cultures seem to have been characterized by a continuing differentiation, and hence proliferation, of parameters.[23] Differentiation has occurred for both conceptual and societal reasons. Conceptual differentiation takes place because prevalent cultural hypotheses (which may be tacit) fail to provide an adequate basis for envisaging and choosing—that is, for understanding and responding successfully to some aspect of nature or culture. Such failure tends to encourage explicit conceptualization and generates a search for more adequate hypotheses, which in turn leads to a new structuring of parameters. From this perspective, much of the intellectual history of Western culture can be understood as the gradual discovery of parametric differences.

As the observation of the physical, biological, and cultural realms gained in precision and sophistication (partly as a result of significant technological development—e.g., the telescope, the microscope, and discoveries in mathematics), the relationship between hypotheses and data led to cycles of refinement and revision.

23. This does not mean, however, that a particular parameter must persist. Formerly differentiated parameters may converge to form a single conceptual realm. Even more important, proliferation does not entail that the dominance relationships among parameters remain constant over time.

Matter was found to be composed of molecules and atoms, atoms consisted of protons, neutrons, and electrons, and these, in turn, were discovered to be made up of quarks, leptons, and other subatomic particles. And to the extent that each level was found to be governed by somewhat different constraints, parametric differentiation took place. In the biological sciences, a comparable differentiation occurred: levels of biological organization ranging from those of animal phyla down to the molecular structure of the gene were distinguished, and each level was defined and specified in terms of somewhat different kinds and levels of constraints. In the social sciences, parameters were distinguished because different kinds and levels of human behavior were found to be governed by somewhat different sets of constraints.

Significant parametric differentiation also occurs because, as cultures develop, becoming both larger and more complex in organization, there is a tendency toward division, specialization, and hierarchic structuring. Food gathering divides from cloth production, and cloth production divides into wool supplying, weaving, and dyeing; the care of illness is allocated among nurse, pharmacologist, and physician, and physicians specialize as diagnosticians and internists, surgeons and pathologists. At the same time there is a tendency for such activities to become more hierarchic in organization. Families are gathered into clans, clans form themselves into tribes, tribes into states, and so on. People involved in the production of goods and services, too, become hierarchically organized according to function—owners, managers, clerks, secretaries, menial labor, and so on. And legal systems, paralleling political ones, are structured according to levels—municipal, county, state, and national laws and courts.

The parameters thus distinguished are not, of course, stipulated by the existential ordering of the world. Rather they are either devised by a culture in order to account for observed differences among phenomena already present or they are created by the culture in order to satisfy human wants and aspirations more effectively. For this reason, the nature and number of parameters will vary from one culture to another and from one epoch to another within a single culture.

The increase has been particularly acute and rapid because differentiation has usually involved not merely tacit behavioral understanding; as just mentioned, it has been accompanied by explicit theoretical conceptualization.[24] As a result, parameters have tended to come in complementary pairs. One member of the pair consists of some phenomenon or activity—some class of relationships in the natural world or in human culture; the other consists of a cultural concept—a theory or hypothesis, however informal—about the constraints or principles governing the phenomenon. Thus the activities of the politician are complemented by the theories of the political scientist or sociologist, and the relationships instantiated by the composer are complemented by the concepts of the music theorist. Though the affinity of such pairs makes

24. This is not to contend that composers, politicians, and businessmen do not conceptualize their activities. But their conceptualizations, which are most frequently ad hoc, do not constitute a coherent, integrated set of constraints. Consequently the conceptualization has the status of a dependent parameter.

their interaction intimate and often rapid, they are not helixlike duplications of one another. Each has an autonomous existence and history, and in the realm of human culture each is often, but not always, the province of a somewhat different group of individuals.[25] In the present context this is important for two reasons: first, it means that parametric proliferation tends to be geometric rather than arithmetic, making change more than merely additive; second, conceptualization allows for an interaction between theory and behavior which itself tends to foster further differentiation.

All this leads to a somewhat outlandish hypothesis about the influence of general cultural conditions on style change and innovation: The tendency toward change, and to some extent possibly the rate of change—but emphatically *not* the *kind* of change or innovation—is correlated with, and perhaps even a function of, the number of parameters differentiated in and conceptualized by a culture. Put the other way around, one of the reasons that change tends to be modest and slow in smaller, less complex cultures is that relatively few parameters have been differentiated; cosmology, religion, medicine, theater, and so on, are basically one.[26] For it seems plausible to suppose that the larger the number of parameters coexisting and interacting within a culture, the greater the probability that any one of them—for instance, musical style—will be noncongruent with some other. And the disequilibrium resulting from such noncongruence will tend to foster change and encourage innovation.

This conjecture is a corollary of the assumption that one of the chief goals of human behavior, and hence of human cultures, is stability.[27] But this goal is seldom realized in cultures of any size and complexity. Thus, though it is important to consider, as structuralists seek to do, how the various parameters of a culture support and complement one another, it is equally important to realize that such integration is seldom unqualified. Often this is so because the constraints governing prevalent cultural parameters (social, economic, intellectual, artistic, and so on) are not congruent either with one another or with those governing external parameters such as other cultures or the physical environment. To put the matter somewhat perversely: a musical style changes precisely because some of its constraints *do not reflect* (are not congruent with) some of the dominant parameters of the culture in which it exists.

Here an analogy with the use of Gestalt theory in aesthetics may help to clarify my conception of the nature of cultural process. Though Gestalt theory posits that shapes will be perceived to be as "good" (stable) as prevailing conditions permit,

25. The mention of history suggests that it should be included in this model. There would then be a tripartite division for many parameters, consisting of a phenomenal relationship on the one hand and systematic and chronological conceptualization (theory and history) on the other.

26. At the opposite extreme, in contemporary Western culture so many parameters have been differentiated and are moving at diverse frequencies that the result is a kind of cultural white noise. It may also be that, because most of the essential principles governing the behavior of the natural world seem reasonably well established, parametric proliferation is slowing down and the rate of cultural change will gradually diminish, with the end result being a relatively closed system of what I have called fluctuating stasis (*Music, the Arts, and Ideas*, chaps. 8 and 9) or, to change metaphors, a kind of high-level Brownian motion.

27. The goal of stability is, of course, related to the axiom of constancy discussed in Chapter 3. For the envisaging that makes choice possible depends on the persistence created by stability.

patterns often fall short of perfection—purposefully so.[28] Similarly, though structural theory posits that cultures will be coherent and integrated, integration is as a rule imperfect. And in both music and culture, the tension of instability tends to generate change. This suggests why synchronic analyses, whether of music or of culture, usually neglect incongruities and disparities. That is, because incompatibilities give rise to change, their significance can be understood only diachronically, and often only in retrospect. More generally, diachronic accounts explain change in terms of the instabilities that arise from the noncongruence of parameters; synchronic ones, as just noted, do not explain change but posit a set of relationships that is essentially stable. As a result, diachronic, narrative accounts and synchronic, structural ones are incompatible in principle.

SPECIFIC CULTURAL/MUSICAL CONDITIONS.

Whether innovation occurs depends not only on the general conditions just considered, but on more specific cultural/musical conditions. Though such conditions may be of many kinds, only four—physical setting, technology, transmission, and theory—will be discussed here.

The *physical setting* of a musical performance may suggest and lead to innovation. For example, Willaert's, and later Giovanni Gabrieli's, use of double choirs responding to one another seems to have been suggested by the two facing choir lofts of the Basilica of St. Mark in Venice. Less specifically, yet perhaps not less importantly, the size and acoustics of concert halls may lead to innovation. For instance, as we shall see, an increase in the size of audiences from the late eighteenth through the nineteenth century led to an increase in the size of concert halls and to a concomitant increase in the size of orchestras and the length of musical compositions. The greater length of compositions made innovations in formal structure necessary.

By making new means possible, *technology* may lead to stylistic innovation. The development of the piano is a case in point. As a result of improved technology, piano frames came to be made of iron, and this made extended registers and increased dynamic range possible. Almost at the same time, the invention of the double escapement action allowed for more rapid performance and greater complexity of piano figuration. The realization of these possibilities led to significant changes in the history of music, not only in the invention of novel pianistic strategies (figurations, sonorities, timbral effects, and so on), but in the role of the piano in the musical culture of nineteenth-century Europe (as it became an important virtuoso instrument as well as the primary performance medium of the middle class).[29]

28. In this connection, see my *Emotion and Meaning in Music*, pp. 86–87.
29. Important though it was, the development of the piano did not, it seems, lead to significant changes in the tonal/formal means shaping musical structure and process. In our own time, however, the development of electronic means has been associated with a search for novel formal and processive relationships, as is the case, for instance, with the attempt to create a syntax of timbres.

Though technology may make change possible, it need not lead to innovation. And certainly it need not do so at once. Our culture, which welcomes change, seems to find the exploitation of technology almost irresistible. For instance, the advent of electronic synthesizers and computers led a number of composers to rush lemming-like in search of new possibilities. But even within a culture receptive to change, whether technological change leads to musical innovation depends on the state of musical style at a particular time and on the values of those who create and patronize a particular kind of music. Equal temperament, for instance, was possible and was discussed by theorists long before it was adopted as the norm of Western music making, and the use of the forearm to perform tone clusters—a twentieth century strategy—was possible on the first keyboard instruments toward the end of the Middle Ages.[30]

The means available for the *transmission* of music and its traditions surely constitute one of the most important constraints affecting the nature of style change. And the most important question about the means of transmission is whether they are primarily oral, written, or recorded in some other way.[31] The significance of the existence of notation in Western music is so obvious that a single instance may stand for a whole history.

> In the second half of the thirteenth century . . . the classical motet began to be altered. The change was intimately related to innovations in rhythmic notation. . . . But as the motet grew in complexity, some means of notating rhythm in syllabic music became a necessity. This was found in a principle that has remained basic for rhythmic notation ever since: different note shapes were given specific rhythmic meanings.[32]

Like any constraint, notation may either encourage or discourage innovation. By making the preservation, replication, and actualization of musical patterns less dependent upon memory, notation facilitates the composition of complex harmonic and polyphonic relationships and of extended works with markedly arched hierarchies. Notation also makes the music of the remote past accessible.[33] For instance,

---

30. Even in hard-core technology, playful invention often precedes explicit employment. For instance, during the Renaissance a tradition of illustrated engineering books developed. Describing one of these by Ramelli, Eugene S. Ferguson writes that as one leafs through the book, "the conviction grows that Ramelli was answering questions that had never been asked, solving problems that nobody but he, or perhaps another technologist, would have posed. There is no suggestion that economic forces induced these inventions. The machines were clearly ends not means. Nevertheless, nearly every one of Ramelli's mechanisms, however elaborate or extravagant, has been put to some use in succeeding centuries" ("The Mind's Eye," p. 829).

31. "Primarily," because there seems to be a continuum of notational precision. Many essentially oral cultures employ mnemonic devices that are protonotational, while even the most meticulously notated score of Western cultures allows leeway for interpretive realization by performers.

32. Hughes, *History of European Music*, p. 62. In Hughes's account, need precedes and fosters invention. But the converse also occurs: invention often precedes need, and in our culture, need is then nurtured by marketing.

33. By ensuring preservation, notation makes the study, if not the existence, of music history possible.

because of notation, Berg could be innovative by replicating a chorale setting by J. S. Bach toward the close of his Violin Concerto.[34]

Preservation may do more than merely facilitate innovation. It may foster novelty. In the twentieth century, the pressing presence of past music, coupled with an ideology that emphasizes the value of individual expression, originality, and change, led composers to search for musical means that distinguished their idiom from that of other composers, past and present. The tendency of past compositions to encourage present innovation has, of course, been intensified by the existence of printing and publication, which are themselves possible only because of notation.

On the other hand, because notation necessarily involves standardization, it also inhibits innovation. For instance, in a traditional score, pitch/time relationships are limited by what can be represented in existing notation. The conservative aspects of notation are evident in the history of twentieth-century music. To represent nontraditional pitch, time, and sonic possibilities, there had to be an increased use of graphic notation;[35] at the same time, synthesizers, computers, and tape players not only obviated the need for written notation but established a new mode of transmission.

Notation influences music history in less direct ways as well. It does so because it facilitates the formulation of *music theory,* which may in turn directly foster innovation.[36] For what theory does, almost always, is to conceptualize the forms and processes of a prevailing musical practice.[37] Once the idea of the triad, of harmonic progression, of the nature of *opera seria,* or of the structure of sonata form was formulated and disseminated throughout the musical community, the informed composer's understanding of musical relationships was forever changed. And what such conceptualization changes is the perception of unexplored possibilities. When the triad, for instance, was conceptualized as an entity rather than as a pair of intervals, the possibilities for manipulation (discussed in the next part of this chapter) were significantly changed: permutation led to the possibility of inversion, while extrapolation gradually led to a piling up of thirds, creating ninth, eleventh, and thirteenth chords.

The kind of music theory formulated, and hence the kinds of innovations made possible, depends on the nature of external constraints such as physics, aesthetics, and ideology.[38] Theories of music formulated in the seventeenth century generally employed philosophic concepts such as clear taxonomic classes, the doctrine of affections, and the deductive method, which were all current at the time; nineteenth-

---

34. In this case, as in most others, notation is a necessary but not sufficient condition for innovation.

35. "Increased use," because traditional notation also involves graphic elements—not only symbols such as ⟨ , but, by deep analogy, the up-and-down position of pitches on a staff.

36. Notation merely "facilitates" because nonliterate cultures have quite sophisticated theories about the nature of music—its origins, its functions, and its powers. In this connection, see Feld, "Metaphors of Kaluli Musical Theory."

37. In my view, one can scarcely exaggerate the importance of the influence of concept (theory) on behavior; it would be fascinating, I suspect, to study a few instances of the effect of theoretical formulations on style change.

38. In this connection, see Balthazar, "Intellectual History and Concepts of the Concerto."

century music theory, employing concepts and metaphors derived from biology, emphasized the importance of gradual development, dynamic processes, and inductive methods; and twentieth-century theories are indebted to Gestalt psychology, linguistics, and various aspects of mathematics. The last of these, mathematics, has obviously had a considerable effect on the kinds of innovations devised by, say, Milton Babbitt and Iannis Xenakis.[39]

## THE SOURCES OF STRATEGIC NOVELTY

External circumstances—political events, economic and social conditions, technology, or cultural ideology—may, as just observed, play an important role in fostering style change by encouraging a search for novel strategies. And such circumstances may, as we shall see, also significantly affect which of the myriad strategies devised by composers are actually used and subsequently replicated. But as far as I can discern, conditions and events external to music can serve as *sources* for novel compositional strategies only under the very special conditions considered later in this chapter in the section "Correlation." The distinction is between the reasons for some change (what caused or influenced it) and the substantive nature of the change (the material and relational means that make the existence of change evident). For what composers build with are not political acts or concepts, social structures or customs, technological means or ideological beliefs. What they manipulate are the materials of music; what they create are relationships among pitches and durations, textures and timbres, registers and dynamics, and so on.

These observations may help to clarify the roles of internal and external constraints in the histories of various disciplines. Since the debate between externalists and internalists has been especially explicit in the history of science, I will consider science as well as music in what follows. Those who seek to account for the *sources* of the concepts that constitute the history of some science are primarily internalists—necessarily so. For even when economic or social conditions encourage the investigation of a specific field of inquiry, the investigation must exploit the concepts and methods of the prevalent mode of scientific thought. Similarly in music, though the ideological goal of aesthetic purity may have influenced the choices made by both J. S. Bach and Anton Webern, prevalent musical means affected the compositional relationships actually used. On the other hand, those who are concerned to explain why at a particular time some problems rather than others engage the energies of the scientific community tend to be externalists—and for the most part, rightly so.[40] As Robert E. Kohler observed, "none of these essays show that social

---

39. Though music theory may affect innovation directly, its most important role is to function as one of the conduits through which parameters external to music influence the thinking and goals of composers.

40. This in no way denies that scientific problems, and musical ones as well, may generate a search for, and perhaps a discovery of, novelty because initial solutions of the scientific or compositional problem were not entirely satisfactory.

organization directly shaped the content of science; rather, its influence was on the direction of science, the selection of certain problems over others."[41] Similarly, as we shall see, realms external to music have influenced its history by affecting the goals and values embodied in ideology. Put briefly, if too broadly, an internalist account of style change is concerned with the ways in which prevalent stylistic *means* affect the choices made by composers, while an externalist account of style change is concerned with the *goals* (ideological, aesthetic, economic, and so on) that affect the choices made by composers. And integrating the externalist and internalist accounts of style change—connecting musical means with ideological goals—is what the last part of this book seeks to do.

The sources of strategic novelty are so many and so varied that an adequate account cannot be attempted here. Nevertheless, as the basis for all style change, some discussion, however brief, is needed, if only to suggest some of the problems and issues involved. For present purposes the sources of strategic novelty are divided into three broad categories: manipulation, simulation, and correlation.[42] An instance of innovation may involve the use of one or some combination of these types.

## Manipulation

Probably the most common and important source of strategic innovation is manipulation—ordering or modifying already existing stylistic means in new ways. Within this category, four subclasses may be distinguished: permutation, combination, displacement, and extrapolation.

PERMUTATION.

In permutation, novelty results from the reordering of the components that make up an existing set of entities—for instance, reordering the letters of the alphabet to make new words, or the words of a language to create new sentences. In music, permutation might involve rearranging the pitches of a scale or the rhythms possible in a style to create new melodies, chords, or harmonic progressions. On the level of the motive—whether in modal, tonal, or serial music—techniques such as augmentation and diminution, inversion and retrograde would produce instances of permutation. As these examples suggest, permutation may occur on different hierarchic levels. For instance, as noted earlier, toward the end of the eleventh century, permutation produced significant novelty when the components of organum changed position: "The organal voice was removed from below the chant and placed above. . . ."[43]

---

41. Review of *Perspectives on the Emergence of Scientific Disciplines,* p. 1197.

42. The first two types may be considered internal modes of innovation, the third external.

43. Hughes, *History of European Music,* p. 49. For the sake of economy and to illustrate that all the kinds of manipulations may occur in a single style period, I will use Hughes's book for a number of examples.

COMBINATION.

Combination involves a novel joining or ordering of two or more already existing stylistic components that previously belonged to different sets. The style of Classic music provides many examples of combinational novelty.[44] One thinks, for instance, of the dice games attributed to Haydn and Mozart, of the use of fugal procedures in sonata-form expositions, as in the last movement of Mozart's String Quartet in G Major (K. 387) of the combining of chorus and orchestra in the Finale of Beethoven's Ninth Symphony, and of the joining of the separate movements of a sonata into a single form, as in the Liszt Piano Sonata. Combination is an important source of novelty not only in the Classic period, but in all periods. In the Middle Ages, for instance, "the classical motet is an ideal type of that sort of counterpoint that brings together in the unity of a single composition separate elements that are in themselves both disparate and complete. . . ."[45] And in the serial music of our own time the combination of different forms of a tone row is a central and explicit aspect of compositional technique.

DISPLACEMENT.

Closely related to both permutation and combination, displacement involves a change in the placement of a pattern in pitch or time or both. When the change is in pitch, or in tonality, the modification will be called *transposition*. Sequences, for instance, result from transposition, and as they show, transpositions can be either conjunct or disjunct.

A kind of displacement that is probably a common source of novelty in all periods is *migration*. Two kinds of migration can be distinguished: positional migration and hierarchic migration. Positional migration involves a change in the place and function of an established pattern or schema: for instance, when what is customarily a closing gesture is used to begin a work, as in the second movement of Haydn's "Military" Symphony, discussed toward the end of Chapter 1;[46] or when a figure usually associated with a processive passage is used as the beginning of a stable melody, as in the theme that begins the last movement of Beethoven's Fourth Symphony.[47]

Hierarchic migration occurs when a set of relationships previously realized on one hierarchic level is used to structure another level. In most cases, the change seems to be from relatively foreground levels to higher ones. In Classic music, for instance, root motion by thirds occasionally occurs on the level of harmonic progression, as in the development section of the Finale of Mozart's Symphony No. 39 in E♭ Major (K. 543). As shown in the sketch in Example 4.1a, the main part of the devel-

44. See Ratner, "*Ars Combinatoria.*"
45. Hughes, *History of European Music,* p. 62.
46. For another instance, see Levy, "Gesture, Form, and Syntax."
47. This instance of migration is discussed in my *Explaining Music,* pp. 222–25.

opment section begins with a harmonic progression by major thirds. And though each root (except the final A♭) is preceded by its dominant, the basic process is mobile and unstable. A similar progression by major thirds forms the basis for the succession of extended tonal areas in many nineteenth-century works. As shown in the abstract in Example 4.1*b,* this is the case in the first movement of Beethoven's String Quartet in B♭ Major, Opus 130.

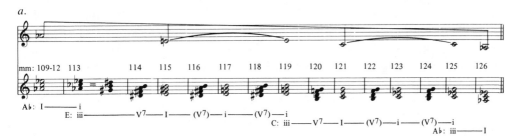

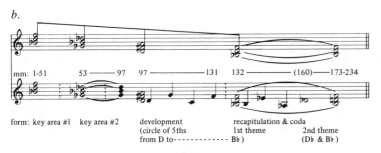

EXAMPLE 4.1. (*a*) Mozart, Symphony No. 39 in E♭ Major (K. 543), iv; (*b*) Beethoven, String Quartet in B♭ Major, Opus 130, i

EXTRAPOLATION.

In extrapolation, some existing means or procedure is extended, usually gradually. Innumerable examples come to mind: in the twentieth century, the extension of serial principles from pitch to rhythm, timbre, and dynamics; in the nineteenth century, the increased emphasis on secondary parameters, the addition of thirds in the construction of chords, and the more extensive use of chromaticism; during the Baroque, the exploitation of the possibilities of tonal counterpoint; and, in the music of the Middle Ages:

> Instead of being restricted to one note for each note of the chant, the organal voice was given the liberty of having two, three, or even more notes to a single one of the chant. With this further possibility available, the newly composed melody could develop almost at will. . . . *The most striking innovation* [of the beginning of the twelfth century] *is an extension of a principle already discussed:* in a few of the St. Martial pieces

the organal voice occasionally has from five to more than a dozen notes to a single note of the cantus firmus.[48]

Finally, there should be a category of manipulation called *retrenchment* that would account for the kind of style change that results from the simplification of means through elimination. One thinks, for instance, of the kind of utter reduction of means that characterized the beginning of opera, of the almost Spartan simplicity sought by a composer such as Erik Satie, and most recently of the music of minimalism. The difficulty with such negative categories is that the ways of *not* doing something are legion. Consequently, unless the constraints (traditions and techniques) denied are specified, accounts of retrenchment will tend to be so general that they will have only weak explanatory power.

## Simulation

Sounds, whether found in the natural world or in culture, have been a significant source of novel patterning in Western music, at least since the beginning of the Renaissance. Simulation occurs when a composer invents musical relationships that are based on, and are similar to, some sound source. The composer's representation of such sounds is itself always partly dependent upon prevalent cultural traditions for "hearing" and conceptualizing the phenomenon in question. Though it may be possible to identify other types of simulation, only three will be considered: imitation, transcription, and mimicry.

IMITATION.
One of the most important sources of innovation in the history of Western art music has been the musics of Western subcultures and, more recently, musics of non-Western cultures. Indeed, one of the most common sources for novel strategies in the retrenchments mentioned above has involved recourse to the constraints of—imitating the styles of—folk and popular musics of the West. One need only recall the influence of such musics on the early history of opera, on the dance music of the Classic style, on the style of such nineteenth-century composers as Berlioz and Dvořák, Musorgsky and Mahler, and on the idiom of such contemporary composers as Bartók and Copland. The music of non-Western cultures has also been a source of novelty, as in Félicien David's use of Arab music and Colin McPhee's use of Balinese music.

But imitation is not limited to the use of Western folk and popular music or the

48. Hughes, *History of Western Music*, pp. 49–50; emphasis added.

musics of other cultures. Earlier styles of Western art music may serve as sources for subsequent innovation. One thinks perhaps of Beethoven's use of the Lydian mode in *Heiliger Dankgesang,* from his String Quartet in A Minor, Opus 132; of the passacaglia that is the basis for the last movement of Brahms's Fourth Symphony; of Schoenberg's use of the Baroque suite pattern; and of Stravinsky's imitation of styles as various as the late Middle Ages (his Mass), the Baroque (*Oedipus Rex*), and the Classic period (Symphony in C). The mention of Stravinsky's music reminds us that imitation is by no means confined to the use of the constraints of the primary parameters. Syntax is frequently, if not invariably, complemented by sonority.

TRANSCRIPTION.

The re-presentation of sonority is what transcription is about. In this case, an attempt to use one medium of performance to simulate or re-create that of some other medium leads to novel modes of sound production and, more importantly, to new kinds of figuration, which in turn become the basis for new strategies for manipulation. Examples of transcription abound from the Renaissance to the present: lute transcriptions of vocal music, harpsichord imitations of lute figuration and ornamentation, organ versions of orchestral concerti, orchestral imitations of mechanical instruments (for instance, music boxes), piano simulations of orchestral sonorities, wind and brass choirs miming the sound of the organ, and most recently, electronic sound generators matching the timbres of orchestral instruments or, conversely, chamber groups mirroring the dry, shallow sounds of electronic music. Transcription has been common both because it makes possible a wider dissemination of the existing repertory and because both performers and audiences revel in displays of virtuosity—in technical skill and a kind of *trompe d'oreille.*

MIMICRY.

Both virtuosity and delight in the pleasure of recognition that follows imitation help to explain the prevalence of mimicry—the simulation in music of what have not, until recently, been considered musical sounds in Western culture. Such re-presentation may be of bird calls or the whining of cats, of forest murmurs or thunderstorms, of battles, factories, or railroad trains—and, above all, of the inflections of human speech, whether in monologue, in chorus, or in responsive interaction, whether expressing love or anger, command or resignation. Once again aural matching is tempered by cultural tradition. And though the musical mimicry of sounds found in the natural or cultural world may seem somewhat less arbitrary than, say, the verbal simulation of the sounds made by animals (English dogs bark "bow wow," French ones bark "oua-oua"), the storms in Haydn's *Seasons,* Beethoven's Sixth Symphony, Rossini's *William Tell*, Wagner's *Die Walküre*, Verdi's *Otello*, and Britten's *Peter Grimes* form part of, and are influenced by (sometimes perhaps negatively), a tradition of re- presentation.

## *Correlation*

Phenomena in nature or culture that make no sound whatsoever may nevertheless be a source of strategic innovation. To be so, however, the composer's interpretation of the phenomenon in question must be complemented by a code for transforming the significant features of the phenomenon into one or more dimensions of sound. And just as simulation is tested by aural matching, so correlation is validated by conceptual correspondence and coherence. Though this ascribes innovation to external sources, there is an important difference between the operation of correlation and that of other kinds of external impingements. For instead of an independent, isolated, and disparate connection between phenomenon and musical pattern, a correlation establishes a coherent, consistent, and continuing relationship between the external realm and that of music. Put briefly, once a correlation is established, the external realm guides the manipulations and simulations that give rise to novelty. This makes it clear that correlation has a tendency to transform music (or some aspect of it) into a more or less dependent parameter. The strong objections—almost righteous indignation—expressed by formalists such as Hanslick to descriptive or narrative music may be related to such transformation; for when the form and process of a composition are dependent upon a program, it is as though the sanctity and integrity of a sacred object have been violated. For instance, instead of being shaped by purely musical constraints, the succession of variations in the tone poem *Don Quixote* is partly dependent upon the pattern of incidents that Strauss's work seeks to depict.

   In what follows, three kinds of correlation are differentiated: metaphoric mimicry, analogic modeling, and metaphoric modeling.

METAPHORIC MIMICRY.
Because the various dimensions of sound (pitch, duration, loudness, timbre, and so on) have counterparts in other realms of human experience, silent features of the phenomenal world can be characterized in sound. The pervasiveness of the correlation between music and other modes of sense experience is evident in the way we describe sounds: pitches are high or low; melodic lines rise or fall, or are sinuous or jagged; rhythms are emphatic or weak, smooth or jerky; timbres (tone *colors*) are brilliant or somber, piercing or dull; volumes are large or small, chords rough or smooth, and textures thick or thin; and, more generally, musical patterns are characterized as regular or irregular, exciting or calm, light or heavy, happy or sad.

These attributes of sound are also the attributes of objects, actions, and affections outside the realm of music. We know perfectly well, for instance, what the attributes of swimming goldfish are: small, light, and brilliantly colored; quietly graceful and smooth but not overly regular in motion; and so forth. Because these attributes of visual experience can, by experiential analogy, be matched in sound, silence can be made audible. Similarly, we can imagine how the pyramids would sound, if they could: very slow and heavily stressed in motion, low and conjunct in pitch, thick in texture, and voluminous in sonority. And we are keenly conscious of the motor/tensional characteristics of affective states such as anger and anxiety, joy and reverence, and of the traditional ways in which they have been translated into musical patternings.

Observe that in order to be re-presented in sound, visual phenomena must be interpreted, not only in the sense that all experience is interpreted, but in the more specific sense that they must be understood as having a characteristic motion or position. Such interpretation is possible because we know from experience how things move: save for special cases (airplanes and so on), large objects move slowly and their position tends to be low—close to the ground; small things generally move more rapidly, often seemingly irregularly, and their position is often high. Such relationships are familiar partly because of the constraints of the physical world. Ordinary experience couples large size with heavy weight, and heavy weight with slow motion and low position. Similarly, the acoustics of sounding bodies links large size with low pitch, slow sound activation, large volume, and dark tone color. With the introduction of attributes such as color, sound, shape (round, sharp), and the like, we begin to border on the realm of cultural metaphor—a realm in which the constraints of the physical and biological worlds become the basis for valuation: *up* (high pitch) is connected with what is "good" (light, life, heaven, birds, sun, and warmth); *down* (low pitch) is connected with what is "bad" (Hades, death, cold, giants).[49]

To be represented in music, then, an object, activity, or concept must be interpreted or traditionally understood as having a characteristic motion, size, location, intensity, or other attribute readily translated into sounds. Pyramids, jumping, heaven, birds, sleeping, and death seem susceptible to such translation and interpretation. But abstract concepts, such as morality or the Pythagorean theorem, and things such as chairs, hats, or noses, which cannot easily be interpreted as having characteristic motion, position, or intensity, are less readily translated into sound. Their representation results not from the natural commonality of human experience, but from more or less arbitrary denotations contrived by the composer, usually in connection with a text.

This difference between what might be called *natural* metaphoric representation and *contrived* metaphoric representation has had consequences for the history of music. It has meant that in the former case a tradition of representations could arise (for instance, the traditions of Hades music, storm music, and pastoral music), while

49. In this connection, see Lakoff and Johnson, *Metaphors We Live By,* chap. 4.

in the latter case no such tradition is likely to arise. There is, for instance, no history of *Tarnhelm* music because the representation, as well as the concept, was contrived by Wagner. And it is worth observing that innovation may involve *denying,* as well as extending, tradition, as is the case in the last movement of Stravinsky's Symphony of Psalms.[50]

For the sake of more specific illustration, let us suppose that a composer wants to represent something in the external world—say, a painting entitled "Great Gate at Kiev." To do so, he must interpret both the silent painting and the noiseless gate that it depicts. He must imagine how such a gate would move, sensing its size and weight, and hence its rate of motion; perceiving its depicted proportions and grandeur, and hence the quality of its motion. The motor imaginings resulting from these perceptions would be complemented by a host of culturally derived concepts and feelings associated with this specific gate, and perhaps the city of Kiev as well. This interactive combining of motor-suggested sensation and concept-induced feeling becomes realized in a specific musical interpretation that is Musorgsky's "Great Gate at Kiev."

In order for this musical interpretation to be realized, sensation and feelings must be transformed into particular pitch and durational relationships, specific tempos and dynamics, and individual textures, registers, and sonorities. The codes that make such transformations possible are modified, but seldom newly invented, by the composers who employ them. Even though they are based on more or less natural modes of metaphoric representation, transformations have generally been particularized by the rich stock of conventions in terms of which musical styles interpret the worlds of culture and nature. In short, using the syntax, grammar, and formal schemata of a prevalent musical style, together with the means established by a culturally sanctioned means of transformation, the composer chooses musical materials by matching his motor/mimetic experience against his interpretation of the visual/cultural phenomenon.

It is important to recognize that very different phenomena may be characterized by quite similar attributes. Take what is probably the most familiar example: the seasons of the year, the ages of man, and the times of day have all been taken as counters for one another. Because winter, old age, and night can be characterized by many of the same attributes—e.g., darkness, cold, low position, somber color, slowness of motion—they might well be mimed by the same music.[51] In other words, what mimicry—whether metaphoric or not—gives us are necessary, but not sufficient, conditions for the specification of the phenomenon being represented in music.

The specification of the phenomenon being represented is by no means a trivial matter. Despite the appealing "purity" of formalism, a title or program that denotes a particular phenomenon is, in my view, just as much an attribute of a composition

50. See above, Chapter 1, note 57.

51. I have called such analogical sets *connotative complexes.* See *Emotion and Meaning in Music,* chap. 8, where the mechanism of metaphoric mimicry is discussed in more detail than is possible here.

as are the pitches, durations, and other relationships notated in the score. The significance of a composition depends on the interactions among a set of stimuli (the sounding music), a competent listener, and a cultural context (including what we know about a composition). Knowledge of what is being represented changes the significance of the composition not only because such knowledge affects human experience,[52] but because by directing attention to particular features of a pattern, such knowledge influences our understanding and response to what is presented. Just as the title of Pieter Bruegel's *Fall of Icarus* directs our attention to a speck of white in the represented water and thereby changes significantly the way in which we relate parts of the painting to one another, so knowledge that the last movement of Berlioz's *Symphonie fantastique* represents a witches' sabbath significantly alters the ways in which we comprehend and respond to, for instance, the tolling of the bells and the presentation of the Dies irae.

An important consequence of this is that what is innovative in the case of Berlioz's "Witches' Sabbath," Musorgsky's "Great Gate at Kiev," or any other piece that represents extramusical phenomena, is not merely the sonorous patterning per se, *but the relation of that patterning to the specified subject matter.* In other words, it is not merely the purely musical relationships devised by a composer that are innovative, but the relation of these to whatever is considered to be represented by them. To make the point more emphatic: were it established that a previously unknown program for the *Symphonie fantastique* were the authentic one—the one Berlioz ultimately wanted for his work—the meaning of the symphony would change and the nature of Berlioz's innovation would, accordingly, be different.[53]

ANALOGIC MODELING.

In mimicry, the source for novel compositional constraints is some aspect of perceptual experience; in modeling, on the other hand, the source of new constraints is a set of relationships present in a conceptual realm. In some cases the consistent use of an explicit formula connects specific dimensions of music with particular features of the model in such a way that new musical relationships are generated. In other cases, a discipline whose terms and concepts seem more familiar or better established functions as a general way of thinking and theorizing about music, and in so doing, it

52. See *Music, the Arts, and Ideas,* p. 57 and chap. 4, passim.
53. The matter is complicated because of the relationship of genesis to significance and history. If the existing program was the one that Berlioz used as a constraint guiding aspects of his simulation, then it would have to be considered in any account of the genesis of the symphony, and in any history of program music as well. Moreover, even if a significantly different program were subsequently substituted for the one we know, the one we know would probably continue to affect our understanding of the symphony's metaphoric/musical meaning. For it seems doubtful that the new, substitute program could entirely obliterate knowledge of the earlier one. As a result, the character of the symphony might in part be a function of the cognitive interplay between old and new, between genesis and phenomenon.

suggests novel alternatives. The first of the possibilities, analogic modeling, is considered in this section; the second, metaphoric modeling, is considered in the next.

Though there is probably no limit on the realms that can serve as models for music, some have, over the course of history, been specially favored. One of these is obviously mathematics. Our own period, characterized as it has been by a somewhat frantic search for viable constraints, is replete with examples: Bartók's supposed use of the golden section as a basis for morphological organization; the widespread use of set theory for the composition of serial music; the use, by Xenakis and others, of statistical methods for generating musical patterns; and the use of tables of random numbers to generate aleatory music. In each case, some realm of mathematics is used to produce a set of numerical relationships, which is subsequently transformed into one or more dimensions of musical patterning (pitch, duration, texture, dynamics, and so on) according to a predetermined formula.

Mention of aleatory music brings to mind one of John Cage's especially striking analogic models, in which astronomical maps were used as a basis for specifying pitch, time, and other relationships. Another discipline, but one more pertinent to music, namely acoustics, has also served as a source of novel compositional means. One thinks perhaps of Vicentino's attempt to make his theory of the Greek modes a basis for musical practice; of Wagner's use in the Prelude to *Das Rheingold* of the relationships among partials to symbolize the unfolding of the natural order at the time of creation (here the use of the "chord of nature," the model, has metaphoric as well as theoretic significance); and of Hindemith's acoustically based theories, which led him to revise a number of his earlier compositions. And there are other cases in which music theory itself has been the basis for novel patterning. For instance, the eighteenth-century theory of key and mode relationships was the basis for the organization of Bach's *Well-Tempered Clavier*.[54] And, going further afield, B-A-C-H reminds us of the possibility that private codes—e.g., equating letters with pitches, as Schumann did, or using Morse code to specify durational relationships, as George Crumb did—may result in the devising of novel patternings.

Earlier, programs were mentioned as instances of correlation. When they are not added later, but instead precede and constrain a composer's choices, programs may act as models that generate novelty. Thus, while the representation of "The Great Gate at Kiev" involves metaphoric mimicry, the overall program of Musorgsky's *Pictures at an Exhibition* involves higher-level analogic modeling. The model is that of the particular succession of paintings with a viewer promenading from one painting to another. Once again, it is important to emphasize that innovation arises from the relationship between the musical stimuli and the program. For our understanding of the quite familiar ritornello procedure of *Pictures* is significantly qualified by our knowledge that the ritornello is a promenade between viewings. Other

---

54. Once a theory has been formulated (usually on the basis of prevalent practice), it may serve, often through a process of logical extrapolation, as a source of novelty. Thus the conceptualization of, say, the triad as an entity easily leads to novel kinds of usage.

programs—for example, those of Berlioz or Richard Strauss—are often more patently narrative than that of *Pictures*. (Again, not only may a narrative program produce purely musical innovations, but the joining of model and musical means will itself be a novel resource.)

Finally, the constraints derived from a specific text may act as a source for innovation. On a high level, for instance, the distinctive structure of a song cycle may be the result of the structure of the group of poems set by the composer, as is the case with Schumann's *Dichterliebe* and Schoenberg's *Pierrot lunaire*. On a more foreground level, the claims of the text per se (together with the prevalent traditions for its interpretation and musical realization) may suggest new musical strategies. For instance, according to Carl Dahlhaus, Wagner's use of alliterative verse—of *Stabreim*—was the source of an important change in his style. Dahlhaus argues that *Stabreim*, with its lack of regular accentuation, led to the "dissolution of musical periodic structure, the syntax that had provided the framework of both instrumental and vocal melodic writing for the past hundred years and more,"[55] and that "the correlative of the musical prose resulting from the discarding of periodic structure was leitmotivic technique, or, to be more precise, the extension of the technique to the entire work."[56]

The second of Dahlhaus's points reminds us that the sources of innovation are not mutually exclusive. Rather, as in the case of the development of the final phases of leitmotivic technique, different types of sources—in this case extension (which I have called "extrapolation") and analogic modeling—may combine to produce a particular innovation.

METAPHORIC MODELING.

In metaphoric modeling the relationship between the model field and music is less exact, consistent, and rigorous than it is in analogic modeling. The metaphoric model serves as a way of thinking about music, and any of its terms or concepts may be translated, either directly or through music theory, into musical practice that is innovative. Language, for instance, has acted as a metaphoric model as well as an analogic one. But while a particular text serves as a basis for innovation in analogic modeling, it is the general notion of "music-as-a-language" that suggests novel possibilities in metaphoric modeling. Yet it is precisely because metaphoric models are not strictly related to musical means that it is difficult to establish explicit connections between the terms and concepts of language and particular musical innovations. Nevertheless, given the pervasive presence of the music-as-language metaphor during the eighteenth century, it is difficult to doubt that notions of musical rhetoric, period

55. *Richard Wagner's Music Dramas*, p. 105.
56. Ibid., p. 107.

structure, and poetic scansion affected compositional practice and the generation of novelty.[57]

Philosophical concepts, too, may act as metaphoric models. During the nineteenth century, for instance, the theorists' and composers' conception of sonata form was evidently influenced by notions of dialectic process: the first key area was thought of as the thesis of the dialectic process, the second key area as the antithesis; the resulting conflict, which was made manifest and intensified in the development section, was resolved (the synthesis) in the recapitulation.[58] Once again, it seems plausible to suppose that thinking about musical form in terms of opposition and resolution encouraged the invention of innovative contrasts and novel reconciliations.[59] In our own century, the metaphor of art as scientific discovery (through experiment and problem solving) not only has strongly encouraged the search for novel means, but has, through metaphoric parallels with particular theories such as that of quantum mechanics, led composers (for example, Stockhausen) to devise novel patterns presumably congruent in some way with the model theory.

The coherent doctrines of established disciplines such as rhetoric, science, and philosophy provide only some of the metaphoric models for music. Others are provided by the more informal beliefs and attitudes that characterize the ideology of a culture. But the chief importance of ideology—of beliefs about mind and body, nature and society, freedom and necessity, genesis and goals—lies not in its effect on the devising of innovations but in its influence on the ways that composers choose which of the available alternatives to use and which to discard, which to replicate and which to reject. And it is to the fascinating problem of choosing that we now turn.

57. In this connection, see Ratner, *Classic Music*, pt. 2, "Rhetoric."

58. It is important to recognize, as I will argue later, that it is probably not the original works of philosophers that primarily influence composers and music theorists. This is why Hegel's name did not appear in this brief mention of sonata form as dialectic process. Rather, what tends to be culturally influential is popularizations of "high-culture" theories and their dissemination as cultural scuttlebutt. See the last part of Chapter 5.

59. This conception of sonata form as dialectic process is still very much alive, as Charles Rosen's description of the form makes evident (see his *Sonata Forms*, p. 17). But this metaphor was not one current in the eighteenth century; then, the metaphor used to conceptualize sonata form was that of rhetorical argument.

# CHAPTER 5

# Choice and Replication

In any reasonably rich culture, novelty abounds. Indeed, it is omnipresent because every act and every artifact that is not an exact replica of an existing one is in some way different and, in that respect, novel.[1] Put in another way, all composers—even those who write the most routine and pedestrian music—are continually devising new relationships. Most of these are historically inconsequential realizations of existing constraints, though some may, of course, be of high aesthetic value.[2] Because cultures are as a rule replete with possibilities, it is not primarily the *advent* of novelty that needs to be explained, but its *use* and, even more importantly, its subsequent *replication*.

Why, out of all the possible alternatives that the composer might have devised or considered for use in some work, was this particular one chosen rather than some other? To make the point forcefully and with only slight exaggeration, the difference between a crackpot and a genius is not primarily a matter of fecund invention; both readily devise novel, imaginative, even eccentric, possibilities. Rather the difference lies in the ability of the genius to choose with perspicacity. On a higher historical level, why did certain patterns, forms, or genres, rather than others that were equally available, appeal to a particular compositional/cultural community, so that they were replicated in a kind of consensus of current compositional choice? Why, in short, do some constraints continue to be chosen while others, however aesthetically satisfying they may have been, disappear, apparently without historical consequences?[3]

---

1. The question of what constitutes an exact replica is more complicated than might at first appear. See the discussion of miming later in this chapter.

2. One can never be certain, however, that some seemingly inconsequential realization will not subsequently be so interpreted that it becomes the basis for a generalized constraint: that is, a new strategy or even a novel rule.

3. "Apparently," because as we shall see it is possible that such rejected alternatives may become consequential at some future time.

## WHY PARTICULAR POSSIBILITIES ARE CHOSEN

### *Goals and Constraints*

Understanding and explaining the replicated choices made by composers is complicated and perplexing not only because of the range and number of alternatives available to a composer, but because the various possibilities may be attractive for very
different reasons. For example, in a specific compositional/cultural situation, some
of the possible alternatives may satisfy the composer's desire for aesthetic elegance
or for expressive richness, others will better serve to please a particular patron or
prospective audience, while still others may be appealing because they are part of the
ideology of the composer's culture.

Composing—and artistic creation generally—always involves balancing such
claims against one another. In some cases a composer will choose to sacrifice one
claim for another; more often there will be compromise—the alternatives will partially satisfy a number of competing claims. For instance, the influence of the music
of the French Revolution on Beethoven's work has been widely acknowledged and
copiously documented.[4] Did Beethoven choose this influence because the music was
popular? Because of his political ideals? Because he was thinking of moving to
Paris? Because it satisfied some inner spiritual need? Or because of some combination of these and other reasons?

The assumption, then, that the single goal guiding compositional choice is aesthetic excellence is usually unwarranted. Most compositions reconcile a variety of
claims—solve a number of problems—some of which cannot be accounted for on
internal grounds alone. And because choices often satisfy multiple claims, criticism
sometimes seems inadequate; it has proved difficult to explain, rather than merely
describe, for example, the relationship between sketches and completed works.

Few choices are optimal from all points of view. Most involve settling for what
is satisfactory—what works well, or very well. In Herbert A. Simon's words, "search
ends when a good-enough alternative is found";[5] and in Alexander Pope's verse,
"Whoever hopes a faultless work to see, / Hopes for what never was, nor is, nor e'er
will be."

But alternatives do not exist in some realm of absolute and eternal first principles. Invariably they are chosen or rejected in terms of goals: The alternative is
good enough for *what?* And what is true of other protagonists of history—princes or
philosophers, clerics or courtesans—is true of composers, whether taken individually or as a community: their choices can be understood and explained only in the
light of some hypothesis about their goals, their intentions. Since emphasis on the
centrality of the intention of composers is perhaps controversial, let me try to make
my position clear by considering the difference between replicating and miming.

---

4. See Solomon, *Beethoven*, p. 138.

5. *Models of Thought*, p. 3. Partly for this reason it is sometimes said that works of art are never finished,
only abandoned.

The distinction between mechanical miming and replication depends on whether or not choice is grounded on an understanding of the constraints that generated the resulting activity or pattern. Suppose, for instance, that an actor watched a grand master playing chess, memorized all his typical moves and gestures, and then performed his miming of them in a play or a film. He would have perceived and re-presented what John R. Searle would call the brute facts of the grand master's behavior.[6] But unless, in addition, he understood the rules and strategies of the game (Searle's institutional facts), he would not have played chess. Max Black makes this point perfectly clear:

> If I say "Jones just made the move, 'pawn to king four,'" a full and suffi-
> cient verification of my claim is that Jones shifted a characteristically
> shaped piece of wood from a certain place on a chessboard to a certain
> other place. Yet, this is only part of the story. I would not say that Jones
> had made the move, should he know nothing of the game, and were merely
> moving the piece at random; nor would I say so if he knew how to play
> chess but were amusing himself by replaying some master's game. . . . In
> using the language of chess, I take for granted the institution of chess
> playing and a host of related facts. Before I can teach anybody how to use
> the language of chess, I must acquaint him with this background of
> presuppositions.[7]

And this holds equally for the arts. In order for a pattern to be replicated in a significant way, rather than being merely mimed or parroted, it must be understood as part of a known (but probably internalized) set of constraints—constraints that establish the goals in terms of which the pattern was chosen. Mere parroting involves presenting the lineaments of a pattern without comprehension of the underlying constraints that generated the relationships.[8] Hamlet's famous lines make this very distinction:

> These indeed seem,
> For they are actions that a man might play;
> But I have that within which passeth show,
> These but the trappings and the suits of woe.

---

6. *Speech Acts*, chap. 2.

7. *Models and Metaphors*, p. 165.

8. The preceding discussion, and the terms developed in this chapter, suggest a reformulation of the idea of imitation. Namely, an imitation is a special kind of replication that borrows elements and relationships (usually ones on a low hierarchic level) from one realm, "real life," but uses them in another realm that has its own set of constraints—its own principles and goals. Thus fictional literature borrows the trappings and the suits of observed human action but plays a significantly different "game" with them. This view owes much to the work of Barbara Herrnstein Smith; see her *On the Margins of Discourse*, chaps. 2 and 5.

To make the point even more forcefully, and paradoxically as well, consider the converse of parroting. Though imaginary, the case is nevertheless instructive. In this instance, the brute facts (the raw stimuli—words, pitches, colors) of two art works are absolutely identical, but the institutional facts (the constraints on which the works are based, and hence the possibilities from which the brute facts were drawn) are significantly different. Then not only would the style and significance of the two works be different, but the intentions of the artists would have been so as well.

This difference is the focus of Jorge Luis Borges's story "Pierre Menard, Author of the *Quixote*." Early in the twentieth century, according to the story, Menard wrote several chapters of a book, the text of which proved to be exactly the same as chapters from Cervantes's *Don Quixote*. As Borges writes: "Cervantes' text and Menard's are verbally identical, but the second is almost infinitely richer. . . . The contrast in style is also vivid. The archaic style of Menard—quite foreign, after all—suffers from a certain affectation. Not so that of his forerunner, who handles with ease the current Spanish of his time."[9] Because the goals implicit in the stylistic constraints he employed were different from those of Cervantes, Menard was not parroting the text of *Don Quixote,* but rather replicating it, albeit in a very bizarre way.

The distinction between merely miming and replicating indicates, then, that far from being irrelevant, comprehending the intentions of composers (collective as well as individual) is crucial for understanding the choices that result in the compositions on which a history of music is partly based. But—and this cannot be sufficiently emphasized—*it is not some kind of idiosyncratic, personal intention that is crucial for such a history, but the sort that is implicit in the stylistic constraints that define the goals of the "game of art" itself.* In short, the historically significant intentions of a football coach, a grand master of chess, or a composer are those that result from choices made among alternative possibilities permitted by the constraints of both the style of the activity and the cultural context.[10]

What follows is concerned with the reasons why some composers choose to use innovative alternatives and why some innovations tend to be replicated while others are not.

## Personal Proclivities and Cognitive Constraints

THE COMPOSER.
Since the difficulties involved in relating the temperament of a composer to his creative style were considered in Chapter 4, only a brief recapitulation will be given

---

9. *Labyrinths*, pp. 42–43.

10. Because "intentions" suggest single, unadulterated goals, it might be better to speak of the "motives" guiding the choices of composers. It is customary to speak of mixed motives, but not of mixed intentions. And this suggests that we have learned to think of aesthetic choices as being pure and unalloyed (intentions) while choices of men of action are devious and mixed (motives). Nevertheless, for the sake of convenience, I will continue to refer to the *intentions* of composers while whispering to myself, "but they are mixed!"

here. Clearly some composers tend to choose more novel relationships than others. Handel seems more adventurous than Bach, Haydn more than Mozart, Berlioz more than Mendelssohn. And though such differences are often attributable to external circumstances and conditions, it seems difficult to doubt that some stem, at least in part, from the personality of the composer—which, I take it, arises from the intricate interaction between innate inclination (accounted for in the seventeenth century by the theory of humors and in the twentieth by hypotheses about such things as body types and hormonal balance) and proclivities ingrained through cultural experience.

Aside from the bald assertion that, because of their personality, some composers tend to choose novel means, three interrelated personality traits seem to favor the use of innovative procedures and relationships: (1) a distaste and disdain for whatever is highly predictable or is sanctified by custom; (2) a complementary propensity to delight in conjoining seemingly disparate and discrepant realms or in turning things topsy-turvy by, say, making old means serve new ends (perhaps in order to mock custom), and (3) an ability to tolerate ambiguity—a necessary condition for the actualization of either of the first two tendencies. The ability to tolerate ambiguity is important because it enables the artist to take time to invent and consider more alternatives, and in doing so to find more satisfactory ones than might otherwise have been chosen.[11]

Once again it is impossible to ignore the insistent and vexing problem of circularity. That is, presumed temperamental proclivities are used to explain the very compositional choices from which they were inferred in the first place. Reason might be rescued if it could be demonstrated that the individual chose novelty in *all* realms of activity. For then generalizations from other realms of behavior might be legitimately used to account for musical choices.[12] As we have seen, however, this is very seldom the case. Until more is known about the nature of personality—about temperament, learning, and human behavior generally—circularity of this sort seems unavoidable. But even if it were possible to ascertain that a particular composer was "by nature" an innovator, that would not explain why, out of the plethora of novelties available or desirable, specific ones were chosen. For particular choices depend more on prevalent cultural and musical constraints than on personal inclinations.

COGNITION AND REPLICATION.
Whether a particular innovation is replicated as a characteristic of the composer's idiom or as a feature of the dialect of the compositional community depends also in

11. A composer's penchant for elegance or richness—his or her level of aesthetic aspiration—may or may not encourage the use of novel means. Where existing stylistic constraints make satisfactory levels of aesthetic significance possible, novelty may involve conserving variation. Nor are the desires for wealth or acclaim necessarily spurs to the invention or use of novel means.

12. This may be one reason why it is so often assumed that a creative artist's personality and behavior are entirely coherent and consistent, and why, despite artistic maturation and impingements from external parameters, it is taken for granted that the artist's personality remains constant over time.

part on psychological constraints.[13] Other things being equal, innovations that are consonant with human perceptual and cognitive capacities—the constraints of the central nervous system—are more likely to be used and replicated than innovations that are not so. For instance, novelties are more likely to be selected and replicated if they do not involve stimuli so extreme—so fast or slow in succession, so loud or soft in intensity, so small or large in pitch difference or temporal separation—that perception is painful or patterning problematic. Equally important, selection and replication are more likely if innovations conform to the Gestalt principles of pattern comprehension—that is, if they are characterized by properties such as similarity and difference, good continuation and symmetry, return and closure, and, above all, functional differentiation and hierarchic ordering. In short, innovations that are compatible with the constraints and proclivities of human perceptual and cognitive processes will tend to be comprehended as coherent, stable, and memorable relationships. As such, they have a reasonable chance of being replicated as aspects of the idiom of a composer or as part of the dialect of the compositional community.

The probability of such replication seems dependent on three other characteristics of patterns: generality, versatility, and redundancy.

*Generality* is a necessary condition for replication. If a pattern is entirely idiosyncratic, later composers may mime its characteristic features, but they will be unable to create comparable stylistic relationships and through replication to transform imitation into influence. Writing about Virginia Woolf, W. H. Auden observes, "I do not know if she is going to exert an influence on the future development of the novel—I rather suspect that her style and her vision were so unique that influence would only result in tame imitation. . . ."[14] In other words, to be replicated a patterning either must be generalizable or must be the realization of some general principle. For example, a number of composers were evidently influenced by Debussy's aesthetic ideals—for instance, an emphasis upon sound per se, achieved through the weakening of syntactic, goal-directed processes and a concomitant increase in the importance of secondary parameters. Others have been influenced by (have replicated) his chord construction through superimposition of thirds. For both these aspects of his style are generalizable. But those who have sought to emulate his harmonic style have only succeeded in parroting, because Debussy's characteristic chord successions were, as far as I can discern, negatively derived. That is, they resulted from *avoiding* progressions normal in the harmonic syntax of tonal music. But because the negation of one set of orderly relationships need not give rise to some other orderly set, Debussy's harmonic language probably cannot be generalized and cannot, through replication, be influential in shaping the development of new harmonic constraints. As William Austin remarks, "Debussy's [harmonic] principle is hard to learn. It is too vaguely general to be taught systematically."[15] It is

---

13. For the most part these function as necessary, not sufficient, conditions for use and replication.

14. *Forewords and Afterwords*, p. 417.

15. *Music in the Twentieth Century*, p. 18. Clearly, by "general" Austin means "lacking identifiable constraints." It should be emphasized that Debussy's antiprocessive/syntactic progressions have been enormously important as liberating, catalytic influences.

important to recognize that the possibility of generalization may itself be dependent on stylistic and cultural considerations, and that, as a result, an innovation not at first generalizable may subsequently become so. Equally important, as the discussion of Example 5.1 later in the chapter will indicate, cultural constraints may prevent a generalizable strategy from being used.

Novel means are more likely to be used and replicated if they have *versatility*—that is, if they can function in a variety of compositional circumstances and stylistic situations. For instance, as Example 2.3 makes abundantly clear, some schemata (in this case a succession of linked triads) not only allow for striking differences in expression, but are able to perform very different compositional functions and work as part of markedly disparate stylistic dialects, in this case as the subject of a forcefully dynamic Baroque fugue in Handel's music and as the delicately insinuating theme of a Romantic symphonic movement in Mahler's. Or, to take another well-established schema, a series of continuous thirds can act as the basis of a fugue subject, as it does in the fourth movement of Handel's Concerto Grosso in F Major, Opus 6 No. 2; of an unstable transition between first and second key areas in a sonata-form movement, as it does in the first movement of Mozart's Sonata in A Major for Keyboard and Violin (K. 305/293*d*); of an opening melody of a large symphonic movement, as it does in the first movement of Brahms's Fourth Symphony; and of a "composed fermata" (a prolongation that does not generate significant implications), as it does in the first movement of Beethoven's String Quartet in B♭ Major, Opus 130 (measures 37–39). Specific figures may also be adaptable in the sense that they have a sort of neutrality that allows them to assume a variety of melodic roles. For instance, the figure given in Example 1.3 occurs as a beginning (Example 1.4*a*), as a parenthetical interruption (Example 1.4*c*, mm. 178–81), and as an end (Example 1.5). As with stock figures from Roman comedy to the present, versatility contributes to survival.

Patterns must have sufficient *redundancy*—internal relational reinforcement—to combat the errors that tend to occur in the transmission of information. This is as true of music as it is of natural languages and biological traits.[16] The syntax of tonality, for instance, involves enough redundancy that, if for some reason one or two pitches in a triadic melody or a cadential chord progression are masked and inaudible, a competent listener has a very good chance of being able to guess what the missing tones would have been. And it seems reasonable to suppose that innovations that can withstand errors in transmission—cultural, as well as acoustical, noise—have a better chance of being replicated than patterns that do not. Such redundancy—the redundancy of melody or harmony or rhythm—occurs *within* a single parameter and is primarily psychological. But there is another kind of reinforcement, a kind of systemic redundancy in which different parameters within some realm support or complement one another by fulfilling necessary but different functions. That is, the constraints of a style complement one another, producing what

---

16. The assumption that music does, or should, communicate has been questioned by those members of the avant-garde whom I have called "transcendentalists." See *Music, the Arts, and Ideas*, chaps. 5, 8, and 9.

might be called *strategy sets*. The sketch-analysis of Wagner's music presented in Chapter 2 attempted to describe such a strategy set. Systemic redundancy is clearly an aspect of style. But before considering the ways in which stylistic constraints and special circumstances influence compositional choices, it is important to be clear about the nature of influence itself.

## CHOICE, INFLUENCE, AND COVERT CAUSALISM

Our understanding of influence has to a considerable extent been biased by the scientific model. That model, which emphasized the importance of the discovery of new data and the devising of new theory, was complemented by nineteenth-century beliefs that stressed the value of innovation (as progress). As a result, our age has conceived of creativity almost entirely in terms of the discovery and use of novelty. Investigators have asked, in repeated studies of little children as well as of famous artists and scientists: How are new ideas generated? Where do they come from? What is the role of the unconscious? and so on. Though doubtless of great psychological interest, this concern with causes and sources of innovation has had unfortunate consequences for our understanding of history. For undue emphasis on the generation of novelty has resulted in the almost total neglect of the other facet of creativity—choosing.[17] Of course choosing is always done by some individual. But the constraints that seem most to influence the compositional choices which shape the course of music history are not those peculiar to the psyche of the individual composer, but those of the prevalent musical style and of the larger cultural community.

This last observation has significant implications for our understanding of influence and, ultimately, for our account of style change in the arts. To begin with, it indicates that, although the term *influence* is generally used to refer to relationships within the history of a particular art,[18] anything that affects the choices made by an artist is an influence. Cultural beliefs and attitudes, the predilections of patrons, or acoustical conditions may, for instance, be every bit as influential as prior musical compositions.[19] And some compositions (perhaps Weber's *Der Freischütz*) may have been influential for cultural rather than purely musical/aesthetic reasons.

---

17. As this was being written, an article making some of the same points and a review concerned with some of the same problems appeared in *Science*. The article was B. F. Skinner's "Selection by Consequences"; the review, by Robert C. Cloninger, was of *Cultural Transmission and Evolution* by L. L. Cavalli-Sforza and M. W. Feldman.

18. For a careful discussion of this kind of influence, see Hermerén, *Influence in Art and Literature*.

19. What is usually meant by influence *within* an art is simply a special kind of replication—one in which a particular patterning can be traced to specific features of some earlier work or to characteristic traits of some composer's idiom. The attribution of *influence* is made because it seems improbable that the similarities between the later (influenced) patterning and the earlier one could have occurred solely as a result of shared stylistic constraints. In this connection, see my *Explaining Music* (pp. 73–74), where it is argued that there is *in principle* no difference between similarities (replications) explicitly devised by the composer and those that arise because the constraints of the style make them probable.

The viewpoint being espoused also makes it evident that just as novelty is omnipresent, so possible sources of influence abound—in prior compositions, in the other arts, in ideology, in political and social circumstances, and so on. Since any specific source of influence—for example, an existing composition or cultural belief—is only one among a large number of possibilities available to a composer, it is never more than a *potential* influence. To be an *actual* influence, it must play a part in the composer's process of choosing. And as with innovation, the central and consequential task for history is not showing that influence *occurred,* or even tracing genetic connection, but explaining *why* it took place. Why, that is, out of the multitude of available possibilities did this one become an influence? To put the matter tersely: a pattern, concept, attitude, and so on, is not chosen because it is influential; rather it is influential because it is chosen.

Finally, the nature of influence, like that of creativity, has been misunderstood because emphasis on the source of influence has been so strong that the act of compositional choice has been virtually ignored. And when the importance of the prior source is thus stressed, there is a powerful tendency unwittingly to transform that source into a *cause,* as though the composer's choice were somehow an *effect,* a necessary consequence of the mere existence of the prior source. This corrupting conception of how influence works is at once confirmed and reinforced by our ordinary way of speaking about such matters: for example, saying "Gluck's operas influenced Mozart's" is equivalent to saying that Gluck's operas are the active agents (cause), Mozart's the passive receivers (effect).

Not only our conceptualization of how influence works and our attitudes toward creativity but also our whole way of thinking about the histories of the arts have been biased and ultimately crippled by what might be called *covert causalism.* In this model of temporal change—and it is virtually the only one available in our culture—prior patterns or conditions are routinely regarded as active causal agents, while later events are regularly relegated to the role of being passive, necessary results or effects. All is post hoc, ergo propter hoc.[20]

But there are, as we saw in Chapter 3, noncausal kinds of explanation. The idea of influence is (or should be) one of these. The reason is simple: causal relationships are necessary; influence relationships are not. To assert that a particular piece of music (*A*) or, more generally, a composer's "way of thinking" (*A'*) was influenced by

---

It should also be recognized that not all instances of influence result in similarities of features. For instance, when a composer explicitly avoids being like some powerful predecessor, *negative influence* occurs; or when some stimulus (musical or other) suggests a novel possibility but no features of the stimulus are found in the resulting music, the influence may be characterized as *catalytic.*

20. The prevalence of causalism may in part be responsible for our culture's almost pathological concern with innovation ( = originality). For when works of art are conceptualized (by composers as well as historians) as necessary effects of prior causes (whether compositional or cultural), artists are in effect denied the freedom to choose. Instead of reveling in their power to select *from*—to exploit—the past, artists become anxious lest they be victimized *by* the past. No wonder, then, that they have sought to escape from such imposed indebtedness, either by repudiating the past or by explicitly rejecting causal explanation.

another piece of music ($B$) or by a parameter external to music ($B'$) is not to contend that $B$ or $B'$ caused $A$ or $A'$. Other composers were in all probability exposed to the same piece of music or external conditions without being influenced, or they might have been affected in quite different ways. What is involved in influence is rather making a new compositional option or alternative available to a receptive artistic intelligence. The "new option" might have existed as a possibility for some time but not have been conceptualized as a viable alternative. For instance, writing a choral finale for a symphony was an option possible for Haydn and Mozart, but one not used by either. Beethoven not only recognized and employed the option, but in so doing he called attention to it, so to speak, and thereby influenced the work of a number of later composers.[21]

Once again the question of choice focuses attention on the central issue. Influence allows choice, causation does not. As J. M. Burgers observes, "A choice cannot be directed by a cause, for then it would not be a choice."[22] For instance, were one to observe that "the poor harvest in England in 1830 was caused by bad weather," the statement would be understood to assert that bad weather was a sufficient condition for the poor harvest. (Plants do not choose to flourish or not to flourish.) And were one to argue that the bad harvest led to economic privation, economic privation may still be understood as having been *caused*. But when economic privation is connected with political unrest (with the rioting and the burning of ricks that took place) and ultimately with the passing of the Reform Bill of 1832, one has moved to the realm of influence. For other alternatives might have been chosen: instead of riots there might have been prayers; instead of reform, repression. Poor harvests just a few years earlier had in fact resulted in neither riots nor reform.

Observe that every instance of influence, whether the source be internal or external to the parameter in question, is the result of an *interpretation* made by the individual being influenced. For instance, whether riots led to political reform or to repression depended on the ways in which they were understood and evaluated by the protagonists who were in a position to make consequential choices—Lord Grey, the Duke of Wellington, King William IV, the leaders and members of Parliament, and so on. Such understanding and evaluation, which involves imagining alternative courses of action, envisaging their probable consequences, and choosing among them, is an act of interpretation. In short, influence is manifest as choice, and choice depends on interpretation.[23]

21. Stephen C. Fisher has called my attention to the fact that it was common in Austrian music (to about 1780) for theatrical overtures in several movements to end with an aria, chorus, or ensemble. (See his "Haydn's Overtures and their Adaptations," pp. 67–83). This usage may, through extrapolation (whether conscious or not), have served as a source of Beethoven's innovation.

22. "Causality and Anticipation," p. 195.

23. And, we may add, interpretation always involves some deformation of prior meaning. This is so because any particular set of relationships is the result of an idiosyncratic interaction among the various parameters defining the phenomenon. Interpretation (on which influence depends) necessarily directs attention to some parameters and some relationships rather than others. As a result, cultural transmission through influence is always distorted by the "noise" introduced by interpretation. Influence, then, is Janus-faced; for in the very act of conserving, it creates change.

Similarly in music, influence invariably involves interpretation. It seems reasonable to suggest, for instance, that the Finale of Haydn's String Quartet in F Minor, Opus 20 No. 5, was influenced by Baroque models—by fugal procedures in general and by a typical fugal subject in particular (see Example 2.4). But the result clearly depended on Haydn's interpretation of the subject (e.g., his subject is closed harmonically and rhythmically, while similar ones by Bach and Handel are open) and of the nature of the fugal structure as a whole (e.g., Haydn uses polyphony to create something comparable to sonata form; Bach and Handel write fugues that are more continuous and processive).[24]

In order for the patterning in one parameter to influence that of some other parameter, there must, in addition to interpretation, be *translation*.[25] For instance, according to the viewpoint adopted in this study, the economic conditions caused by the poor harvest of 1830 could not influence political events directly. Rather, economic grievances had to be related, according to a cultural translation code, to political action so that in addition to praying, petitioning, or emigrating, rioting and other political behavior were understood as possible options. Similarly, as discussed both earlier and later in this book, if economic, political, or other circumstances are to influence the history of musical style, they must be translated in such a way that they can affect the choices made by composers.

The translation codes connecting parameters usually vary from one historical/ cultural situation to another because the nature of the translation code depends on the culture's conception of parametric interaction. For instance, whether economic hardship leads to riots, prayer, or emigration depends on the beliefs of the members of the culture about the way the world works. Since our beliefs about the way the world works are based to a considerable extent on culturally sanctioned metaphors, analogues, and models, translation codes are so as well. For this reason, one of the most important innovations in any culture is a change in favored metaphors, analogues, or models. For instance, the organic model, with its attendant metaphors, served as a central code for translating nineteenth-century political, social, and ideological constraints into musical constraints and compositional choices. On a somewhat less en-

---

24. This analysis suggests that the difference between *influence* and *borrowing* lies in the relative importance of interpretation. For example, one would not, I think, say that Brahms's use of a theme by Handel for a set of variations was per se an instance of influence. Rather, because Brahms presents the theme essentially as Handel wrote it—because no act of interpretation is involved—one would say that Brahms borrowed the theme from Handel. But Brahms's use of fugal procedures at the end of the work does involve interpretation, and one might well contend that at that point Brahms was influenced by Baroque models. Since borrowing and influence lie at opposite ends of a continuum, there may be equivocal cases in which it is impossible to decide whether a similarity is an instance of influence or one of borrowing. In such cases, one can only point to those aspects that might be designated as influence and those that might be best thought of as borrowing.

It should be pointed out that, though every instance of influence involves interpretation, not every act of interpretation is an instance of influence. For example, Stravinsky's *Pulcinella* both borrows from *and* interprets Pergolesi's music. But it would seem strange, I think, to suggest that Stravinsky was influenced by Pergolesi. Stravinsky uses Pergolesi's tunes as a way of exhibiting his own stylistic strategies, but this use does not really change those strategies in any fundamental way. Stravinsky might, one feels, have used someone else's music just as well.

25. See Chapter 3, last section, "Explanation in Music History," subsection b.

compassing level, technology has at times significantly influenced intellectual history by furnishing new metaphors and hence new modes of conceptualization, for example, making the nervous system analogous to the telephone system, or human cognition comparable to computer processing.

When the parameters to be connected are tenuously related, translation codes may be difficult to discover and the steps in the translation hard to trace with precision. Just as a translation between related languages (say, from French to English) involves less radical shifts in semantic and syntactic organization than does a translation between unrelated languages (say, from Chinese to English), so it seems easier, in our culture at least, for economic conditions to be translated into political concepts and choices than for political conditions to be translated into musical concepts and choices.

Of all the metaphors used in Western culture, none has been more persistent than that derived from biological change. Especially since the late eighteenth century, the power and prestige of biological models have strongly encouraged the spread of causalism in history.[26] One consequence of this infection was that in histories of the arts beginnings tended unwittingly to be transformed into quasi-causal agents. That is, the origin of a composition, technique, form, or genre came to be understood as shaping its end. Notions such as the germination (or birth), rise (or development), and decline (or death) of X (the *ars nova, opera seria,* tonal harmony) not only attest to the power of the organic model, but imply that later stages of a historical process were already present in presumed beginnings.[27]

Although still current in popular culture and in the backwaters of musicology, biological metaphors have come to seem somewhat simple-minded. The causal paradigm is so powerful in our culture, however, that most of the new metaphors devised to account for historical change have been characterized by a linear succession that allows for genetic interpretation. For instance, the science-derived concept of artistic creativity as problem solving, mentioned in Chapter 4, is not untainted by covert causalism. The antecedent problem tends to be thought of (perhaps unconsciously) as a kind of generating cause, while the consequent solution is willy-nilly understood to be the resulting effect.

Though initially attractive, the problem-solving model is itself, I think, problematic. In its "strong" form, as it occurs in the hard sciences, mathematics, and formalized games and puzzles (e.g., bridge or chess problems, or crossword puzzles), the very notion of a problem implies the possibility of a single correct solution. But such solutions, though they may be possible in some realms, are seldom encountered in the arts. What single problem is correctly solved by Mozart's Symphony No. 40 in

---

26. In this connection, see Solie, "The Living Work," pp. 147–56.

27. Notice in this connection that psychoanalytic accounts of creativity usually combine the covert causalism of the organic model with the mirror metaphor present in the "art reflects the culture (read 'individual') out of which it arises." That is, the experiences of infancy and early childhood, passing through certain more or less preordained phases of development (like an organism), are the seeds (causes) that shape the psyche of the artist (effect); the psyche, thus formed, is reflected in (causes) the character and organization of the work of art created (effect).

G Minor or by Bartók's Sonata for Two Pianos and Percussion? In its "weak" form, the problem-solving model seems more plausible. For in a broad sense, composers face and solve problems, just as politicians, businessmen, and generals do. Nevertheless, there are difficulties with using the notion of problem solving to explain style changes in the arts.

There seems to be little doubt that individual behavior is guided by goals and that achieving such goals involves more or less continual problem solving. For instance, it seems possible to conceive of the relationship between the opening Adagio of Beethoven's String Quartet in B♭ Major, Opus 130, and the Allegro parts of that movement as constituting a problem that the movement as a whole "solves." But in what sense does the movement or the quartet as a whole constitute the solution, or a steppingstone to the solution, of some more general problem of sonata form? With respect to the history of some strategy, form, or genre, the goals to be reached and the problems to be solved are difficult to discern.[28]

The fact that classes of relationships such as strategies, forms, and genres do not have goals, and hence cannot be said to solve problems, does not mean that the history of music is solely a matter of happenstance. Out of the myriad relationships realized in individual compositions at a particular time, those that work well—for instance, those that are consonant with the cognitive constraints described earlier in this chapter and with the ideological constraints to be considered presently—will tend to form stable constraint sets that will be replicated as part of the dialect of the compositional community. But such stable constraint sets are neither a goal nor the solution of some prior problem. The analogy to biological change, as described by François Jacob, is striking:

> There are two levels of explanation for goal-directed processes in living beings and they have frequently been confused. One deals with the individual organism, of which many morphological, biochemical, and behavioral properties clearly appear as goal-oriented. This applies, for instance, to the various phases of reproduction, to the development of the embryo, digestion, respiration, the search for food, escape from predation, migration, and so forth. . . .
>
> The second level of explanation concerns not the individual organism but the whole living world and its present state. . . . Against the argument from design, Darwin showed that a combination of certain mechanisms could actually mimic design; that it was possible to explain what appeared to be goal-directed activities by the chance variation of characteristics, followed by natural selection.[29]

28. Even in the case of individual compositions, the presence of competing goals—satisfying the simultaneous claims of aesthetics, economics, ideology, and so on—makes a more than metaphoric use of the problem-solving model questionable.

29. *The Possible and the Actual*, pp. 13–14.

The problems posed by works of art are elusive and ambiguous. For what we know are the *solutions*—in music, individual compositions. And what we try to do is to infer what the problems *might* have been. In other words, instead of problem solving, the history of music might better be likened to the parlor game in which the participants, historians, are given answers (a work of art, or a group of works of art) and asked to guess the questions that generated the answers. For instance:

*Answer:* "9-W."
*Question:* "Do you spell your name with a 'V,' Herr Wagner?"
(*Answer,* in the original language: "Nein, W.")

Whatever its guise, covert causalism has tended not only to bias historical inquiry by emphasizing origins at the expense of explanatory accounts of style change, but to misdirect those studies that have sought to trace changes from early instances to subsequent exemplifications. This is so because the model virtually requires that the problem of change be formulated in terms of a linear series of complex entities. That is, it has tended to encourage questions such as, What is the origin (source, seed, cause) of some genre (opera), form (sonata form) or procedure (ostinato bass)? But there seems little warrant for supposing that this is the way in which style change usually occurs. Rather change seems mainly to take place not through the gradual transformation of complex entities but through the permutation and recombination of more or less discrete, separable traits or clusters of traits. And the traits involved may come—*be chosen by the composer*—from sources of disparate stylistic and cultural provenance. Finally, covert causalism inclines musicological studies toward a kind of epidemiology in which mere contact (cause) is tacitly taken to be a sufficient condition for influence (effect). As a result scholarship tends to become overly preoccupied with the past whereabouts of manuscripts and the movements of men.

I close this section by suggesting that it is not so much the past that shapes the present but the present which, by selecting from the possibilities provided by an existing abundance, shapes the kind of past that we construct. The present chooses what will influence it and, in so doing, "decides" what its past will be. It follows from this that our understanding of history is necessarily provisional and uncertain. For such understanding depends on our ability to envisage the future—to imagine, that is, what tomorrow's artists will find worth replicating and building upon: how they will reshape the past.

Such envisaging has not been notably reliable because history is not the result of a causal past but of a selective present. For this reason, too, most historical explanation is retrospective. As we have seen, it consists of an attempt, based on relevant evidence, to reconstruct the alternatives that were available to the composer and—considering such matters as the composer's personality, specific cultural circumstances, and prevalent ideological and stylistic constraints—to formulate hypotheses about why he or she made the particular compositional choices being explained.

Since the choice among alternatives is always a matter of probability, historical relationships cannot be established until the implications of the past are known—that is, until particular choices have been made in some present.

Though choosing to be influenced differs from causation in fundamental ways, they are alike in this: just as causes can be connected to effects only in the light of some relational theory,[30] so influences can be connected to choices only in terms of hypotheses about human behavior in specific cultural/stylistic contexts. As with causation, the relationship between data and hypothesis is reciprocal. For instance, though it might be possible (through painstaking research) to discover precisely what Rossini ate for lunch just before he composed what became the overture to *The Barber of Seville,* such information would not be considered data for a history of music because our cultural beliefs (hypotheses) do not connect the consumption of food with compositional choice.[31] But there may be cultures in which just such a connection is made: in which before composing/performing a ritual song about some totem animal, the shaman conducting the ceremony eats part of the animal. And it is not impossible that developments in neurochemical psychology will one day reveal a connection between eating certain foods—for instance, drug-related ones—and the tendency toward, say, innovation in music.[32]

Though influence, like causation, depends on a hypothesis connecting antecedent and consequent events, *influence is not just a weak kind of causation.* Rather, it involves a significant shift in the positioning of the active agent of change. In causation, that agent (the cause) belongs to the set of prior conditions: $X$ causes $y$ (effect). In influence, on the other hand, the active agent of change—the individual who chooses to innovate or to replicate—belongs to the set of subsequent conditions: $x$ is chosen by $Y$ (the artist/agent).

In sum, what I am suggesting is that, beguiled by the blandishments (the seeming simplicity and certainty) of causal models, we have been looking for the reasons for style change at the wrong end of the creative process. It is not that I want to deny the relevance for music history of innovative invention, sources of influence, or origins of musical means. Rather, I am urging that what are primary and central are the bases and reasons for compositional choice. Of these, the constraints of style and cultural circumstances are obviously of great importance.

---

30. In this connection, see the quotation from Hanson, *Patterns of Discovery,* in Chapter 2, at note 47.

31. Such information might, of course, be relevant in some other history: for instance, that of French cuisine, if it were, say, the first instance of the preparation of "tournedos Rossini." Observe, however, that the original instance is worth recording only because the recipe has been frequently replicated, becoming part of the culinary dialect of continental cooking.

32. I hasten to add that it does not follow from the reciprocity of data and theory that theories *determine* facts. Facts exist apart from the theories that make them relationally significant. Were this not so, intellectual history would not exist or would be merely a random succession. For it is in part the recalcitrant presence of discrepant data that necessitates the revision of theory and thereby results in intellectual history.

## STYLE AND CIRCUMSTANCE

### Stylistic Constraints, Compatibility, and Replication

As observed in Chapter 2, the parameters of a musical style tend to form interdependent constraint sets. The constraints governing one parameter usually affect those governing others. Thus Baroque melodies and rhythms "go together," and both are somehow consonant with Baroque harmonic organization. Looked at negatively, the phrase structure of Classic music tends to be incompatible with certain kinds of polyphonic writing—for example, continuous canons and most fugal themes. And it seems plausible to believe that an innovation is more likely to endure through replication if it is compatible with other constraints of the style being employed. For instance, Antonín Reicha's Fugue No. 28 for piano has a time signature of ⅝ + ⅜, while Fugue No. 30 combines ½ and ¾ meters in the fashion seen in Example 5.1. As Václav Jan Sýkora writes in a preface to Reicha's fugues: "Reicha derives his un-

EXAMPLE 5.1.  A. Reicha, Fugue No. 30 from *36 Fugues for the Piano*

usual time-signatures (⅝, ⅜, ⅞ or composite signatures) from the example of folk music, thus anticipating the creative approach of Béla Bartók." [33] But replication, not origin, is clearly the interesting question here. Few of Reicha's contemporaries or followers in the nineteenth century chose to use meters of this kind. One of the reasons for this was that the Romantics preferred the enchanting mystery of the exotic to what seemed to them  its irregularity; for this reason, composers tended to regularize ("civilize") the music of the folk. Also, because the deep connection between phrase structure and tonality could not be abrogated readily, such irregular meters could prevail only when tonality was considerably weakened in the twentieth century.

This is not to assert that, in order to be replicated, innovation must be entirely compatible with prevalent stylistic and cultural constraints. At times a salient innovation necessitates a significant alteration of the entire set of constraints. In other cases, a series of incremental modifications (usually changes in degree rather than kind) results in a trended change that also leads to adjustments in other features of the style. For example, the gradual increase in the size of symphonic movements that occurred during the late eighteenth and nineteenth centuries led to concomitant changes in the organization of sonata-form movements. [34]

33. Preface to Antonín Reicha, *36 Fugues for the Piano,* 1:iv.
34. See Chapter 6; section, "The Size and Structure of Audiences and of Music."

The speed with which an innovation spreads throughout the compositional community, and the degree to which it is amplified, depend not only on whether the innovation is consonant with external as well as internal constraints, but on whether it is replicated in what I call *exemplary* works. By an exemplary work I mean one whose commanding presence is such that its specific means (whether innovative or not), as well as its more general character, have a compositional/cultural impact and resonance that is widespread and inescapable. One thinks perhaps of such works as Josquin's *Missa "Pange lingua,"* Monteverdi's Fifth Book of Madrigals, Bach's *Well-Tempered Clavier,* Handel's *Messiah,* Beethoven's "Appassionata" Sonata and the Ninth Symphony, Wagner's *Tristan,* and Stravinsky's *Le sacre du printemps.* Put differently: because innovation is independent of aesthetic/cultural significance, the first realization of some constraint may occur in an obscure, and perhaps unprepossessing, work.[35] Only at a later time, when called to the attention of the musical community through its embodiment in an exemplary work, does the innovation become part of the prevalent musical dialect.[36] This would appear to be the case with Ferdinand Fischer's *Ariadne musica.* Fischer's composition employed strategies—for instance, of key scheme and of genre (preludes and fugues)—similar to those subsequently employed in the *Well-Tempered Clavier.* But it was through the latter work that the strategic constraints were disseminated and became influential.

Exemplary works not only may encourage large-scale modeling, but may foster the replication of *individual* traits or groups of traits. As whole works, they may also affect style change in a general way, acting as catalytic influences. On the other hand, exemplary works may also affect style history negatively. That is, their musical/cultural presence may be such that they preempt, as it were, a portion of the available stylistic/strategic space. This was perhaps the case with Beethoven's Ninth Symphony. Precisely because its compelling statement spoke so eloquently for the cultural ideals of Romanticism, for another composer to have written a choral symphony before the end of the century would have seemed an act of high hubris and (because the mythic Beethoven became an almost sacred symbol) rash impiety. It should be recognized that works not at first found to be exemplary may subsequently become so. Bach's *St. Matthew Passion* would seem to be such a work. Conversely, works once found to be exemplary—for instance, Weber's *Der Freischütz*—may cease to be so. And if one asks why this should be so, the answer appears to be that what makes a work exemplary is not primarily the integrity and interest of its musical patternings, but its relationship to external circumstances, and especially to values latent in the ideology of culture.[37]

35. Nevertheless, the work may in retrospect—in terms of the implications it is subsequently understood to have had—be regarded as having had notable historical importance.

36. The notion of an "exemplary" work is similar to George Kubler's concept of a "prime" work. But because an influential realization may not be the first instance, but only an effective proclaimer, of novel means, I prefer the term exemplary. See Kubler, *The Shape of Time,* pp. 39–40.

37. Later works of art, involving changes in aesthetic values, may also transform earlier works into exemplars. As André Malraux has pointed out, it is modern art, not research, that has led to an understanding of El Greco's work and has, in this sense, made his art exemplary. See his "Triumph of Art over History," p. 516.

Needless to say, the role of cultural circumstances in encouraging or discouraging the use and replication of novelty is by no means confined to defining the exemplary. Because they are omnipresent, continually impinging on the choices made by composers, events and conditions external to the realm of music are of prime importance. Such external constraints may influence compositional choice either directly, or may do so indirectly, through the mediation of a translation code.

## External Circumstances

DIRECT CONSTRAINTS.
When the connection between external circumstances and compositional choices requires no translation code, it seems uncomplicated and unambiguous—direct. The connection seems unmediated because it is interpreted in terms of the culturally sanctioned causal model. Thus the fact that Mozart wrote a new slow movement for his Symphony in D Major (K. 297/300a) because he wanted to please the Paris audience tends to be interpreted in causal terms. However, though he wrote the movement for this reason, he *chose* to do so; he was not *compelled* to write it. Moreover, a number of alternative movements might have pleased the Parisian public. Thus, though seeming linearity may encourage causal conception, the possibility of alternatives makes it evident that direct constraints act as influences permitting choice, not as causes precluding it. Reasons, then—even "becauses"—are not causes and should not be so interpreted, even though causality is a central concept in our culture.

Because their relationship to compositional choice appears clear and unproblematic, instances of the action of direct constraints are frequently cited in histories of music. For this reason, and because the usually transient circumstances seldom lead to subsequent replication, only two kinds of direct constraints—the wants of performers and the desires of patrons—will be considered here.[38]

The availability and capability of *performers* have had an important influence on compositional choice throughout the history of music. This is most obvious when the number of performers is in some way restricted, as in the cases of Purcell's *Dido and Aeneas* and Stravinsky's *Histoire du soldat,* or when a particular virtuoso is available or has commissioned a work, as in the cases of the Brahms Violin Concerto and Berlioz's *Harold in Italy.* And this reminds us that the desire of performers for music that shows their special skills to advantage has at times led composers to include left-hand pizzicatos in works for violin, coloratura passages in operatic arias, and so on. The influence of the temperament, as well as the capabilities, of perform-

38. Some of the constraints discussed in Chapter 4 as being reasons for innovation may also affect the choices actually made by a composer (see the section "Specific cultural/musical conditions"). For instance, the physical setting may influence the choice of instruments for a work intended for outdoor performance.

ers on what the composer chooses is strikingly illustrated by the relationship between Mozart and the singer Anton Raaff. As Mozart wrote his father in 1778:

> One must treat a man like Raaff in a particular way. I chose these words on purpose, because I knew that he already had an aria on them: so of course he will sing mine with greater facility and more pleasure. I asked him to tell me candidly if he did not like it or if it did not suit his voice, adding that I would alter it if he wished or even compose another. "God forbid," he said, "the aria must remain just as it is, for nothing could be finer. But please shorten it a little, for I am no longer able to sustain my notes." "Most gladly," I replied, "as much as you like." . . . When I took leave of him he thanked me most cordially, while I assured him that I would arrange the aria in such a way that it would give him pleasure to sing it. For I like an aria to fit a singer as perfectly as a well-made suit of clothes.[39]

Some years later, Mozart composed another aria for the aging Raaff; his care and effort have been described by Daniel Heartz:

> The fragile voice of Raaff required extraordinarily careful treatment. As the voice enters, Mozart switched to the tenor clef, bringing him in on a sustained F, led up to by a little connecting passage in thirds by the clarinets and bassoons. . . . Raaff needed to hear this. The F has no competition because all the strings . . . are scored under the voice. Later the violins climb up and help him by playing (no doubt very softly) in unison with the vocal line. His vocal part is confined to a very small range, from the fifth below middle C to the fifth above.[40]

Not infrequently, peculiarities of *patronage* directly affect the choices made by composers. For instance, not only was Bach's choice of the theme for the *Musical Offering* partly a result of his desire to please Frederick the Great, but, according to David Hughes, "although most of the *Musical Offering* is in a severely Baroque contrapuntal style, there are places in the first fugue and in the trio sonata that show a more open and relaxed manner. Perhaps Bach was here deferring to Frederick's preference for modern simplicity."[41] And, seeking the patronage of a later king of Prussia, Mozart chose to make the cello prominent in all three of his "Prussian" quartets because Friedrich Wilhelm played that instrument.

Patronage may also be institutional. "The army, the navy, the church, and the

---

39. Anderson, trans. and ed., *Letters of Mozart* 2:735–36.
40. "Raaff's Last Aria," p. 527.
41. *History of European Music,* p. 308.

stage," not to mention governments and (in recent years) universities and foundations, have all commissioned works, often for specific occasions, and have all, explicitly or implicitly, stipulated constraints—e.g., about place of performance, number of players, length or character of composition—that in one way or another led to particular compositional choices. Institutions have also influenced compositional choice in broader, more lasting ways by acting as censors, usually conservative ones. Thus the Council of Trent stipulated general sets of constraints that sought to discourage secular influences and generally to simplify musical relationships, while the requirements of socialist realism, which discouraged Soviet composers from experimenting with nontonal means, evidently had a not unimportant effect on the choices made by composers such as Shostakovich.

Audiences, too, are patrons—albeit collective ones—whose special predilections and prejudices tend to affect what composers choose. To cite one well-known instance: to please French taste (as many before him—Lully, Gluck, Mozart, Beethoven, and Meyerbeer—had sought to do), Wagner wrote a ballet for the Paris performance of *Tannhäuser*.

Similarly, performers, whether professional or amateur, are patrons whose needs and taste often influence what composers select. To take the clearest kind of case: sets of pieces—from Bach's Inventions to Debussy's *Etudes* for piano—are designed explicitly to teach by requiring performance in a variety of keys or modes and the practice of characteristic technical problems such as the clear playing of contrapuntal lines or the clean execution of arpeggios and consecutive octaves. The pedagogical desiderata of such patron-performers will tend to affect the choices made by composers.

At times the choices of composers have also been influenced by publishers, sometimes indirectly, because of knowledge of what publishers want, and sometimes directly, through commissions. As is often the case, commissions, though fostering the production of compositions, affect compositional choice by establishing restrictive conditions with regard to matters of genre, duration, difficulty, and instrumentation. Occasionally publishers have interfered directly in the organization of a work. An unequivocal instance involves the Finale of Beethoven's String Quartet in B♭ Major, Opus 130. The publisher, Artaria, had misgivings about whether the quartet would sell with the Grosse Fuge as the last movement. Through a combination of flattery and money, Beethoven was persuaded to compose a new Finale.[42]

Patrons, whether individual, institutional, or collective, are, in a sense, especially powerful critics. Maynard Solomon explicitly connects criticism, patronage, and compositional choice: "The critics did not respond favorably to [*Fidelio*], and Beethoven's friends, led by the Lichnowskys [patrons], urged drastic revisions . . . preparatory to a revival."[43] If critical blame tends to act as a negative influence, favorable evaluation acts as a reinforcing one. Thus Hanslick's praise of Brahms's

42. In this connection, see Solomon, *Beethoven*, pp. 323–24.
43. Ibid., p. 144.

music, or Adorno's of Schoenberg's, probably encouraged those composers to choose within the same broad range of existing possibilities.

INDIRECT CONSTRAINTS.

Although they often affect compositional choice, direct constraints do not for the most part play a central role in the shaping of style history. And unless they significantly change our understanding of the world, this is also true of specific political events, economic conditions, scientific discoveries, and the like. For instance, the Russian Revolution, the Great Depression, and even the control of nuclear energy have led to few deeply significant shifts in the ideological outlook of Western culture.

This is not to deny that particular events and local circumstances may encourage the devising and even the initial use of strategies. We have seen that they do. But such events and circumstances can seldom explain why strategies are replicated, either as part of a composer's idiom or as part of the dialect of the musical community. For instance, while Beethoven evidently included Russian folk tunes in his Opus 59 string quartets in order to please his patron, Count Razumovsky, this short-term, local circumstance cannot account for the prevalence of folk tunes in much of the art music of the nineteenth century.

What accounts for such prevalence is the constraints of ideology—the beliefs and attitudes of the members of some culture, including composers. Occasional events and particular circumstances may transcend their particular confining contexts, however, when they modify ideology. Whether modification occurs depends on the nature and state of the prevalent ideology. Consider, for instance, the influence of a natural event such as an earthquake on human history. Though some cultures may consider earthquakes the result of the anger of the gods at some sacrilegious act, our cultural beliefs tell us that human actions do not influence the occurrence or the force of earthquakes. Nor do earthquakes usually have more than a transient effect on human behavior. But this need not be the case. Because the devastating Lisbon earthquake of 1755 occurred during a time of intense debate between religious orthodoxy and scientific skepticism, it had a significant effect on Western intellectual history. The San Francisco quake of 1906, on the other hand, had virtually no influence on the larger movements of history.[44]

What I am urging, then, is that events in the world of action be considered significant because of what they are understood to *lead* to. And of all the things that they may lead to, none is more important than their influence on ideology. In short, the Lisbon earthquake (casting doubt on religious orthodoxy), the conquests of Napoleon (encouraging nationalism), the publication of Darwin's *Origin of Species* (emphasizing the ubiquity of competition and gradual change), and the detonation of

---

44. Except to the extent that the disaster, like that of Pompeii (as well as Lisbon), came to represent some sort of limit. See the discussion of this aspect of history under "Manifestation," Chapter 3.

the atomic bomb (dramatizing the destructive power of civilization) were momentous events because they influenced ideology by modifying values and goals and, in so doing, somewhat changed the dominance relationships among cultural parameters.

Despite the occurrence of such momentous events, striking changes in institutions, and novel scientific theories, ideologies tend to endure because their most fundamental tenets—about creation and causality, time and human destiny, and so on—are not readily abrogated or replaced. For instance, as argued in the last part of this book, the essential tenets of Romanticism have persisted for some two hundred years. Nevertheless, impelled by the ideological valuing of originality, individuality, nationalism, and gradual (progressive) change, composers of the nineteenth century devised novel strategies for realizing the larger ideological goals of natural, unmediated musical experience.[45]

The persistence of ideology is important for methodological reasons. If it is ideology that most significantly affects compositional choice, then it becomes possible to consider the connection between culture and style history without continually referring the latter to specific political, economic, scientific, and philosophical events and developments. If this viewpoint has merit, it follows that, as long as agreement can be reached about the nature of the ideology being considered, its genesis need not be an issue. Thus if the Marxists, for instance, want to posit that the ideology of a culture is the necessary consequence of the prevalent economic system and its attendant power structure, the music historian need not enter the fray—either for or against. That is, just as the music theorist can take the set of cognitive/perceptual constraints as given, without inquiring into their origins, so the historian of musical style can take a particular set of cultural/ideological constraints as given without inquiring into their origins.[46] The persistence of the basic tenets of an ideology also makes it plausible to suppose that high-level musical constraints—the rules of a style—remain constant over long stretches of time. And this makes reasonable an account of style change in terms of trends and emphases—an account in which fundamental rules and goals remain constant while the strategies for realizing them are modified.

In Part III, I will attempt a rough sketch of what such an account might be by considering how the ideology of Romanticism affected the history of nineteenth-century music. But before embarking on this perilous journey, it seems important to make clear what will be meant by *ideology*.

## CODETTA AND TRANSITION: IDEOLOGY

The term *ideology,* as it is used in this study, refers to a complex network of interre-

45. Perhaps post-Renaissance ideology, of which Romanticism is a part, has endured because no viable alternative has been developed. And until a new way of understanding, envisaging, and choosing is at hand, modification and qualification are preferable to the hazards and uncertainties of untried and unfamiliar substitutes.

46. I am acutely aware that there is a problem with this position: namely, that it is difficult, if not impossible,

lated beliefs and attitudes consciously or unconsciously held by the members of some culture or subculture. As José Ortega y Gasset has put it:

> It follows that man must ever be grounded on some belief, and that the structure of his life will depend primordially on the beliefs on which he is grounded; and further that the most decisive changes in humanity are changes of belief, the intensifying or weakening of beliefs. The diagnosis of any human existence, whether of an individual, a people or an age, must begin by establishing the repertory of its convictions. . . . I have spoken of them as a repertory to indicate that the plurality of beliefs on which an individual, a people or an age is grounded never possesses a completely logical articulation, that is to say, does not form a system of ideas such as, for example, a philosophy constitutes or aims at constituting. The beliefs that coexist in any human life, sustaining, impelling, and directing it, are on occasion incongruous, contradictory, at the least confused.[47]

The deep-seated beliefs, attitudes, and values that form the fundamental basis of an ideology constitute the unconscious categories and often unarticulated premises that channel and direct our perceptions, our cognitions, and our responses, in short, our understanding and experience of ourselves and the world. They involve not only such things as beliefs about the nature of causal relationships and of time, but the ubiquitous metaphors that at once inform and color our outlook, telling us, as observed in Chapter 4, that up, fast, and light are generally "good" while down, slow, and dark are generally "bad." Shading into these fundamental ways of interpreting experience, and perhaps more easily modified, are a culture's more consciously held beliefs about the world. As examples that have been important in recent Western ideology one might mention beliefs about the desirability of social progress, the importance of originality, and the value of aesthetic experience.

Like language, an ideological network is "a composite of elements of very different age, some of its features reaching back into the mists of an impenetrable past, others being the product of a development of yesterday."[48] Thus, while its most fundamental premises may resist modification, an ideology is not "prohibitive of variation and change; it is not a closed logical system of beliefs and premises but rather a historically derived psychological system open to change."[49] In other words, though the strands of the network usually support or complement one another, discrepancies and contradictions may arise within an ideology without destroying it. Our culture,

---

to separate the presumed origins of an ideology (or anything else) from our understanding of its nature. Nevertheless, at this stage of cultural history, such separation may be a prudent strategy.

47. "History as a System," pp. 283–84.

48. Edward Sapir, quoted in Hoijer, "Relation of Language to Culture," p. 557. Hoijer uses the term *cultural metaphysics* to designate what I am calling *ideology*. I prefer the latter term because it carries fewer implications of explicit conscious systematization.

49. Ibid., p. 561.

for instance, has at one and the same time in the past maintained such disparate pairs of beliefs as the following: there are necessary (determinist) laws of historical change, but men have free will; and great works of art are the expression of the innermost being of the individual artist, yet such works are universal.

Moreover, aspects of the larger cultural ideology may be modified, omitted, or contradicted in one or more of the particular subcultures. Or two subcultures may differ even on some fundamental issue. Often such discrepancies within and between subcultures are not apparent even to members of the groups because no direct confrontation of beliefs takes place. But when differences between subcultural ideologies are very marked, or when there is a direct clash between incompatible tenets within an ideology, some sort of accommodation or modification will, as a rule, take place within the larger network. And until such adjustment occurs, the culture involved will tend to be characterized by instability and tension. Witness, for instance, the conflict in our own culture between the claims of equal opportunity and those of individual merit.

Cultural ideologies are not, then, consistent, unitary systems. This is so for two main reasons. First, the myriad economic, political, religious, ethnic, and professional groups that constitute any culture select, combine, and weight in distinctive ways the beliefs and attitudes prevalent in the larger culture; at times, they devise novel variants of their own, which may then become part of the greater ideological composite. And the individuals that make up such groups are not ideological monoliths. Each belongs to a number of subcultures; as he or she moves from one group context to another, assuming somewhat different roles, shifts in the individual's ideological stance take place.[50]

Second, ideological inconsistencies arise because many aspects of culture are hierarchically organized. Individuals combine to form small groups such as the family, part of a business firm, or a string quartet; these groups in turn form larger units such as political communities, corporations, or musicians' unions; and so it continues until national or supranational organizations are formed. As observed in Chapter 4, the constraints governing such hierarchies are usually discontinuous (changing slightly but significantly from one level to the next), and the resulting discrepancies tend to generate ideological inconsistencies and conflicts. In our own culture such differences continually confront us: the values of individual privacy often conflict with the requirements of national security, the ideals of individual choice may be at odds with belief in the need for group solidarity, and so on.

It must be emphasized that, though aspects of an ideology may be linked to hierarchic aspects of culture, the ideologies themselves are not hierarchically structured. That is, there is no reigning Zeitgeist, no single idea or ideal, at the apex of

---

50. Such subcultural ideologies, as pointed out earlier, are fostered and sustained by formal and informal social arrangements—e.g., political parties, artistic movements, professional gatherings. For instance, politicians tend to associate with other politicians, and even ones of different persuasions usually have comparable backgrounds (often legal), read more or less the same literature, and so on. Such subcultures often have their own literatures, which are important for the perpetuation and transmission of the beliefs and attitudes of the subideology.

some ideological tree-structure. Rather, as already observed, ideologies are composites of disparate ages and diverse provenance. Or, to change the image, a cultural ideology is comparable to a complex polyphonic passage performed by an ensemble whose players group and regroup themselves in a variety of ways; the polyphonic texture itself consists of a host of coexisting voices which, while differing in both importance and independence, interact in the presentation of myriad motives—some enduring, others ephemeral, some similar, others contrasting.

This polyphony of beliefs and attitudes should not be confused with what is called the "history of ideas." For the latter realm—mostly comprising the histories of disciplines such as philosophy and natural science, theology and social theory—is, so to speak, only the "upstairs," the salon, of ideology. It is the part characterized by the meticulous refinement of carefully considered hypotheses and coherent argument. What reigns "downstairs" in the scullery is what I have called cultural scuttlebutt—a kind of conceptual gossip that mixes novel terms and ideas from upstairs with already established cultural beliefs and attitudes. Connecting these realms is, to continue the metaphor, the mezzanine of popularization. Beethoven, for instance, did not read Kant. Indeed, he refused even to attend lectures on Kant. Nevertheless,

> this should not be regarded as minimizing Kant's impact on Beethoven. Indeed, Kant's impact extended to all of his educated contemporaries. Heine wrote: "In the year 1789 . . . nothing else was talked of in Germany but the philosophy of Kant, about which were poured forth in abundance commentaries, chrestomathies, interpretations, estimates, apologies, and so forth." . . . As did most of his contemporaries, *Beethoven understood Kant in a sloganized and simplified form.*[51]

And so it has been with theories such as those of Newton, Malthus, Darwin, Einstein, and Freud; and with philosophies such as those of Hume, Hegel, Nietzsche, Peirce, and Dewey.[52]

But popularization does more than merely sloganize and simplify. It makes it possible for upstairs formulations to be transformed into downstairs scuttlebutt. Because meanings are defined, concepts and problems legitimated, and terms established with respect to specific paradigms, the theories and methods promulgated upstairs (in intellectual history) cannot readily interact with one another or with other realms of culture. When a direct "transplant" is attempted a kind of "immune reaction" occurs—the graft cannot "take." By removing high-culture formulations from their highly specific theoretical and historical contexts, popularization at once generalizes and neutralizes, blurring the finely drawn distinctions and the meanings that particular disciplines attach to terms, ideas, and procedures. With their precision

---

51. Solomon, *Beethoven,* p. 37; emphasis added.
52. The popularization of Newton's *Principia* is discussed in Cohen, "The Newtonian Scientific Revolution," pp. 39–42.

thus attenuated, formerly subtle and sophisticated ideas can circulate and find a home in the scullery. There, reworked through metaphor, model, and analogue, they become attached to other disciplines and contexts, some of which belong to the high culture.[53]

Ideology, as I intend the term, is to be found, then, not on any one of the cultural levels, but on all of them. And it includes the interactions that occur when ideas and theories, popularizations and scuttlebutt move up and down the stairs in the cultural mansion, changing meaning and importance as well as position. Finally, it should be emphasized that ideology is not an entity, like a document or an artifact, but a construct devised at a specific time and place by a historian (whether a professional or a layman) with particular beliefs and attitudes. In short, the pattern constructed, selected from the wealth of available data, depends on the ideology of the historian. As I write this book, and especially the next and last part, I am acutely aware of being at once the beneficiary of ideology and its victim. There is no escape.

53. For instance, popularizations of Freud have influenced high-culture novelists and historians, while scuttlebutt about Heisenberg's "uncertainty principle" has presumably affected the thinking of upstairs composers.

Popularization, the removal of an idea or theory from its peculiar connection with its original conceptual context, is analogous to taking verses from a poem or a speech from a play and quoting them separately—for instance, reciting Macbeth's "Tomorrow and tomorrow" speech. The lines are deprived of the context of plot (the death of Lady Macbeth and the approaching battle), but they acquire a kind of universality. And perhaps a great idea, like great lines of poetry, is one that arises out of a peculiar conceptual context yet is general enough to function in a number of other contexts.

# PART III:

## Music and Ideology: A Sketch-History of Nineteenth-Century Music

I have observed that ideologies consist of constraints of very different ages and of significantly diverse provenance. Partly for these reasons they are replete with inconsistencies and contradictions, as well as with connections. This is especially pertinent in the case of Romanticism. As John Warrack points out, one of its salient characteristics

> is its apparent contradictoriness—ambitions for the future mingling with dreams of the past; a determination to overthrow coupled with nostalgia for the rejected world of order and balance; fervent brotherhood yet the exaltation of the individual; proud selfconsciousness yet the sense of acute isolation; the assertion of Man yet an ache for the lost God.[1]

Because Romanticism is so rich and variegated, often characterized by incompatible beliefs and attitudes, many strands of the ideological network as well as many aspects of musical style have necessarily been neglected in the sketch I will present.

These omissions are not, I think, crucial. This is so not only because, as considered in Chapter 3, no history is ever complete or definitive. It is also because my sketch-history is intended to suggest a way of constructing a music history that posits no *a priori* pattern of change yet is more than a succession of essentially discrete synchronic frames chronologically arranged. It is in this area—that of methodology—that problems arise.

In neither music nor ideology is there a single, coherent linear succession. Rather, each consists of a collection of more or less independent, but intricately interrelated, strands that coexist over time. Whatever interactions take place between

---

1. John Warrack, "Romantic," *The New Grove Dictionary* ed. Stanley Sadie, 16:141–42.

the two areas are always mediated by the vagaries of interpretation. Two disparate dangers arise. On the one hand, the enormous richness and variety of each area make it tempting to search for, and easy to find, plausible parallels and presumed homologies between salient features and characteristic processes, simply by picking and matching with indiscriminate diligence. On the other hand lie the hazards of vacuous platitude and vague generality that tend to appear when areas are correlated in terms of overall character, affective tone, and the like.

These difficulties are compounded because, instead of being a coherent and consistent system, culture (including ideology) is like a richly variegated but persisting environment that influences (but does not determine) the choices made by composers. Like local environmental events (storms, droughts, earthquakes), particular political, economic, and social occurrences will, unless they are catastrophic, produce more or less local perturbations. For this reason the influence of commissions, commemorations, local political, economic, or social circumstances, and so forth, will not be considered in the following sketch. But the fundamental beliefs and attitudes of an ideology, once they are established, tend to persist with tenacity, though they may, as we shall see, manifest themselves in a variety of different ways.[2]

This way of looking at ideology will form the basis for how I handle (not solve) the methodological problem of the interaction between coexisting variables. I will treat Romanticism as an essentially stable and enduring network of interrelated beliefs and attitudes. This network will be understood both as the environment in which compositional choices are made and as the generator of stylistic change.[3] The kinds of changes that occur are for the most part what I have called trended changes. Put briefly: my analysis of ideology will be largely synchronic, while my discussion of music will, insofar as possible, be diachronic.

What follows is divided into three chapters. The first is primarily concerned with the ideology of Romanticism: its social and political bases, its central beliefs and attitudes, and some of its general implications for the aesthetics of music. The next two chapters are concerned to show some of the ways in which the tenets of Romanticism were translated into and influenced the musical choices made by nineteenth-century composers.

2. It might be objected that ideology cannot account for the particular patterns and features of a specific composition. But the objection is not well taken. For unless a particular pattern or trait is replicated, especially on the level of dialect, it is of little interest for style history. And, one might add, the more a trait is replicated, the more we want to know why it was chosen.

3. Influence is not, of course, a one-way street, running only, say, from politics to ideology to music. It runs the other way as well. For while our cultural beliefs and the dominance of parameters make it difficult to discern an instance in which music changed ideology or politics, there is little doubt that music has often confirmed beliefs and attitudes, acting as a reinforcing influence.

# CHAPTER 6

# Romanticism—The Ideology of Elite Egalitarians

It seems probable that Western culture has from its beginnings been marked by a tension between the claims of Apollonian classicism and those of Dionysian romanticism. Classicism has been characterized by a valuing of shared conventions and rational restraint, the playful exploitation of established constraints and the satisfaction of actuality (Being), the coherence of closed forms and the clarity of explicit meanings; while romanticism has been characterized by a valuing of the peculiarities of individual innovation and the yearning arising from potentiality (Becoming), the informality of open structures and the suggestiveness of implicit significance.

> Classic art was conceived by the German critics as "beauty"; romantic art as "energy." Classic was universal and ideal; romantic was individual and "characteristic." Classic was plastic (like sculpture), finite, closed, pure in genre. Romantic was picturesque (like painting), infinite, open, mixed.[1]

Countless critics and historians of the arts have remarked upon the continuing oscillation from one of these general outlooks to the other.[2]

Each romantic phase, like each classic one, is, of course, different from every other one. This is so not only because the stylistic constraints governing the actualization of characteristic values are different for each phase, but because, even when they exhibit similar traits, the phases will have had different histories.[3] But the romanticism that we will be concerned with—the movement begun in the eighteenth

---

1. Wimsatt and Brooks, *Literary Criticism*, p. 368.

2. Particular traits taken to be typical of one outlook may, of course, occur in works otherwise grouped with the other. For instance, characteristics of romanticism have been found in Mozart's music, and classic ones are said to occur in the music of Brahms.

3. In other words, as observed in Chapter 1, what something is—what it means to us and how we comprehend it—is inextricably linked to what led to it and what follows it.

century and continued into our own time—is not merely different. It is not just that it seems more extreme and pervasive. Rather it constitutes a radical departure—a difference in kind.

The latest romanticism differs from all other romanticisms in this: Instead of being but a phase within a periodic swing in the inclinations and beliefs of the artistic/intellectual community, this romanticism formed part of a profound change—revolution is not too strong a term—in social, political, and ideological outlook. "It was a reorientation, along many lines, as fundamental as that of the Renaissance, and its results are still being worked out." [4] At its core, I will argue, was an unequivocal and uncompromising repudiation of a social order based on arbitrary, inherited class distinctions. This rejection was not confined to the arts or philosophy; rather it penetrated every corner of culture and all levels of society. It was, and is, Romanticism with a capital *R*.

Although the roots of this Romanticism extended back to the Renaissance and Reformation—for instance, to the growing emphasis on the worth of the individual, the widened perspective fostered by the discovery of new lands and cultures, and the dazzling achievements of the natural sciences—its prime driving force was a political and social radicalism that defined itself "as the antithesis of feudal Christianity . . . Jules Michelet, the great republican historian and polemicist, pitted the old regime, which was based upon Arbitrary Grace—ascriptive hierarchies reigning according to *bon plaisir*—against a new society grounded in Necessary Justice." [5] As Rousseau, its most polemical and influential spokesman, explicitly avowed, "I had attained the insight that everything is a bottom dependent on political arrangements, that no matter what position one takes, a people will never be otherwise than what its form of government makes it." [6] The revolt against rules and conventions that sanctioned political prerogative and social privileges—against an unjust, arbitrary "system that subordinated useful talent to mere birth" [7]—was economic as well as political; for "all inequalities can be reduced to rich and poor." [8]

## REPUDIATION OF CONVENTION

Though Rousseau's views are familiar, almost to the point of being cultural clichés, the denigration of convention so profoundly affected the choices made by Romantic composers that a capsule summary is warranted:

    4. Artz, *Renaissance to Romanticism*, p. 223. Some will doubtless disagree with the breadth that I will be giving to the concept of *Romanticism*, preferring to restrict the term to the movement in philosophy and the arts that took place in the late eighteenth and early nineteenth centuries. But I simply do not know what else to call the profound revolution that I am attempting to characterize and to relate to the changes that have taken place in music since the last part of the eighteenth century and are still occurring at the end of the twentieth.
    5. Auspitz, *The Radical Bourgeoisie*, p. 4.
    6. *Confessions*, quoted in Cassirer, *Rousseau, Kant, Goethe*, p. 27.
    7. Shklar, "Jean-Jacques Rousseau and Equality," p. 14. Thus in 1792 Beaumarchais valued the applause of "citizens who recognized no superiority but that accorded to merit or to talent" (quoted in Porter, "Notes on *Le Nozze di Figaro*," n.p.
    8. Shklar, "Jean-Jacques Rousseau and Equality," p. 15.

Man was born free, equal, self-sufficient, unprejudiced, and whole; now, at the end of history, he is in chains (ruled by other men or by laws he did not make), defined by relations of inequality (rich or poor, noble or commoner, master or slave), dependent, full of false opinions or superstitions, and divided between his inclinations and his duties.[9]

But the repudiation was by no means confined to social, political, and economic realms. Whatever was deemed arbitrary or artificial, grounded in convention, or the basis for distinction and privilege was called into question. Philosophy, religion, and language, and above all, beliefs about art were involved.

The revolution in thought represented by the Enlightenment received enormous impetus from the convincing success of science, which had long since repudiated the authority of the Church and Scripture. What was crucial was not so much new knowledge as the new method of acquiring knowledge and understanding. For the deductive, *a priori* method characteristic of Scholasticism—a method used to rationalize the organization of the ancien régime—science had substituted an empiricism that was egalitarian in the sense that it depended on no antecedent knowledge of texts and hermeneutic traditions. Rather, it was presumably based on the direct, virtually naïve, observation of what was there in nature for all to see. The philosophical psychologies that came to be associated with this empiricism were also essentially egalitarian. Whether constrained by Kantian categories, ordered by the unmediated observation of positivism, or shaped by the pure perceptions of phenomenology, experience rather than authority was considered to be the source of true knowledge.

Already weakened by the skeptical spirit of the Enlightenment—coupled with the prestige accorded science—established religious beliefs, texts, and institutions were also repudiated: "In religion also Rousseau rejects any dependence on external authority and any subjection to it. This at once excludes tradition as a religious source. . . . The principle of mere Scriptural authority is hence abandoned once and for all."[10] This abandonment had important consequences for the Romantic ideology of art. For the cultural niche previously occupied by traditional religious belief and ritual came to be filled, at least in part, by pantheism.[11] One learned moral truth not from authority ("sages") but directly from God, who was omnipresent in nature:[12]

One impulse from a vernal wood
May teach you more of man
Of moral evil and of good
Than all the sages can.
        (Wordsworth, "The Tables Turned")

9. Bloom, "Education of Democratic Man," p. 135.
10. Cassirer, *Rousseau, Kant, Goethe*, p. 45.
11. The niche was filled also in part by a devout reverence for art and the adoration of artists as divinely inspired creators.
12. The central importance of Nature in Romanticism is discussed below in the section entitled "The Glorification of Nature: Organicism."

Language, too, was suspect. First, differences in vocabulary, dialect, and pronunciation were inescapable and invidious signs of class distinctions. Second, the growing awareness of the diversity and variability of languages made it obvious that they were more or less arbitrary and artificial. Particularly in literature, the paraphernalia of grammatical rules and rhetorical devices exemplified conventionality. To cite but one device, allegory was rejected because it was

> arbitrary: the connection between the signifier and the signified is imposed by the mind or fancy, while the eye and imagination are aware primarily of the difference. The symbol, on the other hand, is a motivated sign, a synecdoche, in which the signifier is naturally connected to the signified. Allegory for Coleridge is an instance of "mechanic form" . . . whereas the symbol is a case of "organic form" based on the intuitive grasp of *natural relationship.*[13]

The depreciation of language had especially important consequences for music. It not only encouraged the view that music was the exemplary art. As Robert Schumann put it, "Music speaks the most universal language which arouses the soul in freedom, without specific constraints, yet the soul feels itself at home in it."[14] It also contributed to the growing prestige of instrumental music: "Music has developed into a self-sufficient art, *sui generis,* dispensing with words."[15] Perhaps even more important, the denigration of language was in part responsible for a significant change that occurred in the aesthetics and theory of music: the change from a conceptual model derived from language to one based on organic growth.[16]

The denigration of language as a collection of arbitrary rules supporting class distinctions was more than matched by the ideology's vehement repudiation of the artificial and conventional in art. Anton F. J. Thibaut, for instance, writes, "How easy it is for art to become unnatural . . . and how often do we find music, laboriously composed by mere artifice, uninspired by any real spontaneous emotion."[17] Victor Hugo observes that whatever is systematic becomes "false, trivial and conventional," and he condemns "our petty conventional rules."[18] Franz Liszt declares that Chopin "did violence to the peculiar nature of his genius when he endeavoured to subject it to rules, to classifications and to regulations not of his own making."[19]

---

13. Culler, "Literary History, Allegory and Semiology," p. 263; emphasis added.

14. Schumann, "Music as a Universal Language," excerpted in *Music and Aesthetics in the Eighteenth and Early Nineteenth Centuries,* ed. Peter le Huray and James Day, p. 489. Hereafter *Music and Aesthetics in the Eighteenth and Early Nineteenth Centuries* will be referred to as "le Huray and Day."

15. Herder, *Kalligone,* quoted in le Huray and Day, p. 257.

16. In this connection, see below. When the use of language was inescapable, as it was in many songs and operas written in the nineteenth century, it was to be "natural" rather than artificial. Thus Wagner, for instance, considered that "the kind of verse he was soon to write for the *Ring* dramas was a return to the language of a Golden Age before it was spoiled by the sophisticated overlay of a more complex civilization" (Stein, *Richard Wagner,* p. 71).

17. *On Purity in Musical Art,* p. 67.

18. "Preface to *Cromwell,*" pp. 357, 363.

19. *Life of Chopin,* p. 13.

And according to Wagner, "The most perfect form of art . . . is that wherein all vestiges of conventionality are completely removed from the drama as well as from the music." [20]

## ACONTEXTUALISM AND EGALITARIANISM

Despite the fact that political beliefs and attitudes gave it force and direction, Romanticism did not include an explicit program of social change. [21] Nevertheless, the rejection of the older order profoundly affected ideology. One of the most important consequences of this rejection was the emphatic denial of the relevance of origins and contexts. In the ancien régime, artificialities of birth and lineage established one's position in society and determined benefits and rights available to each individual. The new ideology not only repudiated such hereditary privileges, but insisted on the irrelevance of *all* origins, lineages, and contextual connections whatsoever. Inheritance was to be replaced by inherence—an inherence that was at once natural and necessary. This significant and continuing tenet of Romanticism I will call *acontextualism*.

### Acontextualism and the Past

To repudiate lineage—to espouse acontextualism—would seem to deny the relevance of the past. Yet the nineteenth century was intensely concerned with history, not only as a field of inquiry but as a subject for works of art. To understand how acontextualism was integrated with an intense concern with history, it is necessary, first of all, to distinguish between the beliefs of historians and the theories of history proposed by philosophers. The historians believed that writing history could and should be an objective, positivistic act of discovery that, like scientific investigation, apprehended and recounted the facts without prior prejudice or preconception. Influential historians such as Michelet, Ranke, Tocqueville, and Burckhardt "all agreed that a true history should be written without preconceptions, objectively, out of an interest in the facts of the past for themselves alone, and with no aprioristic inclination to fashion the facts into a formal system." [22] From this point of view, the ideals of historical scholarship were consonant with the ideas of acontextualism.

General theories of historical change were also compatible with acontextualism, but for other reasons. In this case, it is necessary to consider the change that occurred during the eighteenth century in the culture's beliefs about the natural and social worlds. The old order conceived of the world as a fixed, eternal hierarchy,

---

20. Quoted in Stein, *Richard Wagner*, p. 167.

21. It needed none since its promulgators and supporters had already attained the power they sought and now favored only gradual, incremental change.

22. White, *Metahistory*, p. 142.

each component of which—rocks, plants, and animals; serfs, burghers, and no-bility—had a preordained place in the divine plan. During the Enlightenment this fixed hierarchy of Being gave way to views that emphasized the ubiquity of change and development—a world of Becoming. The preeminent manifestation of this change in ideology was, of course, the theory of evolution, which received its classic formulation toward the middle of the nineteenth century.

What needs to be recognized was that the theory of evolution was one of *natural* change and development. Lineage, it seems, could be allowed if it was natural and necessary rather than artificial and arbitrary. And it is scarcely surprising that many philosophers of history searched for inherent, and hence natural, patterns of historical change—organic growth (Herder), dialectic development (Hegel and Marx), and cyclic processes (Wölfflin). History was, in short, to be rescued from the fortuitous and arbitrary and to become a study of necessary, natural change.

Inherent change, whether in nature or in culture, was conceived as being gradual and continuous, without radical breaks or revolutions. This belief in incremental change was wholly consonant with the interests of the reigning elite egalitarians.[23] Thus, according to Stephen Jay Gould, the great British geologist Charles Lyell "in part . . . merely 'discovered' his own political prejudices in nature—if the earth proclaims that change must proceed slowly and gradually . . . then liberals might take comfort in a world increasingly threatened by social unrest."[24] Evolution, too, was influenced by and, at the same time, supported the gradualism favored by the ruling elite.[25]

Gradualism was consonant with the egalitarian side of Romanticism as well. For it posited an unbroken continuum that masked—indeed, denied—clear hierarchic differentiation. In principle, and to a significant extent in fact, social differences became matters of degree (amount of wealth) rather than of kind (inherited title). A famous exchange between F. Scott Fitzgerald and Ernest Hemingway captures the contrast concisely. Implying the prevalence of differences in kind, Fitzgerald observed that "the very rich are different from us." For Hemingway, the egalitarian Romantic, on the other hand, the matter was one of degree; he replied, "Yes, they have more money."[26]

---

23. I do not mean to suggest that "gradualism" was a conscious political ploy. When the world came to be understood as a changing order rather than a fixed one, some way had to be found that made envisaging (for the sake of choice) intelligible. Gradualism, the theory of evolution, the ideas related to organic development, and historical necessity were all chosen because they implied the possibility of envisaging the future in the face of change.

24. *Ever Since Darwin,* p. 192. Gould also observes that science was used to call the ideology of the ancien régime into question. For example, the biologist Ernst Harckel used the notion that ontogeny recapitulates phylogeny "to attack nobility's claim to special status—are we not all fish as embryos?—and to ridicule the soul's immortality—for where could the soul be in our embryonic, wormlike condition?" (ibid., p. 217).

25. Evolution was also used to rationalize the competitive nature of capitalist economy, which was likened to the survival of the fittest.

26. Quoted in Trilling, "Manners, Morals, and the Novel," p. 19. Put in terms developed elsewhere in this study (Chapter 1 and especially Chapter 8), statistical relationships become relatively more important than syntactic ones during the nineteenth century. Seen thus, it is tempting to speculate that music based primarily on statistical processes is the ultimate capitalist art. For what counts is amount, whether of money or of sound.

In the arts, the past—not history[27]—served at once to exemplify the values and predilections of the elite egalitarians, to disguise conventionalities of concepts and means, and to affirm the universality of human behavior. As with every age, the Romantics valued most, and chose to identify themselves with, those pasts that seemed to exemplify their own beliefs and attitudes. They singled out for special attention those aspects of each past that could most readily be interpreted in terms of such interests. They were, for instance, drawn to the Middle Ages by a feeling of kinship with the exuberance, restlessness, and informality of the period, and with what they took to be the childlike naïveté of its art. The concepts and metaphors used to interpret the past were, however, those of Romanticism: "The young Goethe, under the influence of the ideas of Herder, described Gothic architecture, in contrast to buildings constructed according to rules, as *the organic product of growth in the mind of genius.*"[28]

The past—and at times the exotic as well—not only reflected the present, it also tended to disguise conventions of language and plot, character and concept. Like a costume, the historical setting of a novel such as Scott's *Ivanhoe* affirmed, yet at the same time masked, the predilections of the British upper classes: the forthright honesty and innate goodness of Cedric, the Saxon, represent the values and self-image of the English egalitarian elite, while the duplicity of Brian du Bois-Guilbert typifies the attitude of nineteenth-century Englishmen toward foreigners—and especially the French. Similarly, in *Die Meistersinger* Wagner celebrates the wisdom and virtue of the *volk,* disguises a familiar plot schema (boy-meets-girl/trial/boy-wins-girl) in exotic dress, and, masking ideology in a Medieval setting, dramatizes the opposition between empty convention (Beckmesser's pedantic rules) and fecund nature (Walter's untutored genius).[29]

Romantic artists chose to use those pasts with which they felt a special kinship, and they simultaneously shunned those they found offensive, the most notable being classical mythology.[30] Several factors seem to have been involved. First, classical

The continuousness of a statistical hierarchy also seems to suggest that the very notion of a class struggle in capitalist society is mistaken because it presumes a set of fixed hierarchic (class) distinctions. And perhaps it was because gradualism, coupled with an abiding faith in the working of beneficent Progress, became an article of faith (not just for the ruling elite but for the working classes) that radical change occurred in feudal Russia rather than in industrial Europe. Romanticism, not religion, was the opiate of the masses. Ironically, then, the very ideology that nurtured Marx undermined the predictions that he made, because ideology posited that change was gradual and evolutionary, not radical and revolutionary.

27. See the section "The Past as Manifestation" in Chapter 3.

28. Abrams, *The Mirror and the Lamp*, p. 205; emphasis added.

29. Turning to a different past and espousing other values, Jacques Louis David employs Roman history and Roman sculpture to proclaim the virtue, courage, and ideals of contemporary French republicanism.

30. It seems possible that the prizing of folk tales and legends by the elite egalitarians was a result not only of the intensification of nationalism but of the lacuna caused by the repudiation of classical mythology. Such acknowledged fictions are needed because they at once express and reinforce the values and attitudes of the ruling elite of the culture. And since the repertory of such tales probably remains quite constant over time—and even territory—one can study the values of a culture by seeing which tales, myths, or legends are most frequently replicated. In addition, such stories are usually varied and modified in such a way that they more precisely represent the predilections and values of a particular culture. In this connection see Darnton, *The Great Cat Massacre*, chap. 1.

mythology was closely associated with, and had served to support, the political structures of the ancien régime, and the hierarchy of Gods and mortals had been related by analogy to these political structures.[31] Second, classical mythology was connected with neoclassical art, whose aesthetic rules, dramatic conventions, and prosodic practices seemed patently unnatural and contrived. Third, understanding stories based on classical mythology required explicitly learned knowledge about names and functions (who, after all, was Hebe?) and actions (what were the labors of Hercules?) that were unfamiliar to a considerable segment of the elite egalitarians.[32] Manet's famous painting *Le déjeuner sur l'herbe* (1863), which was based on a portion of Raimondi's engraving (after a painting by Raphael) *The Judgment of Paris* (ca. 1520), exemplifies the changes that have occurred. Reference to mythology is eliminated; the subject is acontextual in the sense that appreciation is not dependent upon knowledge of the characters or event being represented. The painting, as the art-for-art's-sake formalists might say, can be enjoyed "in its own terms." And the increasing importance of still life and landscape painting may in part be related not only to the sentimental yearning of urbanites for the bucolic, but to their unease with representations that required knowledge of mythology, or for that matter, of history.[33]

Finally, history was an important concern of the elite egalitarians because it could be used to justify the present: both the inequalities and injustices of industrialism and the innovations that produced the burgeoning diversity characteristic of nineteenth-century culture. That is, the idea of historical progress—of the basic beneficence of change—meant that each change was, as it were, required by history. Thus, in the later stages of Romanticism, Schoenberg and Webern justified the radical novelty of serialism by finding antecedents (in the music of Bach, for instance) and by claiming that it was a necessary consequence of the history of music. According to one story, when asked by a border guard whether he was the famous composer, Schoenberg is said to have replied, "I didn't want to be, but someone had to be."

### Acontextualism and Aesthetics

Both acontextualism and egalitarianism are clearly exemplified in the Romantic view of genius and the tenets of the ideology with which genius was associated. Geniuses,

---

31. Observe that Wagner's pantheon, though hierarchic, was associated with native rather than alien myths. Even more significant was the moral of the story: in the end, the artificial laws and contrived conventions of the gods are overwhelmed by the force of natural man, represented by Siegfried, the hero/genius.

32. By way of contrast, Shakespeare's plays, which seldom rely heavily on knowledge of classical mythology, became enormously popular and were frequently chosen by nineteenth-century artists as subjects for painting, operas, and program music.

33. In historical novels, dramas, and operas, the necessary background or context could easily be provided; this was not so in painting or sculpture. The ultimate state of this deprecation of reference occurs in abstract expressionism, which considers all traditions obstacles to genuine aesthetic experience. "As examples of such obstacles," Mark Rothko mentions "(among others) memory, history or geometry" (quoted in Miller, ed., *Fifteen Americans*, p. 18).

so the saying goes (and it is thoroughly Romantic in spirit), are born, not made. As Anton F. J. Thibaut wrote, "Mozart, as a true genius, would have been a brilliant example of any style, whether he had lived earlier or later, among Alpine goatherds, or in a cloister, or in regal luxury."[34] Context, then, is irrelevant, and so is learning:

> There are neither rules nor models; or, rather, there are no other rules than the general laws of nature, which soar above the whole field of art. . . . Genius, which divines rather than learns, devises for each work the general rules from the general plan of things, the special rules from the separate *ensemble* of the subject treated.[35]

Thus, paradoxically, the concept of genius is also egalitarian. For though geniuses are endowed with extraordinary powers and special sensibilities, these gifts are understood to be innate rather than dependent on lineage or learning. In brief, the accomplishments of genius, like those of the elite egalitarians, were a result of the natural talents of the individual rather than of inherited wealth or social position.[36] Supposedly, too, the appreciation of the best Romantic music—the works of geniuses—depended not on acquired taste but on natural musical sensitivity. For instance, George Bernard Shaw argued that Wagner was not concerned with

> first subjects and second subjects, free fantasias, recapitulations, and codas. . . . And this is why he is so easy for the natural musician who has had no academic teaching. . . . The unskilled, untaught musician may approach Wagner boldly; for there is no possibility of a misunderstanding between them; the *Ring* music is perfectly single and simple.[37]

Like exemplary members of the egalitarian elite, geniuses were innovators. Change was valued, as Tennyson's famous lines make clear:

> The old order changeth, yielding place to new
> And God fulfills himself in many ways,
> Lest one good custom should corrupt the world.
> ("Mort d'Arthur," 1842)

(Notice that even *good* customs corrupt!) And just as change was incremental in nature and in the social order, so it was thought to be in the history of the arts as well.

---

34. *On Purity In Musical Art,* p. 62.

35. Hugo, "Preface to *Cromwell,*" p. 368.

36. The insistence on the importance of innate ability, emphasizing the irrelevance of learning, may in part explain why the idea of inherited musical talent appealed to nineteenth-century thinkers. In this connection, see Chapter 4, note 6.

37. *The Perfect Wagnerite,* pp. 2–3.

Art, like nature, is made up of gradual transitions, which link together the remotest classes and the most dissimilar species and which are necessary and natural, and hence also entitled to live.

Just as there are in nature no gaps . . . so between the mountain peaks of art there yawn no steep abysses and in the wondrous chain of its great whole no ring is ever missing. In nature, in the human soul, and in art, the extremes, opposites and high points are bound one to another by a continuous series of various varieties of *being*.[38]

And if "society" is substituted for "art" in the quotation, the sentiments expressed are clearly those of the elite egalitarians.

In the nineteenth-century view, the craftsman clings to established stylistic constraints,[39] the innovative genius overturns them. As early as 1757 Chevalier Louis de Jaucourt wrote:

The man of genius is cramped by rules and laws of taste. He breaks them so that he can fly upwards to the sublime. . . . As far as he is concerned, taste is a love of the eternal beauty that characterizes nature. . . . He is constantly thwarted in his desire to express the passions that excite him, by grammar and convention.[40]

Though de Jaucourt pays lip service to the eighteenth-century idea of taste, he effectively drains it of meaning by subsuming it, making it nothing more than "a love of eternal beauty." Indeed, in the aesthetics of Romanticism, taste and beauty are virtual opposites. Taste depends on education and is learned; thus, we speak of cultivated and acquired tastes. But beauty, the sine qua non of value for Romanticism, cannot be learned. Its presence is immediately and intuitively experienced through natural sensitivity. As opposed to taste, it is both acontextual and egalitarian. It is the province of genius: "in the domain of the Beautiful, Genius alone is the authority."[41] In Keats's famous words, "Beauty is truth, truth beauty." More mundanely, "beauty is only in essence a revelation of truth."[42] And both are one with nature, which cannot lie.

---

38. Franz Liszt, quoted in Strunk, ed., *Source Readings in Music History,* p. 852. That these views affected the conception of music history is evident in Hubert Parry's article, "Sonata," in the second edition of Grove's *Dictionary of Music and Musicians* (1904–10): "There is no such thing as leaping across a chasm on to a new continent, neither is there any gulf anywhere, but continuity and inevitable antecedents to every consequent" (4:507).

39. Observe that the word *craft,* at least in its adjectival form, crafty, has taken on pejorative connotations involving notions of guile and duplicitous calculation.

40. De Jaucourt, *Encyclopédie . . . ,* quoted in le Huray and Day, p. 65. The idea that geniuses innovate by breaking the rules while lesser composers conform to stylistic norms has led to the belief that the essence of a style is to be found in the work of minor masters. Though this view appealed to the academy because it made research about the work of minor masters seem especially significant, my own study (partly reported in the following chapters) suggests that it is mistaken. It is the major composers who most effectively exploit, and therefore represent, the constraints of a style.

41. La Mara, *Letters of Franz Liszt* 1:152.

42. Hughes Félicité Robert de Lamennais, *Esquisse d'une philosophie* (1840), in le Huray and Day, p. 518.

The equation of beauty with truth, and of both with whatever is natural, helps to explain a number of Romantic beliefs and attitudes. First, it accounts for what Arthur Lovejoy refers to as the "naturalization in art of the 'grotesque.'"[43] it was not merely that Romanticism valued diversity, as Lovejoy seems to suggest. Rather, because no one would deliberately or consciously contrive them, the grotesque, the imperfect, and even the deformed were necessarily free from all artifice. Their indubitable naturalness guaranteed, as it were, their truth and hence their beauty.[44] In the words of the great satirist of Romanticism, W. S. Gilbert:

> Are you old enough to marry, do you think?
>     Won't you wait till you are eighty in the shade?
>         There's a fascination frantic
>         In a ruin that's romantic;
>     Do you think you are sufficiently decayed?
>                         (*The Mikado,* Act II)

And the many stories in which the ugly is transformed into the beautiful—for instance, "Beauty and the Beast" and "The Frog Prince"—not only express deep, though suppressed, longings for status, but symbolize the kinship of truth and beauty.

Here, at least in part, lies the connection between Romanticism and realism. Because it was supposedly based on purely objective observation (as in positivistic science or history), realistic representation was in principle uncontrived and without artifice. It was true and hence, almost by definition, beautiful. Even if what was represented was repugnant it was understood that natural beauty transcended cultivated taste.[45]

Nature does not (indeed, cannot) lie.[46] Only human beings are duplicitous, disingenuous, and deceitful.[47] They are not so by nature, however, but because they have been corrupted by customs, laws, and institutions. Those not thus sullied by society—who are without guile, pretense, and affectation—know and speak the truth. Hence the infatuation with the "innocence" of children, the faith in the "simplicity" of the folk, and the belief in the "naïveté" of genius.[48]

---

43. *Great Chain of Being,* p. 293.

44. Curiosity, too, probably plays a part in this interest. But curiosity is seldom idle; for the deformed and fantastic—like the unusual or the exotic—serve to establish limits for conception of probability and thereby facilitate envisaging and choice.

45. From this point of view, impressionism can be considered a late stage of realism in which the artist's dispassionate eye captures solely what it *sees,* not what the prejudiced mind knows.

46. In the *Discourse on Inequality,* Rousseau observed that he tried to read the history of mankind "in nature, which never lies" (quoted in Cassirer, *Rousseau, Kant, Goethe,* p. 24). And because it can never deceive, those unrelentingly committed to nature are seldom witty or humorous.

47. The prime mode of lying is language. One can, of course, deceive using other conventional, gestural signs—e.g., smiling despite dislike. But language is the most familiar and successful medium for deception. And it is partly perhaps for this reason, as well as those noted earlier, that it was regarded with so much suspicion by the Romantics. Conversely, music may have become the exemplary art of Romanticism partly because it could not lie.

48. Joseph Featherstone makes a distinction "between low and high varieties of Romanticism. Low Roman-

Unfettered by cultural convention and free from class distinction, the child symbolizes the ideals of acontextuality and egalitarianism. Once again, Thibaut is concise as well as characteristic:

> Culture . . . is by no means always a true development of nature; and, in this sense, it is quite possible for an educated man to rank beneath a child. It is said of children in the Gospel that of them is the kingdom of God; and herein lies an eminent truth. Perfect openness, sincerity, and truthfulness are the noblest traits of the human character. But education, and the circumstances of life, generally make a man more or less close, calculating, disingenuous, and deceitful; whereas a child stands before us with his virtues and his faults, a fresh and virgin specimen of nature's handiwork.[49]

The prevalence of these beliefs is evident in the art of the "high" culture: in the compositions for and about children (for instance, those of Schumann, Saint-Saëns, and Debussy) and in literature (from Blake's *Songs of Innocence* to Kipling's *Just So Stories*). The truths of innocent childhood result from a closeness to the divinity of nature and are gradually dissipated through the weight of custom, as Wordsworth's "Ode: Intimations of Immortality from Recollections of Early Childhood" makes clear:[50]

> But trailing clouds of glory do we come
> From God, who is our home:
> Heaven lies about us in our infancy!
>
> .   .   .   .   .   .   .   .   .   .   .
>
> Thou little Child, yet glorious in the might
> Of heaven-born freedom on thy being's height,
> Why with such earnest pains dost thou provoke
> The years to bring the inevitable yoke,
> Thus blindly with thy blessedness at strife?
> Full soon the Soul shall have her earthly freight,
> And custom lie upon thee with a weight,
> Heavy as frost, and deep almost as life!

---

ticism exalts the intuitive and disdains rationality. High Romanticism, on the other hand, is a quest for a proper mediated balance between reason and feeling" ("Rousseau and Modernity," p. 177). Thus Rousseau did not endow children with special prescience. "It was Wordsworth and later Romantics (many of them much lower Romantics than Wordsworth) who took the radical step of talking as though the child were a philosopher already" (ibid., p. 178). Perhaps every ideology begins as a "high" version of a concept and moves lower, becoming part of cultural scuttlebutt.

49. *On Purity in Musical Art*, pp. 66–67.

50. The connection of childlike innocence with divinity is, of course, not a new idea. What is important for history is its increased replication and the changed ideological network within which it is embedded—its connections with nature, acontextuality, and egalitarianism.

These ideas were prevalent in the popular culture as well. The story "The Emperor's New Clothes," for instance, is an almost perfect distillation of the Romantic view of the virtues of childlike innocence. Unlike the other spectators, who are constrained by class distinction and subservient to tired custom, the child spontaneously sees (quite literally in this case) and speaks the naked truth. And just as childlike naïveté was, as we shall see, considered an attribute of genius, so untutored children were thought to be touched by a kind of genius—a belief still with us today as we exhibit gauche gouaches in which the young "express" their presumably true and unvarnished versions of reality.

Because they were supposedly untainted by artificialities of civilization, the folk (ordinary people, especially those associated with things rural), and "primitives" as well, were believed to be endowed with the traits surrounding natural innocence. Indeed, they were often characterized as being simple, guileless, and childlike. Their art was, accordingly, thought to be natural, free from calculation and contrivance.[51] The result was a telling change in pastoral music: the conventions of the mythic, arcadian pastoralism of the ancien régime were gradually replaced by the egalitarian folk-pastoralism of Romanticism. Thus, though folk art expressed the inner being of a people, it was not nationalism alone that encouraged the use of folk elements in art music. Equally important was the Romantic view that, whatever its provenance, folk music was the spontaneous burgeoning of natural song.[52]

As with both children and the folk, what guides the art of the genius is not knowledge of rules or learned skills or calculated choices, but spontaneous inspiration coupled with heartfelt emotion. Like Shelley's skylark, a genius pours forth a "full heart / In profuse strains of unpremeditated art." Or, more prosaically, according to Schilling:

> The *creative musician,* the true tone-poet, experiences . . . in much the same way as do all those in whom any kind of divine creative fire is kindled. . . . Hence he becomes all soul, all feeling. The notes come to him vividly, with uncommon facility, clarity and immediacy. They become symbols of his own natural language, expressing effectively, spontaneously and in undiluted purity the emotion latent within him. This is the origin of that intensity and expressive power, that urgent, intimate eloquence of tender emotion, that savage turmoil of vehement passion, that rich store of multifarious images, that subtle shading of emotion, that strange, often dreamlike juxtaposition of widely differing things, that note

---

51. Romanticism affected the kind of folk music initially collected and studied. For the belief that rural "folk" were more natural (less corrupt) than urban "folk" led early investigators to the country rather than the city.

52. Romanticism ultimately leads to a change in the use of folk materials. In the eighteenth century composers such as Haydn and Beethoven found ways to make folk music conform to the constraints of the Classic style. But as time passed—and clearly in the twentieth century—composers sought to make the constraints of art music compatible with, or even subservient to, those of folk music.

exactly suited to each emotion, and everything else that inspiration brings
out in the artist. . . . In the moment of inspiration, he snatches his pen
and captures for posterity in an act of composition the vision of pristine
beauty that his prophetic eye has discerned.[53]

Composers also subscribed to this view. Schumann, for instance, wrote, "The first
conception is always the most natural and the best. *Reason errs, but never feeling.*"[54] And Leon Plantinga observes that "in a review of Cherubini's second string
quartet, [Schumann] says he suspects that the composition is really a reworking of an
unsuccessful symphony. 'I am averse to all such transformations,' he writes, 'for
they seem to me like a sin against the divine first inspiration.'"[55]

What guarantees the truth and beauty of art is the natural, unmediated spontaneity of the feeling that generates it. Art should be natural, like a man "whose
speech, gestures and movements are governed with perfect sincerity and spontaneity
by his emotions, without reference to any acquired system of conduct."[56] Echoing
these sentiments, Wagner wrote, "The combining intellect must have nothing to do
with the dramatic work of art. In the drama we must become knowers through feeling. . . . This feeling, however, becomes intelligible to itself only through itself; it
understands no language other than its own."[57] The contrast of these views with the
attitude of neoclassical aesthetics could scarcely be more striking. To take but one
instance: in his preface to *All for Love,* a play based on the story of Anthony and
Cleopatra, Dryden wrote, "That which was wanting to work up the pity to a greater
heighth, was not afforded me by the story: for the crimes of love which they both
committed, were not occasion'd by any necessity, or fatal ignorance, but were
wholly voluntary; *since our passions are, or ought to be, within our power.*"[58] The
Romantic affirmation of the primacy of unconscious, spontaneous inspiration growing out of individual emotion, and the concomitant denial and denigration of the
claims of consciousness and shared rationality, result in a curious, almost paradoxical, dichotomy between the creative act and the aesthetic object. For though reason
plays virtually no role in inspired creation, the relationships that are prized in works
of art result from the inevitability and inner logic of organic development.[59]

---

53. Gustav Schilling, *Encyclopädie de gesammten musikalischen Wissenschaften* . . . (1834–38), excerpted in le Huray and Day, pp. 467–68. These observations help to explain why a letter spuriously attributed to
Mozart (describing the instantaneous nature of his compositional conception) was readily accepted throughout the
nineteenth century. Namely, it supported important beliefs of Romanticism. Note, once again, that the central question (for history at least) is not where the ideas come from, but why they were so frequently replicated.

54. Quoted in Plantinga, *Schumann as Critic,* p. 131; emphasis added.

55. Ibid., pp. 130–31.

56. Johann Georg Sulzer, *Allgemeine Theorie der schönen Künste* . . . (1771), excerpted in le Huray and
Day, p. 137.

57. Quoted in Stein, *Richard Wagner,* p. 68.

58. In *Works of John Dryden* 13:10; emphasis added.

59. See below, at note 132 and following pages.

References to "divine creative fire" and to the composer's "prophetic eye" in the quotation from Schilling call attention to a facet of Romanticism alluded to earlier: the devout reverence for art and the correlative adoration of the creative artist, whether composer or performer.[60] "The content of music, then, is a rich world, a world of the living soul and of the mysterious power of divine natural life."[61] And Liszt quotes Manzoni as "defining genius as 'a stronger imprint of Divinity.'"[62] The relationship is reciprocal: not only were artists considered godlike in their creation, but God was said to be artistic in His. Thus Schiller refers to "the work of the Divine Artist."[63] And just as God is worshiped for the mystery of his creation in all its multiplicity, so artists should be revered in the wonder of theirs.[64] The religious aura that surrounded artistic creation was also consonant with Romanticism because, like God's creation, it was unmediated and unencumbered by prior doctrine or established constraints.

Unfettered by man-made constraints, geniuses are natural innovators (the "Walters," not the "Beckmessers," of the world).[65] And this innate proclivity was encouraged by an ideology that not only placed a premium on originality and change, but highly prized individual expression. These views and values tended to foster the burgeoning of diversity that has been so characteristic of Western culture during the past two hundred years or so. Finally, because there are innumerable ways of avoiding a prevalent practice, diversity was also intensified by the tendency of Romanticism to denigrate convention.[66]

It is fortunate that diversity, which was fostered by ideology, was itself a value of Romanticism. Like God's creation, the "rich world" of art was to be characterized by what Lovejoy calls "plenitude."[67] "The world is wide," wrote August Wilhelm von Schlegel, "and many things can coexist in it side by side."[68] Indeed,

---

60. These beliefs and attitudes manifested themselves (and continue to do so) in the ritual behaviors accompanying the performance of "classical" music (both in the concert hall and the opera house): e.g., the lowering of house lights, the special dress of the performers, the reverent hush as the conductor raises the baton, the devoted attention expected of the audience. Such behavior served also to enhance belief in the value and seriousness of the aesthetic experience. The development of devoutly reverent concert behavior, which was a symptom of a change in ideology, is discussed in Weber, "Learned and General Musical Taste."

61. Eduard Krüger, "Hegels Philosophie der Musik" (1842), quoted in le Huray and Day, p. 533.

62. La Mara, *Letters of Franz Liszt* 1:152.

63. Lovejoy, *Great Chain of Being*, p. 299.

64. To continue the analogy with only slight irony: rare book rooms become the reliquaries of contemporary scholars, and sketches, manuscripts, and letters act as the holy relics of what Brahms called "the sacred memory of the great musicians" (quoted in Brodbeck, "Brahms as Editor and Composer," p. 16).

65. As is so often the case with tenets of an ideology, this view seems incompatible with the notion that geniuses overturn rules and flout convention, since the truly naïve and innocent genius—a kind of artistic Siegfried—presumably never really had (learned) any constraints in the first place. On the other hand, at least in the natural sciences, there appears to be a relationship between naïveté and originality. See my essay "Concerning the Sciences."

66. Seen thus, the pluralism of twentieth-century music is to a considerable extent a consequence of the diverse strategies devised to eschew or disguise convention.

67. *Great Chain of Being*, chap. 10.

68. Ibid., p. 306.

according to Victor Hugo, "it is of the fruitful union of the grotesque and the sublime types that modern genius is born—so complex, so diverse in its forms, so inexhaustible in its creations."[69] As Lovejoy puts it, Romantic poetry must be universal,

> not in the restrictive sense of seeking uniformity of norms and universality of appeal, but in the expansive sense of aiming at the apprehension and expression of every mode of human experience. Nothing should be too strange or too remote; . . . no *nuance* of character or emotion can be so delicate and elusive, or so peculiar, that the poet or novelist ought not to attempt to seize it and to convey its unique *quale* to his readers.[70]

These views were not confined to the "upstairs" realm of intellectual history, but find expression in works such as Robert Louis Stevenson's *A Child's Garden of Verses:* "The World is so full of a number of things, / I'm sure we should all be as happy as kings."

The valuing of diversity is related not only to the prizing of innovation and change, but to the repudiation of hierarchies and classes and to a correlative concern with what is unique about a person or work of art. The latent logic of these relationships would seem to be somewhat as follows. When the world is conceived of in terms of stable, recurrent types and classes (as it generally was before the end of the eighteenth century), diversity appears to be diminished. Taxonomy subverts diversity (and hence plenitude) because grouping plants and animals, human beings, or works of art into classes—and such classes into higher-level orders—entails emphasizing those traits that are shared and disregarding whatever is peculiar and idiosyncratic about a phenomenon. Put more forcefully, it is the goal of taxonomies and theories to reduce existential diversity by subsuming particular instances under some general principle.

Conversely, when the relevance of hierarchies and taxonomies is denied, as it was in Romanticism, attention is willy-nilly directed to what is individual about phenomena.[71] Thus hierarchies and classes were repudiated not solely because of their political connections with the ancien régime, but because the ideology was deeply concerned with what was peculiar to each phenomenon, be it a human being, an emotion, a landscape, or a work of art. In the absence of classes and hierarchies, all phenomena coexist in a kind of one-dimensional cognitive space, and as a result, the impression of diversity and plenitude is markedly enhanced. Succinctly stated, even

---

69. "Preface to *Cromwell*," p. 358.

70. *Great Chain of Being*, p. 306.

71. Though apparently plausible, the coupling of esteem for uniqueness with the rejection of classes gives rise to one of those paradoxes so characteristic of Romanticism. For what is unique is known to be so only in relation to some class of objects or events. To conceive of something (a flower, a sunset, a person, or a piece of music) as being unique entails considering it as a member of some class.

if the totality of existing phenomena had remained constant, the sense of diversity, unmitigated by taxonomy, would have seemed greater.[72]

The depreciation of genres was another corollary of the denigration of class and hierarchies. For genres are kinds of classes.

> The attack on the genres by the romantic artists betrays one of their deep-est ambitions: the achievement of "immediacy," of forms of expression *directly understandable without convention and without previous knowl-edge of tradition.* It was no doubt an unrealized ambition, but one that goes back to Rousseau, to his deep distrust of language, and the way it betrayed and deformed one's inmost thoughts and feelings. The romantics wanted an art that would speak at once and to all. The attack on the sys-tem of genres is *an attack on a tradition that made intelligibility depend upon connoisseurship. . . .*[73]

As Charles Rosen and Henri Zerner observe in this passage, the denial of the rele-vance of genres "was . . . an unrealized ambition." The depreciation of genres seems to have little effect on musical practice. For though mixed genres (for in-stance, the symphonic poem) became more common, the presence and importance of genres—old (opera, oratorio, symphony) as well as new (tone poem, program-matic overture, nocturne)—were far from diminished during the nineteenth century.[74]

Preoccupation with what is individual and peculiar about a work of art is re-lated not only to the denigration of hierarchies and classes, but to the depreciation of rules and theories. I have argued elsewhere that rules and theories are devised to deal with recurring relationships, not with unique ones.[75] As a result, they can never *fully* account for what is peculiar, ineffable, and transcendent about works of art. In short, if interest is in the truly idiosyncratic, theory is necessarily inadequate.

Concern with the individual and idiosyncratic may also be connected with the interest of Romanticism in the mysterious. For if the entirely unique becomes the exclusive focus of attention, then art is inexplicable—and hence mysterious.[76] One

72. The depreciation of class distinction is also related to a facet of Romanticism already touched upon: the view that change was incremental and gradual. If this is believed—that there are no decisive divisions in the world—then all classifications are essentially arbitrary, conventional fictions.

73. Rosen and Zerner, "The Permanent Revolution," p. 27; emphasis added. Note that Rosen and Zerner make two of the tenets of Romanticism that I have emphasized—acontextuality and egalitarianism—central to their argument.

74. Indeed, it seems that as the nineteenth century continued, composers became more conscious of the distinctions among genres. That is, they tended to emphasize genre differences stylistically; songs were differenti-ated from sonatas, sonatas from tone poems, tone poems from operas.

The critical/analytic methods that grew out of Romanticism did tend, however, to ignore the constraints peculiar to genres; in the analysis of the *Ursatz*, the motivic relationships creating coherence, or the "sets" display-ing economy, it is irrelevant whether a composition is a fugue, a minuet, or an impromptu.

75. See my "Concerning the Sciences," pp. 191–202.

76. Analysis tends to be denigrated by Romantics not only because it destroys the organic unity of the works of art, but because it robs art of its mystery by trafficking in generalization.

suspects that at times minor Romantic masters, affirming the consequent, supposed that mystery guaranteed transcendence:

> And every one will say
> As you walk your mystic way,
> "If this young man expresses himself in terms
>     too deep for me,
> Why, what a very singularly deep young man
>     this deep young man must be!"
>                     (W. S. Gilbert, *Patience*)

And the emphasis on the mysteriousness of art and creativity is also connected with the religious aura surrounding art and artists.

The rejection of classes and hierarchies is related to yet another important facet of Romanticism, one that will be considered more fully later in this chapter. It is *organicism,* which emphasizes gradual transformation rather than fixed classes, processive development rather than formal differentiation, and continuous Becoming rather than established Being. Of the many writers who emphasized the centrality of organicism, none, perhaps, was more important than Goethe. For he combined the authority of the artist with the prestige of the scientist. As Ernst Cassirer wrote:

> The generic view of the plant world found its classic expression in Linnaeus's system of nature. It holds that we have understood nature when we have succeeded in arranging it in the pigeonholes of our concepts, dividing it into species and genera, into families, classes and orders. . . . According to [Goethe], what we grasp in this way are only the products, not the process of life. And into this process he wanted, not only as poet but also as scientist, to win insight.[77]

As the plethora of quotations used to illustrate the tenets of Romanticism indicate, artists as well as aestheticians believed in and fostered the ideology of Romanticism. Indeed, at times their reports of how they composed conform to the Romantic image of the creative act rather than to the facts. For example, Wagner wrote:

> Before I go on to write a verse or plot or scene I am already intoxicated by the musical aroma of my subject. I have every note, every characteristic motive in my head, so that when the versification is complete and the scenes are arranged the opera is practically finished for me; the detailed musical treatment is just a peaceful meditative after-labour, the real moment of creation having long preceded it.[78]

77. *Rousseau, Kant, Goethe,* p. 69.
78. Quoted in Coren, "Genesis of Wagner's *Siegfried,*" p. 266.

But as Daniel Coren has shown, it is doubtful that Wagner actually conceived of music and text simultaneously. Rather, important musical ideas were conceived years after the text was written. As Coren observes: "With characteristically nineteenth-century eyes, Wagner saw himself as a mythic figure; he delighted in the role of composer as mystic visionary."[79] And evidently, we may add, he sought to exemplify the Romantic ideal of the inspired genius creating as a result of spontaneous feeling.

Another doctrine that often led to departures from strict verity was the myth of the unappreciated genius. As Hans Lenneberg remarks, "ever since the nineteenth century, the martyrdom of an artist has been taken for granted."[80] At once saint and seer, the genius through inspired vision reveals new worlds and, because he is "ahead of his time," is misunderstood, neglected, and vilified. Here is Berlioz's version of the suffering martyr syndrome:

> The great musicians share the fate of almost all humanity's pioneers. Beethoven was lonely, misunderstood, looked down upon, and poor; Mozart, forever in pursuit of the necessaries of life, was humiliated by unworthy patrons, and at his death left nothing but six thousand francs' worth of debts; and so with many others. If we look outside the domain of music, at poetry for instance, we find Shakespeare, tired of the lukewarmness of his contemporaries; . . . We find Cervantes crippled and poor; Tasso also poor and dying insane from wounded pride as much as from love, in a prison.[81]

Though the myth of the neglected composer suffering for the good of mankind was consonant with belief in the mystery and sanctity of artistic creation, it does not seem to be a corollary of acontextualism. Rather it is, I think, related to the change in the nature of patronage and of the audience for music, a change that had begun in the late eighteenth century.

"The composer's patronage relationships had continued their rapid evolution. . . . New forms of patronage—by the public theater, by members of the financial nobility, by groups of connoisseurs—had emerged."[82] The new patrons were less musically experienced and sophisticated than those of earlier times. Benjamin Lumley, who was manager of the King's Theater, the traditional opera house in London, wrote:

> The Opera House—once the resort and the 'rendezvous' of the *élite* of rank and fashion, where applause received its direction from a body of cultivated, discriminating 'cognoscenti', and the treasury of which was

79. Ibid, p. 210.
80. "Myth of the Unappreciated Genius," p. 227.
81. *Evenings with the Orchestra*, p. 307.
82. Solomon, *Beethoven*, pp. 145–46.

furnished beforehand by ample subscriptions . . . now mainly depends for support upon miscellaneous and fluctuating audiences. . . . Boxes, which of yore were lent to friends if not occupied by the possessor, are now . . . sold for the evenings to any stranger who wishes to attend the performance.[83]

And in Paris, as his *Mémoires d'un Bourgeois de Paris* makes clear, Dr. Louis Véron, Director of the *Opéra,* was "instrumental in the development of a form of opera calculated to exploit the taste of the well-to-do bourgeoisie." [84]

What the myth of the suffering, sacrificing artist did was enhance the new audience's belief in the sincerity of the composer's inspiration and in the seriousness and value of the works of art he created. And such beliefs at once encouraged listeners to attend devotedly to the music and fostered receptivity and a tendency to respond affectively.[85]

Central for the argument being explored here, however, was the fact that the new audience enthusiastically embraced the ideology of Romanticism. This new elite did so because the ideology was in full accord with their ideals and self-interest. *For Romanticism is, as I have been urging, fundamentally egalitarian.*[86] Thus Wagner's *Art Work of the Future* "proclaims the doctrine of an art of the people, by the people, and for the people, an art which would necessarily appeal to the masses because it was an expression of their own thought, feelings, aspirations." [87] The ultimate triviality of privilege and power and, correlatively, the essential egalitarianism of all mankind are repeatedly emphasized—for instance, in Shelley's "Ozymandias" and in the following famous lines from Gray's "Elegy Written in a Country Churchyard":

> The boast of heraldry [lineage], the pomp of power,
>     And all that beauty, all that wealth e'er gave.
> Awaits alike the inevitable hour.
>     The paths of glory lead but to the grave.

Before considering the embodiment of Romanticism in works of art, some qualifications and distinctions may help to put my position in perspective. First,

83. From his *Reminiscences of the Opera,* quoted in Raynor, *Music and Society Since 1815,* p. 70.
84. Raynor, *Music and Society Since 1815,* p. 71.
85. In this connection, see my *Emotion and Meaning in Music,* pp. 73–75.
86. The beginnings of egalitarianism, of course, date back at least to the Enlightenment. And I suspect that it was (and continues to be) a more important historical force than reason, with which it was initially associated.
87. Stein, *Richard Wagner,* p. 62. Egalitarianism pervades more than the social order and the arts. According to Philip Rieff, Freudian psychology (which is a late manifestation of Romanticism) "declassifies human society, creating an essential democracy within the human condition. Even the Greek tragedy—the most aristocratic context—was leveled out by Freud; the unique crime of the tragic hero becomes an intention of every heart, and in the most ordinary of plots, the history of every family. . . . The aristocratic bias of the 'heroic' myth is replaced, in Freud, by the democratic bias of the 'scientific' myth: Oedipus *Rex* becomes Oedipus Complex, which all men live through" (*Freud: The Mind of the Moralist,* p. 354).

nineteenth-century societies were not *in fact* egalitarian; their behavior toward women and ethnic minorities makes this emphatically evident. Most members of the newly powerful middle class, however, professed and valued the ideal of equal opportunity, though acknowledging differences in native ability.[88] Second, desires for distinction, position, and privilege should not be minimized. Artists wanted to be different and special, and their claims to singularity were supported both by the mysteries of musical creation and by the mythic opposition of the Philistines. Yet even as they scorned and mocked the middle class, the artists of the nineteenth century created for it, representing subjects, symbolizing beliefs, and advocating values consonant with those of the elite egalitarians.

## ARTISTIC REPRESENTATIONS OF ROMANTIC IDEOLOGY

As will by now be evident, the dissemination of Romanticism was by no means confined to the ideas explicitly formulated in the disquisitions of philosophers, critics, and composers. Rather, the most pervasive and insinuating ideological indoctrination was probably that which stemmed from encounters with works of art.[89] Only a few of the various embodiments that, often unbeknownst to them, simultaneously shaped and expressed the beliefs and attitudes of the audiences of the period can be considered.

During the nineteenth century, there was an increasing preoccupation with the representation of nature in all its wondrous diversity. This manifestation of Romanticism is so well known that only the briefest mention seems necessary. In the visual arts, landscape painting, still life, and scenes depicting ordinary people engaged in commonplace enterprises were frequently replicated. Conversely, mythological and historical subjects tended to be avoided unless they were familiar (e.g., national heroes or well-known events) or symbolic of the values of Romanticism (e.g., scenes from Shakespeare's plays). In music, too, natural phenomena tended to be represented more frequently. One thinks, for instance, of Beethoven's "Pastoral" Symphony, Berlioz's "Scene in the Country," the "Forest Murmurs" in *Siegfried,* and Debussy's *La mer.* In literature, examples of nature poetry abound from Wordsworth (and before) into the twentieth century. Though the attitude toward nature and the emphasis it received were new, its representation was not.

The themes that were new and most important for the propagation of Romanticism were those surrounding acontextualism and egalitarianism. But in art, these themes had to be embodied in represented action rather than philosophic assertion or argument.

---

88. One can scarcely fail to notice that the conflict between the claims of equal opportunity and those of native ability are still very much with us.

89. Note that works of art become canonic—are repeated and replicated in anthologies and the school curriculum—not solely because of their aesthetic qualities, but because they are consonant with the ideology of the reigning elite.

Let us begin with Wagner's *Parsifal,* which strikingly symbolizes many of the themes of acontextualism. The hero's parentage is unknown; consequently lineage and class are irrelevant to his achievement.[90] He is at once naturally good, innocent of learning, and without guile—a naïve child of nature. His opposition, the villainous Klingsor, is an envious magician who contrives an artificial world, a spurious garden of pleasure, and compels Kundry (basically good, but fallen from grace) to tempt our hero and bring about his disgrace and downfall. But innate virtue triumphs over the falsehood and corruption of secular society, and the true social order of the knights of the Grail is saved by the purity of natural innocence.

Such symbolizations are by no means confined to the art of the high culture. Stories in which a naturally gifted but naïve hero triumphs over privileged, sophisticated opposition were replicated time and time again in the popular literature of the nineteenth century.[91] For instance, like Parsifal, the hero of the Horatio Alger stories is often a "poor, uneducated street boy—sometimes an orphan, more frequently the son of a widowed mother." And the villain "usually has some important hold over the hero. . . . Whatever his mask, he [the villain] invariably attempts to assert his tyrannical authority over the hero, and fails."[92] On their way to success, the heroes of such tales are usually tested by temptation: "Henry Ward Beecher and T. S. Arthur revel in the dangers of extravagance, drink, and 'strange women.' In somber but glowing, almost loving, detail they set forth the awful degradation which awaits the young man who unwarily sets his feet on the primrose path."[93] Here is the description of the escape from the temptations of some humble Kundry made by Edwin Fairbanks, the hero of A. L. Stimson's novel *Easy Nat; or, The Three Apprentices* . . . (1854): "The spell was broken, and Edwin was enabled to tear himself away from the siren, who had held him for some minutes, lost to all self-consciousness by the power of her fascination."[94] The resemblance to Parsifal (1877–82) could scarcely be more striking.[95]

The writers of popular literature were not unaware of the values they were espousing. Nature was good; the artificial conventions of society were corrupting. According to James Fenimore Cooper, Natty Bumppo, the hero of his Leatherstocking

90. Wagner's implicit denial of the relevance of origins in *Lohengrin* and *Parsifal* may be related to his doubts about his own legitimacy and that of his mother as well. (See Curt von Westernhagen, "Richard Wagner," *The New Grove Dictionary,* ed. Stanley Sadie, 20:104.) But the irrelevance of origins was a fitting subject for representation and replication because it was consonant with the tenets of the prevalent ideology.

91. To emphasize the view that neither wealth nor social position nor degree of education was necessary for success, the opposition that had to be overcome was often bourgeois and capitalist. But it was not, as far as I can see, the system and its ideology that were denigrated and deplored; rather it was the unseemly behavior of those who misconstrued the values of the elite. This interpretation is supported by the fact that the heroes of such sagas were often aided and abetted by a kindly capitalist. As with melodrama generally, correction was the implied moral.

92. Cawelti, *Apostles of the Self-Made Man,* pp. 111, 113.

93. Ibid., p. 50.

94. Quoted in ibid., p. 56.

95. The immense popularity of the American western in Europe may be due in part to its accord with the ideology of the elite egalitarians.

tales, was "removed from nearly all the temptation of civilized life." [96] And the irrelevance of lineage is made clear in Calvin Colton's *Junius Tracts* (1844):

> Ours is a country, where men start from an humble origin . . . and where they can attain to the most elevated positions. . . . No exclusive privileges of birth, no entailment of estates, no civil or political disqualifications, stand in their path; but one has as good chance as another, according to his talents, prudence, and personal exertions. [97]

Wagner's *Der Ring des Nibelungen* is, according to Carl Dahlhaus, "about nothing less than the downfall of a world of law and force, and the dawn of a utopian age"—an age of freedom. [98] In the *Ring,* Wotan and the Gods represent the world of laws, contracts (with the Giants), and conventions (marriage obligations violated by Siegmund and incest committed by him with his sister, Sieglinde); Siegfried symbolizes the new order, one that dispenses with convention and law because it is founded upon nature. As Shaw describes it:

> The most inevitable dramatic conception, then, of the nineteenth century, is that of the perfectly naïve hero upsetting religion, law and order in all directions, and establishing in their place the unfettered action of Humanity doing exactly what it likes, and producing order instead of confusion thereby because it likes to do what is necessary for the good of the race. [99]

Siegfried learns about the world (about Mime's treachery and about Brünnhilde) not through experience or social acculturation, but through the magic of nature—the awareness coming from Fafner's blood and from the revelations of a woodland bird that symbolizes the union of nature and truth. But he remains free of guile, and it is this innocence, the power of nature, that enables him to break Wotan's spear and with it the reign of artificial law and convention. [100] Dahlhaus observes:

> Siegfried must be the "instinctive," unreflecting hero who obeys nothing but his own impulses. But though one face of this kind of self-reliance is

96. Quoted in Cawelti, *Adventure, Mystery, and Romance,* p. 200.

97. Quoted in Cawelti, *Apostles of the Self-Made Man,* p. 39.

98. *Richard Wagner's Music Dramas,* p. 81.

99. *The Perfect Wagnerite,* p. 60. Shaw goes on to connect this Romantic view with Adam Smith's *Wealth of Nations.* And this suggests, once again, how central political economy was to the greatest creators of the nineteenth century. For as Stephen Jay Gould has observed, Darwin, too, was significantly influenced by Adam Smith. See Gould's book *The Panda's Thumb,* pp. 65–66.

100. Wagner replicated rather than invented these dramatic "themes," though his disguising of them in mythic garb was largely his own devising. But—and this is the crucial point—he did choose them. He did so because he was essentially in accord with the ideology of his audience. In other words, I disagree with Shaw's view that their message was revolutionary. Rather the message both reflects and supports the values and prejudices of the elite egalitarians. Siegfried was one of them, not an anarchist.

liberty, another is limitation, confinement in the moment, in the here and now. Inasmuch as Siegfried, a "poor fool" like Parsifal, belongs undividedly to the present, the past fades for him; lacking any faculty of memory, he falls victim to Hagen's plot.[101]

In *A Communication to My Friends* (1851), Wagner wrote that "Lohengrin sought a woman who would believe in him: who would not ask who he was or whence he came, but would love him as he was and because he was what he appeared to her to be. He sought a woman to whom he would not have to explain or justify himself, but who would love him unconditionally."[102] What Wagner here described is what is quite properly called *Romantic love,* an egalitarian love to which lineage and social position are irrelevant:

> Nie Sollst du mich befragen
> noch Wissen Sorge tragen
> wo her ich kam der Fahrt,
> noch wie mein Nam' und Art!

Or, to quote W. S. Gilbert once again,

> Never mind the why and wherefore
> Love can level ranks and therefore . . .
>                 *(H. M. S. Pinafore)*

Like inspiration and creativity, true love is natural, guileless, and spontaneous. As Dahlhaus remarks, "Love is always at first sight in Wagner."[103] In short, Romantic love is a manifestation of both egalitarianism and acontextualism.[104]

But the course of Romantic love seldom runs smoothly. The obstacles almost always come from the constraints of society—from custom, law, or political connivance. In *Lohengrin,* for instance, convention (the social prizing of lineage) makes it impossible for Elsa to resist the insinuations of Ortrud, whose motives are at least partly political. Because such external impingements are a common source of dramatic action—notably in the operas of Verdi (for example, in *La traviata* and *Don Carlos*)—romantic love is very seldom fully acontextual. But there is one opera—and it is generally regarded as the epitome of musical Romanticism—in which love is in effect insulated from significant impingement: it is, of course, *Tristan and*

---

101. *Richard Wagner's Music Dramas,* p. 91.
102. Quoted in ibid., p. 40.
103. Ibid., p. 67.
104. Though love is excluded from his adventures, and though he rides a white horse instead of a white swan, the origins of the Lone Ranger, Lohengrin's counterpart in popular culture (fighting for justice in the West instead of in Brabant), are equally mysterious: "Who was that masked man?"

*Isolde.* For the power of the love potion frees the lovers not only from moral blame, but from the constraints of their own pasts and those of the prevailing social order.

> When Wagner tried to outline *Tristan* in words, the external action involuntarily shrank to a few sparse allusions, and the inner action emerged as the only important one. . . . His intention was to show that the inner drama, which is the essential action, is freed in *Tristan* from the encrustation of outer action, the business of events.[105]

Wagner himself recognized this radical acontextualism when he wrote that, as a result of the love potion, "there were no bounds to the longing, the desire, the bliss and the anguish of love: the world, power, fame, glory, honour, chivalry, loyalty, friendship, all swept away like chaff, an empty dream; only one thing is left alive: yearning, yearning, insatiable desire, ever reborn—languishing and thirsting; the sole release—death, extinction, never more to wake."[106] And because all this is familiar in the popular culture, W. S. Gilbert is able to poke fun at the extremes of Romantic love. When Bunthorne asks Patience: "Do you ever yearn?" she replies with ironic innocence, "I earn my living."

Despite the egalitarianism of Romanticism, a surreptitious nostalgia for the distinctions of class and privilege is present in nineteenth-century ideology. This seems evident in favorite folk tales ("Cinderella," "The Princess and the Pea," "Beauty and the Beast," and so on), and in the plots of popular culture in which a child of unknown parentage proves to be well born (for instance, Ralph Rachstraw in *H.M.S. Pinafore*).[107] And in the United States, where *inherited* class distinctions did not exist, comparable "success" involved marrying the proverbial boss's daughter (as in Horatio Alger stories) or, if one was a woman, marrying the boss (as in *True Confessions*).[108] In short, though love should be pure and acontextual, it is best when the beast turns out to be a handsome prince or the light of the hero's life happens to be the boss's darling daughter. Thus are the ideals of egalitarianism reconciled with the benefits of class and privilege.

## Formalism

Acontextualism is a central theme not only in the art of Romanticism but, particularly late in the nineteenth century and in the twentieth, in aesthetics and criticism as

---

105. Dahlhaus, *Richard Wagner's Music Dramas,* pp. 49, 50. Dahlhaus goes on to remark that "*Tristan* has outgrown its conventions" (p. 52). But in the view I am arguing for, Wagner is repudiating not merely the conventions of the theater but also the conventions of society. He is presenting acontextualism in its purest form.

106. Quoted in ibid., p. 50.

107. Observe that earlier, when the parentage of a presumed orphan is discovered (as, for example, in the case of Figaro or in Shakespeare's comedies), there is seldom a change of class.

108. The American yearning for class is evident both in the enormous interest in the fortunes of the British royal family and in the tendency of American heiresses to marry titled Europeans.

well. For the aesthetics of formalism is an almost exact counterpart of Romantic love. " 'Art for art's sake, not art for life's sake,' is the watchword of formalism. Art is there to be enjoyed, to be savoured, for the perception of the intricate arrangement of lines and colours, of musical tones, of words, and combinations of these." [109] Like a beloved, an artwork is to be adored—even worshiped—for itself alone. Societal claims for religious, political, or even emotional significance are irrelevant, and they ultimately corrupt and detract from the purity of aesthetic experience. Thus, according to Carl Dahlhaus, Hanslick "argues that beauty is complete in itself, that a musical work of art represents 'a specific esthetic structure not conditioned by our feeling,' and that this structure must be 'comprehended by scientific observation, set free from any psychological subsidiaries relating to its origin and its effect.' " [110]

History is irrelevant. In the words of Clive Bell:

> Great art remains stable and unobscure because the feelings that it awakens are independent of time and place, because its kingdom is not of this world. To those who have and hold a sense of the significance of form what does it matter whether the forms that move them were created in Paris the day before yesterday or in Babylon fifty centuries ago? [111]

Far from being aristocratic, as it might seem to be, formalism, like Romantic love, is essentially egalitarian. It affirms that knowledge and experience, cultural and historical context—which tend to depend on the privilege made possible by wealth and social position—are unnecessary for the comprehension and appreciation of works of art. [112] All that is required is the gift of natural sensitivity.

According to the aesthetics of formalism, each work of art contains its complete meaning within itself and, correlatively, the principles appropriate to its own analysis. These attitudes still pervade music theory and criticism, leading to the belief that "the good composition will always reveal, on close study, the methods of analysis needed for its own comprehension." [113] This facet of formalism is also related to the idea that the critic is the "servant of the text," since one can be a servant of the text only if the mode of criticism is, as it were, "ordered" by the text.

For a strict formalist, all kinds of representation (especially program music) are illicit, and even conventions of grammar, syntax, and form are ultimately suspect.

109. John Hospers, "Philosophy of Art," *The New Encyclopedia Britannica*, 15th ed. (Chicago, 1974), 2:49. Like most tenets of Romanticism, the "art for art's sake," idea begins in the eighteenth century. Cf. Woodmansee, "The Interests in Disinterestedness."

110. *Esthetics of Music*, p. 54. The internal quotations (single quotation marks) are from Hanslick, *The Beautiful in Music*.

111. *Art*, p. 34.

112. The striking growth of criticism during the nineteenth century is related to changes in the composition of the audience; for the audience needed more guidance than had previously been necessary. And this need was intensified by the increasing diversity of styles, especially in the fine arts and music.

113. Cone, "Analysis Today," p. 187.

The greatest works of art can be "comprehended by scientific observation" because they are based on universal, natural principles. Thus the notion that music is a universal language is connected with both formalism and egalitarianism, because universality requires that cultural experience, learning, and history be irrelevant for understanding and appreciation. By way of summary, here is M. L. Abrams's description of the Romantic viewpoint: "Acting thus under 'laws of its own origination' . . . the genius gives the laws by which his own products are to be judged; yet these laws are universal laws which he himself must necessarily obey because his composition proceeds in accordance with the order of the living universe." [114]

Belief in the existence of a purely natural and hence universal basis for music pervades the psychology and theory, as well as the aesthetics, of nineteenth- and twentieth-century music. Thus Helmholtz and, later, the first psychologists sought to explain the power of music in terms of acoustical stimuli, which were presumably independent of time and place because they were natural. And as a rule, this was true of music theories as well. For instance, Heinrich Schenker's theory, based on the universality and necessity of the *Ursatz*, is fundamentally ahistorical; it is unconcerned with and unable to account for style differences (between musics of different cultures) or style change (within the music of Western culture). [115]

Finally, the beliefs and attitudes of formalism can be related to the idea that art is a form of play. If art is "for art's sake" alone—like Romantic love, unsullied by utilitarian goals—why do people create it and attend to it? The answer is because of the pleasure, both innate and instinctual, of play for its own sake. Two corollaries follow from this. The nonutilitarian pleasure of art confirms the distinction between art and craft (which almost by definition has a purpose), and it also confirms, as it were, the childlike innocence of the creative artist. For, eschewing the worldly temptations of patronage, fame, and fortune, the artist plays the game of art for its own sake. [116]

## THE GLORIFICATION OF NATURE: ORGANICISM

Though Romanticism owed its peculiar power and impetus to the radical rejection of the constraints of the political and social order of the ancien régime, a positive side

114. *The Mirror and the Lamp*, p. 225.
115. Similarly, as we shall see, motivic analysis and its progeny, set theory, are based on the assumption that patterning by similarity (of motive or of pitch-class organization) is an innate mode of apprehension independent of learning and history.
116. It is, I think, significant that while animals play mostly when they are young, human beings play throughout their lives. Perhaps this is because animals are acquiring competencies—kittens play "catch-a-mouse," puppies play "beat-you-up," etc.—needed for survival; once the behavior is ingrained, play ceases. That human beings continue to play is perhaps because we need to practice envisaging and learning for the sake of effective choosing all our lives. In short, the notion that play is "useless activity" "for its own sake" is at once deeply Romantic and profoundly mistaken.

complemented the repudiation of convention.[117] "Modernity arrived in the West pro-claiming a return to nature. It was the appeal to nature and basic human nature, the recovery of nakedness, that ended by sweeping away tradition, the older roles, patri-archal forms of authority, the ancient hierarchies of privilege."[118] The nature to which the Romantics turned was not one of fixed, hierarchic ordering, as it had been in earlier times, but one of change and growth, development and openness. The core concept of this Romantic view of nature was the metaphor of *organicism.*

> Form is mechanical when it is imparted to any material through an exter-nal force, merely as an accidental addition, without reference to its char-acter. . . . Organic form, on the contrary, is innate; it unfolds itself from within, and reaches its determination simultaneously with the fullest de-velopment of the seed. . . . In the fine arts, just as in the province of na-ture—the supreme artist—all genuine forms are organic.[119]

Although some of its tenets had been present in Western thought since ancient Greece,[120] organicism was "politicized" and received its most forceful and thor-oughgoing formulation as part of the ideology of Romanticism. Organicism was cru-cial for the history of music because it furnished the central metaphors of Romantic aesthetics.[121] Its influence was so profound and pervasive that it has persisted, with occasional and minor remissions, throughout the twentieth century, not only in such high-culture manifestations as formalist aesthetics, abstract painting, and avant-garde music,[122] but in such mundane realms as organic food and hippie culture.[123]

Because the organic is *natural,* as opposed to mechanical or artificial, many of the ideas associated with organicism were touched on in the preceding sections. The organic is associated with genius and inspiration, as opposed to craftsmanship and calculation; with spontaneity and freedom, as opposed to deliberation and restrictive rules; with innocence and artlessness, as opposed to sophistication and deceptive

117. This was—had to be—the case, because choice is impossible without constraints, whether in society or in art. This need for constraints calls attention to an interesting point. Without in any way minimizing the politi-cal component of gradualism, it should be recognized that gradualism itself is related to choosing. For, as mentioned in Chapter 3, envisaging and choosing are possible only if the world is either static or characterized by ordered (nonrevolutionary) change. And it is perhaps partly for this reason that as people and revolutions grow old and are obliged to make responsible, consequential choices, they tend to become more conservative.

118. Featherstone, "Rousseau and Modernity," p. 187.

119. August Wilhelm von Schlegel, *On Dramatic Art and Literature (1809–11),* quoted in Abrams, *The Mirror and the Lamp,* p. 213. That Schlegel's formulation of organicism was widespread is indicated by Coleridge's paraphrase of this quotation: "The form is mechanical when on any given material we impress a predetermined form. . . . The organic form, on the other hand, is innate; it shapes as it develops itself from within, and the fullness of its development is one and the same with the perfection of its outward form." (from *Shakespearean Criticism,* quoted in Abrams, pp. 172–73).

120. See, for instance, Nisbet, *Social Change and History.*

121. It is interesting to note that Romanticism tended to influence music through philosophical aesthetics rather than through music theory. That is, the composers replicate the ideas of philosophers and their popularizers.

122. In this connection, see the last chapter, "Epilogue: The Persistence of Romanticism."

123. In part, of course, the persistence of organicism is made possible by the persistence of the politi-cal/economic elite that fostered it in the first place.

guile; with innate knowledge and feeling, as opposed to labored knowledge and cold reason; with uncontrived beauty and goodness, as opposed to cultivated taste and unnatural custom; and with relationships and meanings that are acontextual, as opposed to ones that are dependent on context. Our virtually unconscious tendency to value the earlier terms in each of these sets of oppositions is eloquent evidence that the power of the organic model is still very much with us.

Despite its long history, the organic model was not the main basis for conceptualizing musical relationships during the preceding centuries. Rather, language was the favored model: musical structure was described in terms of phrases, sentences, and periods; expression was discussed in terms of rhetoric and characteristic figures; and unity was understood as a function of both expression and structure. In *L'Essai sur le beau* (1741), Yves Marie André writes that "music becomes a kind of sonorous rhetoric which has its grand gestures to inspire the soul, as words do, its charms to move it, and its playfulness, its jokes and its games to divert it." [124] In music as in language, then, grammar, syntax, rhetoric, gestural expression, and even formal schemes—particularly when explicitly differentiated and classified, as they were in the seventeenth and eighteenth centuries—were understood to be learned and significantly conventional; and, like language, such learned conventions were associated with lineage, class, and hierarchic authority. [125] Thus the shift from the language model to the organic model is both a symptom and a consequence of the repudiation of convention and class discussed earlier. [126] At the risk of exaggeration, it may be

124. Excerpted in le Huray and Day, p. 33. In this connection, see Ratner, *Classic Music,* pts. 1 and 2. André's views are obviously far from those of the Romantics. And the reference to playfulness, jokes, and games is especially telling. For these facets of human behavior are intimately dependent on the shared understanding of convention. The absence of the witty and comic in much of the music of the nineteenth century is virtually a corollary of the repudiation of convention. (It is perhaps also related to the Romantic valuing of gradual transformation as opposed to the abrupt contrast characteristic of the comic.) Put in relative terms: to the extent that the music of the nineteenth century is playful or witty, nature has surrendered to convention.

125. As one peruses the writings of aestheticians and theorists from the beginning of the eighteenth century to, say, the middle of the nineteenth, there is a striking change in the grounds used to justify assertions about art and music, a change from the authority of the ancients and the Bible to the direct and democratic "observation" of nature.

126. I do not mean to suggest that the idea that music is akin to language was abandoned. It persisted. But the basis of the kinship changed: in both models, emphasis was placed on individual expression, which, as we have seen, was presumed to be a natural and spontaneous consequence of human feeling. Cf. the quotation presented earlier from Shelley's "Ode to a Skylark."

Note that the turning of some contemporary music theorists to linguistics does not involve a return to the language model favored in the seventeenth and eighteenth centuries. For the *linguistic* model posits the existence of a "deep" and (presumably) natural basis for language, rather than a conventional one. For this reason, it is at least as much a symptom of continuing Romanticism as it is of neo-Cartesianism, as its partisans pretend.

It is important to distinguish between aesthetic theory and musical practice. Though instrumental music was exalted and the language model was rejected by Romanticism, there was in practice no "decisive break between music and language," as Rose Rosengard Subotnik suggests ("Cultural Message of Musical Semiology," p. 747). To be sure there was some decline in the production of choral music, but this had more to do, I think, with changes in patronage than with changes in models. The *lied* (from Schubert through Schoenberg) flourished, as did opera in Italy, Germany, and France. This is not to suggest that the compositional relationship between tones and texts remained constant. As the viability of musical constraints became attenuated, texts become a more and more important source of constraints until, in early Schoenberg, music verges on becoming a dependent parameter: that is, musical choices depend more and more on the structure and interpretation of the text being set.

said that the language model for music represents a prizing of societal constraints while the organic model celebrates the felicities of natural constraints.

The core metaphor of organicism is that of a seed germinating and developing into a full-blown flowering plant:

> In the world we see every where evidences of a Unity, which the component parts are so far from explaining, that they necessarily pre-suppose it as the cause and condition of their existing *as* those parts; or even of their existing at all. . . . That the root, stem, leaves, petals, etc. . . . cohere into one plant, is owing to an antecedent Power or Principle in the Seed, which existed before a single particle of the matters that constitute the *size* and visibility of the crocus, had been attracted from the surrounding soil, air, and moisture.[127]

That this metaphor was subscribed to by composers as well as aestheticians is evident in Wagner's account of the composition of *The Flying Dutchman* and, more particularly, of Senta's second-act ballad:

> In this piece I unwittingly *planted the thematic seed* of all the music in the opera. . . . When I came eventually to the composition, the thematic image I had already conceived *quite involuntarily* spread out over the entire drama in *a complete, unbroken web;* all that was left for me to do was to allow the various *thematic germs* contained in the ballad *to develop to the full, each in its own direction.*[128]

And in the same vein, Wagner tells us that the composition of *Lohengrin* grew "out of the construction of the scenes, out of their *organic growth* one from another."[129] Some fifty years later, Anton Webern reports and endorses Mahler's belief that, "just as the whole universe has developed from the original cell—through plants, animals, men, to God, the highest being—in music, too, a whole piece should be developed from a single motive, a single theme, which contains the germ of all that is to follow."[130]

From these beliefs "grow" a host of interrelated ideas (to use the metaphor to explain it). The most important, and most obviously relevant, for aesthetics was that of organic unity. Because the work of art was understood to be the result of the gradual unfolding of a single underlying principle or germ, division into parts invariably violated the integrity—the unity or oneness—of the whole. All analysis, whether of organisms or ideas or works of art, is destructive:

127. Samuel Taylor Coleridge, *Aids to Reflection*, quoted in Abrams, *The Mirror and the Lamp*, p. 171.
128. Quoted in Dahlhaus, *Richard Wagner's Music Dramas*, p. 18; emphasis added.
129. Quoted in ibid., p. 44; emphasis added.
130. Quoted in Blaukopf, ed., *Mahler: A Documentary Study*, p. 240.

The labours of anatomy cannot be practised on a living body without destroying it; analysis, when attempted to be applied to indivisible truths, destroys them, because its first efforts are directed against their unity. . . . In whatever way this division takes place, it deprives our being of that sublime identity.[131]

Organic development is not only gradual, it is necessary. According to Constantin Julius Becker:

Truth, on which the arts are based, necessarily excludes chance and coincidence. . . . It follows, then, that what we experience as surprising, or, as we call it, original in music is none the less *necessary;* anything that is contrived or irrelevant to the idea either makes no impression on us or causes disquiet.[132]

The contrast with earlier beliefs and attitudes is striking. One can scarcely imagine a Romantic composer constructing dice games, as Kirnberger, Haydn, and Mozart did. For composers of the seventeenth and eighteenth centuries, the *ars combinatoria* was a way of thinking about melodic manipulation and invention.[133] And in actual eighteenth-century composition, as opposed to dice games, what constrained the choice of figures were the claims of taste, coherent expression, and propriety, given the genre of work being composed, rather than the inner necessity of a gradually unfolding, underlying process.

Related to the postulate of necessity were two correlative beliefs that are still prevalent in the aesthetics of music and the thinking of many composers and critics. The first of these was the belief that, because whatever occurs in a composition is (or should be) the necessary result of "an antecedent Power or Principle in the Seed," each and every note and pattern, texture and timbre, is determined and inevitable. To change a single note is to violate the organic integrity of the whole. When inevitability becomes a test of value, whatever seems arbitrary or capricious is either ipso facto found wanting or more likely (because critics generally deal with unassailable masterpieces) found to be a mere surface idiosyncrasy that masks an underlying inevitability.[134]

131. Mme de Staël, *De l'Allemagne* (1810), excerpted in le Huray and Day, pp. 307–8. That countless music-lovers, as well as a number of scholars, have expressed similar sentiments is evidence of the persisting presence of Romanticism in twentieth-century culture.

132. "Ideen über Baukunst und Musik," (1838), excerpted in le Huray and Day, p. 493.

133. In Johann P. Kirnberger's words: "It is possible for this method to be useful in the composition of larger pieces, for example symphonies. Those who truly understand musical composition will at least not be displeased by the manifold elaborations upon the same harmony over a single bass line. A beginning student of composition can derive advantage from the store of variations of the musical figures" (*Der allezeitfertige Polonoisen-und-Menuett componist* [1757], quoted in Ratner, *Classic Music,* p. 101). Also see Ratner's "*Ars Combinatoria.*"

134. The idea of artistic necessity is also related to the conception of the artist as a genius whose creations, like God's, are at once inscrutable, infallible, and inevitable. One of the consequences of these beliefs is the growing

The correlative of organic unity and necessity was the belief that economy is an important aesthetic value. Just as nature was thought to be economical,[135] so was art.[136] For when every relationship grows from a single germinal idea, nothing is wasted.[137] Like gradual, evolutionary change and natural, acontextual understanding, the notion of artistic economy had a patent appeal for the "up and doing" middle class.[138] Celebrated in stories and poems such as Ann Taylor's "The Pin" from *Hymns for Infant Minds* (1810), the valuing of economy was ideological pablum fed to the young: "And willful waste, depend upon 't, / Brings, almost always, woeful want!"[139] Economy meant that, generally speaking, whatever was understood to be "merely" ornamental was deprecated because it lacked inner necessity—because it seemed an arbitrary and wasteful addition to the unfolding of the inherent germinal process. And the general decline in the use of ornaments in the music of the nineteenth century was partly a consequence of these attitudes.[140]

The depreciation of ornament was but a superficial manifestation of the belief that the significant relationships of the world—those that gave it meaning and coherence—lie concealed beneath surface features and relationships. This was part of biological as well as aesthetic doctrine. During the last part of the eighteenth and the beginning of the nineteenth centuries, according to François Jacob, "the very nature of empirical knowledge was gradually transformed. . . . It was within living bodies themselves that the very cause of their existence had to be found. . . . The surface properties of a living being were controlled by the inside, what is visible by what is

---

emphasis on "authentic editions." For if, as posited by the aesthetic of Romanticism, every sign and symbol chosen by the composer is the necessary and inevitable outcome of his inspiration, then it becomes virtually a moral imperative to establish and perform from a definitive text. It should perhaps be mentioned, however, that composers often appear to have been less concerned with inner (organic) necessity than were critics and theorists: Beethoven seemed quite unconcerned about the inner necessity and unity of, say, the "Hammerklavier" Sonata; and Mozart's arias were influenced by the needs of singers (see Chapter 5, at notes 39 and 40).

135. Whatever may be the case in art, the notion that nature is economical was surely a wish-fulfillment fantasy of the elite egalitarians. What, after all, could be more profligate than using millions of sperm to fertilize a single egg?

136. I do not intend to imply that economy in art is not important; for it clearly serves the central cognitive constraint of memory.

137. The valuing of economy, coupled with the denigration of hierarchies, leads to the view that absolutely everything counts (nothing is wasted)—and counts equally (is nonhierarchic). This outlook ultimately leads to the Freudian view of the unconscious in which everything is significant (slips of the tongue, lapses of memory, dreams, etc.), and to strict serialism in which every note counts (and is counted!) so that nothing is superfluous or redundant—and analysis consists in demonstrating the economy and necessity of the pitch structure of compositions. In this connection, see Levy, "Covert and Casual Values," pp. 7–13.

138. The phrase "up and doing" is from Longfellow's "Psalm to Life," which is a virtual distillation of the values of the Romantic elite egalitarians. The line runs, "Let us, then, be up and doing, / With a heart for any fate."

139. *Bartlett's Familiar Quotations*, p. 546a.

140. Clearly, there are notable exceptions, as in the music of Chopin (Example 8.12) and Schumann (Example 8.23b). But as the sequential repetitions in the examples indicate, these "ornaments" are no longer ornamental; they have motivic significance. As is almost always the case, a combination of circumstances was responsible for the decline in the use of ornaments. One important circumstance was the weakening of syntactic constraints. For ornaments are intelligible in nonreferential music only when there is functional differentiation between structural and nonstructural tones.

hidden."[141] Emphasis on the centrality of concealed underlying processes or principles has continued, affecting twentieth-century thought in many fields of inquiry,
including, for example, linguistics (deep structure), psychology (Freudian theory),
and anthropology (structuralism). In aesthetic theory, as elsewhere, there tended to
be reification; the concealed principle, instead of being understood as provisional
hypotheses inferred from actual perceived phenomena, became what was real, while
the sights and sounds of the world were appearance—surface manifestations of a
more fundamental principle. From this point of view, organicism is Platonism in biological clothing.[142]

Both the composition of music and especially the concepts informing theory
and criticism were, as we shall see, significantly affected by this strand of Romanticism. In composition, the ultimate consequences were methods such as those of
serial and statistical music in which the precompositional "seed" was explicitly and
consciously contrived—an ironic outcome for an ideology that particularly valued
unconscious, spontaneous inspiration! The same ideological strand was at least
partly responsible for the exegetic character of much music theory and criticism. For
if the principles governing relationships in music lie concealed behind less important
surface features, then it becomes the task of the theorist and critic to reveal this inner
essence, whether it be a Schenkerian *Ursatz*, a motivic germ, or a Fibonacci series.
Thus theorists and critics become comparable to theologians or seers interpreting the
divinely inspired message of the creator.

It is relevant to observe in passing that the search for—and the importance accorded to—underlying processes and principles was (and continues to be) significantly a consequence of the need to stabilize the "conceptual/behavioral" world for
the sake of envisaging and choosing. This need became especially pressing because
of the presence of rapid and radical cultural change beginning with the second half of
the eighteenth century. Ways of reducing the number of kinds of change characteristic of the phenomenal world were needed. This is what deep structures, whether linguistic, psychological, or musical, seek to provide. In principle, the more a culture
changes, the greater the need (the more intense the search) for concepts and theories
that make envisaging possible.

In addition to being gradual and necessary, organic processes were conceived
of as being goal-directed, a view that was also incorporated into nineteenth-century
biological theory, as François Jacob makes clear:

> The very idea of organization, hereafter implicit in the definition of a
> living organism, is inconceivable without the postulate of a goal identi-

141. *Logic of Life*, p. 74.
142. To make underlying principles more important (somehow more "real") than the surface features that
significantly shape experience is to commit the genetic fallacy—to confound the genesis of a phenomenon with its
existent actuality. It is almost like confusing knowledge about the DNA molecule that shapes and colors daffodils
with our experience of the flowers, "Tossing their heads in sprightly dance." For a discussion of this aspect of
organicism in contemporary literary criticism, see Smith, "Surfacing from the Deep," in *On the Margins of
Discourse*.

fied with life: a goal no longer imposed from without, but which has its origin in the organization itself. It is the notion of organization, of wholeness, which makes finality necessary, to the degree that structure is inseparable from its purposes.[143]

And Jacob continues by quoting Goethe: "Each being contains the reason for its existence within itself."[144] The goal is emergent self-realization on all levels of the natural order. Instead of a fixed order of kinds and classes established once and for all time by God's creation, there is a continuing process in which the innate potentialities of nature gradually realize themselves. According to Lovejoy,

> one of the principal happenings in eighteenth-century thought was the temporalizing of the Chain of Being. The *plenum formarum* came to be conceived by some, not as the inventory but as the program of nature, which is being carried out gradually and exceedingly slowly in the cosmic history. While all the possibilities demand realization, they are not accorded it all at once. Some have attained it in the past and have apparently since lost it; many are embodied in the kind of creatures which now exist; doubtless infinitely many more are destined to receive the gift of actual existence in the ages that are to come. . . . The Demiurgus is not in a hurry; and his goodness is sufficiently exhibited if, soon or late, every Idea finds its manifestation in the sensible order.[145]

The goal of the individual, like that of the natural world, is self-realization. As Schleiermacher put it,

> every man should exemplify humanity in his own way, in a unique mixture of elements, so that humanity may be manifested in *all* ways and everything become actual which in the fullness of infinity can proceed from its womb. . . . Yet only slowly and with difficulty does a man attain full consciousness of his uniqueness. Often does he lack courage to look upon it, turning his gaze rather upon that which is the common possession of mankind, to which he so fondly and gratefully holds fast; often he is in doubt whether he should set himself apart, as a distinctive being, from that common character.[146]

143. *Logic of Life,* p. 88.

144. Ibid., p. 89. This calls attention to one possible connection between organicism and formalism. For if a true—that is, organic—work of art "contains the reason for its own existence within itself," then, as my formalist friends at the University of Chicago were wont to argue, a work of art can (indeed, should) be understood "in its own terms."

145. *Great Chain of Being,* p. 244.

146. Friedrich Schleiermacher, *Monologen* (1800), quoted in Lovejoy, *Great Chain of Being,* p. 310. The rise of individualism obviously antedates the ideology of Romanticism. On the other hand, it seems more than coincidental that a nineteenth-century scholar, Jacob Burkhardt, should have found individualism to be the core idea of what he considered to be a crucial and salutary change in Western culture.

And it is from this point of view—in terms of full realization of potentiality—that Schumann criticizes Chopin:

> Now Chopin could publish everything anonymously; everyone would recognize him anyway. In this there is both praise and blame—praise for his talent, blame for his effort. . . . Always new and inventive in externals, in the shape of his compositions, in his special instrumental effects, yet he remains in essence the same. Because of this we fear he will never achieve a higher level than he has already reached. . . . With his abilities he could have achieved far more, influencing the progress of our art as a whole.[147]

In short, to realize oneself is to become differentiated from others—to be original—and to continue the "progress" of art. This search for self-realization and originality is one of the important forces for change during the nineteenth century.[148]

But, at the same time, according to Romanticism, complete self-realization is an unachievable—and in the end, improper—goal. For man's true nature is one of restless striving after a perfection that can never be his. Just as the world is forever in a state of Becoming, so man is—and so his art should be.

> Romantic poetry is constantly developing. That in fact is its true nature: it can forever only *become,* it can never achieve definitive form. . . . It alone is infinite. It alone is free. Its overriding principle is that the poet's fantasy is subject to no agreed principles. Romantic poetry is the only poetry that is more than a poetic genre. It is, so to speak, the very art of poetry itself. Indeed, in a certain sense, all poetry is—or should be—romantic.[149]

As we shall see, this valuing of Becoming—of continual growth and unfolding—finds musical expression in the use of open forms and implied structure.

Becoming is related to the yearning so characteristic of Romantic music. Wagner's description of the feelings of Tristan and Isolde (quoted above at note 106) epitomizes this facet of the ideology. And the persistence of the "ethos of longing" is evident in Schoenberg's attitude toward aesthetic value:

> There is only one content, which all great men wish to express: the longing of mankind for its future form, for an immortal soul, for dissolution into the universe—the longing of this soul for its God. This alone, though

147. Quoted in Plantinga, *Schumann as Critic,* p. 321.

148. Though teleology no longer plays a part in biological theory, the importance of individual self-realization (discovering one's "real" self) is still part of cultural scuttlebutt, clear evidence of the force and persistence of Romanticism in our time.

149. Friedrich von Schlegel, *Kritische Schriften,* excerpted in le Huray and Day, pp. 246–47. Notice the derogation of "agreed principles"—that is, conventions.

reached by many different roads and detours and expressed by many different means, is the content of the works of the great; and with all their strength, with all their will they yearn for it so long and desire it so intensely until it is accomplished.[150]

Yearning is a characteristic of Romantic art not only because perfection—whether in love, beauty, or the soul—is an unrealizable ideal, but because, paradoxically, realization would itself be an imperfection. For the closure and consummation required for realization transform Becoming into Being—into "definitive form," in Schlegel's words; and such form, flawed by the imperfections of material embodiment, can never be ideal and transcendent. In short, perfection can be a possibility only as long as the potentiality of Becoming precludes the actuality of Being.[151]

Becoming is a continuous, incremental, and unending process without clear articulations or significant discontinuities. In place of what it rejects as the artificial and mechanical part/whole relationships of syntactic structures, Romantic "theory" substitutes what might be called *emergent* structures—ones that, as we shall see, emphasize motivic development and statistical processes. Although significantly a matter of emphasis, since syntax invariably underlies emergent structure in Romantic music, the distinction between these kinds of organization seems to be somewhat as follows.

In a syntactic structure, more or less clearly defined, separable formal units on lower hierarchic levels combine with one another, usually processively, to form larger, more extensive formal entities. This combining of units continues until the highest level being considered is reached. The organization of such structures depends on the criteria for closure provided by syntax. And though process creates coherence on each level of the structural hierarchy, the constraints governing organizational processes tend to change from one level to the next. (Turning for clarity's sake to language, the principles governing the organization of sentences are somewhat different from those structuring paragraphs, and those structuring paragraphs are not identical with those shaping chapters—and so on, until the level of plot is reached.) This is what I have called *hierarchic discontinuity*.[152] The unity of such syntactic structures primarily depends not on similarity relationships, but on *subsumption*. Consequently, differences and contrasts in pattern, function, and expression can be comprehended as real and consequential relationships because lower-level events can be subsumed within higher-level ones.

Emergent structures, on the other hand, are characterized by continuous, seamless development. Mobility and openness, rather than stability and closure, are emphasized. Because the unity of emergent structures is the consequence of the ac-

---

150. *Style and Idea*, p. 26.

151. Perhaps part of the appeal of fragments and sketches, and of compositions beginning *in medias res* or ending without decisive closure, was that they preserved the possibility—the promise—of perfection.

152. See my *Explaining Music*, pp. 89–90, and *Music, The Arts, and Ideas*, pp. 96–97, 257–59, 306–8, and passim.

tualization of a single compelling, though perhaps hidden, constraint (principle or seed), subsumption is not structurally significant. However striking they may seem, differences and contrasts, as well as relationships of part and whole, are deemed inessential and inconsequential (though not fortuitous) manifestations of the underlying principle, the gradual unfolding of the work.

The discontinuities experienced in the world or in a work of art are illusions that arise because we have failed to discover or properly understand the principles governing phenomena:

> If the march of Nature seems to us sometimes uncertain and ill-assured, if she seems sometimes to operate in a fumbling, devious, equivocal manner, it is a false appearance, due only to our ignorance and our prejudices. We forget that she should not and cannot let any *nuance,* any variation, go unrealized. . . . Nature does nothing useless, her course is minutely graded, and each *nuance* is necessary in the total plan. The forms which we so ineptly take for irregularities, redundancies, inutilities, belong to the infinite order of beings and fill a place which would be empty without them.[153]

Since in this view all stages of development—from seed to plant to all of nature—are governed by a single principle, hierarchic discontinuity does not exist. Somehow (and on this point Romantic theory seems silent) all significant relationships, whether in nature or in culture, are manifestations of a single, encompassing process that shapes the "Becomingness" of everything. Thus, even though a theme or composition may seem to be a discrete formal entity, it is really but a stage in the realization of the work, the composer's stylistic development, and the history of music. Franz Liszt writes:

> For all that it is the creature of man, the fruit of his will, the expression of his feeling, the result of his reflection, art has none the less an existence not determined by man's intention, the successive phases of which follow a course independent of his deciding and predicting. It exists and flowers in various ways in conformity with basic conditions whose inner origin remains just as much hidden as does the force which holds the world in its course, and, like the world, it is impelled toward an unpredicted and unpredictable final goal in perpetual transformations that can be made subject to no eternal power.[154]

Though Liszt doubts the possibility of predicting the future, many nineteenth-century philosophers of history sought to understand change in terms of inherent,

---

153. J. B. Robinet, *De la Nature* (1761–68), quoted in Lovejoy, *Great Chain of Being,* p. 280.
154. Quoted in Strunk, ed., *Source Readings in Music History,* p. 854.

natural, and hence necessary processes. The connection between the emphasis on Becoming and the search for such processes was not fortuitous. As already observed more than once, understanding the present depends significantly on the ability to envisage the future (as well as on the construction of a past). When the world order was believed to be fixed and stable, as was the case in pre-Romantic times, the meaning of the present was patent because the future was known: it would be essentially like the present. But when the world order came to be understood as emergent, open, and continually Becoming, then the present seemed uncertain because the future was unclear. Only if some inherent, natural process or dialectic could be found to govern the course of historical change could the significance of the present be comprehended.

Notice that the present, like the past, can be *definitively* comprehended only if the future is, in fact, closed in the sense of reaching some final stable, steady state. And this may at least in part explain the tendency toward some form of historical eschatology. The irony is obvious: the philosophy of Becoming ultimately ends in a state of Being, and on the highest level of history, a single inherent process—for instance, a series of repeated cycles—precludes change.

Because Becoming is characteristic of all stages of organic processes, innovation is a consequence not only of the goal of individual self-realization but of inherent historical forces. For this reason, being "original"—that is, contributing to the actualization of natural and necessary change—is a kind of aesthetic/moral obligation, virtually a historical imperative. This seems the basis for Schumann's "blame" when he writes that Chopin "could have achieved far more, *influencing the progress of our art as a whole.*"[155] Thus, through the idea of Becoming, organicism is connected with the valuing of innovation, which is itself a corollary of the belief in historical progress—an ideal entirely consonant with the interests of the elite egalitarians.


## *Unity*

Although increasing emphasis on open, emergent structures (in relation to syntactic ones) was a matter of degree, the consequences for the aesthetics, theory, and composition of music were substantial. One of the most important of these was that the need for and sources of unity became a more pressing problem. The strategies chosen by composers to deal with this problem will be considered in the following chapters. But a preliminary discussion of the need for and sources of unity, as well as some mention of general kinds of solutions, seems appropriate here.

Before and during the eighteenth century, the basis of unity was not a pressing problem for two main reasons. First, differences and contrasts in musical patterns and expression could be subsumed as part of functional, syntactic hierarchies; and

155. See above, at note 147; emphasis added.

second, such relationships could be understood and explained in terms of the conventions of form and genre. For instance, the relationships among the different movements of a symphony were not problematic; they were taken for granted as being in the nature of the genre. But the Romantic repudiation of convention (and especially of neo-Aristotelian aesthetics, which had been associated with the ancien régime), coupled with the denigration and weakening of syntactic relationships, highlighted the presence of diversity.[156] As a result, the basis of coherence and unity became an issue: How did disparate and individualized themes, diverse modes of organization, and contrasts of expression—all intensified by the valuing of originality—form an organic whole? How did the several parts of a set of piano pieces or the different movements of a symphony or chamber work constitute a cohesive composition?[157]

The problem was especially acute in the aesthetics of music. In literature, significant weakening of syntactic constraints and hierarchic organization were never really viable options, and in the visual arts, at least until the twentieth century, coherence was significantly dependent upon iconicity. In both realms, the representation of human and physical nature—often with convention disguised by historical or ethnic exoticism—played an important role in creating artistic unity. But in instrumental music, "unity through representation" was not a possibility, except of course in program music. And it is not implausible to argue that program music flourished in the nineteenth century partly because the use of a program was a way of establishing coherence and, in particular, accounting for the juxtaposition and succession of palpably different moods, connotations, and the like.[158]

In "pure" instrumental music, the strategies chosen by composers to create unity were responsive to the tenets of Romanticism. One of the most important strategies involved creating coherence through similarity, usually motivic or thematic. Because they were similar in significant respects or were derived from a common source (seed), seemingly disparate patterns could be understood as forming a unified composition. Even in the absence of an explicit program, motivic continuity created a kind of narrative coherence. Like the chief character in a novel, the "fortunes" of the main motive—its development, variation, and encounters with other "protagonists"—served as a source of constancy throughout the unfolding of the musical process.

The concept of motivic unity, which is considered further in Chapter 8, was compatible with Romanticism not only because thematic coherence, like nature, was considered economical and its changes gradual, but, most importantly, because

156. See the discussion of plenitude below.

157. For audiences and critics, unity may to some extent have been warranted by the presumed integrity of the composer's psyche. That is, belief in the unity and oneness of the individual—particularly if the individual was a genius, since truth and authenticity were, so to speak, guaranteed—meant that whatever discontinuities and contrasts occurred in a work were ultimately manifestations of a single, underlying psychic process.

158. In this connection, see my *Emotion and Meaning in Music,* p. 171. This and other aspects of program music are discussed at the end of the present chapter.

similarity relationships are, in principle at least, acontextual—that is, they are not significantly dependent on learned syntactic convention. (A simple example will help to make the connection between similarity and acontextuality clear. Suppose that an intelligent American college student were asked to arrange a number of cards of various sizes, shapes, and colors, each with some Chinese character on it. He or she might group the cards according to color or size or shape, and even perhaps in terms of the similarity between the characters. But unless the person knew Chinese, it is doubtful that the arrangements would result in intelligible, grammatical sentences. The arrangement would involve classification, but it would be based on physical similarity rather than on functional differentiation. In a comparable way, motivic similarities constituted the building blocks that enabled the new audience of elite egalitarians to comprehend the coherence of musical compositions.)[159]

The role of similarity relationships in ensuring unity—usually through derivation from, or transformation of, a single germinal motivic cell—was emphasized by theorists and composers throughout the nineteenth century.[160] Carl Czerny's description of Beethoven's Third Piano Concerto is representative of this conception of coherence. He writes that, following the first tutti, "all other passages are drawn from the principal theme, by which means the composition obtains that characteristic *unity,* by which it is so highly distinguished."[161]

Because they are not structured syntactically, similarity relationships are synchronic. Consequently, temporal order is theoretically irrelevant. Our experience of motivic similarities, however, invariably involves temporal ordering. And though the relationship between a motive and its variants can be described in "objective" terms, the diachronic ordering of such variants was and is more difficult to explain.[162] Indeed, virtually all diachronic accounts of motivic variation are metaphoric or analogical.[163] Thus, complementing the largely synchronic view of unity quoted

159. From this point of view, the whole history of music from, say, Berlioz to Boulez can be understood as one in which nonfunctional class membership becomes increasingly important, ending in serialism, set theory, and the compositions arising from them. Thus, in the analysis of much contemporary music, the "pitch-class" of a tone is more important than its function.

160. This emphasis is still very much with us today, not only in the writings of Rudolph Reti and his followers, but, to the extent that they have any relevance for perception, in serial theory and set theory as well.

161. *School of Practical Composition* 1:164. Other affirmations of this conception of unity are given in Chapter 8, at notes 152–155.

162. See Chapter 8, the section entitled, "Unity and Motivic Relationships."

163. The concept of unity through class similarity seems incompatible with that of organic unity. For organisms are invariably characterized by functional differentiation: for example, there are components responsible for sustenance, movement, and reproduction. Motivic similarities are not thus differentiated, however. The coexistence of the two views in the aesthetics of Romanticism can be explained, at least in part, by observing that both are conceived of as being natural and in some sense acontextual. And this observation accounts for a twentieth-century coupling of ideas that has puzzled me: the disciples of Schenker, whose theories are putatively organic, also espouse set theory, which is based on class similarities. Both theories are essentially acontextual and presumably based on natural relationships.

above, Czerny proposes an essentially narrative metaphor to account for diachronic unity:

> Just as in a romance, a novel, or a dramatic poem, if the entire work shall
> be successful and preserve its unity, the necessary component parts are:
> first, an exposition of the principal idea and of the different characters,
> then the protracted complication of events, and lastly the surprising catas-
> trophe and the satisfactory conclusion:—even so, the first part of the
> sonata-movement forms the exposition, the second part the complication,
> and the return of the first part into the original key produces, lastly, that
> perfect satisfaction which is justly expected from every work of art.[164]

The tendency to make narrative analogies is evident in the proclivity of nineteenth-century critics, theorists, and composers[165] to interpret the themes of a sonata-form movement in terms of a *conflict* between an emphatic ("masculine") first theme and a lyric ("feminine") second theme.[166] Often this conflict was thought to be resolved in the recapitulation. This metaphoric account is in turn related to the kind of diachronic unity created by dialectic processes. As M. L. Abrams points out, this view of unity was seen as being organic: "Following Schelling, [Coleridge] formulates [the nature of organic unity] in terms of the polar logic of thesis-antithesis-synthesis. 'It would be difficult to recall any true Thesis and Antithesis of which a living organ is not the Synthesis.'"[167]

As a condition of culmination, synthesis can be related to another important facet of Romantic thought and composition: the concept and expression of the *sublime*. Although it had figured prominently in aesthetics since Burke's influential essay,[168] the sublime came to play an even more important role in the art and aesthetics of Romanticism. Contrasted with the pleasing proportions and controlled clarity of the beautiful, it was the transcendent aspect of experience:

> The term sublime is generally applied to whatever in its way is much
> greater and more powerful than might have been expected; for this rea-
> son, the sublime arouses our astonishment and admiration. We enjoy

---

164. *School of Practical Composition* 1:34.

165. Cf. Schindler's report of Beethoven's interpretation of the "Pathétique" Sonata recounted in Newman, *Sonata in the Classic Era*, pp. 513–14.

166. It seems symptomatic of the change in attitude from the eighteenth to the nineteenth century that in the Classic period the relationship between themes or key areas was thought of as being one of *contrast*, which is a formal relationship that could be hierarchically subsumed, while in the Romantic period the relationship was conceived as being one of *conflict* that required resolution through thematic rather than harmonic processes.

167. Abrams, *The Mirror and the Lamp*, p. 174; the quotation is evidently from Coleridge, though this is not entirely clear.

168. *A Philosophical Inquiry into the Origin of our Ideas of the Sublime and the Beautiful* (1747).

those things which are simply good and beautiful in nature; they are pleasurable or edifying; they create an impression that is tranquil enough for
us to enjoy without disturbance. The sublime, however, works on us with
hammer-blows; it seizes us and irresistibly overwhelms us.[169]

It is this difference between the beautiful and the sublime that Mahler seems to have
in mind when he contrasts Brahms's Variations on a Theme by Haydn (which show
"an unparalleled musical mastery. . . . He takes the *seed* out of its matrix and con-
ducts it through *all the stages of development* to its highest degree of perfection")
with Beethoven's variations (which "are of a totally different nature. Carried away
by his own soaring imagination and flights of fancy, Beethoven is incapable of stick-
ing to the details of the theme. . . . Brahms's variations are like an enchanted stream,
with banks so sure that its waters never overflow, even in the sharpest bends").[170]
There is covert criticism here which Mahler makes more explicit elsewhere: "Brahms
is not concerned with breaking all bonds and rising above the grief and life of this
earth to soar up into the heights of other, freer and more radiant spheres. . . . [H]e
remains imprisoned in this world and this life, and never attains the view from the
summit."[171] Clearly what Mahler finds wanting in Brahms's music—the soaring to
the freer, more radiant spheres—is the expression of the sublime.

Mahler's criticism indicates that while Romantic composers and their audiences
found the intimacy of the small piano piece and the modest *lied* affecting, what they
most valued was the mystery and awe of the sublime. And the expression of the
sublime depends not on perfection but on magnitude. Following Kant's formulation,
Peter Lichtenthal observes, "whereas the beautiful relates to the *form* of things, that
is to say to their *quality,* the sublime is a matter of their *size,* or *quantity,* and may be
found in objects that are devoid of form."[172] In Romantic music, the expression of
sublimity took the form of huge cumulative climaxes—either high points of intense
and complex activity (which I call *statistical climaxes*) or, following such intensifications, powerful statements of majestic affirmation (which I call *apotheoses*).

Such climaxes constitute a new source of unity. For by literally overwhelming
the listener, their force and magnitude make prior unrealized implications, diversity
of materials, contrasts of expression, and even gaucheries of technique irrelevant.
Unity is established, so to speak, by the transcendence of the sublime—a kind of
statistical, rather than syntactic, subsumption.

Huge climaxes became a favored strategy not only for aesthetic and composi-

169. Johann Georg Sulzer, *Allgemeine Theorie der schönen Künste* (1771), excerpted in le Huray and Day,
p. 138.

170. Quoted in La Grange, *Mahler* 1:560–61; emphasis added. Notice the explicit use of the organic metaphor. I am grateful to David Brodbeck for calling this quotation and the following one to my attention.

171. Quoted in Bauer-Lechner, *Recollections of Gustav Mahler*, pp. 142–43.

172. *Dizionario e Bibliografia della Musica* (1826), excerpted in le Huray and Day, p. 372. In Kant's
words, the "pleasure in the beautiful is a matter of quality, and the pleasure in the sublime a matter of quantity"
(*Kritick der Urteilskraft* [1790], in le Huray and Day, p. 223).

tional reasons but because, like motivic unity (and, as we shall see, many other aspects of Romantic music), they were significantly egalitarian. That is, even the many somewhat unsophisticated members of the new middle-class audience could scarcely fail to appreciate and respond to the enormous force and power of, say, the third movement of Tchaikovsky's Fifth Symphony, the "Transfiguration" from *Tristan and Isolde,* and, even more obviously, the gigantic climaxes characteristic of French grand opera. Writing about this last genre, Henry Raynor observes that the librettist Scribe "had an infallible sense of what was theatrically effective in terms that Vérnon's audience could accept. . . . [His] libretti also integrated ballet into the dramatic action and built each to a climax which involved a scene of pageantry, huge dramatic choruses and the participation of several principal singers with fine voices." [173] And he goes on to point out that in Meyerbeer's operas "each act must achieve a great climax involving crowds of people and a huge orchestra." [174] In short, though as a rule social circumstances influenced compositional choices through the mediation of ideology, at times social circumstances affected style change more directly. Foremost among these circumstances were changes in the character of the audience for music.

## Social Circumstances, Style, and Ideology

"The era of the connoisseur aristocracy which had nurtured Gluck, Mozart, Haydn, and Beethoven had come to an end. The nobility's private orchestras and ensembles, its salons and palaces, now belonged to the history of the *ancien régime.*" [175] The facts are familiar and have frequently been recounted: the decline in noble and ecclesiastical patronage, complemented by the growth of an affluent upper middle class that believed in the value of, and developed a liking for, music, led to the burgeoning of public concerts and opera performances. Though these changes in patronage and concert life have been documented and described, they have seldom been related to specific changes in musical style. Perhaps the connections seemed so obvious that they were not deemed worthy of notice. Yet they were by no means inconsequential.

### *The Size and Structure of Audiences and Music*

Public concerts meant, quite simply, larger audiences, which in turn required larger concert halls and opera houses. "To insist upon the importance to nineteenth-century concerts of the size of the auditoria they frequented is not, of course, to note a mere triviality; concerts which had to survive more or less entirely through takings at the box perforce depended either on high prices or on the availability of a hall large

173. *Music and Society Since 1815,* p. 75.
174. Ibid., p. 78.
175. Solomon, *Beethoven,* p. 228.

enough to allow the sale of tickets at prices within the financial reach of the more or less poor." [176] Larger halls and houses affected both the size and the composition of orchestras and operatic productions, and these in turn affected the size and nature of the compositions presented.

The need to fill larger halls with sound—and especially the sound needed for the expression of the sublime—led not only to an increase in the number of performers in relation to those present in a normal Classic symphony or opera performance (more strings, winds, and brass; larger choruses, and so on), but to the use of instruments that extended the range of the orchestral sound (e.g., contrabassoons and piccolos). More importantly, the growth in the number of performers tended to encourage the composition of longer, more massive works. To put the matter negatively and much too crudely, it seemed somewhat incongruous (at least until the middle of the twentieth century) to gather a large group together to play a relatively brief composition. The increase in the size of both performing groups and compositions was, as we have seen, also encouraged by the valuing of the sublime and by the ability of the more diverse, less sophisticated audience to appreciate the huge climaxes that created transcendence. (Conversely, it seems possible that the existence of large performing groups fostered the composition of such climaxes.[177]) But the appeal of magnitude transcends ideology; for size is, and has generally been, a sign of power. And perhaps especially in the absence of inherited, fixed class distinctions, *amount* was increasingly associated with social status until size and value became virtually synonymous.

Not all compositions, of course, were monumental, and the division that developed between public display and private consumption led to a marked separation between the character of works meant for concert halls and that of works intended for the intimacy of the home. One need only think of the contrast between Mendelssohn's oratorios and his *Songs Without Words*. Yet for a considerable number of elite egalitarians one could, without too much exaggeration, paraphrase an old rhyme:

> Good, better, best
> Never let it rest,
> For the big is better
> And the biggest best.

In addition to facilitating monumental climaxes, the increased size of instrumental works may well have affected foreground compositional choices. As works became larger (and in some respects more complex), remembering the several musi-

---

176. Raynor, *Music and Society Since 1815*, p. 106.

177. This perhaps partly explains the tendency to play the choral works of the Baroque period with larger forces than they were written for. As Ruth A. Solie pointed out to me (in a personal communication), large forces were used in part because of the huge number of singers in the amateur choral groups that performed such works in the nineteenth century. And, in more cynical moments, one suspects that the success of Mendelssohn's revival of Bach's *Passion* was partly due to its monumentality.

cal ideas presented in the work became more difficult. And the more striking, peculiar, and patently delineated a musical idea—and in the notion of "idea" I include not only melodic/rhythmic/harmonic patterning, but register, orchestration, dynamics, texture, and so on—the more likely that it will be remembered.[178] The marked individuality of, say, the ideas that begin Schubert's "Unfinished" Symphony, Berlioz's *Symphonie fantastique,* Wagner's *Tristan and Isolde,* or Debussy's *Afternoon of a Faun* not only shapes expression and generates implicative processes, but is especially memorable.[179]

The valuing of highly individualized ideas is also related to the strategy of unity-through-diversity described in the discussion of organicism. The connection seems to be more or less as follows. Highly individualized ideas—ones that significantly modify, disguise, or dispense with prevalent convention—are more difficult to create than those that exploit, but do not basically change, such convention. It is partly for this reason, as well as for ones having to do with unity, that thematic conservation through similarity became an important strategic means in nineteenth-century music. Put briefly, the composers of the period not only made necessity a virtue, but made a virtue of necessity; economy, that is, was not only a value of organicism but an exigency. Note, too, that such conservation also serves musical memory; for varied recurrence both impresses an idea upon memory and reduces the number of different ideas to be stored.

The interdependence of size and memory also affected formal and tonal organization. Because of the constraints of human memory, the duration of temporal patterns is limited.[180] As a result, the length of the units of musical structure (generally speaking, phrases) is not solely a matter of convention. Depending partly on "density of information" and tempo, musical phrases (defined by some degree of closure) tend to range from four to eight measures. Consequently, forms grow longer not primarily because structural units become longer but because there are more of them. For instance, the exposition section of the first movement of Brahms's First Symphony is approximately twice as long as the exposition of the first movement of Haydn's Symphony No. 99 in E♭ Major, and Brahms's exposition contains more than twice as many structural units.[181]

The increase in the number of phrase units in turn affects tonal organization and formal structure. This is so because phrase units are not, generally speaking,

178. And the more likely that "imperfect" (varied) exemplifications and exact ones will be clearly distinguished from one another, emphasizing the nature of formal and processive relationships.

179. As always in history, there are too many reasons—in this case for the invention and prizing of distinctive musical ideas. Clearly the repudiation of convention and the correlative valuing of innovation and individual expression also played an important role in encouraging the invention of distinctive ideas—as the characteristic ideas of shorter piano pieces indicate. Nevertheless, I suspect that distinctiveness in the service of memory was especially important for large-scale works.

180. See Miller, "The Magical Number Seven."

181. The figures are as follows: (*a*) number of measures: Brahms, 151; Haydn, 71; (*b*) number of units: Brahms, 37; Haydn, 15; (*c*) average length of units: Brahms, 4.7 mm.; Haydn, 4.08 mm. The obvious methodological problem is that of establishing criteria for determining structural units. In this case, the same general criteria were used for both works. I am grateful to Justin London, who is studying the problems of structural lengths in Classic and Romantic symphonies, for these figures.

strung together like beads in a necklace, but combine with one another to create higher-level sections. This organization has two important consequences. First, because one way of defining such sections and, at the same time, enhancing their integrity is through tonal differentiation, the increased number and variety of tonal areas employed in nineteenth-century music are a consequence not just of the valuing of innovation, but of the fact of magnitude as well. Second, when such sections combine with one another to become still higher-level structures, there is a tendency for forms either to become tripartite or, perhaps more often, to function as elements in the cumulative, statistical form that is characteristic of much Romantic music. What I am suggesting—and much more careful study is needed to confirm these speculations—is that many of the changes in the formal and tonal organizations of nineteenth-century music can be traced to the increased size of compositions and through this to changes in audience and ideology.

## Declining Audience Sophistication

In the preceding discussion, the increased size of the audience was related to an overall decline in the level of its musical sophistication. To put the matter bluntly, the syntactic constraints—the rules and strategies—of a style are to a considerable degree learned and conventional. Insofar as a larger proportion of nineteenth-century audiences lacked familiarity with these constraints, the ability of members of an audience to respond sensitively to the nuances of syntax and the subtleties of form suffered. This decline cannot, unfortunately, be documented directly or unequivocally.[182] Though indirect evidence abounds, it usually involves problems of logic. On the one hand, characteristics of nineteenth-century music serve as evidence for a decline in audience sophistication; on the other hand, a decline in audience sophistication is used to explain the prevalence of the characteristics in question. I know no way out of this impasse, so I will assume that a decline in audience sophistication took place and then show that such a decline can be related to a number of characteristics of nineteenth-century music. The credibility of the network of relationships among music, ideology, and audience will, I hope, make the assumption seem reasonable.

THE INCREASED IMPORTANCE OF SECONDARY PARAMETERS.
One of the most important means employed by Romantic composers to compensate for the decline in the ability of many members of the audience to respond sensitively

---

182. This is not solely a problem of historical documentation. Because of the problems of testing and of interpreting verbal reports, which are necessarily biased by cultural beliefs, it is impossible to ascertain with reliability and precision what even present-day listeners comprehend—how they pattern and respond to the flow of musical stimuli.

to the subtleties of syntactic process and formal design was the increase in the relative importance of secondary parameters in shaping musical process and structure—and hence musical experience. To understand this change in emphasis, it will be helpful to review the differences, described in Chapter 1, between the primary and secondary parameters of music, especially because their respective roles in nineteenth-century music will be important in the discussions in Chapters 7 and 8.

The primary parameters of tonal music—melody, harmony, and rhythm—are syntactic. That is, they establish explicit functional relationships (such as tonic and fifth, subdominant and dominant, accent and weak beat) and specific kinds of closure (authentic or deceptive cadences, masculine or feminine rhythms) that make articulated hierarchic relationships possible.[183] Secondary parameters, on the other hand, are statistical in the sense that the relationships to which they give rise are typically ones of degree that can be measured and counted. Because secondary parameters establish continuums of relative, not stipulative, states of tension and repose—that is, louder/softer, faster/slower, thicker/thinner, higher/lower—music based on them can cease, or end, but cannot *close*.[184] Consequently, secondary parameters cannot readily act as the basis for articulated hierarchies, but only for continuous, emergent ones. Some of the compositional/stylistic consequences of these differences will be considered in what follows. In the present context, however, the crucial point is this: the syntax of tonal music, like other kinds of syntax, is rule-goverened, learned, and conventional. The secondary, statistical parameters, on the other hand, seem able to shape experience with minimal dependence on learned rules and conventions. Even in the absence of syntactic structuring, gradually rising pitches, increasingly loud dynamics, faster rates of motion, and a growth in the number of textural strands heighten excitement and intensity; while descending pitches, softer dynamics, slower rates of motion, and so on, lead toward relaxation, repose, and cessation.

I do not mean to imply that ordinary listeners did not understand the rudiments of syntax and form; most listeners probably understood how cadential progressions functioned, knew when melodies reached closure, and were able to experience the larger effects of stability/instability relationships. But for many listeners, the power of sheer sound—as music slowly swelled in waves of sonic intensity, culminating in a statistical climax or a plateau of apotheosis, and then quickly declined toward cessation and silence—in a very real sense shaped experience "naturally." To cite an unalloyed, though relatively recent, instance: it requires only a very modest degree of musical sophistication to understand the culmination processes created by dynamics, orchestration, texture and sonority, rate of activity, and so forth, in Ravel's *Boléro*. In short, without in any way disparaging the many exquisitely composed statistical climaxes in nineteenth-century music, it seems reasonable to argue that

183. Although rhythmic structure results from the interaction of a number of parameters, including secondary ones such as tempo and dynamics, it is considered a syntactic parameter here because it can create clearly defined closure.

184. The termination created by secondary parameters will be referred to as *cessation* to distinguish it from closure.

such means were chosen and similar patterns were replicated not only because they were consonant with the values of romanticism and its elite adherents, but because the resulting music could be appreciated by the less sophisticated members of the audience—in short, because such music was egalitarian.[185]

As the nineteenth century continued, the roles of the secondary parameters—the "natural" means of music—came to be more and more important relative to the primary, syntactic ones in shaping musical process and structure. One symptom of this trend is the increase in both the frequency of notational signs having to do with secondary parameters (dynamic and tempo markings, special timbres and modes of performance—pizzicato, con sordino, sul ponticello —and expressive markings such as *morendo* and *grazioso*) and their extent (more extreme dynamics and tempos, a greater range of pitches and sonorities, and so on).[186]

Ordinary language also supports the connection between an emphasis on secondary parameters and Romanticism. What is customarily characterized as a "Romantic performance" of a piece (of whatever style) is usually one that emphasizes the role of secondary parameters in the delineation of process, form, and affect. And it seems likely that the "romantic" style of performance was more than a matter of taste; it was one of change of audience. For as the familiarity of the audience with syntactic and formal conventions of tonal music diminished, performers turned to the secondary parameters that they could control—mainly dynamics and tempo—in order to make processive and structural relationships unmistakable.

Though I have emphasized the relative increase in the role of secondary parameters in the shaping of musical process and form, the part played by the primary parameters—the tensions and closures created by melody, harmony, and rhythm—is by no means insignificant. Clearly there are patent closures as well as cessations. Yet even the primary parameters bespeak the influence of ideology. Often closure is less

---

185. The enormous prestige and popularity of instrumental virtuosos can be attributed to the decline in audience sophistication on the one hand and to the tenets of ideology on the other. Let us take ideology first. Virtuosos were welcomed to the pantheon of the aesthetic elect because their abilities, like those of genius, were considered to be the result of natural endowment rather than privileged learning. The ideological importance of native endowment also accounts for the enormous interest in the feats of child prodigies. Thus the accomplishments of virtuosos were compatible with the ideals of egalitarianism. With regard to audience sophistication, without denying the perennial appeal of incomparable performance skill, it seems evident that relative tyros can be enthralled by stunning feats of instrumental agility, almost in the same way that they are entranced by prodigious feats of prestidigitation. Such feats are particularly striki﹐g when there is some standard of comparison. This may in part explain the penchant of nineteenth-century virtuosos and audiences for potpourris based on familiar tunes, often from operas. For what appealed was not merely hearing what was familiar (the pleasure of recognition), but the realization that what had been done by a large group of performers was now being done by one superplayer (the pleasure of economy?).

186. In a sketch such as this, it is obviously impossible to present a comprehensive account of the ways in which the secondary parameters of music act to create process and form, both alone and in interaction with primary parameters. Fortunately, the effects of tempo and rate of activity, dynamics and instrumentation, are quite familiar and have been considered, though not always explicitly so, by a number of scholars, including Wallace Berry (*Structural Functions in Music*), Deryck Cooke (*The Language of Music*), Donald N. Ferguson (*Music as Metaphor*), Leonard B. Meyer (*Emotion and Meaning in Music*), Jan LaRue (*Guidelines for Style Analysis*), and Robert G. Hopkins ("Secondary Parameters and Closure in the Symphonies of Gustav Mahler").

than decisive; for instance, when final cadences are plagal or when the melody ends on the fifth of the scale rather than on the fully stable tonic, there is an openness that implies continuation beyond the substantiality of sound into the ambiguity of silence.

It should be apparent from this discussion that the relationships among ideology, expression, and technique are far from simple. For example, it is often suggested that the frequency of dying-away endings is a more or less direct expression of the spirit of nineteenth-century culture. Without denying the expressive character of "*morendo* abatements," their relationship to ideology is both more interesting and more subtle. The denigration of convention involved both the rejection (or disguise; see below) of traditional closing formulae and, correlatively, the increased use of natural signs of ending. (From this point of view, nineteenth-century composers made an expressive virtue of ideological/compositional necessity.) In addition, these inclinations—these compositional choices—were encouraged by the ideological climate. Both the dying-away effect and the openness of the primary parameters imply the possibility of endless Becoming, a state especially valued by Romanticism, rather than the realized actualities of mere Being that result from complete, closed patternings.

PROGRAM MUSIC.

The heightened prestige of instrumental music, coupled with a decline in the audience's level of sophistication, is in part responsible for another of the many ironies and inconsistencies in nineteenth-century musical aesthetics and practice. Ideologically, the goal of art is the expression of "spirit," disembodied and pure. As Gustav Schilling wrote:

> Romantic art springs from man's attempt to transcend the sphere of cognition, to experience higher, more spiritual things, and to sense the presence of the ineffable. No aesthetic material is better suited to the expression of the ineffable than is sound, the stuff of music. All music is in its innermost essence romantic. . . . The proper realm of true music only begins where speech leaves off. E.T.A. Hoffman says that instrumental music is the most romantic of all the arts; and he is right.[187]

In practice, however, instrumental music tends more and more to be linked with literature and representation through titles, programs, and the like.

As is almost always the case, there were a number of reasons for this trend toward representation. An obvious one is that as the social status of composers

---

187. *Encyclopädie de gesammten musikalischen Wissenschaften* . . . (1834–38), excerpted in le Huray and Day, p. 470. Instrumental music is often referred to as pure because it appears to be independent of external reference and the conventions of language.

changed from servant/craftsman to independent artist, so did their education, out-look, and interests. Composers such as "Liszt, Berlioz, Schumann and Wagner were not only widely read; they mixed with literary and artistic people. They not only mixed with literary men; they were literary men themselves." [188] And it seems a small and not unnatural step from reading Dante, Shakespeare, or Norse mythology to emphasizing the referential and narrative possibilities of music. Nevertheless, this step was inconsistent with the Romantic ideal of pure instrumental music. The feel-ing that representation—especially when coupled with verbal description—violated the purity of musical expression may in part explain why composers tended either to deny the existence of programs or to question their aesthetic propriety.

Reference and programs were attractive for other reasons as well. In a period that placed a premium on originality and innovation—a period characterized by a significant increase in the number of alternative compositional possibilities and by a correlative deprecation of conventions and norms—devising and choosing musical relationships became problematic and time-consuming. [189] And it seems probable that extramusical ideas, whether literary or other, often served at once to stimulate musical invention and to limit the number and range of possible alternatives. For instance, ac-cording to Donald Mitchell, "the problem of the continuation of the Second Sym-phony was not solved until Mahler had, as it were, alighted on a programme that enabled him to round the work off." [190]

Extramusical reference also served the needs of the growing middle-class audi-ence. Henry Raynor observes:

> To declare any essential connection between the composer's new aware-ness of literature as a musical stimulus and the search for new audiences forced upon him by social and political conditions, would be to state more than we can ever have sufficient information to know. But it may well be that subconsciously—for no composer of programme music has sug-gested that his approach to literature was a deliberate attempt to create a community of feeling with an audience which might otherwise find it difficult to come to terms with what he had to communicate—the roman-tic composer realised that the shared experience of literature was a means of approach to listeners otherwise hard to reach. [191]

It was not, however, merely a matter of "sharing." As I have already argued, human beings seek to make the world as coherent, understandable, and predictable as pos-sible. And when the constraints governing some realm of nature or culture are

---

188. Abraham, *A Hundred Years of Music*, p. 24.

189. One circumstance that suggests this was indeed the case was the decline, mentioned earlier, in the number of works written by nineteenth-century composers as compared with eighteenth-century ones.

190. *Gustave Mahler: The Wunderhorn Years*, p. 165.

191. *Music and Society Since 1815*, p. 22.

known—usually in the sense of being internalized as a set of behavioral dispositions and attitudes—its characteristic processes and forms seem understandable. When, on the other hand, the constraints governing some realm are only weakly internalized, so that the music seems less coherent and understandable, there is a search for a conceptual framework that will make relationships seem more comprehensible.

The decline in the general level of sophistication most affected the audience's ability to comprehend large-scale processes and forms. Even quite inexperienced listeners could (and still do) respond to the ethos—the affective character, which Schumann called "moods of the soul" (*Seelenzustände*)—of a stable thematic passage. But they had difficulty following the less stable, modulatory processes that related stable parts to one another. In addition, the largely conventional relationships among key areas and formal returns tended to be more or less problematic.[192] What a program provided was a narrative in terms of which successive passages, both processive and formal, could be understood.[193] In other words, what a program made understandable was not primarily the ethos of the individual themes or gestures of a composition (though it necessarily gave these "A local habitation and a name"), but the composition's large-scale processive/structural relationships. That the function of a program is to clarify the music is suggested by Schumann: "The music does not denote or portray the program; something like the reverse is true: the program suggests and clarifies certain qualities of the music."[194]

These problems in comprehension were compounded by changes taking place in musical style. Several interrelated tendencies were present. One involved the direct juxtaposing of disparate affective (ethetic) states. While such juxtapositions, which occurred most often in collections of character pieces (usually for piano), served ideological ends by heightening the delineation of feeling and ethos, they also intensified the problem of mood succession. The question was, what was the basis for, the significance of, the succession? Programs and titles constituted a "solution" of this problem. One further feature of such character pieces should be mentioned here. It is well known that such pieces—Schumann's *Carnaval* is an exemplary instance—often employ a unifying motive or theme. The pertinent point here is that such motivic constancy emphasizes contrast of character and mood. Just as differences in expression and mood in a play are most patent and poignant when manifested in the behavior of a single protagonist, so differences in ethos and expression in music are especially salient when a single motive is the basis for successive parts.

192. Again, I must emphasize that the attribution of these characteristics to less sophisticated members of the audience is a speculative inference, which is very difficult to verify or support with hard data.

193. I discussed this matter at greater length in *Emotion and Meaning in Music*, chap. 8.

194. Quoted in Plantinga, *Schumann as Critic*, p. 120. This is why, for Schumann at least, the same work could be consonant with a number of quite different programs: "I will not attempt to provide [Schubert's C-Major Symphony] with a foil, for the different generations choose very different words and pictures to apply to music" (quoted in Plantinga, p. 124). As Plantinga observes, in Schumann's view a program was "a supplement to a composition, not a subject of it" (p. 125).

Thus in *Carnaval,* the expansive dignity of the "Valse noble" is more striking because its opening motive (A–E♭–B–C–D, etc.) is a variant of that which began the piquant "Arlequin" (A–E♭–[C]–B–C–D, etc.).[195]

Anomalies of form or genre also tended to elicit programs and title tags. In some cases, that is, it may not have been primarily the relationship between ethetic states that was problematic but the nature of form or genre. This supposition is supported by the observation that when the nature of a genre was familiar (as in the case of a nocturne or ballade) or the structure of a movement (e.g., a sonata form or a theme and variations) was unambiguous, extramusical reference was unlikely. Conversely, whatever seemed especially striking, unusual, or anomalous—for whatever reason—tended to elicit a title tag, a biographical reference, or a program.[196] This is the case, for example, with the sudden *forte* in the slow movement of Haydn's "Surprise" Symphony and the striking dialogue between orchestral (string) unison and solo piano in the second movement of Beethoven's Fourth Piano Concerto.[197]

What programs and title tags do, then, is provide psychic security; what seemed an anomaly, threatening our ability to comprehend the world (for the sake of envisaging and choosing), is made understandable and restores our sense of control, either through reference to genesis (the story behind the "surprise" in Haydn's symphony) or through reference to some source of order beyond the musical relationships per se (the Orpheus program for Beethoven's concerto). I have already mentioned the relationship between the proliferation of programs and the decline in audience sophistication. The reciprocal relationship between the tendency to devise programs and the valuing of originality and innovation should also be noted. That is, the valuing of innovation resulted in the very anomalies that elicited explanatory programs and mythic anecdotes. Conversely, as we shall see, the delineation of the extramusical encouraged (and in instrumental music virtually required) the use of means that were out of the ordinary. As Robert Morgan observes, "those nineteenth-century works that most severely strained the syntactic conventions were almost always programmatic."[198]

The subjects of program music—whether autobiographical, imitative of natural events, or taken from literature, history, and mythology—were those consonant with the ideological beliefs and aesthetic attitudes of both composers and audiences. For instance, Greek and Roman myths were seldom chosen as subjects, not only because they were unfamiliar and seemed irrelevant to the new egalitarian audience, but be-

195. Obviously, differences in character are dependent upon rhythm, tempo, dynamics, phrase structure, and so on.

196. In a sense, the composer's "life and hard times"—e.g., illness, disappointed love, financial distress, and the like—serves as a surrogate program.

197. My point is not whether, for instance, Beethoven actually had a program in mind when he wrote the slow movement of the concerto, as Owen Jander argues ("Beethoven's 'Orpheus in Hades,'" pp. 195–212). Rather it is that the proclivity to create a program (on the part of Czerny, A. B. Marx, and Jander—or Beethoven himself, if Jander is right) is related to the special affective and structural characteristics of the movement. As Jander himself observes, "to try to relate this work to any of the recurring forms of slow movements of Classical concertos is futile" (p. 205).

198. "Analysis of Recent Music," p. 48.

cause of their association with the political/social structure and the rule-governed aesthetic of the ancien régime. Instead, composers turned to the vernacular literature, to Dante, Shakespeare, Byron, and Scott, to local mythology and history, and to Norse gods and national heroes, as well as to personal reminiscences and experiences.

Such general subjects were chosen because they were consonant with the constraints of ideology and culture. But which of the events from a novel or history were actually depicted in a composition depended to a considerable extent on the types of representation already available as part of existing musical/pictorial tradition. More specifically, any moderately complex story depicts a large number of diverse incidents, characters, settings, and so on. Those chosen for musical representation were so not primarily because of their special narrative importance, but because a concatenation of musical traits for their delineation already existed. This is why the same musical "scenes" (e.g., military and funeral processions, battles and storms, pastoral and sea scenes, fairies and demons, religious solemnity and peasant dancing, contemplative soliloquies and violent assertions) are represented time and again during the nineteenth century. It is as though the characteristic styles (heroic, military, pastoral) prevalent in eighteenth-century music served as "source sets" for the events in the program. In so doing, they influenced which incidents, scenes, and sentiments from the original, nonmusical subject were chosen for representation.[199] Put differently, in the eighteenth century, musical modes of representation were associated with one another in terms of *class* relationships (various aspects of the heroic or different facets of the pastoral, and so on); in the nineteenth century, essentially the same modes of representation were associated with one another in terms of narrative, developmental processes—processes specified by a program. An analogy with the practice of the singing of folk epics is suggestive. As Albert Lord has observed, folk singers have stock texts ready to insert into particular narratives, such as texts for wedding scenes, competitions, and messengers.[200] In short, cultural constraints (values) generally influenced the subjects chosen for musical programs, while prevalent musical constraints played an important role in determining which incidents from the program would be represented.

It should be observed, finally, that there is a connection between the incidents chosen for musical representation and the statistical forms favored by nineteenth-century composers and audiences. That is, events such as storms, battles, marches, and dance scenes—events that generally have or can be given a statistical shape (the music begins with low pitches and soft dynamics, slow rates of activity and uncomplicated textures; this section is followed by gradual intensification of all parameters, then slight subsidence, and again further intensification until the statistical climax is

---

199. The means of representation were, of course, partly conventional, though their delineation was significantly enhanced through the more salient use of secondary parameters. For the conventions of eighteenth-century music, see Kirby, "Beethoven's Pastoral Symphony"; Ratner, *Classic Music,* chap. 2; and Allanbrook, *Rhythmic Gesture in Mozart,* pp. 1–70.

200. *The Singer of Tales,* chap. 4.

reached; finally there is rapid abatement to the end of the event)—tend to be replicated with special frequency.[201]

Extramusical reference was, needless to say, scarcely new. At least since the Renaissance, music had been thought capable of depicting ideas and actions, character and passions. What was new in the nineteenth century was that delineation, which had previously depended to a considerable extent on conventional signs or on the complementary relationship between language and tone, was now made mainly the responsibility of instrumental means alone.[202] But if tone alone, independent of convention, was to be the chief basis for musical delineation, compositional strategies had to be devised or existing ones modified. The changes that took place were trended: reference was made more palpable and understandable through the extension of existing modes of representation.[203] Influenced by the ideological valuing of natural means, the extension took the form of an increasing emphasis on the role of secondary parameters.[204]

Increasing emphasis was not, however, a matter of using a greater *number* of secondary parameters. For whenever there is any sound at all, most of the secondary parameters are necessarily present: that is, there are always timbre, texture, some general pitch level (even for nonpitched percussion) and duration, and some dynamic level. Rather, emphasis took the form of increased deviation from more or less normal states for each of the several parameters. For instance (to choose examples where the reference is explicit), the ethereal and poignant sadness of Violetta's impending death is represented in the preludes to acts 1 and 3 of *La traviata* with extreme states of all parameters: unusually high registers, very soft dynamics (*ppp*), very slow tempo (MM. = 66), largely conjunct motion, concordant harmonies, and simple choralelike durations and texture. By way of contrast, satanic malevolence is delineated in Liszt's Mephisto Waltz No. 2 by almost the opposite configuration of extremes: predominantly low register, loud dynamics, rapid tempo, discordant harmony and disjunct motion, and ironically irregular waltz rhythms. F. H. J. Castil-

---

201. I will put forward another unsubstantiated hypothesis: In nineteenth-century virtuoso potpourris, the original numbers from an opera are so arranged that the incident most amenable to statistical shaping is put at the end.

202. Obviously, the complementary relationship between text and tone continued and flourished in the *lied* and *chanson*.

203. This is not to assert that no new strategies were devised. Clearly, Wagner's invention of "leitmotif-narration" was a major innovation.

204. The understanding of musical reference always involved learning. This is so in two respects. First, many references (for instance, that of brass instruments to the Last Judgment or of drone fifths to the pastoral) are matters of almost Pavlovian association, having little that is "natural" about them. Second, even more natural means are given specific references through culturally learned metaphors. On the other hand, reference is often partly natural, again in two respects. First, it seems indisputable that there are deep-seated connections between the shapes and actions of music and those of extramusical phenomena: to scale a mountain and to ascend a musical scale are, because of similarities of tension and effort, experientially comparable. Second, the tendency to associate music with extramusical phenomena seems an innate human proclivity, as is indicated by a wealth of cross-cultural data. Moreover, the tendency to make such associations is, as noted above, especially pronounced when the musical patterning is unusual, given prevalent stylistic norms.

Blaze describes the expressive effect of the use of secondary parameters on even inexperienced listeners:

> The first person to create a powerful effect, not only by giving the harmony an unusual and unexpected twist, but by scoring it for full orchestra, doubtless made a great impact. The first person to prolong an expression of terror by the use of low, repeated notes on the strings, doubtless petrified his audience; and if someone had then tried to describe this effect he could justifiably have said that in listening to those terrifying sounds his hair stood on end. If soft, slow and sustained notes followed those violent shocks they would have produced a kind of enchantment. Such alternation of gentleness and strength would give inexperienced and sensitive listeners much satisfaction.[205]

Though deviation enhanced delineation,[206] the most important means of representation was through some similarity—either by correlation or metaphoric mimicry (see Chapter 4)—between musical relationships and extramusical ones. Similarity was the favored choice because, once the idea of representation was an accepted cultural belief, the recognition of similarities was a natural way of "relating"—that is, relative to conventional reference, it was largely independent of privileged learning.

Though the secondary parameters were of primary importance in the delineation of reference, deviation from prevalent syntactic norms also played a part in program music.[207] But delineation was not the sole—or even the primary—reason for changes in tonal syntax, for the avoidance of patently conventional relationships, and for the use of means that were less directly dependent upon privileged learning. These changes occurred in "pure" as well as program music. Nor was the change of audience alone responsible; ideology, and in particular the repudiation of convention, was of central importance. Strategies devised to mask both patent conventionality and the means employed to diminish dependence upon learning will be considered in the next chapter. The weakening of tonal syntax and the changes in musical form that took place during the nineteenth century are considered in Chapter 8.

---

205. François Hénri Joseph Castil-Blaze, *Dictionnaire de musique moderne* (1821), excerpted in le Huray and Day, p. 356.

206. For a discussion of these matters, see my *Emotion and Meaning in Music,* chaps. 6, 7, and especially 8.

207. See Robert Morgan, quoted above at note 198.

# CHAPTER 7

# Convention Disguised—Nature Affirmed

A crucial question for the history of music is how ideological values are transformed into musical constraints and specific compositional choices. In this chapter and the next, I hope to describe some of the ways in which the beliefs and attitudes of Romanticism influenced the choices made by composers from the beginning of the nineteenth century well into the twentieth.

The changes that occurred from the late eighteenth to the early twentieth century involved, not decisive breaks on the level of rules, but rather general trends on the level of strategies. As with a change of season, there may be marked fluctuation within such a trend. Thus, though there is, for instance, a tendency for the range of melodies to become greater during the nineteenth century (until one reaches the extremes, say, of early Schoenberg), the process is not one of necessary, unremitting increase. Above all, the process implies nothing about any individual instance; the melody of the first movement of Mahler's Fourth Symphony (Example 2.3a), for example, is relatively limited in range.

My sketch is explicitly limited in two important ways. First, the discussion of musical relationships will be concerned with relatively foreground levels of structure. This is not really surprising since we know that competent listeners can usually recognize that a work is Romantic after hearing only a few measures.[1] Though the style changes that took place during the nineteenth century were largely on the foreground level, it does not follow that they were trivial or inconsequential. As I hope to show with respect to form, essentially surface features may have important effects on compositional practice. Second, for the most part instrumental, rather than vocal,

---

1. Attention to foreground levels is appropriate for ideological reasons as well. Generally speaking, the expression of individual choice—a prerogative highly prized by Romanticism—increases as one moves from higher to lower structural levels. That is, on the level of laws, individual choice is precluded; on the level of rules, only radical novelty is possible; but on the level of strategies, in the realms of idiom and intraopus form, individual choice can be freely exercised.

music will be used to illustrate the salient features of the Romantic style. I imposed this limitation not only because of the Romantic valuing of "pure" instrumental music, but also because the connection between compositional constraints and ideological ones can be more easily traced when it is not complicated by the further, not necessarily congruent, constraints of text setting and theatrical performance.[2]

## CONVENTION, ORIGINALITY, AND INDIVIDUALITY

Ideologically, whatever seemed conventional (familiar cadential gestures, commonplace melodic schemata, stock accompaniment figures, and so on) was anathema to Romantic composers. Distaste for, and disparagement of, established rules and routines was, as we have seen, evident in the writings of the period. The following sampling from Berlioz's memoirs is typical:

> "the appalling quantity of *platitudes* for which the piano is daily responsible . . ." (p. 41)

> "the *lure of conventional* sonorities . . ." (p. 41)

> "hence those convenient vocal *formulas* . . ." (p. 212)

> "that eternal *device* of the final [authentic] cadence . . ." (p. 212)

> "the deadliest enemies of genius are those lost souls who worship in the *temple of Routine* . . ." (p. 218)

> "those *perfect cadences, recurring every minute,* account by themselves for some two-thirds of the score . . ." (p. 317)

> "[Cimarosa's *Secret Marriage*] is an opera fit only for fairs and carnivals." (p. 317)[3]

Yet, from a practical point of view, those who composed tonal music could no more dispense with the norms of grammar, syntax, and form than could poets and novelists. For such conventions were, after all, their native language—the way in which they had learned to "hear," to understand the relationships among sounds.

The problem of reconciling the ideological rejection of conventions with the practical need for them was intensified by another dilemma. Two of the prime values of Romanticism were originality and individuality. Thus Liszt tells us that, in the Romantic view, "the merit of perfecting a process can never equal the merit of inventing it,"[4] and, according to Leon Plantinga, Schumann believed the characteristics of Romantic music to be "an emphasis on originality rather than the normative,

---

2. In addition, because it is usually easier to discern and discuss Romantic traits in a text or a plot than in "pure" music, there is a temptation to allow their analysis to act as a substitute for an analysis of the connections between the constraints of ideology and those of music per se.

3. *Memoirs of Hector Berlioz;* emphasis added.

4. *Chopin,* pp. 139–40.

an interest in the unique effect and individual emotion."[5] But the existence of originality and the expression of individuality are invariably dependent upon—are defined and comprehended in relation to—some norm or convention of behavior, whether in everyday life or in art.[6] And because of the lack in humankind of an adequate complement of innate (genetic) constraints, a large majority of such norms are necessarily established by learned, cultural conventions. Put aphoristically: radical individualism seeks to undermine the norms on which its expression depends. Since, for Romanticism, originality and individuality are virtually inseparable and often indistinguishable—one even speaks of someone of striking individuality as an "original"—I will treat them as more or less interchangeable notions.[7] Their expression in and effects on nineteenth-century music are worth exploring briefly.

It is significant that, together with other facets of nineteenth-century thought such as the belief in progressive development, the prizing of originality and individuality probably served to foster the kind of trended change described in Chapter 3. Because the indispensable constraints of tonality severely limited the *kinds* of innovations possible, changes were, for the most part, matters of *degree*. Something comparable to what political scientists call *outbidding* took place.[8] That is, if a composer or a compositional community employed a particular kind of musical means in a relatively modest manner, later composers seeking to affirm their originality and individuality were virtually obliged to intensify the degree or increase the frequency of the means. For instance, over the years there was a general tendency for chromatic progressions, registral limits, and what I am calling melodic/rhythmic "stretching" to become more common and more extreme. Thus ideology affected both the kinds of strategies employed (favoring those capable of difference in degree) and the pattern of change (trended) that occurred during the nineteenth century.

The valuing of originality and individuality was reciprocally related to the denigration of convention. A convention is a shared, common property; it belongs to the compositional community, not to the individual. And it does not seem too farfetched to suggest that the emphasis on the importance of novel musical ideas was related to the concern of the elite egalitarians with the power of possession. Musical ideas constituted the main "capital" possessed by composers, and these ideas could be made manifest only to the extent that they were in some way different—that is, original.[9]

5. *Schumann as Critic,* p. 108. And much later, Schoenberg asserts that "in higher art, only that is worth being presented which has never before been presented" (*Style and Idea,* p. 39).

6. Appropriately, the distinctive dress and sometimes wayward behavior of some of the artists of the period seem to be telling evidence of the dependence of individuality on established norms and customs.

7. In the ultimate music of Romanticism—for instance, that of John Cage—there are no norms in terms of which the individual can be known or personal expression defined. Originality remains. But it is defined not through play with and deviation from prevalent, and usually conventional, norms, but through the devising of categorically novel means. As such it becomes an important (at times exclusive) basis for criticism.

8. I am grateful to my friend Sidney Verba, a political scientist, for calling this concept to my attention.

9. The valuing of originality is also related to the notion that musical ideas—and even stylistic constraints (rules as well as strategies)—become exhausted. That is, the hypothesis of exhaustion serves as a supplementary reason for the imperative of innovation: new means are needed because old means become worn-out. The relation of exhaustion to the organic model is obvious.

The valuing of individual inner experience is evident in the shift from the eighteenth-century idea that music *represented emotions* (affects) to the nineteenth-century belief that music *expressed the feeling* of the composer. For emotions are classlike, social, and hence nameable. Love and hate, anger and fear are states that depend on social context for their identification and (at least in part) on convention for their musical delineation. Feelings, on the other hand, are personal, idiosyncratic, and unnameable. Thus, defining the nature of God, Goethe's Faust says:

> Feeling is all in all;
> The name is sound and smoke,
> Obscuring heaven's pure glow.[10]

Feelings, as distinguished from emotional states, are natural—even acontextual.[11]

Feeling is prized not only because it is individual and natural, but because it unites, creating the *oneness* valued by Romanticism. "Whereas reason can only comprise each object separately," writes Schlegel, "feeling can perceive all in all at one and the same time."[12] Moreover, unlike reason, which is governed by artificial rules and conventions, feeling is spontaneous, unmediated, and natural. Hence it is the primary way of knowing. Writing to Wagner, Liszt affirms that "we must become *wise* by means of *feeling*," and that "Reason tells us *so it is,* only after feeling has told us *so it must be.*"[13]

Again there seems to have been a disparity between ideological belief and the exigencies of compositional practice. According to Romanticism, the *real* self of an individual was not manifest in the externals of conscious behavior—especially not in cultivated cultural norms. Rather, it lay buried in an inner realm of personal longings and desires, private dreams and fantasies. But because the fundamental stylistic constraints of tonality were an indispensable basis for composition, the deep, inner realms of feeling could be realized only through the devising and use of foreground strategies. Such realizations of the inner self of the composer tended to be replicated

---

10. Quoted in Artz, *Renaissance to Romanticism*, p. 223.

11. But because "pure," acontextual feeling seems eerie and disembodied, there is a tendency to refer pure feeling to an external source. Paradoxically, then, the avoidance of conventional representation of emotion encourages the devising of referential contexts (programs) in terms of which pure feeling can be specified and comprehended.

12. Quoted in Artz, *Renaissance to Romanticism*, pp. 223–24.

13. Hueffer, trans., *Correspondence of Wagner and Liszt* 2:170. And perhaps it is partly for this reason that instrumental music came to be considered the Romantic art par excellence. Literature almost of necessity represents human beings in social contexts that suggest that experience is more or less classlike. This suggests that lyricism was especially favored—because it is more concerned with individual feeling than with interpersonal relationships. (Perhaps this is why Dostoevski's novels, which are centrally concerned with the inner soul of individual characters, have generally been considered more profound than those of Dickens or Thackeray, which are more concerned with social interaction. The ultimate triumphs of the inner life occur, of course, in symbolist poetry and the stream-of-consciousness novel.) In the visual arts, the change from, for instance, mythological and historical subjects (representing human beings in social interaction) to landscape and still life (which do not) may have occurred not only because of the valuing of nature and the change in audience discussed in the previous chapter, but because these subjects presumably evoked individual feelings in each viewer. (Again, the ultimate appeal to the peculiar, idiosyncratic response of the individual viewer takes place in the twentieth century, especially in abstract expressionism.) In this, the lyric and the landscape are symptoms of egalitarianism.

throughout his or her *oeuvre*. Thus the valuing of individuality and originality led not only to the outbidding mentioned earlier, but to a kind of "stylistic territoriality." Composers tended to define such territories through the use of what might be thought of as surface self-markers—e.g., idiomatic rhythms, melodic gestures, harmonic relationships, instrumental usage—and, in the twentieth century, novel precompositional constraints. Partly for this reason, it is more likely that a work by Haydn would be mistaken for one by Mozart than that a work by Schumann would be mistaken for one by Schubert, or that one by Mahler would be mistaken for one by Bruckner.

Nevertheless, similar strategies were employed by most nineteenth-century composers. Broadly speaking, these involved ways of making the claims of ideology compatible with the inescapable conventions of tonal syntax. Though no fundamental reconciliation between these claims took place in the nineteenth century, workable arrangements were found. Two different but related strategies will be considered in this sketch. The first reconciled the claims of ideology with the conventions of tonal syntax through what I call *disguise*. The second, discussed later in this chapter and in the next, involved the use of means less definitively dependent upon syntactic constraints and ones less patently conventional.

## CONVENTION DISGUISED

In music, one of the discoveries of Romanticism was how to hide convention, yet have it too. Established patterns—the cadential gestures, harmonic progressions, and formal structures of the Classic style—could be used but were generally disguised in some way.[14] Though there are probably many ways of disguising convention, only two are discussed in what follows: disguise through *emergence* and disguise through *divergence*.[15] Convention was not, of course, invariably veiled. This was clearly the case in French and Italian opera from Rossini through Verdi.[16] At times, too, convention could be forgiven because it served the ends of parody and satire. For instance, Hugh Macdonald observes that "Berlioz regarded strict contrapuntal forms as mechanistic and inexpressive. He parodied the Handel-Cherubini style of fugue in *La Damnation de Faust* and *Beatrice et Benedict*."[17] And Donald

---

14. Perhaps it was an unconscious awareness of the act of disguising that led to the celebration of the hidden, underlying forces proposed by organicism. And what was hidden was the lineage, the origin, of the patterning. If this suggestion has merit, Freud was profoundly mistaken; what was (and is) repressed in our Romantic culture was not the id but the superego.

15. The subject of disguise—its uses and kinds—needs much more careful study than can be attempted here.

16. See, for instance, Gossett, "Gioachino Rossini"; and idem, "Verdi, Ghislanzoni, and *Aida*." The use of conventional schemata such as sonata form in instrumental music is considered in the next chapter.

17. Hugh Macdonald, "Berlioz, (Louis-) Hector," *The New Grove Dictionary*, ed. Stanley Sadie, 2:599. Wagner and Strauss also used fugue to parody the artificial and academic: the former in the Overture to *Die Meistersinger*, the latter in *Also sprach Zarathustra*.

Grout suggests that the fugal chorus ("Tutto nel mondo") at the end of Verdi's *Falstaff* satirizes the entire Romantic century.[18]

### Disguise Through Emergence

Not surprisingly, the most decisive closure in Debussy's *Prelude to the Afternoon of a Faun* is that created by the last cadence (Example 7.1). Closure is articulated by an ostensibly normal ii–$V^7$–I progression that accompanies two coordinate melodic closing gestures. Each of these gestures is disguised by both emergence and divergence.

The first gesture (Example 7.1, middle staff) is built on a figure (*m*) that descends sequentially from B♭ to E. This figure is equivalent and similar to that leading to the first cadence of the *Prelude* (Example 7.2*a*). Moreover, as part *b* of the example shows, the B♭ (= A♯) at the end of measure 103 could be regarded as continuing (growing out of) the linear descent begun in measure 3 (analytic graph 1). From this point of view, the opening can be understood as generating a descending linear motion from the C♯ in measure 3 (or even m. 1?) to the E in measure 106.[19]

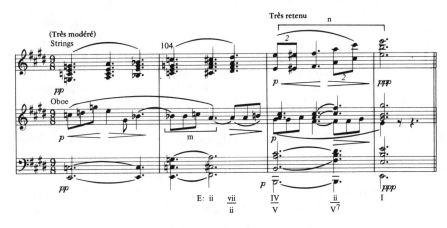

EXAMPLE 7.1. Debussy, *Prelude to the Afternoon of a Faun*

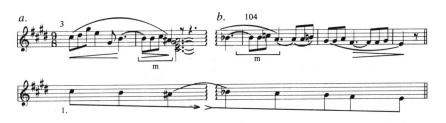

EXAMPLE 7.2. Debussy, *Prelude to the Afternoon of a Faun*

18. *History of Western Music*, p. 607.
19. Note that the descent from B♭ to E parallels the striking motion of the main motive from C♯ to G (m. 1).

A comparable process occurs in the clear cadence from measure 29 to 30 (Example 7.3*a*). That process, which also begins on A♯ (= B♭), reaches the dominant rather than the tonic. But the dotted rhythm makes credible what one already suspected: that the descending figure is a deformation of a closing gesture common in the Classic style. An instance of such a gesture, from the second movement of Mozart's String Quintet in E♭ Major (K. 614), is given in Example 7.3*b*. The similarities are obvious. What concern us here are the differences. For Mozart's cadential gesture, unlike Debussy's, does not grow out of earlier events. Indeed, nothing resembling it occurs earlier in the movement, nor does it complete a process begun before. The gesture signifying closure is not essentially part of the intraopus style of this movement, but rather part of the dialect of Classic music. As such, it is unequivocally and unashamedly conventional.

EXAMPLE 7.3. (*a*) Debussy, *Prelude to the Afternoon of a Faun*; (*b*) Mozart, String Quintet in
E♭ Major (K. 614), ii

The presence of a second closing gesture (*n*) is less obvious. It begins with the half-step motion to the supertonic (E♯ to F♯ in measure 105; Example 7.1, top staff, and Example 7.4*a*), which is extended through A and C♯. This gesture is common in Classic music. But as Example 7.4*b* (from the last movement of Mozart's String Quintet in E♭ Major) shows, in the Classic style the fifth of the supertonic triad skips down to the tonic, becoming part of a I⁶₄–V progression. In Debussy's cadence, the fifth of the supertonic also moves to the tonic, but instead of skipping down, the line continues to rise and the tonic (E) is accompanied by tonic rather than dominant harmony. Because the gesture grows out of the melodic, orchestral, and textural processes that precede it, its identity and integrity are masked. And so, as a result, is its conventionality.

EXAMPLE 7.4. (*a*) Debussy, *Prelude to the Afternoon of a Faun*; (*b*) Mozart, String Quintet in
E♭ Major (K. 614), iv

Although this closure is the most decisive in the *Prelude,* it is not very forceful. In addition to the veiling of cadential gesture, two other features of the patterning weaken closure. First, because the harmony in measure 105 (see Example 7.1) contains a strong subdominant component above dominant harmony, the motion from measure 104 to 105 lacks articulative force,[20] despite the dominant-tonic motion in the bass. The second feature of the pattern that weakens closure is the lack of a reversal breaking the momentum of the ongoing, divergent wedge (Example 7.5).[21] All of these aspects of Debussy's cadence enhance openness, contributing to the sense of Becoming characteristic of nineteenth-century music and consonant with the ideology of Romanticism.

EXAMPLE 7.5.  Debussy, *Prelude to the Afternoon of a Faun*

The connection between compositional choices such as these and other tenets of the ideology of Romanticism—organicism, disdain for convention, and the valuing of originality/individuality—is not difficult to discern. Organicism, which posits the naturalness and virtues of gradual transformation, encourages the emergence of a syntactic gesture from earlier materials; such emergence, at the same time, tends to disguise the presence of the conventional. The individuality of the composer is made evident by the kind of strategy chosen for disguising. One further comparison will serve to emphasize that disguise-through-emergence is a strategy characteristic of nineteenth-century music.

The closing gesture given in Example 7.6a (motive *m*) occurs twice at the very end of the slow movement of Mozart's "Haffner" Symphony (K. 385). Following

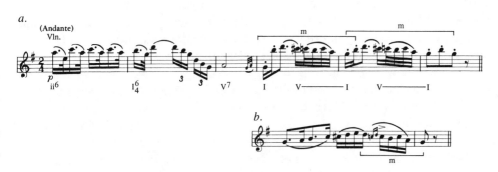

EXAMPLE 7.6.  (*a*) Mozart, Symphony No. 35 in D Major (K. 385), "Haffner," ii; (*b*) Mahler, Symphony No. 4, i

20. The importance of the subdominant/dominant relationship in defining tonality is discussed in the next chapter.

21. The nature and use of divergent wedges in the music of the nineteenth century are also discussed in Chapter 8.

the chief cadential closure of the movement, the gesture seems patently conventional (Example 7.6*a*). As we saw in Chapter 2, virtually the same gesture ends the opening theme of the first movement of Mahler's Fourth Symphony (Example 7.6*b*). But the conventionality of Mahler's version is significantly mitigated by context. For as the analytic staffs in Example 7.7 show, the gesture in Mahler's symphony forms part of—emerges from—a larger motion of continuously linked triads. The conventional motion of linked triads is itself disguised both by the passing tones of the melody and by the rhythmic/metric displacement of some of the structural tones (for instance, the E in m. 5).

EXAMPLE 7.7.  Mahler, Symphony No. 4, i

## Disguise Through Divergence

Many of the schemata that are indispensable for the perception and understanding of Classic and Romantic music are dependent for their delineation on the conventions of tonal syntax.[22] The disguise of the conventionality of such schemata through divergence will be the chief concern of the ensuing discussion. Other schemata and strategies less intrinsically linked to the syntactic constraints of tonality will be considered in the next section of this chapter, "Nature Affirmed."

To show how divergence disguises, I will discuss instantiations of a schema frequently replicated in the music of the eighteenth and nineteenth centuries. What I call a *changing-note* schema occurs in three versions, which differ mainly in melodic structure. These versions are given in abstract, unembellished form in Example 7.8. In each, the harmonic motion is from tonic to dominant (V or vii), and then back from dominant to tonic (I or vi); often, as shown in the examples, the bass revolves around the tonic and is in contrary motion to the melody, though other bass notes are possible, especially the fifth. The form of the schema is strophic (A A'), but on the next hierarchic level, the first two elements of the schema frequently form

---

22. The role of schemata in the perception and understanding of music was discussed in Chapter 2.

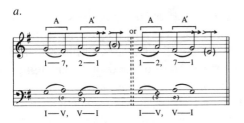

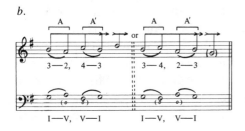

EXAMPLE 7.8. Changing-note schema: (*a*) tonic; (*b*) mediant; (*c*) disjunct (mixed)

part of a larger bar form (A A' B, not shown in the example). The melodic process is always sequential.[23]

In the tonic version of the changing-note schema, the melody revolves around the first degree of the scale, usually moving 1–7/2–1, but sometimes using the opposite order (1–2/7–1). The first of these possibilities rises sequentially, implying continuation to the third of the scale or beyond, as indicated by the arrows in the example. The second possibility is much less common, probably because the closure that the leading-tone-to-tonic motion (7–1) creates is too strong for the generation of more extensive melodic structures. For this reason, instead of being the basis for beginnings of patterns, it tends to be the basis for cadential gestures.[24]

The mediant changing-note schema revolves around the third degree of the scale. Like the tonic version, it usually rises sequentially, implying motion to the fifth degree of the scale or beyond. In this case, too, the prevalence of rising motion probably occurs because descent leads to the tonic and the tendency toward closure.[25]

23. All of these changing-note patterns are obviously prolongations of tonic harmony. But what is of interest stylistically is not such similarities, but rather the differences in structure and usage that result in differences in frequency of occurrence and in modes of disguise.

24. See, for instance, Haydn, String Quartet in F Major, Opus 77 No. 2, ii, mm. 73–74; Mozart, Clarinet Quintet in A Major (K. 581), iv, mm. 7–8; and a divergent version, Dvořák, String Quartet in F Major, Opus 96 ("American"), iii, mm. 5–8. Though closing versions of the tonic changing-note schema (1–2/7–1) are not discussed in what follows, they do occur. An instance from the first movement of Mozart's Oboe Quartet in F Major (K. 370/368*b*) is analyzed in my *Explaining Music*, pp. 192–96. A witty use of the cadential aura of this version also occurs at the beginning of the Trio of Haydn's String Quartet in F Major, Opus 74 No. 2. There, the pattern D♭–E♭–C–D♭ (1–2/7–1) constitutes a kind of pun on the gesture that closed the Minuetto section of the movement—F–G–E–F (1–2/7–1)—and will close it again when the Minuetto is repeated.

25. Examples of the descending mediant changing-note schema (3–4/2–3) will not be considered in what follows. For a nineteenth-century version, see Schubert's Piano Sonata in G Major, Opus 78 (D. 894), iii (Trio), mm. 1–4.

The third version of the schema combines the first half of the tonic version (1–7) with the second half of the mediant version (4–3).[26] As a result, its patently disjunct elements (a fourth apart) combine aspects of the gap-fill schema with those of the changing-note pattern. Since I have discussed instantiations of the disjunct changing-note schema elsewhere,[27] its history will not be considered in this sketch.[28]

Since several Classic instantiations of the tonic changing-note schema have already been presented,[29] only two are given here. In these relatively simple instances, the presence and nature of the schema should be clear. Nevertheless, a few brief comments will facilitate the discussion of examples from later music. First, although the changing-note bass shown in Example 7.8a and in the Andante of Haydn's String Quartet in D Major, Opus 33 No. 6 (Example 7.9a) is common, it is by no means invariable, as Examples 2.1 and 7.10 indicate. Second, weak afterbeats—as in measures 2 and 4 of the theme of the last movement of Beethoven's String Quartet in F Major, Opus 18 No. 1 (marked m in Example 7.9b)—are not uncommon. By anticipating the next structural tone of the schema, these afterbeats seem to act as signs

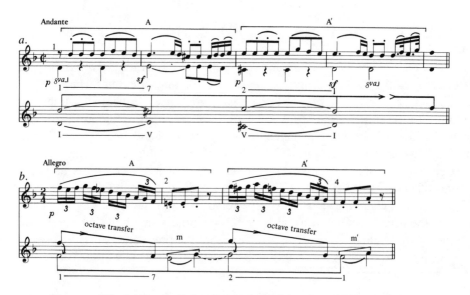

EXAMPLE 7.9. (a) Haydn, String Quartet in D Major, Opus 33 No. 6, ii; (b) Beethoven, String Quartet in F Major, Opus 18 No. 1, iv

26. Sometimes, but very infrequently, changing-note patterns occur on the fifth degree of the scale. Examples of this version of the schema are not considered in this sketch.

27. "Exploiting Limits." For a more comprehensive discussion, see Gjerdingen, A Classic Turn of Phrase.

28. Once again, because the inverted order of the schema (3–4/7–1) usually descends, creating closure, it generally occurs as a cadential gesture. For an example, see Haydn's String Quartet in E Major, Opus 54 No. 3, ii, mm. 8–9.

29. See Examples 1.1a and b, 2.1, and 2.2f (no analytic graph is given for this last example, but the changing-note pattern, E♭–D/F–E♭, is unmistakable). Notice that the changing-note schema can be combined with the Adeste Fidelis one (as in Examples 1.1b and 2.2f) without obscuring either.

confirming the nature of the pattern.[30] Last (and typically), closure is not very de-cisive in most instantiations of this schema. This is so because in most cases the changing-note pattern is part of a higher-level melodic process and because of the absence of a subdominant-to-dominant harmonic progression.[31]

Now consider some examples from the nineteenth century. The Allegro theme from the first movement of Beethoven's String Quartet in B♭ Major, Opus 130 (Example 7.10), is also an instantiation of the tonic changing-note schema. The general parallelism of the parts (A and A') and the harmonic process (I–V⁷/V–I⁶) conform to the norms of the model. And its initial descending gesture is not unlike that of the theme of the finale of Opus 18 No. 1 (Example 7.9*b*). But there are striking differ-

EXAMPLE 7.10. Beethoven, String Quartet in B♭ Major, Opus 130, i

ences, and because of these, the presence of the schema is much less apparent. The most important factors masking convention are, of course, the competing schema of sequentially rising fourths (in the second violin) shown in graph 3[32] and the auxiliary but very important rising line shown in graph 2. Melodic elaboration also disguises the schema. Both the beginning and the ending of the parts (A and A') of the pattern are equivocal. The beginning is so because the first structural tone (B♭) is differ-entiated neither motivically nor dynamically (for instance, by a *sforzando*) from the preceding anacrusis or the following weak beats. It is, so to speak, buried in the continuity of the rapidly descending line. The end of each part of the schema is am-biguous because, unlike the patterning in Opus 18 No. 1, there is no slowing of the rate of motion and because the duration of the structural A is very short. Though

30. The notion of a confirming sign is suggested in Levy, "Texture as a Sign," pp. 519*f.*
31. As will be discussed in the first section of Chapter 8, I–V/V–I does not result in forceful closure.
32. For a more patently thematic use of this schema, see Beethoven's Piano Sonata in A♭ Major, Opus 110, fugue theme.

there is a suggestion of a confirming sign (*m*), the motion from A to C seems more like a triadic connection than an aspect of the schema. Finally, the normal balance of the schema, in which the several elements have the same duration, is disturbed because, instead of consisting of 4 + 4 beats, the first part consists of 5 + 3 beats and the second of 5 + 2 beats.

The opening theme of the first movement of Schubert's Trio in B♭ Major, Opus 99 (D. 898), written about two years after Beethoven's String Quartet in B♭ Major, Opus 130, also diverges from and disguises the tonic changing-note schema, but in significantly different ways (Example 7.11). The very first melodic motion is from 1 to 7. But this is no more than a passing suggestion of the kind of schema being presented because A is a nonstructural neighbor note. As in Examples 7.9 and 7.10, what follows is an octave transfer (rising, however, rather than falling) through the tonic triad, which is prolonged by an axial motion around F (see the analytic graph).

EXAMPLE 7.11. Schubert, Piano Trio in B♭ Major, Opus 99 (D. 898), i

Then in measure 4, the B♭ (functioning as an appoggiatura) resolves to A, in effect completing the first part of the schema—though the A, too, is prolonged through a descending triad on the dominant. (Observe that though the B♭–A in measure 4 replicates that in measure 1, there is a compensatory reversal of function; that is, the B♭ is now ornamental, the A structural.)

The second part of the schema begins quite normally on the second degree of the scale (C) and exhibits the characteristic motivic parallelism. But the harmony begins on the subdominant instead of the usual dominant. This suggests that the theme will have to be further extended to reach closure. That is, had the second part of the theme begun on the dominant, then the high C might have resolved to B♭ in measure 9, with a rhyming extension to measure 12. As it is, however, the subdominant leads to clear dominant harmony only in measure 10. This is followed by a complete cadence ii$^6_5$—V$^{6-5}_{4-3}$—I) in measures 11 and 12, which is accompanied by a conventional melodic closing gesture (3–2–1)—including even the stock signal of a trill. The internal extension in measures 9–11 creates a special tension by stretching the length of the second part of the theme—a strategy that is, as we shall see, characteristic of much nineteenth-century music.[33]

A number of divergences disguise the presence of the schema in Schubert's theme. The first of these occurs when the second part begins with subdominant, rather than dominant, harmony. The stretching that results from this harmonic change somewhat disturbs the parallelism between the parts of the schema. In addition, the very conventionality of the closing gesture—coming, as it were, from custom rather than internal generation—tends to obscure the rhyme at the end of the theme and hence the presence of the schema. These differences result in a change in the relationship between schema and theme. In the Classic style, as observed above, changing-note schemata are usually only part of a theme whose full form is A A′ B. But the presence of subdominant harmony, the stretching, and clear cadential closure make it evident that in Schubert's Trio the schema is coextensive with the theme, not just part of it.

Of the many factors serving to disguise the presence of schemata in nineteenth-century music, perhaps none is more obvious than magnitude. Schubert's realization of the tonic changing-note schema is a case in point. In the realizations given in Examples 1.1*a*, 2.2*f*, 7.9, and 7.10, for instance, the structural tones delineating the schema occur in consecutive measures. Partly because of magnitude, the structural tones (B♭ and A) of the first part of Schubert's realization are separated from each other by four measures, while those of the second part (C and B♭) are separated by seven measures. This alone tends to obscure the presence of the schema.[34]

Magnitude tends to mask schemata—especially those defined by syntactic relationships—because of the constraints of aural memory. For a schema is a kind of replicated style-"chunk."[35] And the greater the temporal separation between the elements defining such a chunk (in this case, the stipulated structural tones), the more difficult it is to connect them to one another and, hence, the harder it is to recognize the nature and presence of the schema. It is also relevant in this connection to observe that size also seems to affect which parts of a pattern are best remembered. In general the beginnings and ends of temporal events are remembered better than middles, and the longer the event, the greater the tendency to remember the beginning.[36] It is partly for this reason that, though the beginnings and ends of Classic

33. Extensions are, of course, common in eighteenth-century music as well, but there they generally occur *after* thematic closure has taken place.

34. For an example in which magnitude, coupled with melodic and harmonic elaboration, disguises a formal schema, see Chopin's Prelude in E Minor, Opus 28 No. 4, which is an extended antecedent (mm. 1–12)–consequent (mm. 13–25) period.

35. See Simon, "How Big Is a Chunk?" Also see above, Chapter 6 at notes 180 and 181.

36. See, for instance, Wright et al., "Memory Processing of Serial Lists," pp. 287–89.

melodies are remembered more or less equally well, with Romantic melodies the beginnings are usually much better remembered than the ends.[37] Of course, when openness is especially prized, as it was in Romanticism, ends tend to be weakly articulated and minimally marked.

But the perception of connection between parts of a schema is not merely a matter of proximity and magnitude. For instance, in the opening theme of Mozart's Piano Quartet in G Minor (Example 1.1*b*), although the first and last notes of each part of the schema (G–F♯ and A–G) are separated by two measures, the presence of the schema is not masked. There are several reasons for this. First, the opening G and the one leading to the F♯ closing in the first part of the schema are in the same register, as is the case in the second part in which A leads back to G. Moreover, the ends (measures 4 and 8) are specially marked both by the sudden *piano* and by the cadential trill. As a result, the rhyme between parts is unmistakable. Second, and most important for present purposes, the intervening gap-fill pattern (mm. 2–3, graph 4) is strongly differentiated from and contrasts with the first and last events of the schema, even though the descending scale pattern leads into the cadence.

In Schubert's theme, on the other hand, the striking axial figure (around F in the first part and G in the second) does not contrast strongly with the rest of the patterning. Rather, it grows out of the initial gesture and, becoming the focus of attention, somewhat weakens the connection between the structural tones that define the schema. This, together with the divergences described above, masks the conventionality of the schema underlying Schubert's melody. More generally, when the intervening material that separates parts of a processive pattern is strongly contrasting, the relationship between such parts tends to be more patent than when intervening material is similar to that of the parts that are separated.[38] If this view has merit, it would appear that while the gradual growth and organic transformation favored by Romanticism enhance motivic connectedness (as is surely the case with Schubert's melody), they tend to obscure the syntactic relationships on which such schemata are based.

In Beethoven's String Quartet in B♭ Major, Opus 130 (Example 7.10), not only is the schema itself veiled, but its presence is further masked by a strong competing pattern. Sometimes, however, a competing pattern diverts attention away from the presence of an otherwise evident schema. This is the case with a melody in Chopin's Waltz in A Minor, Opus 34 No. 2 (Example 7.12). As graph 1 indicates, the tonic changing-note schema occurs on the weak beats of each of the first four measures of the eight-measure antecedent phrase (A A′ B) of the melody. Neither durational sep-

---

37. I am indebted to Janet Levy for this suggestion.

38. The most obvious example is that of cadenzas, which separate a I$^6_4$ from its resolution and are strongly contrasting in texture and material with what immediately precedes and follows. Other examples are the parentheses and interruptions of which Haydn was especially fond (see, for instance, his Symphony No. 104 in D Major ["London"], iv, mm. 84–101). This phenomenon is particularly apparent when one medium of communication is interrupted by another—for instance, tones by words. In this connection, see Deutsch, "Tone and Numbers."

EXAMPLE 7.12. Chopin, Waltz in A Minor, Opus 34 No. 2

aration nor significant melodic elaboration disguises the schema. Indeed, the tones delineating the patterning seem somehow too emphatic, as though the schema were a piquant parody of itself.[39]

This is so for several reasons. The offbeat metric position of the tones of the schema is incongruous given both the potential importance of the tones and the regularity of the conventional accompaniment figure. In addition, rhythmic and melodic continuities are repeatedly denied. The initial upbeat, E, suggests subsequent anacrustic motion—from weak beat to strong across the bar line. This implication is reinforced by the ♩. ♪ rhythms in measure 17 and 19. But the strong downbeats implied are denied by the rests on the first beats of measures 18 and 20.

Two competing patterns divert attention from the changing-note schema. The first consists of successive falling gaps (E–A and F–B), each followed by the beginning of a rising linear fill that implies continuation (see graph 2). The linear motion, A–B and B–C, is not continued.[40] Instead, the main fill follows from the more important rising line in the soprano (graph 3). This process, reinforced by parallelism with the bass, is reversed and closed by the small gap from F to A, which moves to G to begin the fill. The descending motion of the second half of the phrase provisionally fills the various gaps present in the first half.[41] In the extended consequent phrase (not shown in the example), a more normal presentation of the schema is followed by a satisfactory fill-process that descends conjunctly on the measure level from high A down to the lower tonic.

Not all melodies of the Romantic period disguise schemata. Some capitalize on their familiarity, varying them in such a way that conventionality is not blatant. Not surprisingly, such melodies tend to be particularly well loved. The opening theme of the slow movement of Tchaikovsky's Fifth Symphony is a case in point

39. These parodistic emphases are not present in the consequent phrase of the waltz.
40. The eighth-note scale from A up to E (mm. 22–23) is on too low a hierarchic level to satisfactorily fill the higher-level gaps.
41. "Provisionally," because many of the tones are not structural.

*a.*

*b.*

EXAMPLE 7.13. (*a*) Tchaikovsky, Symphony No. 5 in E Minor, Opus 64, ii

(Example 7.13*a*). Undisguised by length or competing patterns, the schema is in the foreground. The main divergence is the lack of parallelism between the two parts; that is, the beginning of motive A′ does not correspond to that of motive A. (Had such correspondence existed, the melody would have been stale, flat, and vulgar indeed, as Example 7.13*b* makes evident.) It should also be mentioned that the effectiveness of the theme owes a considerable debt to a secondary parameter—instrumentation; repressing its potential for vigorous assertion, the french horn makes this lyric melody seem especially expressive and tensely tender.

The mediant changing-note schema is of interest both because it seems especially common in the music of the nineteenth century and because it is closely related to another kind of melodic patterning—the axial schema—frequently encountered in music of the period. This version of the schema was a favored compositional choice of Romantic composers for several reasons. First of all, it generates a slight tension that is affective and expressive. This is so because the patterning, which involves a prolongation of the third rather than the tonic, is mildly equivocal. On the one hand, the melodic motion (3–2/4–3) produces a rising sequence implying continuation to the fifth; on the other hand, the third of the scale implies descending motion to the tonic. Second, the absence of the leading tone makes considerable harmonic variety possible—indeed, the schema can be realized without any use of dominant harmony, and as a result, closure can be attenuated. This leads to the third possible reason for the prevalence of this schema in the nineteenth century. Closure on the third is generally less decisive than closure on the tonic, and such openness is consonant with the general cultural valuing of continuousness, gradual transformation, and eternal Becoming associated with the organic metaphor.

Realizations of the mediant changing-note schema, as it occurs in music of the Classic style, are given in Example 7.14. The first, the opening of Sammartini's Symphony in D Major (JC 15), begins with a prolongation of the tonic (Example

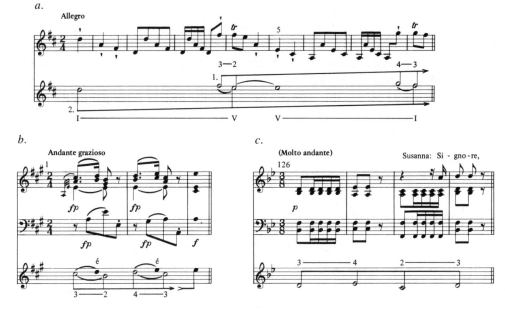

EXAMPLE 7.14. (*a*) Sammartini, Symphony in D Major (JC 15), i; (*b*) Mozart, *La finta giar-diniera* (K. 196). Overture; (*c*) Mozart, *The Marriage of Figaro* (K. 492), Act 2, Finale

7.14*a*). But the pattern governing the syntactic process is that from the third of the scale to the second and from the fourth back to the third (graph 1).[42] The predominance of the changing-note schema is emphasized by three features of the passage: (1) the composed *accelerando* (from quarter- to sixteenth-notes) that prolongs the tonic triad makes the slower eighth-notes of the schema especially conspicuous; (2) the first downbeat of each part of the schema is marked by a trill; and (3) the striking registral change, following the triadic pattern, throws the changing-note schema into high relief.[43]

In the Andante grazioso from Mozart's Overture to *La finta giardiniera* (Example 7.14*b*), the mediant changing-note schema is ornamented only by the sixteenth-note *échappés* (*é* in the graph) that follow the first and third structural tones. This ornamentation is frequently associated with the schema—as, for instance, in the Trio of Mozart's Symphony No. 40 in G Minor (K. 550)[44] and in the theme of the last movement of Beethoven's Eighth Symphony, discussed below.

The instantiation of the schema that occurs in the Finale of act 2 of Mozart's *Marriage of Figaro* (Example 7.14*c*) is an unadorned instance of the less common, inverted version (3–4/2–3). It provides a striking example of the amusing effect that can be created when one convention denies another. The passage occurs just as

42. I do not mean to deny the presence of the linear motion beginning on D, shown in graph 2.

43. For comparable realizations of this schema, see Haydn's Keyboard Sonata in D Major (XVI:33), i, mm. 13ff., and his String Quartet in D Major, Opus 64 No. 5, i, mm. 8–16; for a tonic changing-note schema preceded by triadic patterning, see Mozart's String Quintet in C Major (K. 515), i, mm. 1–10.

44. See my "Grammatical Simplicity and Relational Richness," pp. 693–761.

Susanna, much to everyone's amazement, steps out of the closet. But instead of dramatizing surprise through a crashing, conventional *forte* or an unusual, unexpected harmony, Mozart creates a delicious double surprise as he combines an unmistakable version of the conventional schema with the rhythm of "a paradigmatic late eighteenth-century minuet."[45]

The opening of the last movement of Beethoven's Eighth Symphony (Example 7.15*a*) is also a realization of the mediant changing-note schema. However, al-

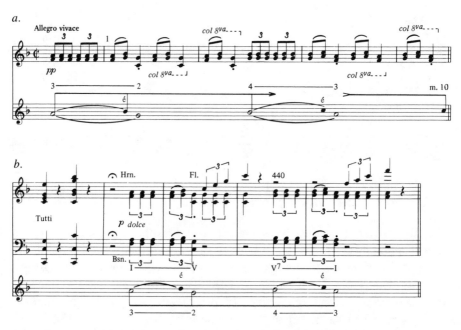

EXAMPLE 7.15. Beethoven, Symphony No. 8 in F Major, Opus 93, iv

though all the basics of the schema are present, including the characteristic *échappée* figure, the main motions from 3 to 2 and from 4 to 3 are hurried over, minimized, and left open by playful, almost perfunctory, repetition. In addition, openness is emphasized by the absence of the leading tone, E, in the harmony. Even when the theme is presented by the whole orchestra (at m. 18, not shown in the Example), the E is notably weak. And this weakness is compounded by the presence of a strong tonic pedal.

But, as is often the case, Beethoven's Classic proclivities ultimately prevail. As Joseph Kerman observes, "Again and again there seems to be some kind of instability, discontinuity, or thrust in the first theme which is removed in the coda."[46]

45. Allanbrook, *Rhythmic Gesture in Mozart*, p. 123.
46. "Notes on Beethoven's Codas," p. 149.

The fourth movement of the Eighth Symphony is a clear example. For at the last large articulation in the coda, following a forceful fermata, Beethoven presents an essentially undisguised version of the changing-note schema (Example 7.15b).

The same schema is replicated throughout the nineteenth century. Early in the period, for instance, it forms the basis of the opening passage of Chopin's Étude in F Major, Opus 10 No. 8 (Example 7.16);[47] later in the century, it is instantiated as the main theme of the fifth movement ("Fandango asturiano") of Rimsky-Korsakov's

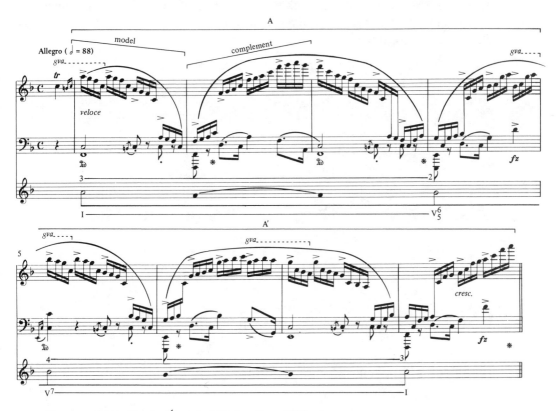

EXAMPLE 7.16. Chopin, Étude in F Major, Opus 10 No. 8

*Capriccio espagnol* (Example 7.17a) and as the famous march tune from the first movement of Mahler's Fifth Symphony (Example 7.19a).

In Chopin's Étude, the presence of the schema is masked by foreground figuration, which creates complementary relationships between successive measures, by precipitous octave changes (for instance, in m. 1 from $A^6$ down to $A^3$), and by the competing pattern in the left hand. Nonetheless, the parallelism between parts of the schema is evident, as is the typical harmonic progression.

---

47. For other early nineteenth-century examples, see Beethoven, Piano Sonata in E Minor, Opus 90, ii, mm. 1–4; Schubert, Piano Sonata in E Major (D. 157), ii, mm. 1–2; and Example 7.20 below.

The melody that Rimsky-Korsakov uses for the fifth movement of his *Capriccio* is a folk tune taken from a collection compiled by José Inzenga.[48] It is also an instantiation of the mediant changing-note schema. As in many folk tunes, there is a lack of strict parallelism between the two halves of the melody. What is interesting about the lack of parallelism is not that it saves the tune from banality (as is clear from Example 7.17*b,* part *A'*) or that it obscures the changing-note schema, since such obscuring would be minimal were it not for the very fast tempo. Rather, what is interesting is that the history of such tunes illustrates the kind of change in which a strategy belonging to one set of constraints comes to play a part in a significantly different set of constraints.

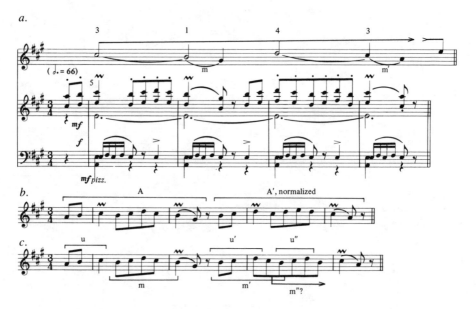

EXAMPLE 7.17.  (*a*) Rimsky-Korsakov, *Capriccio espagnole,* v

48.  I have been unable to locate a copy of this collection. According to David Lloyd-Jones, it was published by Don Andres Vidal y Roger with a title page reading: "Ecos de Espana. / coleccion / de cantos y bailes populares / recopilados / por José Inzenga." But Lloyd-Jones asserts that the first presentation of each of the borrowed tunes "is stated by Rimsky-Korsakov exactly as he found them in Inzenga's collection." Lloyd-Jones's notes are for the miniature score of the *Capriccio* published by Eulenburg (No. 842).

Let us begin by "normalizing" the tune that Rimsky borrowed (Example 7.17*b*). When this is done, the rhythmic/metric parallelism between parts is constant and the pitch pattern is varied; that is, part *A'* is a step higher than part *A*. This mode of variation by pitch displacement (sequencing) is typical of Western art music. In the folk tune that Rimsky chooses to use, however, the sequential structure of the second part of the schema is undermined by the rhythmic/metric displacement of motive *m* (Example 7.17*c*). The displacement results from the following circumstances. When we first hear the last two eighth-notes of measure 6 and the downbeat of measure 7 (bracket *u'*), the group is interpreted as the sequential beginning of the second half of some sort of antecedent-consequent pattern. But as the melody descends through C♯ to B, a parallel with the end of measure 5 and the first beat of measure 6 (motive *m*) emerges. The result is a cognitive conflict, analogous to the rabbit-duck images used by Gestalt psychologists, between the perceptual primacy of motive *m* and motive *u*. But in either case the repetition of the pattern involves a shift in metric position.

In the *Capriccio,* motivic ambiguity and metric displacement occur because they were present in the particular folk tune that Rimsky chose to use.[49] For this reason, their occurrence constitutes an individual instance. In the music of Rimsky's student Stravinsky, however, these modes of variation become generalized as a stylistic strategy. That is, their use ceases to be confined to, or warranted by, their folk-related origin. Rather, variation in the internal ordering of a group of pitches or intervals, coupled with metric displacement, occurs throughout Stravinsky's *oeuvre,* as it does, for instance, in the variation movement of the Octet for Winds (Example 7.18*a*) and in the fugue subject of the second movement of the *Symphony of Psalms* (Example 7.18*b*). This strategy becomes a compositional resource for many twentieth-century composers—Bartók's music is another case in point. In short, some of the relationships previously prevalent in Western art music become reversed: pitch collections tend to be treated as constants, while temporal displacement and pitch reordering become indispensable variables.

EXAMPLE 7.18. Stravinsky: (*a*) Octet for Winds, ii; (*b*) *Symphony of Psalms,* ii

49. Such usage was warranted by the Romantic valuing of the putative naturalness and innocence of the folk. The repeated open fifth (A–E) in the bass and the dronelike pedal in the horns were also considered characteristic of folk music.

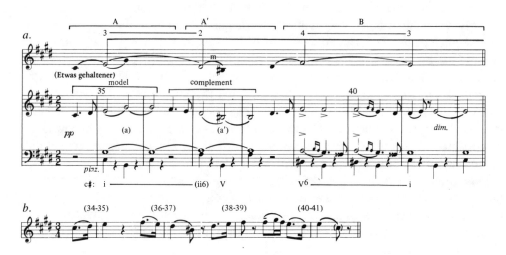

EXAMPLE 7.19. (*a*) Mahler, Symphony No. 5, i

In the march melody from the first movement of Mahler's Fifth Symphony (Example 7.19*a*), the lack of parallelism between the parts of the schema is much more marked. Instead of the strophic form (A A′) characteristic of most realizations of the changing-note schema, Mahler creates a bar form (A A′ B). He does so by giving the first structural tone an afterbeat comparable to that which follows the second structural tone. That is, just as the D♯ in measure 37 has a falling afterbeat (B♯), so the E in measure 35 has a corresponding, though rising, afterbeat (G♯). As a result, what is customarily a single melodic motion (3–2) divides into two parts, a model (motive A) and its complement (A′). To accommodate this restructuring, the second part of the schema (the motion from 4 to 3) is stretched to four measures by the addition of measures 39 and 42. The presence of the schema is further obscured by the lack of a rhyming afterbeat at the end of the melody. Despite signal contrasts in ethos (partly the result of differences in tempo, mode, volume, and so on) as well as form, Mahler's melody belongs to the same schema family as Rimsky's, as is clear if Mahler's extra afterbeat and its stretching are removed (Example 7.19*b*).[50] Although parallelism between parts of the schema is somewhat weakened in Rimsky's melody and more so in Mahler's, it is by no means destroyed. In both cases the upbeat-to-downbeat parallelism is preserved; in addition, in Rimsky's melody the rhyming of the ends of the parts is patent, while in Mahler's theme both parts (A A′ and B) have the same basic rhythmic shape.

There are melodies that are essentially without parallelism, however, even though they move around (away from and back to) a single structural tone. Such melodies are superficially similar to changing-note schemata, but there are funda-

50. Other changes in melody and meter have also been made.

mental differences. Because these differences provide a clear example of the ways in which the Romantic valuing of natural means affected both the inventions and the choices of nineteenth-century composers, they will be considered in the next section.

## NATURE AFFIRMED

While changing-note melodies can be found in both eighteenth- and nineteenth-century music, as far as I have been able to discover *axial* melodies occur only in nineteenth-century music. Before considering why this should be so, it is important to be clear about the differences between the two kinds. Let us begin with two melodies from the music of Schubert and then consider examples in which the nature of the axial schema becomes more clearly defined. In so doing, I hope not only to illustrate the concept of trended change but to show that axial melodies are consonant with values of Romanticism such as openness, reliance on natural rather than learned means, and appeal to less sophisticated members of the elite egalitarian audience.

The opening melody of the slow movement of the Piano Trio in B♭ Major, Opus 99, begins with what seems to be an unadorned instance of a mediant changing-note melody (Example 7.20). In a way it is too pure. That is, the absence of any melodic elaboration, taken together with the presence of a tonic pedal, minimizes both the sense of cadential progression[51] and the sense of formal structuring into parallel parts.[52] Because of the lack of differentiation,[53] it is unclear whether the pat-

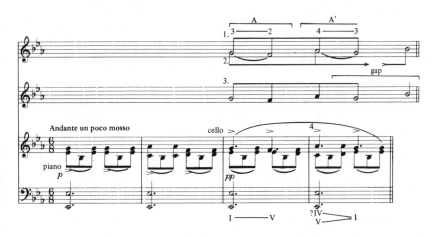

EXAMPLE 7.20. Schubert, Piano Trio in B♭ Major, Opus 99 (D. 898), ii

51. The harmony of the first beat of measure 4 is ambiguous: at first it seems subdominant, but since the C might be interpreted as an appoggiatura, the harmony might be thought of as dominant.
52. When the melody is repeated in the violin (mm. 13–14, not given in the Example), the counterpoint in the cello further weakens the sense of division into parts.
53. Cf. Examples 7.14*b* and *c*, in which differentiation (an *échapée* in the first, and rhythmic structure in the second) makes the presence of the schema clear.

tern is a changing-note melody (graph 1), a sequence leading to B♭ (graph 2), or something like an axial prolongation of G that skips to B♭ (graph 3), creating a gap that is filled by what follows.

No such ambiguity, however, characterizes the melody of the second key area of the first movement of Schubert's String Quintet in C Major, Opus 163 (Example 7.21). For though the characteristic pitches (3–4/2–3) are emphasized and the har-

EXAMPLE 7.21. Schubert, String Quintet in C Major, Opus 163 (D. 956), i

monic progression (I–IV–V⁷–I) is partly as stipulated by the schema, form and process are not coordinated in parallel phrases as they are in typical realizations of the schema.[54] Rather, the effect is of a prolonged G (as part of the E♭-major triad), which functions as the axis around which higher and lower tones revolve and toward which they tend to gravitate.

The melody that begins "Pierrot" from Schumann's *Carnaval* is also an axial pattern that revolves around the third, G, over a tonic (E♭) pedal (Example 7.22). Because motivic organization, harmonic progression, and rhythmic grouping are ambiguous, process and form are weakly defined. To the extent that the pattern is closed, it is so because of the natural psychological satisfaction of *return* (to the opening G), the relative concord of the E♭ triad, and the interjection of the contrasting and parenthetical *forte* figure on the last beat of measure 3. In short, learned syntactic constraints do not play a crucial role in the perception of the process and form of this pattern.[55] Like most axial melodies, this one lacks clear implication and

54. In this instance, as in the previous one, the tonic pedal tends to weaken still further whatever parallels are latent in the patterning.

55. Indeed, the one tone that would have been a "resolution"—namely, B♭ following F♯ and C— is scrupulously avoided (it becomes the axis of the next phrase).

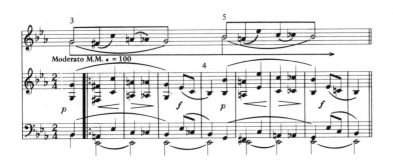

EXAMPLE 7.22.
Schumann, *Car-naval*, Opus 9,
"Pierrot"

strong closure; and what follows—a repetition of the axial motion a third higher—is by no means uncommon, as the next two examples make clear.

Neither the lyrical melody from Liszt's *Les préludes* (Example 7.23*a*) nor the somber theme that begins the slow movement of Brahms's Fourth Symphony (Example 7.23*b*) requires much comment. Both are plainly axial, and after less than decisive closure, both repeat their axial pattern a major third higher. Though Liszt's theme is more clearly defined harmonically—there is an unambiguous progression

EXAMPLE 7.23.  (*a*) Liszt, *Les préludes*; (*b*) Brahms, Symphony No. 4 in E Minor, Opus 98, ii

of dominants ($V_4^6$–V/IV–IV)—the closing cadence is plagal; the melodic motion around E consists mainly of the stable tones of the tonic triad. On the most foreground level, Brahms's theme is much more strongly implicative both melodically and rhythmically, but on the level of motivic units (the half-measure), structuring depends on changes in secondary parameters (additional instruments, new registers, and so on). Closure is signaled by the *diminuendo* and is confirmed by the repetition of the axial pattern beginning on G♯.[56]

We can now attempt to answer the question posed earlier: Why were axial melodies invented and chosen by nineteenth-century composers? First, not only was the generally weak closure of axial patterns consonant with the valuing of open forms, as already mentioned, but it made the composition of quite long musical structures relatively easy. That is, because such melodies were not decisively closed, they could easily be repeated, at either the same pitch level or a new one; in this way four measures of music could be extended to eight, sixteen, or even more. And for composers who chose to rely on convention as little as possible and consequently had to make many more or less conscious, and time-consuming, compositional choices, this was not a trivial consideration. For the audience—particularly its less sophisticated members—themes of this sort had obvious advantages; though a thematic section might be long, the amount of material to be perceived and remembered would be relatively small. Not only are relationships between statements of an axial pattern redundant, but so are many of the relationships within the pattern. For on a high level the pattern is reducible to a single tone, while on lower levels the second part of the axial pattern is often understood as an inverted repetition (or complement) of the first part.

There are other reasons—ones that illuminate important facets of Romantic music—for the prevalence of axial melodies. A comparison of the constraints governing axial and changing-note patterns will help to make these reasons clear. Like axial patterns, changing-note melodies return to the tone(s) on which they begin. When they do so, however, it is to a considerable extent felt to be attributable to the learned constraints of tonal syntax. In axial melodies, on the other hand, the satisfaction of return to a central focal tone can be attributed to innate (natural) cognitive constraints.[57] One might put the contrast in this way: in changing-note melodies nurture (syntactic convention) dominates nature,[58] while in axial melodies nature dominates nurture. Or to emphasize the contrast still further, axial patterns are possible in nontonal music, but changing-note schemata are not.

---

56. For a further discussion of axial patterns and other examples, see my *Explaining Music*, pp. 183–91; also see Narmour, *Beyond Schenkerism*, pp. 22–23. I am indebted to Narmour for both the concept and the term *axial*.

57. For a discussion of the law of return, see my *Emotion and Meaning in Music*, pp. 151–56.

58. The principle of return plays a part in our understanding of changing-note melodies. But syntax is not merely an added, supplementary force. Rather it takes cognitive primacy.

## *Plans Versus Scripts*

The differences between changing-note melodies and axial ones call attention to a broader distinction—one that may help to account for other choices made by nineteenth-century composers. The distinction is one made by psychologists Roger C. Schank and Robert P. Abelson between *scripts* and *plans*.

> A script is a structure . . . made up of slots and requirements about what can fill those slots. The structure is an interconnected whole, and what is in one slot affects what can be in another. . . . Scripts allow for new references to objects within them just as if these objects had been previously mentioned; objects within scripts may take 'the' without explicit introduction because the script itself had already implicitly introduced them.[59]

Plans, on the other hand, are repositories

> for general information that will connect events that cannot be connected by use of an available script or by a standard causal chain expansion. . . . A plan explains how a given state or event was prerequisite for, or derived from, another state or event. . . . The point here is that plan-based processing is different in kind from script-based processing. . . . [Script-based processing] takes precedence over plan-based processing when an appropriate script is available.[60]

Put in terms that I have been using, syntactic relationships and the schemata associated with them—e.g., changing-note melodies, antecedent/consequent phrases, full authentic cadences (subdominant-dominant-tonic), and sonata-form structures—are scriptlike. Thus, once the first part of a changing-note pattern is comprehended, subsequent parts of the pattern are largely predictable.[61] To the extent that the syntactic constraints shaping some script are unfamiliar, however, the listener will tend to understand that script in terms of a more general plan. Such a listener might, that is, interpret a changing-note melody as an axial schema. For axial melodies are plan-based patterns that provide for general kinds of relationships, such as "move around (above and below) some central tone, and then return to it."

Implicit in these observations is a hypothesis that needs much more careful documentation. While music of the Classic period employs plan-based patternings, these are almost always coordinated with and dominated by syntactic scripts. In the

---

59. *Scripts, Plans, Goals and Understanding*, p. 41. I am grateful to Robert Gjerdingen for calling this distinction and the work of Schank and Abelson to my attention.
60. Ibid., pp. 70, 77, 99.
61. It is this very predictability that makes deviation affectively and intellectually engaging.

nineteenth century, the situation is more or less reversed: what had been specific syntactic scripts tend to be subsumed within or transformed into general plans. For instance, from this very broad point of view, the history of the practice and theory of sonata form during the nineteenth century might be interpreted as the transformation of a script—a tonally defined hierarchic schema of slots—into a thematic plan, often of a dialectic or narrative sort (thesis/antithesis → synthesis; opposition/conflict → resolution). More generally, as suggested earlier (and argued later), the role of secondary parameters in the shaping of musical forms and processes becomes increasingly important during the course of the nineteenth century. The forms and processes thus shaped are based on plans, not on scripts.[62]

It also seems probable that, relative to their predecessors, nineteenth-century composers tended to choose plan-based patterns such as axial, complementary, and gap-fill melodic types more often than script-based patterns.[63] Let us consider some examples.

Though the incidence of complementary melodies increases during the Romantic period, notable instances of such melodies can be found in Classic music. The theme that begins the last movement of Mozart's Piano Concerto in G Major (K. 453) is a clear example of a melody based on a complementary plan or schema (Example 7.24).[64] The second four-measure phrase is an almost exact inversion (complement) of the first (model). This relationship is perceptually clear because the second phrase duplicates the rhythmic structure of the first and because, if the complementary phrase is analyzed as being on the dominant, the harmonic progressions are similar as well.

Though perceptually less striking, the basic parallelism between the opening phrases of the Minuetto of Mozart's String Quartet in A Major (K. 464) is even more

EXAMPLE 7.24.  Mozart, Piano Concerto in G Major (K. 453), iii

62. This calls attention to a relationship that may be more than coincidental: as the relative importance of scripts declines and that of plans increases, programs (which quite literally provide scripts) become more common.

63. Notice in this connection that since plan-based patterns are less dependent on conventions of syntax, there is less need for disguise. In the eighteenth century, conversely, plans were script-dominated, and the syntactic coherence provided by such scripts allowed for playful variation that often tended to veil the underlying plan.

64. As this remark indicates, two different kinds of schemata can be distinguished: script-based schemata and plan-based ones.

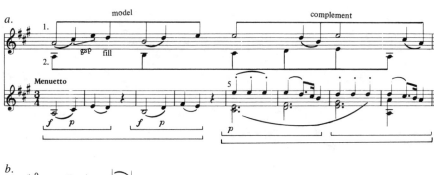

EXAMPLE 7.25.  (*a, b*) Mozart, String Quartet in A Major (K. 464), iii

exact (Example 7.25*a*). For the fundamental structure of the complementary phrase is both a slightly varied inversion and a quite precise retrograde of the model (graph 1). But on a foreground level, this melodic parallelism is disguised.[65] Disguise is possible because coherence can depend on the conventions of tonal syntax; this is evident in the linear bass pattern (graph 2) that links model to complement. One advantage of this sort of varied parallelism can be seen in the very next measure and throughout the remainder of Mozart's Minuetto. It is the possibility of contrapuntally combining the motive of the model with that of the complement (Example 7.25*b*).

The opening phrase of the second movement of Beethoven's String Quartet in A Minor, Opus 132 (Example 7.26), is remarkably similar to that of Mozart's Minuetto (Example 7.25).[66] Both consist of a pair of two-measure motives played in unison (with the cello an octave below) by all the instruments of the quartet. And, though somewhat disguised by appoggiaturas on the first beat of each measure, Beethoven's model motive (*m* and graph 3), like Mozart's, rises a perfect fourth (A–D) and is repeated a step higher (B–E).

65. Rhythmic parallelism—(2 + 2) + (2 + 2)—is maintained, as the brackets under the example indicate. For a more detailed analysis of the example and of other complementary melodies, see my *Explaining Music,* pp. 175–83.

66. I am not the first to remark on the similarities between these themes. See, for instance, Kerman, *The Beethoven Quartets,* p. 253.

EXAMPLE 7.26. Beethoven, String Quartet in A Minor, Opus 132, ii

But Beethoven's version of this pattern is much more mobile and open than Mozart's. On the lowest level, the appoggiaturas create a conflict between tonal/rhythmic syntax and the notated meter—a conflict performers must take seriously.[67] That is, the meter forces the A and the D to function as stressed weak beats in a dactylic rhythmic group (Example 7.27a) instead of as accented structural tones in an amphibrach (Example 7.27b).[68] As a result, the weak beats in each measure are

EXAMPLE 7.27.

especially mobile, and the pattern as a whole is very open and somewhat unstable.[69] In Mozart's theme, on the other hand, not only are meter, rhythm, and melody congruent with one another so that motivic structure seems stable, but the change in melodic motion from rising to falling (the descending E–D), the filling of the C♯–E gap, and the closed trochaic rhythm of the second measure create clear, if modest, closure. I have considered these foreground relationships in some detail because the kinds of rhythmic/metric displacements present in Beethoven's version of this patterning are characteristic of Romantic music more generally.

67. If the notated meter is to be audible and effective, dominating the rhythmic/metric organization that would otherwise arise, the first beat of each measure must be somewhat stressed.

68. The amphibrach group latent in this pattern becomes manifest only at the close of the first section of the movement (Example 7.27c).

69. Closure is preemptive. That is, the end of a pattern is recognized because of its repetition (a "natural" mode of structural definition) at the one-measure and, even more forcefully, two-measure levels, not primarily because of its syntactic structuring.

The openness of Beethoven's theme is not merely a matter of low-level patterning. For while the descending motion of the second motive (Example 7.26, mm. 5–6, c) makes it and its repetition (in a lower octave) seem like complements to the first pair of motives, the second phrase actually continues the linear process begun in the first. That is, the structural tones of the first phrase, A and B, move on to C♯ and D in the second, although the D is displaced down an octave (Example 7.26, graph 1). The harmonic progression in measures 7 and 8 (ii–V) might have been a half cadence ending the first period, but there is no closure beyond the level of the motive. This is not primarily because of the registral displacement,[70] but because the rising sequential motion continues beyond what would have been the normal four-measure length of the complementary phrase;[71] the rise is not only to E (m. 9), but through a weak F♯ to G♯ (m. 13) and A (m. 15).[72]

One consequence of these continuities is that, while the extent of each motive is clearly defined (significantly by repetition and registral change, as well as by harmonic progression), the structure of the theme as a whole is ambiguous. Because it is continually Becoming—at least until the close of the first section (mm. 19–22)—the theme seems to drift off toward quiescence (m. 14). Following this abatement, there is a modest reversal of harmonic motion. Finally, a strong progression creates cadential closure that marks the end of the section.

The complementary relationship of action/reaction seems naturally understandable; moreover, once the relationship is established, one element of the pattern tends to imply another. Particularly when each element is represented by a brief motive (as in Examples 7.25 and 7.26), the interaction between model and complement may be playfully witty and amusing.[73] But the laws of human cognition are such that even when no model/complement pattern has been established within a work, a repeated action that has patent melodic direction tends to imply a compensatory reaction—that is, motion in the opposite direction.[74]

70. On the contrary, the displacement, returning to the register of the opening phrase, may suggest closure.

71. This kind of sequencing is facilitated by the fact that the basic intervallic structure of the complement is an inversion (descending a fifth) of that of the model. As a result, model and complement move together in parallel tenths and thirds (as shown in Example 7.26, graphs 1 and 2).

72. Measures 11–15 are not shown in Example 7.26.

73. This may help to explain why this type of melodic structure seems especially prevalent in dance movements and fast finales. For in witty exchanges, repartee is rapid. (In this connection, see my *Music, the Arts, and Ideas*, pp. 11–12, n. 12.) For examples from Beethoven's *oeuvre*, see the Piano Trio in B♭ Major, Opus 97, iii, mm. 1–8; String Quartet in E♭ Major, Opus 127, iii, mm. 3–10; and Symphony No. 5 in C Minor, iv, mm. 45–48.

74. The implication of reaction is a special case of what has been called *saturation* (see my *Emotion and Meaning in Music*, pp. 135–38), which is, I suspect, itself a special case of subjective probability (e.g., the *feeling* that the more often a tossed coin comes up heads, the more likely it is that the next toss will come up tails).

The beginning of the Scherzo of Schumann's Piano Quintet in E♭ Major, Opus 44 (Example 7.28), capitalizes on this cognitive proclivity. A rising scale pattern of an octave plus a fourth is presented three times in measures 1–6. By the third statement, the probability of a reaction seems quite high. And when the next action (mm. 7–8), which returns to the opening scale, is followed by a descending scale, the implied complementary pattern is actualized (see graph 1).

EXAMPLE 7.28.  Schumann, Piano Quintet in E♭ Major, Opus 44, iii

EXAMPLE 7.29.

As in the second movement of Beethoven's String Quartet in A Minor (Example 7.26), characteristic traits of Romanticism are present. Though the theme does not exactly "drift off," its closure is ambiguous. Mostly this is because there are two different, competing processes: that is, the phrase structure of the second complementary pattern (Examples 7.28, graph 1-b and 7.29, graph 1-b) is not congruent with that of the cadential segment of the theme (Example 7.29, graph 2).[75] Disparity between metric placement and melodic importance creates a kind of noncongruence on a foreground level. As I have analyzed it, the first important tone of model and complement occurs on the last eighth of the measure, while the second important tone occurs in the second half of the measure (Example 7.29, graph 1).

This kind of melodic/metric noncongruence, creating what I have called *potential structural tones,*[76] is not, I think, a mode of disguise. The complementary nature of the melodies of Beethoven and Schumann is, after all, quite clear. Rather, such noncongruence creates a kind of natural implication that is not necessarily dependent on syntax. That is, when a pitch whose prominence suggests that it should be structural occurs in a weak rhythmic/metric position, the implication is that the tone will subsequently occur as, or will lead to, an accent.

This is the case in the first phrase of another complementary melody—that which begins Chopin's Waltz in E♭ Major, Opus 18 (Example 7.30, graph 1). The lilting gaiety of the music is due in large part to the fact that the most prominent melodic tones come on weak beats. These potential structural tones (marked ‿ in Example 7.30, graph 2) are actualized by the B♭ in measure 8, which, as a result, is especially emphatic.

EXAMPLE 7.30. Chopin, Waltz in E♭ Major, Opus 18

<hr/>

75. Despite an authentic cadence on the dominant, the closure of the section is rather weak, both because of the absence of subdominant harmony and because there is no significant reversal of harmonic/melodic activity.

76. See *Explaining Music,* pp. 196–201.

One last example illustrates the influence of Romantic plans on Classic scripts. Brahms's Intermezzo in A Major, Opus 118 No. 2, begins with a four-measure phrase which, ending with a half cadence, is understood to be an antecedent (Example 7.31). This inference is strengthened when the next phrase (not shown in Example 7.31) begins like the first: that is, we assume that it will be a consequent. But this phrase is deflected away from the tonic to the dominant, which is weakly tonicized. The eight-measure period is repeated but without tonic closure. Then, after a transition of eighteen measures, a variant of the melody appears (Example 7.31, complement). It is a consequent phrase, but its characteristic opening and closing motives make it clear that it is also the complement of the opening phrase. This join-

EXAMPLE 7.31. Brahms, Intermezzo in A Major, Opus 118 No. 2

ing of the contours of a complementary plan with the syntactic stipulations of an antecedent-consequent script seems to symbolize Brahms's so-called classicizing Romanticism.[77]

Gap-fill melodies, too, are plan-based,[78] and of the myriad melodies employed in tonal music, none perhaps are more readily and immediately understood. There is no waiting for cadential progression (as in a changing-note melody) or for the shaping of the second phrase (as in an antecedent-consequent period or in a complementary pattern). The initial gap makes the nature of the pattern apparent from the outset. Moreover, though tonal syntax underlies the melodic relationships, its stipulations are not crucial for an understanding of the process. Consequently, it is not surprising that gap-fill melodies are very common in the music of both the eighteenth and the nineteenth centuries.

In the eighteenth century, however, realizations of the schema tend to be subservient to syntactic scripts, such as antecedent-consequent harmonic and melodic structural organization. That is, each phrase of the melody contains a gap that is followed by a fill, but the first fill reaches only partial closure on some note of the dominant triad, while the second reaches considerably greater closure on one of

77. The separation of antecedent and consequent is not a peculiarly Romantic strategy, since it is used in Classic music as well. See, for instance, Example 1.5.

78. The plan consists of two parts. The gap—which may be a single skip (usually within the octave), a coherent pattern of skips (such as a triad), or some more complex structure perceived as disjunct—creates a sense of incompleteness that implies the fill. In the fill, most of the tones skipped over in the first part are presented in more or less conjunct motion. As a rule the gap involves rising motion and the fill involves descending conjunct motion, but other combinations are possible.

I have discussed the nature of gap-fill patterns and given examples in *Emotion and Meaning in Music* (chaps. 3 and 4, and especially pp. 130–35) and *Explaining Music* (pp. 145–57 and passim).

the notes of the tonic triad. For instance, the antecedent and consequent phrases of the Minuetto of Mozart's Flute Quartet in A Major (K. 298) both begin with a gap of a fifth (Example 7.32),[79] but the first fill, instead of returning to the tonic, ends with a half cadence on E. The syntactic script, as it were, prevents the gap-fill plan from reaching completion. Then, in the second phrase, the conjunct fill is complete and coordinate with syntactic closure.[80]

EXAMPLE 7.32. Mozart, Flute Quartet in A Major (K. 298), ii

In the music of Romanticism, script constraints tend to be attenuated and, late in the period, even disappear. Often, as though to compensate for the weakening of syntactic implication, the generating force of an initial gap is renewed through *subsidiary gaps* or through *gap reiteration*. For instance, the main melody of Chopin's Waltz in C♯ Minor, Opus 64 No. 2, begins with a patent skip from G♯ up to E (Example 7.33). Conjunct descending motion follows, and embedded within are subsidiary gaps (*s/g*) which serve to strengthen the sense of goal-directed motion.[81] Though a tonic cadence (m. 4) divides this first part of a long antecedent phrase into two parallel subphrases (mm. 1–4 and 5–8), melodic continuity takes precedence

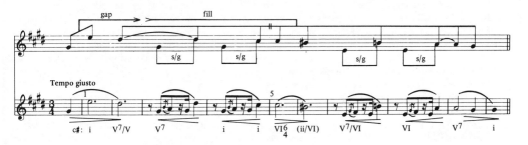

EXAMPLE 7.33. Chopin, Waltz in C♯ Minor, Opus 64 No. 2

79. For purposes of this discussion, I ignore the first A, which makes the gap into an octave; this gap is filled at the beginning of the second part of the rounded binary form.

80. Also see Example 1.5, in which script constraints prevent the gap-fill pattern from reaching completion in measure 8.

81. For another instance of gap renewal, see the opening melody (mm. 1–17) of the first movement of Schumann's Symphony No. 3 in E♭ Major, in which an extended gap (E♭–G–C) is followed by a fill containing a succession of subsidiary gaps (mm. 5–15).

over harmonic articulation: the gap-fill plan dominates the syntactic script. One consequence of this is that, as in many Romantic melodies, closure at the end of the fill is weak.[82]

As Romanticism increasingly influences compositional choices, the gap-fill schema tends to function mainly as a plan. Often the gap consists of exact or sequential reiteration (A A'), while the fill may descend either more or less directly or sequentially, often with auxiliary gaps.[83] Plan rather than script governs comprehension, and plans give rise to contour-governed relationships such as "pure" gap-fill, axial, and complementary patterns.

The second movement of Mahler's Fifth Symphony provides a clear example of gap reiteration (Example 7.34). The gap—a skip of a minor sixth from C (through F) up to A♭—is followed by descending motion (A♭–G–F) that is initially thought to be the beginning of a fill but is subsequently (when the melody returns to A♭) understood as ornamental.[84] The gap is reiterated, but this time the descent has an aura of the axial about it. The third statement of the gap—the nature of the plan could scarcely be more patent—is followed by a fill that moves conjunctly down to the initial C. But closure is masked by the strong countermelody in the bass clarinets and is attenuated by the lack of a strong point of syntactic arrival.[85]

Gap reiteration may also be sequential, as it is in the Andante mosso theme of the Overture to Verdi's *La forza del destino* (Example 7.35).[86] The first gap, a major sixth (D up to B), is followed by a partial fill down to G.[87] The G also functions as the first note of a second gap. The second gap process is more intense than the first. This is so for two main reasons: (1) the second gap-fill pattern is both higher and louder (notice the *crescendo* mark); and (2) in order for the dissonance of the second

82. Nor is the end of the whole antecedent phrase (m. 16) very forceful, though for quite different reasons. (Neither the remainder of the antecedent nor the consequent is given in Example 7.33.) A switch takes place: harmonic progression creates clear syntactic articulation, but melodic patterning and rhythmic grouping are somewhat equivocal. Closure is enhanced, however, by abatement in the secondary parameters: descending chromatic eighth-notes (nonsyntactic pitch) are accompanied by a *decrescendo*—and probably in many performances by a *ritardando* as well. What really marks the end of this drifting-off of the antecedent phrase is the beginning of the consequent. And its close, though clear and secure, is scarcely emphatic.

More generally, because musical "rhyming" at the ends of phrases enhances closure, Romantic composers employ antecedent-consequent schemata less often than do Classic ones; when such patterns are used, formal parallelism is usually minimized (as in Chopin's melody) or disguised (as in Mahler's variant of a changing-note schema in Example 7.19). In addition, "pure" antecedent-consequent relationships are less common in nineteenth-century music because they have no late high point and, partly for this reason, seem to lack organic development.

83. From the point of view of Romanticism, one advantage of a sequential gap followed by a relatively brief fill (as in Example 7.35) is that the high point (the statistical climax) occurs relatively late in the pattern.

84. The A♭ has been included as part of the possible fill (see analytic graph) because of the impetus created by downbeats, played by the double basses in measures 80 and 84.

85. Melodically, C, which should have been a goal-tone, occurs on the weakest beat of the measure, and the line moves on to B♭; harmonically, the cadence is plagal and takes place on the weak half of measure 89; rhythmically, the closed, end-accented grouping ( ⏑⏑⏑ )—or, alternatively, the bar form (A A' B: 4 + 4 + 8)—suggested by the first two phrases is aborted by the brevity of the final phrase.

86. For other instances, see Mozart, *Marriage of Figaro,* Overture, mm. 25–35; and Brahms, Symphony No. 3 in F Major, iii, mm. 70–77.

87. Because the B is an appoggiatura implying further motion downward, it is included as part of the fill portion of the plan. The fill process is not merely potential, as it was in Example 7.34.

EXAMPLE 7.34. Mahler, Symphony No. 5, ii

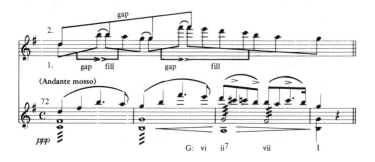

EXAMPLE 7.35. Verdi, *La forza del destino*, Overture

appoggiatura, F♯, to match that of the first, B (a major seventh above C), the gap of a sixth must be stretched to a seventh.[88] Even though it never reaches the initial D of the theme, the fill that follows is felt to be satisfying and complete. Compared to the two previous examples, closure is unequivocal: harmonically, the cadence is strong (ii[7]–vii–I); rhythmically, the low- and high-level groups are end-accented;[89] melodically, the fill seems satisfactory because the stability of the tonic, G, takes closural precedence over the claims of a complete fill (down to D),[90] and because, owing to greater intensity, the second gap-fill process tends to preempt the implications of the

88. The seventh is also a stretch and intensification relative to the preceding statement of the theme in which the second gap was a sixth (G up to E). Stretching, which is a very important expressive resource of Romantic music, is discussed in the next section.

89. On the lowest level, the stresses in measure 74 suggest iambic groups for the eighth-notes and for the last quarter; on a high level, an anapest group or bar form (1 + 1 + 2 measures) enhances closure.

90. Eugene Narmour calls this kind of precedence "substitution by rank." I am indebted to him for this concept. See his "Melodic Structure of Tonal Music," pp. 235, 244, 274–80.

first. Notice, too, that the sequence in Verdi's melody creates a hierarchy of gaps, both within motives (graph 1) and between them (graph 2). When this occurs, the presence of the gap-fill plan is particularly powerful, perhaps because greater cognitive/motor effort is required to "lift" whole motives than single pitches.

Such hierarchic gap-fill patterning can be the basis for extended melodic structures such as the solo cello melody from the first scene of act 1 of Wagner's *Die Walküre* (Example 7.36). The gap part of the schema consists of a three-measure motive that moves sequentially through the tones of the C-minor triad (see graph 1). Each of these statements contains a subsidiary gap (*s/g*) that reinforces the sense of disjunct motion. The last statement of the motive is varied so that the G, which might have closed it (see staff *a*) is passed over in favor of the B♭, which would have begun the next step had the sequence continued. This has three important consequences: first, the change signals that the sequential process is ended (there will not be a fourth statement); second, the larger motion to B♭ creates a tensive stretch suggesting that a descending motion will follow; and third, the "early" B♭ prepares the suspension that begins the fourth-species counterpoint (7–6) characteristic of the fill (graphs 1 and 2, mm. 10–18). The downward pull of the fill is strengthened both by the suspensions and by the succession of subsidiary gaps. As is characteristic of

EXAMPLE 7.36. Wagner, *Die Walküre*, Act 1, Scene 1

Wagner's music, and more generally of Romantic works, the end of the schema is not decisively closed.

The next, and last, gap-fill melody is included as a telling illustration of the relationship between schemata and characterization. The tune that opens the first act of *La traviata* (Example 7.37*a*) is a clear instance of a gap-fill melody. To be sure, the schema is elaborated, as comparison with a fugue theme by Geminiani (an almost unadorned instance) makes evident (Example 7.37*b*).[91] But the elaboration does not really disguise the schema; rather, the inverted rhythms and offbeat stresses impart a dramatically appropriate feeling of somewhat contrived gaiety. And it is precisely because the basic plan—the schema—is manifest and familiar that the exuberance seems a bit forced and frenetic.[92]

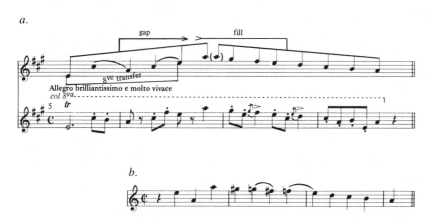

EXAMPLE 7.37. (*a*) Verdi, *La traviata,* Act 1, Scene 1; (*b*) Geminiani, Concerto Grosso in E Minor, Opus 3 No. 3, i (transposed)

Part of Verdi's genius was his ability to endow with verve melodies based on such frequently encountered schemata. This ability is perhaps what Charles Rosen had in mind when he wrote that Verdi "had the knack . . . of writing a melody that seems long-familiar at first hearing."[93] But it by no means follows that such melodies are, as Rosen suggests, "banal." Rather, the presence of a patent schema, such as a gap-fill plan (and they are plentiful in Verdi's music), provides a structural/processive norm in terms of which character and feeling can be effectively delineated.

The preceding section has been concerned with the use of schemata—the tendency to disguise their presence and the preference for general plans over syntactic scripts—in the music of the Romantic period. Though all parameters are involved in

91. For the sake of this comparison, I have transposed Geminiani's theme (from the Concerto Grosso in E Minor, Opus 3 No. 3, i, mm. 7–10) to A minor. For a discussion of this theme in relation to a gap-fill fugue theme by Bach, see my *Music, the Arts, and Ideas,* pp. 24–32.

92. Obviously other parameters—orchestration, tempo, dynamics, and the like—are important for the delineation of character.

93. "Verdi Victorious," p. 33.

the patterning of schemata, attention was directed to melody. Such attention seems warranted not only because the histories of harmony and form during the Romantic period have been much more extensively discussed than that of melody, but because both the composers and the theorists of the Romantic period considered melody to be the heart and soul of musical expression. In the words of Schopenhauer, the philosopher who perhaps best represented Romantic thinking about music:

> In melody, in the high, singing, principal part, which dominates the whole and progresses freely in a single, uninterrupted, coherent and meaningful idea from start to finish, a complete entity in itself, I recognize the highest stage of the objectivication of the Will, the conscious life and strife of man. . . . [Melody] tells the story of the Will as illuminated by self-awareness, the Will which imprints upon the phenomenal world its successive actions. But melody expresses still more: it reveals the Will's secret history, portrays its every movement, its every endeavour, everything that reason comprehends under the broad pejorative concept of emotion, being incapable of further abstraction.[94]

Melody received prime place in the pantheon of parameters because it seemed consonant with the ideals most highly prized in the ideology of Romanticism. It was associated with inspiration and genius, as opposed to learning and craft, and with spontaneity and feeling, as opposed to calculation and rationality. Harmony could be taught and learned—its rules could be found in treatises—and forms could be classified and analyzed into hierarchies of parts and subparts. But the art of writing a beautiful melody, progressing "freely in a single uninterrupted, coherent and meaningful idea from start to finish," could be neither learned nor taught; such a melody followed the natural laws of expression, not the artificialities of syntactic convention.[95]

Thus Rousseau, who denigrated the conventions of syntax, whether in language or music, considered that "the pleasure that springs from melody and song is a pleasure of interest and feeling that speaks to the heart."[96] And, by way of summary, Schopenhauer once again: "The composition of melody . . . is the work of genius, whose action, which is more apparent here than anywhere else, lies far from all reflection and conscious intention, and may be called an inspiration."[97]

---

94. Arthur Schopenhauer, *Die Welt als Wille und Vorstellung* (1819), in le Huray and Day, p. 327.

95. These notions—that melody cannot be taught, etc.—are still very much with us today. See Solie, *Metaphor and Model*, chap. 7. Because of its relationship to melody, counterpoint is privileged despite the fact that it, like harmony, can be codified in rules. For instance, unruly harmony can be excused on the grounds of voice leading or counterpoint. Cf. Levy, "Covert and Casual Values," pp. 20–22.

96. Jean-Jacques Rousseau, selection from *Dictionnaire de musique* (1767), in le Huray and Day, p. 116.

97. Arthur Schopenhauer, *The Philosophy of Schopenhauer*, pp. 204–5, quoted in Solie, *Metaphor and Model*, p. 301. It is pertinent to observe that the Romantic view of melody seems to involve a self-confirming prophecy. That is, if the relevance of convention (for instance, schemata such as those considered in the preceding selection) is denied, then melody cannot be analyzed, taught, or explained; it must be left to the realms of genius and inspiration.

## MEANS EXTENDED: STRETCHING

The avoidance or disguise of the familiar and formulaic, and the choice of musical patternings less dependent on syntactic constraints were not entirely compatible with another value central to Romanticism: that which assigned a place of prime importance to emotional expression—especially to that of the individual. The difficulty arose because, whether in life or in art, the expression of feeling and the delineation of individuality are inescapably dependent on norms of some sort (we recognize the signs of emotion, just as we diagnose the symptoms of disease, in terms of deviation from some normal state), and in the Classic period (and before) such norms were to a very significant degree matters of learned syntactic constraints and shared rhetorical strategies. To reconcile the claims of nature with those of expression, modes of deviation less dependent upon syntactic constraints were needed. One of these— perhaps the most important—was *stretching*.[98]

For any parameter of music, stretching involves an increase *in degree* relative to some nonsyntactic standard or precedent. The precedent may be established on any level of the stylistic hierarchy. For instance, the extensions of secondary parameters considered earlier—e.g., higher and lower pitches, louder and softer dynamics, faster and slower tempos—are, from this point of view, kinds of stretchings that serve both to delineate character and connotation and to heighten expression. The standards in these cases are not only the stylistic norms of the prevalent dialect, but transcultural norms set by the constraints of psychoacoustics and human physiology.[99]

Thus the extension of secondary parameters mentioned in Chapter 6 served expressive as well as programmatic ends. The opening measures of *La traviata* are poignantly expressive, not merely because of what they connote, but because the high registers, combined with unusually soft dynamics, create a tensive implication of change to acoustically more "normal" conditions. Composers of the Romantic period also tended to choose larger disjunct and smaller conjunct (chromatic) intervals than their predecessors had. Similarly, discordant harmonies and widely spaced sonorities were chosen more frequently than had previously been the case. The resulting aura of heightened tension is cognitive as well as psychoacoustical in origin. For what is involved is the effort—motor as well as mental—of making pitches that are separated in space or "incompatible" in frequency into coherent, comprehensible relationships.[100] These "natural" means of expression were, of course, not new. What was different was the degree and frequency of deviation.

Melodic stretching does occur in the music of the Classic period. The transition passage from the first movement of Mozart's String Quintet in G Minor (K. 516)

---

98. I am sure that there are other modes of nonsyntactic deviation that I have not recognized as such.

99. For instance, the limits of pitch and loudness perception or the range of the normal human heartbeat.

100. In twentieth-century music, not only have these disparities been increased, but temporal disjunction has heightened the problems of pattern perception.

provides a clear instance (Example 7.38). An initial skip of a minor sixth, D up to
B♭, is established as the standard in measures 30–31, and at the beginning of the
second part of the phrase, the initial interval is stretched to a minor ninth, while
the duration of the accent is lengthened from a dotted quarter to a dotted half-note.
The closure of this phrase establishes a bar form of 1 + 1 + 2 measures—a pattern
and length that is normal in the Classic style. The second phrase begins by repeating
the first two measures of the first, but instead of a two-measure continuation, an internal extension stretches the duration of the second part of the pattern to four
measures.[101]

The expressiveness of these stretches requires little comment. The interval
stretch is commonly to an appoggiatura, which at once delays the arrival of the implied structural tone and heightens the sense of impending fill. The durational stretch
(mm. 37–38) is emphasized by a stressed, syncopated amphibrach ⌣–⌣ . Notice that
in this passage the stretching is used primarily in the service of syntactic structure.[102]
That is, the tension of stretching is part of the modulation to the relative major.[103]

In the famous melody of Schumann's "Träumerei," however, stretching clearly
serves the needs of expression (Example 7.39).[104] There is no modulation here. The
period consists of two phrases: an antecedent and a consequent. The consequent begins like the antecedent and could easily have risen once again to F (m. 22) instead
of A;[105] just as in the melody of the Minuetto of Mozart's Flute Quartet (Example
7.32) where the A (m. 1) of the antecedent phrase is repeated in the consequent
phrase (m. 5). Instead, Schumann stretches the fourth (C to F) to a sixth (C to A).
The expressive tension of the stretch is heightened by the tensive character of the
harmony (V⁷/V) and by the fact that the resolution of the very discordant appoggiatura, A, implying a descending fill, is delayed by the fermata.[106] But these inten-

101. Durational stretching is a special case of phrase extension in which the extension occurs *within* the
phrase and the motivic materials are not differentiated from, but grow out of, the main body of the melody. Thus
durational stretching occurs in the opening melody of Schubert's Piano Trio in B♭ Major (Example 7.11) and the
opening period of the Prelude to *Tristan und Isolde* (discussed in my *Explaining Music*, pp. 237–39), but not where
the extension occurs after clear closure, as in the slow movement of Mozart's "Haffner" Symphony (Example 7.6a).
For though extensions after closure prolong, they do not usually affect the listener's understanding of the length of
the modules out of which structure is built. They act as confirming signs which, instead of heightening tension,
relieve it, allowing the musical momentum to diminish.

This general distinction between internal and external extensions must be qualified, however. There are internal extensions that do not create stretching. For instance, in the last movement of Haydn's String Quartet in E♭
Major, Opus 50 No. 3, a four-measure *parenthesis* extends what might have been an eight-measure phrase. But
because the music of the parenthesis is not related to the main melodic motion, it seems discrete, a kind of alien
aside. (For a discussion of this passage, see *Explaining Music*, pp. 240–41.)

102. I say "primarily" because the stretch also has expressive significance. Indeed, the syntactic process
and the expressive tension can scarcely be separated.

103. The modulation creates no definitive arrival—indeed the arrival does not occur until measure 64—
because no subdominant harmony precedes the V–I cadence.

104. The version of the melody used in the example is the one that occurs at the end of the piece.

105. The harmony could have been the same, with the F (instead of the high A Schumann wrote) moving
exactly as it did in the antecedent phrase.

106. The fermata here functions as a kind of nonpatterned durational stretch, delaying continuation. Its
function is, consequently, different from that of the fermata that closes Schumann's piece.

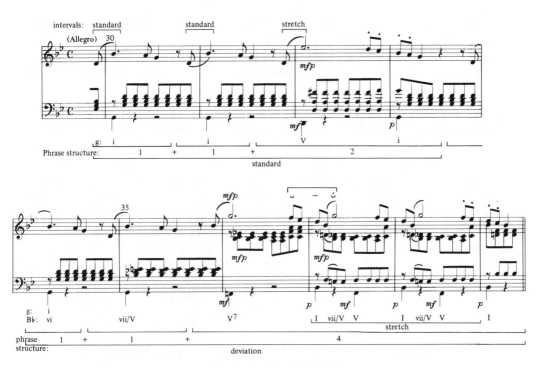

EXAMPLE 7.38. Mozart, String Quintet in G Minor (K. 516), i

sifications are largely local. The basic syntax of the period is not affected by the larger gap. Rather, what the restructuring does, in addition to increasing expressive tension, is to give the melody a point of culmination, a high point or statistical cli-

EXAMPLE 7.39. Schumann, *Kinderszenen,* Opus 15 No. 7, "Träumerei"

max characteristic of Romantic form.[107] The close of the period is, in typical Romantic fashion, characterized by abatement—descending pitches, probably coordinate with a modest *diminuendo* to the *piano* stipulated in the score, and a *ritardando* to the final fermata.

When stretching occurs within a composition, its force depends on the listener's ability to compare the standard pattern with the stretched version.[108] For this reason, the closer the standard and stretch are to one another in time, the more effective the stretch, other things being equal. It follows from this that stretches should occur more frequently within phrases than between them, especially as syntactic relationships become less clearly defined. This appears to be the case. As the nineteenth century moves on, stretching tends to occur as a reiteration in which the increase in interval size, as well as the repetition of the gap, serves to make the nature of the process patent. The fill part of the schema is, in turn, emphasized by the fact that the skipped-to notes are almost always appoggiaturas.[109]

Observe, too, that the more individually shaped the standard event against which the stretch is measured, the more manifest the fact of stretching. For instance, in both the theme that begins the third movement of Brahms's Third Symphony (Example 7.40) and the famous "Kiss" theme from Verdi's *Otello* (Example 7.41*a*),[110] the patterning *before* the interval to be stretched is well formed and characteristic. And proximate comparison creates an expressive tension that does not depend di-

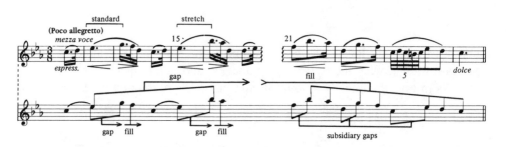

EXAMPLE 7.40. Brahms, Symphony No. 3 in F Major, Opus 90, iii

107. See Chapter 8. High points such as this should be distinguished from the high pitches that often precede closure in Classic music: for instance, the kind of rise to the sixth above the tonic that occurs near the end of the last movement of Mozart's String Quintet in E♭ Major (Example 7.4*b*) or the pre-cadential upper tonic that precedes closure in the first movement of Haydn's "Surprise" Symphony (mm. 232–34). In such cases—and they are legion in Classic music—the high pitch is not part of a "natural" culmination, but is instead a conventional sign of impending closure.

108. Though it depends on cognitive comparison, stretching also involves motor behavior: a literal experience of physical tension.

109. Needless to say, stretching occurs in other kinds of schemata. For instance, the melody of the second key area of the first movement of Caesar Franck's Piano Quintet in F Minor is an axial melody whose intervals above and below the axis tone are stretched. For a discussion of the axial nature of this theme, see my *Explaining Music*, pp. 187–89.

110. From act 1, rehearsal letter YY, Schirmer vocal score.

*a.*

EXAMPLE 7.41. (*a*) Verdi, *Otello*, Act 1, Scene 3

rectly on the presence of conventional tonal syntax. In Brahms's theme, each phrase of the antecedent-consequent period begins with a highly characteristic figure followed by a reiteration in which the gap is stretched. The final part of the period skips to B♭ again, and the ensuing linear descent is reinforced by a succession of subsidiary gap-fill motions.[111]

Verdi's melody is more complex and more intense (Example 7.41*a*). Its complexity is both contrapuntal and harmonic. Contrapuntally, a chromatic bass line descends against the ornamented B, the first (standard) part of the pattern;[112] harmonically, the chromaticism of the bass, together with emphasis on nonchord tones

111. The middle part of the period presents a provisional linear fill.

112. Juxtaposing a descending bass line and a relatively constant upper voice is a traditional strategy found not only in the Baroque period but in the music of the nineteenth century. See, for instance, Chopin's Prelude in E Minor, Opus 28 No. 4.

(appoggiaturas and neighbor notes) in the upper voice, creates an environment of instability and ambiguity. This background tension is both heightened and characterized by the manifest, yet tender, ardor of the melody. The stretching that expresses desire is compounded: not only does the second presentation of the "Kiss" motive stretch the interval of the first (the standard; see graph 1), but the third presentation of the motive stretches the stretch of the second, reaching the upper octave (m. 6). But it is not these "natural" tensions alone that characterize this theme. The motion of the reiterated standard is the beginning (somewhat disguised) of a conventional cadential gesture, as Example 7.41b, the main closing cadence of the first movement of Beethoven's String Quartet in F Major, Opus 18 No. 1, indicates. For Verdi, this gesture was associated with death and parting.[113] This is illustrated by two cadences from *La traviata:* the first from the duet between Violetta and Germont in act 2, scene 1 (Example 7.41c); and the second accompanying Violetta's final words of act 2 (Example 7.41d). But the potentially stark close of a turn around the dominant down to the tonic (Example 7.41e) is softened in *Otello* by a linear descent from the third (Example 7.41f).[114]

The prevalence of appoggiaturas in the music of Romanticism can scarcely be exaggerated. The reasons for this prevalence are many, and only some need be considered here. It should, first of all, be observed that to the extent that sonic tensions and melodic tendencies are generated by acoustic discord, the expressive and processive power of appoggiaturas is "natural"—independent of explicitly syntactic convention. The sense of downward pull toward a tone of greater concord gives such figures a strongly affective character—a character that, generally speaking, becomes more pronounced as the relative duration of appoggiaturas increases during the nineteenth century. In Liszt's words, what is expressed is "all that relates to the inaccessible depths of imperishable desires and longing for the infinite."[115] From a rhythmic point of view, appoggiaturas create mobile, ongoing groups that are readily associated with the Romantic valuing of openness, Becoming, and continuous growth.

113. It is so for Wagner (and many other nineteenth-century composers) as well. See, for instance, Lohengrin's last "Lebewohl" (act 3) and references to death in *Die Walküre* (act 1, scene 2; Siegmund's narrative) and *Tristan and Isolde* (act 1, scene 4; "Tod nun sag' ihr Dank!"). The association seems both natural and appropriate. For what the gesture at once presents and represents is an abrupt drop in energy level coupled with the finality of forceful closure.

114. The juxtaposition of Examples 7.41e and f suggests that the whole "Kiss" theme might be analyzed as a greatly stretched I$^6_4$–V–I cadence. (I am cognizant of the fact that I have not touched on many important facets of this melody—for instance, the striking use of C major in measure 7.)

115. Franz Liszt, from the preface to the *Album d'un voyageur, Années de pèlerinage* (1842), in le Huray and Day, p. 537. It is impossible not to mention in this connection that *Tristan and Isolde,* which epitomizes the expression of yearning (see Chapter 6, note 106), is replete with stretched, structure-shaping appoggiaturas.

EXAMPLE 7.41. (*b*) Beethoven, String Quartet in F Major, Opus 18 No. 1, i; (*c*) Verdi, *La traviata*, Act 2, Scene 1, "Dite all giovine"; (*d*) Verdi *La traviata*, Act 2, Scene 1

The proclivity of composers of the nineteenth century to choose more "natural" constraints—for instance, gap-fill melodies, stretching, and patent appoggiaturas—may help to explain why Adeste Fidelis melodies, so frequently encountered in the music of the eighteenth century (see Chapter 2), are seldom found in that of the nineteenth. The subject is pertinent here because Adeste Fidelis melodies, like stretch/gap-fill ones, involve skips from a standard tone. Whether it begins on the downbeat with a descending skip (as in "Voi che sapete" from Mozart's *Marriage of Figaro;* Example 7.42*a*) or with an anacrustic skip up (as in the opening measure of Haydn's String Quartet in E♭ Major, Opus 50 No. 3; Example 7.42*b*), the Adeste Fidelis schema is defined by a rising succession of syntactically related diatonic structural tones (**1**–5/**2**–5 or 5–**1**/5–**2**) that imply continuation to the fourth or fifth of the scale. Though gaps are present, the rising line takes precedence and is the primary focus of attention. Had the structural tones been ornamented by appoggiaturas (as in Examples 7.40 and 7.41), however, a descending fill would have been strongly implied and the nature of the schema would have been different.[116] In brief, then, Adeste Fidelis melodies are seldom found in the music of the nineteenth century because composers favored planlike schemata over scriptlike ones.

*a.*

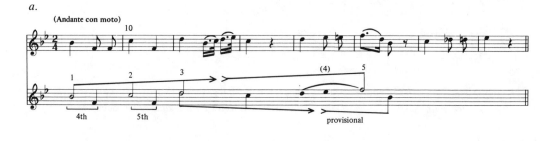

*b.*

EXAMPLE 7.42.  (*a*) Mozart, *The Marriage of Figaro* (K. 492), Act 2 No. 11, "Voi che sapete"; (*b*) Haydn, String Quartet in E♭ Major, Opus 50 No. 3, i

116. In other words, the absence of appoggiaturas makes it possible for the scriptlike aspects of the Adeste Fidelis schema to dominate its planlike potential. The gap-fill schema is subservient but not entirely negated. In both melodies (as in the tune "Adeste Fidelis" itself), a fill pattern does occur later in the music.

One last example from late in the Romantic period will serve to summarize many of the points already discussed. A passage from the third movement of Mahler's Symphony No. 4 in G Major (Example 7.43) is an unequivocal instance of an initial gap that is reinforced through reiteration and stretching. Though the nature of the plan is emphatic and unequivocal, the syntactic goal is ambiguous. The dominant harmony, instead of resolving, is dissipated when the highest notes are reached. The sense that the G♯–F♯ (m. 210) is a goal is a result not primarily of syntactic relationships, but of the organization of secondary parameters: the G♯–F♯ is the highest and the longest descending second, implying fill; the F♯ resolves an acoustic tension (discord); and the high point is marked by a change of orchestration and tempo.

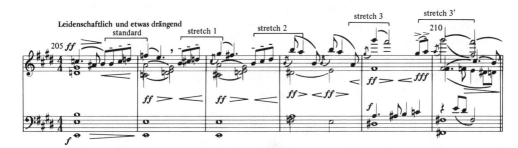

EXAMPLE 7.43. Mahler, Symphony No. 4, iii

Despite the intensity of successively stretched gaps and forceful appoggiaturas, the implied fill does not follow until some hundred measures later (m. 320, not shown in the example). There, following a monumental affirmation of the local tonic, E major (with G♯ in the top voices; mm. 315–19), the melody descends through a pentatonic scale that is only weakly syntactic because the two tones most important for defining tonality (the fourth and the leading tone) are missing. The entire end of the movement consists of a process of gradual abatement or subsidence in which the music dies away in a *morendo,* without decisive melodic, rhythmic, or harmonic closure. As the final harmony—the dominant—makes evident, the end is open, leading to the last movement of the symphony.

Taken by itself, this final fill seems a feeble response to the forceful tensions of stretched intervals and discordant appoggiaturas. And though the nature of the plan is not in doubt, the myriad different gaps (none adequately closed by a fill) make it impossible to know which, if any, is the gap that establishes criteria for a satisfactory fill and, consequently, what, if anything, would constitute such a fill. The end of the movement is paradoxical: while the abatement of secondary parameters creates closure, syntax suggests continuation. Nevertheless, the end is satisfying. For tension is more than merely dissipated in abatement. A sense of satisfaction is possible, I suspect, because the apotheosis-like affirmation (mm. 215–319) serves to cancel all previous implicative debts. That is, all the unrealized implications of melodic and harmonic invention, all the unresolved tensions of syntactic and nonsyntactic processes, and all the ambiguous formal juxtapositions are absorbed and "absolved" by the sheer intensity and size of the statistical climax, the apotheosis-like affirmation.

This discussion calls attention to a relationship between the local and the global aspects of large-scale musical forms. Put succinctly, there are two "schools" of stretching, a classicizing one and a romanticizing one. In the former, the initial gap, together with the stretch that enlarges the gap, are followed by a satisfactory fill. As in the case of the opening theme of the third movement of Brahms's Third Symphony (Example 7.40), the fill is satisfying because syntactic closure is also involved. In the latter school, stretching creates a succession of highly tensive gaps, but the adequacy of subsequent fill is in doubt, partly because abatement often takes the place of clear syntactic closure. In terms of large-scale form, what this suggests is that for classicizing composers, such as Brahms, strong statistical climax is unnecessary; for romanticizing composers such as Mahler, however, statistical climax or apotheosis is a way not only of achieving a sublime turning point in the form, but of dealing with the problem of prior implicative obligation.

Though stretching tends to become more common (and the resulting gaps larger) during the course of the nineteenth century, not all composers choose this strategy for shaping melodic structures. Indeed, two of the most important composers of the period, Wagner and Debussy, seem deliberately to avoid stretching, though for very different reasons.

Wagner's avoidance is, as I see it, related to the development and use of the leitmotif as a narrative and symbolic device. Because they have a referential function—symbolizing people, concepts, and objects—leitmotifs must be readily recognizable in a variety of musical and dramatic contexts. And to be recognizable, they must be relatively constant.[117] Stretching is avoided partly because it tends to disturb such constancy.[118]

It follows from this that in passages not essentially concerned with motivic narrative, melodic stretching should be possible. This appears to be the case. For instance, patent stretches occur toward the end of Walter's "Prize Song" in the last act of *Die Meistersinger* (Example 7.44a). Observe, too, that the chromatic descent (G–F♯–F♮) is reminiscent of a closing gesture (c/g) often found in Classic music (see Example 7.44b, from the first movement of Mozart's Keyboard Sonata in C Minor [K. 457]). But in the "Prize Song" the conventionality of the gesture is somewhat veiled both because the second degree of the scale is missing and, more

117. In Schoenberg's words, "Wagner, in order to make his themes suitable for memorability, had to use sequences and semi-sequences, that is, unvaried or slightly varied repetitions differing in nothing essential from first appearances, except that they are exactly transposed to other [scale] degrees" (*Style and Idea,* p. 185).

118. That the significance of motives changes depending on context does not gainsay their referential/ symbolic function. For the same may surely be said of words and visual images. And because symbol recognition depends not only on shape but on context, some degree of pattern variation is possible. What the limits of variation are probably cannot be the subject of general theory but must be dealt with on an ad hoc basis.

*a.*

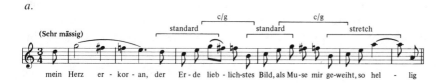

*b.*

*c.*

EXAMPLE 7.44. (*a, c*) Wagner, *Die Meistersinger von Nürnburg*, Act 3, Scene 5, "Prize Song";
(*b*) Mozart, Keyboard Sonata in C Minor (K. 457), i

importantly, because the gesture grows out of the preceding phrase.[119] It seems likely that Wagner felt free to use convention here because Walter's song is a traditional aria. This supposition is confirmed when the final stretch—both in interval and in duration (the long A)—is followed by an undisguised, stock closing formula (Example 7.44*c; s/c/f*),[120] the same pattern that so frequently occurs in Classic music (Example 7.44*b*).[121]

Debussy, too, chooses motivic constancy rather than stretching, transformation, or gradual variation. He does so, however, not because his motives have a semantic function to perform, but in order to emphasize the sensuous qualities of sound, creating a music more like a lyric tableau than a narrative action. More generally, Debussy tends to avoid patterns that strongly suggest goal-directed motion. The reasons for this were discussed earlier: because of the imperative of choice, human beings almost instinctively attend to whatever seems a basis for envisaging. Only by explicitly weakening the processive aspects of experience can we be forced, as it were, to attend primarily to the qualities of sense experience—the sound of a particular instrument, the specifically sensuous shape of a motive, the changing qualities of such sounds as they follow one another.[122]

119. This gesture also occurs near the end of the *idée fixe* in the first movement of Berlioz's *Symphonie fantastique*. It is discussed in my "Exploiting Limits," pp. 199–200.

120. Wagner's cadence at the end of Example 7.44*c* is deceptive. The assertion of C major is reserved for the music of the mastersingers.

121. It should be observed that though Wagner seldom uses intervallic stretching, stretches in duration are not uncommon in his music. See note 101 of this chapter.

122. In this connection, see my *Music, the Arts, and Ideas*, p. 74.

Debussy avoids not only stretching, whether intervallic or durational,[123] but melodic forms that are strongly processive. For instance, as far as I can tell, there is not a single instance of a gap-fill melody in all of his *Nocturnes,* nor are there instances of a syntactic schemata such as changing-note melodies. Finally, more than any other composer of the nineteenth century, Debussy avoids syntactically active harmonic progressions—especially the subdominant (IV or ii)/dominant relationship, which defines tonal centers and creates goal-directed motion.

Though Debussy's reasons for avoiding stretching are quite different from Wagner's, and though his motives are not explicitly semantic, his music tends, nonetheless, to evoke extramusical reference. For in the absence of emphatically goal-directed processes and conventional formal schemata, the ordering of successive events often seems problematic. Events come *after* one another, but they cannot readily be understood as following *from* one another. And when the raison d'être for a particular succession is in doubt, there is a tendency (fostered, again, by the need for envisaging) to search for a rationale that makes sense of the perceived patterning. Often extramusical reference, whether suggested by the composer or conjectured by the listener, provides the desired cognitive connection. Thus Debussy's compositional strategies (weakening syntactic and hierarchic structure in order to emphasize the primacy and facticity of sound) link him to the impressionists, while the cognitive consequences of his choices (creating the need for an interpretive reference) link him to the symbolists.

Debussy's "suggestive symbolism" does not depend on the semantic specificity of the motives he employs.[124] Rather it arises from the forms and processes of the sound patterns and their juxtaposition as they interact with the cultural environment and psychological dispositions of listeners. Wagner's motives, on the other hand, are explicitly semantic and iconic. For though a motive—for instance, the spear motive from the *Ring*—always refers to a network of associated ideas, persons, and objects, its significance is no more indefinite than that of a word such as *earth* or a visual image such as that of a crucifix. As a result, Wagner's music dramas might be said to employ "stipulative symbolism."[125] But the concern of this sketch is

---

123. In the absence of patent tonal syntax, morphology tends to be structured by motivic/metric modules, and the resulting patterns are generally additive rather than cumulative. Consequently, it is difficult to know what constitutes a durational stretch as distinguished from a simple addition.

124. Debussy does employ recurring motives in *Pelléas and Mélisande.* But as Roger Nichols points out, "Everything lies in the mode of suggestion to which the orchestra is dedicated and in the sparing (and often misunderstood) use of recurring themes. Debussy docs not use these as material for any symphonic argument essential to the opera, still less as agents of what he called the 'visiting card' technique of the *Ring*" ("Debussy, [Achille-] Claude," *The New Grove Dictionary,* ed. Stanley Sadie, 5:295).

125. Joseph Kerman reports that "what most interests most Wagner scholars today is definitely not [the semantics of Wagner's leitmotifs] . . . but larger questions of form and process. They are interested in the principles of structure in Wagner: principles involving leitmotifs as functional rather than as semiotic elements, and involving rhetorical modeling, narrative strategies, ambiguities of tonality and phraseology, and much else" ("Wagner and Wagnerism," p. 27). Such formalism—itself but a tired vestige of Romanticism—is mistaken not only because rhetoric, narrative, and all the rest are inseparable from the semantic significance of Wagner's motives, but because the view tends to obscure important aspects of nineteenth- and twentieth-century music history.

with history, not semiotics. So I close this chapter with a brief, if perhaps somewhat eccentric, account of the history of the leitmotif.

In his early operas—*The Flying Dutchman, Tannhäuser,* and *Lohengrin*—Wagner uses motives as adjectival adjuncts to the text and stage business, which are mainly responsible for shaping the dramatic action of the work. In other words, motivic relationships constitute what I call a *dependent* parameter (Chapter 1). Subsequently, beginning with the *Ring,* these roles are, if not reversed, at least more equal. That is, leitmotifs become an important means for shaping the aesthetic/dramatic action, while text and stage relationships serve to illuminate and explicate motivic processes. In Carl Dahlaus's words, "From *Rheingold* onwards, the basis of Wagner's musical form is no longer primarily syntactic but motivic."[126] The increasing importance of motivic relationships during the nineteenth century was in part a response to a gradual attenuation of the structuring provided by tonal syntax, a change that will be considered in the next chapter. Early in the twentieth century, composers—Richard Strauss and Schoenberg, among others—wrote works that continued to explore the aesthetic possibilities of leitmotif structure, though always in conjunction with some degree of tonal syntax and some sort of extramusical reference.

Though leitmotifs became more than mere adjuncts of extramusical action—though their role in shaping and characterizing musical relationships increased—their order could not be fully comprehended apart from extramusical reference and the constraints of tonal syntax. Nor did this situation change.[127] Motivic relationships never developed into an independent set of syntactic constraints that governed the possibilities and probabilities of variation, combination, and succession. This failure had important consequences for the history of musical Romanticism in the twentieth century, consequences that will be explored in the Epilogue.

126. *Richard Wagner's Music Dramas,* p. 107. Put in the terms developed in Chapter 1, there was a change in the dominance relationships among parameters.

127. I do not mean to imply that the final curtain has been lowered on the possibility of a narrative syntax of motivic structures. Since history is open-ended and full of surprises, Wagner's innovation may still prove consequential.

# CHAPTER 8

# Syntax, Form, and Unity

## THE WEAKENING OF SYNTACTIC IMPLICATIONS

The gradual weakening of syntactic relationships, coupled with a correlative turning toward more natural compositional means, was perhaps the single most important trend in the history of nineteenth-century music. It is generally agreed that of the many factors contributing to this attenuation none was more influential than the increased use of chromatic harmony. Without questioning the validity of this received opinion, it should be recognized that other alternatives were available for reaching the same aesthetic goals. A number of different strategies were used to mitigate and mask cadential closure. For instance, the increased use of plagal cadences at once avoids the conventionality of the authentic cadence and fosters a sense of openness;[1] marked abatement (descending pitches, thinning of texture, *decrescendo*, and *ritardando*) following arrival at dominant harmony weakens cadential closure, and as a result, the ensuing tonic is understood not as closing the preceding phrase but as beginning a new one;[2] striking, sudden changes in secondary parameters (usually from high to low intensity) can also mask the presence of conventional closure, so that the tonic sounds like a new beginning.[3] Other strategies such as phrase-elision, contrapuntal overlapping, and deceptive resolution also mitigate conventionality and weaken closure.[4] But none of these compositional means diminish or undermine the shaping force of tonal syntax.[5]

It should be recalled that even the profligate use of less probable syntactic alternatives will not change our understanding of tonal relationships. As noted in Chapter 1, though deceptive cadences weaken closure, even their frequent use does not undermine tonality. Indeed, the most eloquent evidence of the continuing power of foreground tonal syntax in nineteenth-century music is the ubiquity of deceptive ca-

---

1. See, for instance, Example 7.23*a*. Openness is especially marked in those closing cadences in which the minor subdominant precedes the tonic major (iv–I). This cadence is discussed below at Examples 8.5, 8.8, and 8.9.

2. This strategy is very common throughout the nineteenth century. See, for instance, Liszt's *Les préludes* (mm. 178–82) and Scriabin's *Le poème de l'extase* (mm. 15–19).

3. See, for instance, Example 7.15.

4. See, for instance, Examples 7.34 and 7.43 (following m. 210).

5. It should be emphasized again that none of these strategies was new. What was different was the increased frequency of their use.

dences. For the possibility of deception entails the presence of stipulative harmonic implication. Seen thus, one of the unequivocal signs of the dissolution of tonality is the absence of deceptive cadences—as, for instance, in the music of Debussy, though his music is essentially diatonic.

Chromatic harmony per se is neither a sufficient nor a necessary cause for the weakening of tonal syntax.[6] That chromatic harmony is not a sufficient condition for such weakening is evident in the fact that chromaticism and strong tonal syntax are by no means incompatible: witness such works as the "Ricercare" from Bach's *Musical Offering,* the "Introduzione" of Beethoven's Piano Sonata in C Major, Opus 53 ("Waldstein"), Chopin's Prelude in E Minor, Opus 28 No. 4, and countless other compositions from the seventeenth through the nineteenth century. That chromaticism is not a necessary condition for attenuated tonal syntax seems clear from the pentatonic musics of many diverse cultures and the relatively weak syntax of some of the basically diatonic works of, for instance, Debussy, Bartók, and Stravinsky.

To argue that the weakening of syntactic relationships cannot be directly attributed to the intensification of chromaticism is not to assert that there was no connection between these trends. To understand the connection, it is necessary to consider the basis for the definition of tonal syntax. For, not surprisingly, the weakening of syntactic relationships resulted in considerable part from the disuse of relationships essential for the specification of a tonal center.

In broadest terms, the specification of a tonal center—the definition of syntactic relationships of whatever kind (septatonic, pentatonic, and so on)—depends on the presence of *nonuniformity* in the repertory of pitches being employed. Put the other way around: complete uniformity—e.g., exclusively chromatic or whole-tone collections—cannot be the basis for tonal syntax. For instance, the passage from Debussy's "Nuages" given in Example 8.1 consists of four measures combining

EXAMPLE 8.1. Debussy, *Nocturnes,* "Nuages"

6. Obviously the validity of this claim depends in part on one's definition of chromatic harmony—and the hierarchic level being considered. I am using the term here in quite a straightforward sense: a chromatic progression is one that involves chords that do not occur diatonically in the established key and mode.

whole-tone with chromatic relationships, followed by two measures built on diminished triads. Though not tonal, the passage is highly processive. But the process has no tonal goal; that is, no particular pitch or harmony establishes a preferred point of closure or arrival. Similarly, neither a uniform succession of secondary dominants (Example 8.12*b*) nor a series of augmented sixth chords (Example 8.12*d*) will define a tonal center.[7]

On the other hand, uniformity supports values and goals central to the ideology of Romanticism: the continuous unfolding (Becoming) of process, the heightening of expression through deviation, and the intensification of uncertainty through ambiguity.[8] The conflict between the claims of syntactic relationships and those of ideology is of central importance for an understanding not only of the history of nineteenth-century musical practice, but of the special expressive quality of much of the music of the period. For the pervasive sense of restless yet unconsummated striving arises in part from the paradox that increased uniformity enhances mobility and the feeling of goal-directedness, even as it undermines the diatonic relationships that stipulate specific goals. Isolde's "Transfiguration," which is discussed toward the end of this chapter, is an exemplary instance of the connection between uniformity and ethos—the restless striving toward an unknown goal.

## *The Role of the Subdominant*

What is, I believe, one of the most important trends in the harmonic practice of the nineteenth century is related both to the intensification of uniformity and to the weakening of syntactic processes. The trend involves a turning away from the progression from subdominant (IV or ii) to dominant (V or vii).[9] To understand why the shift away from this progression is important, it is necessary to recognize that it is precisely this progression that specifies particular tonal centers.[10] The view that the most important harmonies of tonal syntax are the dominant and the tonic is, as I see it, both mistaken and misleading. That it is mistaken is evident in the fact that, for any competent listener to tonal music, a progression from subdominant to dominant unambiguously defines a specific tonal center *whether or not* the tonic of that center is actually presented. And it is equally obvious, even to a tyro in music theory, that a dominant to tonic progression does not define a tonal center, since that progression

---

7. The succession in Example 8.12*b* consists of dominant seventh chords, and as a result, the stability of each potential tonic is attenuated. On the other hand, had there been no sevenths, tonal centers would have been only tenuously defined because there would have been no tritones (4 to 7) between successive triads. Consequently, no preferred tonal realm would have emerged. If a tonal realm had emerged, it would have done so because of the patterning of other parameters. The mobility of the augmented sixth chords (Example 8.12*d'*) is intensified by the uniformity of the implied fourth-species counterpoint shown in Example 8.12*b'*.

8. For the role of uniformity in music, see my *Emotion and Meaning in Music,* chap. 5 and passim.

9. By "subdominant" I mean chords built either on the fourth degree of the scale or on the second degree (most often in the form of a seventh chord in first inversion, ii$^6_5$).

10. As I remember it, I learned this from William Mitchell, to whom I owe debts that should long since have been acknowledged.

can be interpreted as I to IV in another key.[11] The view has been misleading because it has masked the importance of changes in the use and prevalence of the subdominant in the history of tonal music.

The misconstruing of the importance of the subdominant is of particular interest in the present context because the interpretation is symptomatic of an ideological outlook that prizes nature rather than nurture—an outlook, that is, that seeks to base musical relationships on natural, rather than conventional, constraints. Indeed, the very notion of a *sub*dominant was derived from an acoustical account of the nature of musical relationships. And though Rameau eventually recognized that the subdominant could not be explained on acoustical grounds, it was his first formulation, together with his terminology, that persisted.[12] Subsequently, many theorists have struggled to "naturalize" the subdominant; taking another tack, Heinrich Schenker considered the subdominant merely ancillary (an embellishing neighbor chord) to the fundamental, natural order of the *Ursatz*.

I cannot satisfactorily explain why the progression from subdominant to dominant specifies a tonal center.[13] Fortunately, for the present purpose it is unnecessary to do so. It is enough to recognize that the progression does perform this function, adding perhaps that, despite our almost unconscious ideological biases, the constraints provided by nurture are usually at least as important in guiding human behavior as those provided by nature[14]—witness the force of religious belief, political doctrine, and scientific faith.

Why the subdominant/dominant progression was explicitly avoided and thus fell into disuse is both easier to explain and more germane to the present inquiry.

11. Consequently, the dominant/tonic progression does not create unequivocal closure. This is evident in eighteenth-century practice. For instance, although the *parlante* section of the buffo finale in eighteenth-century opera often consists of a long string of tonic and dominant chords, closure is not signaled until subdominant harmony precedes the dominant, creating a IV–V–I progression. In this connection, see Platoff, "Music and Drama in the *Opera Buffa* Finale."

12. See Cohen, "Rameau, Jean-Philippe: Theoretical Writings," *The New Grove Dictionary*, ed. Stanley Sadie, 15:569. Rameau was evidently enough of an empiricist to recognize that a natural explanation would not do, and enough of a rationalist to admit the possibility that the progression from subdominant to dominant involved learning.

13. The central importance of the subdominant/dominant progression in the definition of tonal closure may help to explain the prevalence of the $I_4^6$–$V_3^5$ progression, especially in cadences in which the melodic voice descends linearly from the fourth of the scale to the tonic. For if the subdominant is to be followed by the dominant, the third of the scale cannot be harmonized by I (in root position or first inversion), III, or VI because the subdominant/dominant progression would be interrupted and destroyed. But the $_4^6$–$_3^5$ appoggiatura pattern harmonizes 3 while keeping the subdominant/dominant relationship intact.

14. It seems probable that the tonal definition created by the subdominant/dominant progression has something to do with the fact that the fourth and the seventh uniquely delimit the sharp and flat sides of a diatonic collection. In this regard, see Browne, "Tonal Implications of the Diatonic Set"; and Butler and Brown, "Tonal Structure versus Function." The experiment of Butler and Brown indicates that the pitches 7 and 4 are crucial for the definition of a tonal area, and since 4 is a component of subdominant harmony while 7 is a component of dominant harmony, their conjunction may play a part in the definition of tonality. Yet questions remain: viz., why should the order subdominant/dominant (rather than the reverse) be crucial, and why shouldn't a progression from the subdominant to the mediant (III), which also involves both the fourth and seventh degrees of the scale, define a tonal area? Perhaps the presence of the tritone (whether successive or simultaneous, but especially the former) is a necessary condition for key definition, but learning may also be indispensable.

Ironically, it was precisely the power of the progression to specify a tonal center that ultimately discouraged its use. For that power had previously, in the eighteenth century, led to its frequent replication. As a result, it came to seem almost the quintessence of the conventional.[15] The subdominant/dominant progression was avoided because, in addition to being conventional (impersonal, unoriginal, and inexpressive), the unequivocal closure that it created was at odds with the ideological valuing of openness and emergent hierarchies.[16]

Nowhere is the avoidance of the subdominant/dominant progression more patent than in cadential gestures where subdominant harmony, which would have formed part of the melodic/harmonic pattern, seems almost explicitly excised. For instance, the melodic patterns that close phrases in Donizetti's *Lucia di Lammermoor* and Verdi's *Attila* (Examples 8.2*a* and *b*) are very similar to closing patterns in Mozart's Keyboard Sonata in E♭ Major (K. 282/189*g*) and his String Quartet in A Major (K. 464) (Examples 8.2*a'* and *b'*). And the final phrase of Lohengrin's "Farewell" (Example 8.2*c*) is similar to that which closes the first theme of the second movement of Mozart's Keyboard Sonata in B♭ Major (K. 333/315*c*) (Example 8.2*c'*). But while in the Mozart examples the fourth and sixth degrees of the scale are harmonized by the subdominant, in the Donizetti, Verdi, and Wagner examples that harmony has been eliminated. Instead, the fourth degree of the scale is treated as the seventh of the dominant, and in the Wagner example the sixth of the scale is transformed into an appoggiatura.

Another comparison also points to a shift in the relative importance of syntax in the articulation of closure. In the Donizetti and Verdi examples, the final melodic figure (*m*) prolongs the tonic without harmonic change, whereas in the Classic period the same figure is typically harmonized by a cadential $I_4^6 - V^7 - I$ progression, as in the second and third Mozart examples (8.2*b'* and *c'*).[17] "Liberated" from syntac-

---

15. See the quotations from Berlioz's *Memoirs* near the beginning of Chapter 7. I suspect that it was not merely the frequency of replication that made the subdominant/dominant progression seem a cliché. Rather, the progression seemed especially marked because the bass motion rose by a second (IV or ii[6] to V) and, in so doing, contravened and reversed more common kinds of bass movement (by thirds, fourths, or fifths—often descending). In other words, the subdominant/dominant progression was avoided not solely because of its frequency, but because it was particularly conspicuous.

16. Emergent hierarchies are discussed in Chapter 6. To forestall misunderstanding, let me emphasize that I am *not* suggesting that subdominant harmony was per se avoided. Quite the opposite. Once it became, so to speak, uncoupled from the dominant, it was more important in the delineation of structure and the articulation of closure than it had previously been. (The increased frequency of plagal cadences is discussed below.)

For an interesting discussion of some aspects of subdominant usage in the late nineteenth century, see Stein, "Expansion of the Subdominant." Because Stein's theoretical orientation is Schenkerian, she has trouble accounting for the increased use of the subdominant, and she seems to consider it a defect that "the subdominant does not define the tonic as forcibly or precisely as the dominant" (p. 164). It seems questionable, however, whether the dominant taken alone defines the tonic more forcefully than the subdominant does. Rather, the dominant defines the tonic unambiguously only when preceded by some sort of subdominant harmony.

17. This change is probably a consequence of the fact that, instead of using subdominant harmony (as Mozart does), Donizetti and Verdi harmonize the preceding measure with $I_4^6 - V^7$, which makes that harmonizing of motive *m* redundant.

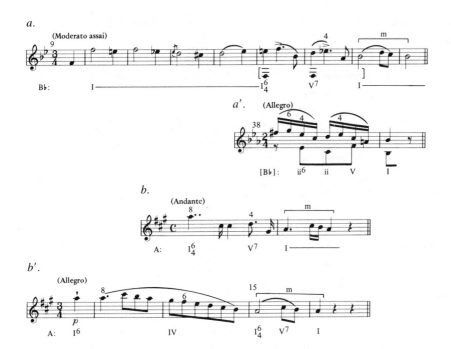

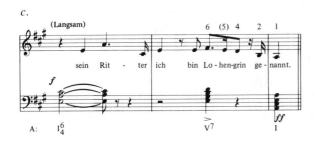

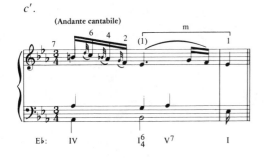

EXAMPLE 8.2. (*a*) Donizetti, *Lucia di Lammermoor,* Act 1, Finale, "Verranno a te sull'aure"; (*a'*) Mozart, Keyboard Sonata in E♭ Major (K. 282/189*g*), iii; (*b*) Verdi, *Attila,* Act 1, Scene 1, "Si quello io son, ravvisami"; (*b'*) Mozart, String Quartet in A Major (K. 464), i; (*c*) Wagner, *Lohengrin,* Act 3, Scene 3 (Lohengrin's "Farewell"); (*c'*) Mozart, Keyboard Sonata in B♭ Major (K. 333/315*c*), ii

tic constraints, the closing gesture has, ironically, become more conventional—a kind of purely formulaic style structure signifying closure.[18]

This calls attention to a general point of some interest. When replicated foreground patterns (such as stock gestures and ornaments) have a syntactic function as they normally do in Classic music,[19] their conventionality is minimized; conversely, when syntax is weakened, conventionality is emphasized.[20] The weakening of syntax during the nineteenth century affected the use of both replicated figures and ornaments. For instance, not only are ornaments used less often, but, when they are used, their function tends to change. Instead of contributing to the shaping of rhythmic/melodic relationships, they often have a referential/characterizing function (in the last movement of Berlioz's *Symphonie fantastique,* for instance, ornaments enhance the sardonic character of the E♭ clarinet's version of the *idée fixe*), serve as a kind of sonic coloring and increase the statistical intensity of a passage (as in the opening measures of Rimsky-Korsakov's *Capriccio espagnol*), or perhaps serve simply as a way of exhibiting the virtuosity of a performer (as in, say, Donizetti's elaborate coloratura passages).

Of course, subdominant/dominant progressions do occur in nineteenth-century music. Especially in music such as Italian opera, where structural articulation is aesthetically indispensable, the progression continues to play a vital role in the creation of closure. Yet even here there are some signs of the shift that I am trying to describe. For instance, though a strong subdominant/dominant progression (IV–I⁶₄–V⁷–I) emphasizes the closure of act 2, scene 1 of Verdi's *La traviata* (Example 8.3a), the final closing gesture excludes the subdominant. That is, the sixth of the scale, which would probably have been accompanied by subdominant harmony in eighteenth-century music (as in Example 8.3b), is transformed into an appoggiatura whose tension depends on acoustic discord (also see Examples 7.41c and d). In short, conventional syntactic relationships tend to give way to natural acoustical ones.[21]

The use of the sixth degree of the scale as an appoggiatura and the avoidance of the subdominant are, I suspect, reciprocally related. That is, when the sixth degree occurs over dominant harmony, it creates a ninth chord, and particularly when the seventh is also present, three of the constituents of the harmony (the fifth, seventh, and ninth) form an acoustic complex comparable to a chord built on the second degree of the scale (see Example 8.3c). Because the dominant ninth chord already con-

18. The term *style structure* is borrowed from Eugene Narmour's *Beyond Schenkerism,* chap. 11. For much later instances of this kind of nonsyntactic usage, see Stravinsky's *Rake's Progress*—for example, at the end of Anne's Arioso in act 2, scene 2 (see Example E.2).

19. The role of ornaments in shaping melodic/rhythmic patterns is discussed in Cooper and Meyer, *The Rhythmic Structure of Music,* pp. 21–22 and 48–49.

20. It follows from this that the weaker syntax becomes, the greater the tendency either to disguise convention or to employ radically novel means.

21. Though the appoggiatura-sixth to the fifth becomes somewhat formulaic in Italian opera (the avoidance of one convention leads, somewhat paradoxically, to the cultivation of another!), it is by no means absent from other repertories—witness Example 8.2c from Lohengrin's "Farewell."

tains crucial tones of the subdominant, any progression from the subdominant to such a ninth chord will tend to lack syntactic force and articulative power. More generally, to the extent that any piling up of thirds increases the number of tones common to successive chords, it tends to weaken the sense of syntactic progression.[22]

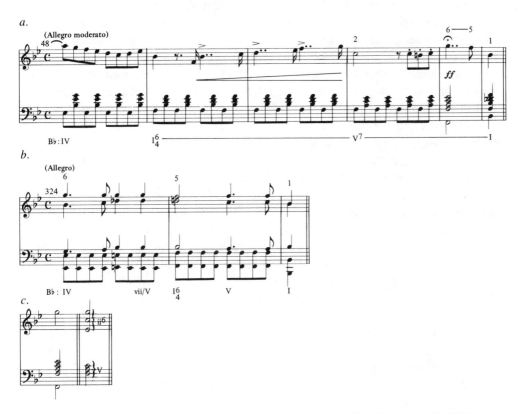

EXAMPLE 8.3. (*a*) Verdi, *La traviata,* Act 2, Scene 1, "Morrò! la mia memoria"; (*b*) Mozart, *The Marriage of Figaro* (K. 492), Act 2, Finale

22. "Piling up" of thirds refers, of course, to the principles of grammatical construction of chords, not to their actual compositional disposition.

This may in part explain some of Debussy's compositional choices. In order to emphasize the sensuous qualities of sound, he uses means such as ninth and eleventh chords, which tend to weaken the feeling of syntactic progression.[23] As noted in Chapter 7, subdominant/dominant progressions seldom occur in his music; this observation is strengthened by the fact that one searches in vain in his music for unequivocal deceptive cadences. His inclination to avoid this most syntactic of harmonic progressions seems evident in his revision in 1892 of the song "En sourdine" ten years after its initial composition. One of the changes made involves the elimination of all subdominant/dominant progressions.[24] This is not to contend that Debussy's music is not at times processive and goal-directed. But the processes usually either depend on nontonal sequences, as in the passage from "Nuages" discussed earlier (Example 8.1), or they create a sense of implication through *saturation*—the repetition of a single figure, as in measures 17–20 in *Afternoon of a Faun*.[25]

This account of the weakening of syntactic connection is supported by Laurence Berman's observation that Debussy's harmonic style bespeaks "a certain motivation, not so much to create a new language, as to avoid an old one. We must recognize a certain negative aspect of his art at this time in his abhorrence of the basic functional relations. . . ."[26] On the positive side, Debussy not only uses harmony to enhance sonic quality but, as William Austin points out, he uses "chords to support the onward movement of the melody."[27] But Austin's further observation that Debussy's harmonic "choices cannot be explained by any rule"[28] should not be taken to imply that Debussy's harmonic progressions are random. Instead of being a primary parameter fully governed by syntactic rules, harmony in Debussy's music often functions as a secondary parameter,[29] governed both by dependency rules (having to do with sonic enhancement, melodic support, and so on) and by contextual rules (having to do with major structural articulations).[30]

Why, as Austin asserts and Berman implies, Debussy's music sounds so "right" is a question beyond the scope of this sketch. But one facet of the problem does seem relevant here. Namely, the absence of a full complement of syntactic constraints

23. See the discussion of Debussy's music at the end of Chapter 7.

24. In addition, Debussy removes the "high points" in verses 2 and 3, leaving only the final one in verse 5; this makes the form more "statistical." I am indebted to Marie Rolf, whose paper "The Emergence of the Symbolist Aesthetic in 'En sourdine,'" read at the annual conference of the American Musicological Society in 1985, provided the basis for these observations.

25. And in this case, abatement (*decrescendo, ritardando,* thinning of texture, change of register, etc.) attenuates the sense of arrival when the flute melody returns. The concept of saturation is discussed in my *Emotion and Meaning in Music,* pp. 135–38.

26. "Evolution of Tonal Thinking," p. 243.

27. "Toward an Analytical Appreciation," p. 82.

28. Ibid.

29. Chapter 1, in the section "Rules."

30. See Chapter 7, at the beginning of the section "Disguise Through Emergence."

means that no harmonic progression per se is either wrong or right. In this situation, listeners tend to base their sense of propriety on other parameters such as chord sonority (construction), melodic interval, rhythmic/metric patterning, instrumental color, and so on. These parameters have two important characteristics: they are used with great consistency, and they are seldom irregular, unusual, or disturbing. As a result, we accept Debussy's harmonic relationships, much as we do a cool breeze, a passing cloud, a fragrance, or the sounds of the sea.

## Nonchord Tones and Syntax

As observed in Chapter 7, syntactic relationships were also weakened by the durational stretching of nonchord tones, especially appoggiaturas. Not only did the frequency of appoggiaturas increase,[31] but to enhance their palpability and expressive power, so did their duration relative to the chord tones they embellished. Psychologically, however, longer tones seem more important than shorter ones, and for this reason, they tend to be understood as structurally and syntactically more significant. As a result, durational stretching may make it doubtful whether a particular tone embellishes harmony (is an appoggiatura) or is a structural component of the harmony. The functional relationship among pitches becomes more ambiguous.

But even markedly stretched appoggiaturas need not be syntactically ambiguous. The long appoggiatura in the excerpt from *La traviata* (Example 8.3*a*) creates virtually no syntactic ambiguity. This is so because the contrast between timbres, together with the disposition of the texture—that is, the high vocal part placed against the orchestra bunched in a low register—leaves no doubt about the essentially melodic function of the long high G. The presence of two features characteristic of most appoggiatura figures also helps to clarify function. First, the discordant G *descends* so that retrospectively, at least, its function is clear.[32] And second, the final high G is, in effect, prepared by the last sixteenth-note of measure 50; such preparation leaves no doubt about the origin, and hence the function, of the long G.

When some or all of these conditions do not prevail, the function of a long discordant tone may be in doubt. In Schumann's "Träumerei" (Example 7.39), for instance, the function of the high A in measure 22 is somewhat ambiguous. Although the anticipation and the following descending motion argue for its interpretation as an appoggiatura—as does the fact that the A is the top of a stretched interval—the parallelism with the F in measure 18 (clearly *not* an appoggiatura) and

---

31. Reasons for the ubiquity of appoggiaturas in nineteenth-century music were considered in Chapter 7.

32. I suspect that descending appoggiaturas are the norm because acoustic/harmonic resolution (to a chord tone) and descending melodic motion are both associated with closure, and hence with each other.

the absence of clear timbral and textural differentiation argue against it. But the most notorious case of functional ambiguity involves the most famous single chord in all of nineteenth-century music. I refer, of course, to the *Tristan* chord (Example 8.4*a*).

That this chord is functionally ambiguous is evident in the alternative analyses given by different critics. Which alternative is preferred seems to depend largely on the interpretation of the function of the G♯. Thus Leonard Ratner (Example 8.4*b*)[33] and William Mitchell (Example 8.4*c*)[34] consider the G♯ to be structural.[35] Ratner does so by implication; Mitchell does so by explicitly arguing for the structural status of the G♯.[36] For Carl Dahlhaus (Example 8.4*d*),[37] Walter Piston (Example 8.4*e*),[38] and Felix Salzer,[39] the G♯ is an appoggiatura.[40] The ambiguity of the G♯ is

*a.*

EXAMPLE 8.4. (*a*) Wagner, *Tristan and Isolde*, Prelude

33. *Harmony: Structure and Style,* p. 313.

34. "The Tristan Prelude," p. 170.

35. Also see Bailey, "An Analytic Study of the Sketches and Drafts," in his edition of Wagner's *Prelude and Transfiguration from "Tristan and Isolde,"* pp. 124, 127.

36. "The Tristan Prelude," pp. 174–76.

37. "Harmony," *The New Grove Dictionary,* ed. Stanley Sadie, 8:181.

38. *Harmony,* p. 306.

39. *Structural Hearing* 1:176 and 2:144 (example 371). Though Salzer does not discuss the G♯, his classification of the chord indicates that he considers it to be a nonchord tone.

40. Roger Sessions, Ernst Kurth, Alfred Lorenz, and Roland Jackson also interpret the G♯ as an appoggiatura. See the excerpts from their writings in Bailey, "An Analytic Study" (see n. 35 above), pp. 164, 187, 222, and 269 respectively. The entry " 'Tristan' chord" in *The New Grove Dictionary,* ed. Stanley Sadie, 19:153–54, gives two interpretations of the chord. The first considers the G♯ to be an appoggiatura; the second considers it to be structural—part of a iv chord in A minor with an added sixth: "(e.g. *d–f–a+b,* inverted to *f–a–b–d'* with lowered 3rd and a raised 6th = *f–a♭–b–d♯*)."

the result of a concatenation of the factors already mentioned: its relative length (5:1), its lack of preparation, the fact that it moves up rather than down, and its timbral and textural relationships that do nothing to specify function.[41] Since I introduced the *Tristan* chord in a discussion of the role of nonchord tones in the weakening of syntactic process, context seems to suggest that I prefer the appoggiatura interpretation. And while I do tend to favor this view for criticism because the character and affective quality of the chord seem inextricably linked to its continuation to A (that is, its dependence), the analysis of the G♯ as a structural element in an independent harmony is perhaps preferable historically.[42] For what has been called the emancipation of dissonance begins with unprepared appoggiaturas and continues with unresolved dissonances that are eventually transformed into acoustic entities (discords) in relation to which the notion of syntactic resolution is meaningless.

For most historians, *Tristan* and its representative, the *Tristan* chord, have a special significance in these changes. As Carl Dahlhaus describes it:

> It is not that Wagner anticipated Schoenbergian atonality; there was never any question of his abandoning the principle of tonality. . . . Yet the harmonies of *Tristan* point the way that was to lead eventually to the dissolution of tonality, the emancipation of melody and counterpoint from preformed chordal associations. *Tristan* is a primary source in the history of modern music.[43]

Though the harmonies of the opera may have played a part in the dissolution of tonality, the significance of the *Tristan* chord is, I think, different. It seems to me to signal that the primacy of *generalized syntactic function,* which makes chord inversion possible, has begun to give way to the claims of sonority and voice leading. From this point of view, it is misleading—at least historically—to analyze the *Tristan* chord as an inversion of, say, an augmented sixth chord with a long appoggiatura. For unlike the chord from *La traviata* (Example 8.3a, m. 52), it is not fully defined by syntactic function but is significantly a *sonority.*[44] This is evident in the fact that the same "interval collection" occurs in many other compositions during the nineteenth century—for instance, in Chopin's Prelude in F♯ Minor, Opus 28 No. 8.[45] But the chord in Chopin's Prelude is *not* by any stretch of the imagination the

41. Nor do orchestration and dynamics serve to clarify ambiguity. The emphasis on the first four eighth-notes in measure 2 (not shown in the Example) might be interpreted as enhancing the mobility of the G♯ (its appoggiatura function) or its structural importance (its harmonic function).

42. Aesthetic and historical significance are not, in other words, necessarily identical.

43. *Richard Wagner's Music Dramas,* p. 64.

44. My views here are close to those of Werner Karsten, excerpted in Bailey's edition of Wagner's *Prelude and Transfiguration from "Tristan and Isolde,"* p. 235. Though Ernst Kurth emphasizes the importance of the dynamic tensions inherent in the *Tristan* chord, he too recognizes the significance of its sonority. More generally, Kurth discusses the increasing individualization of chord-sound during the nineteenth century. For him, the dynamic tension of harmony leads to expressionism, while the sensuous aspect leads to impressionism (in this connection, see Rothfarb, *Ernst Kurth as Theorist and Analyst,* chaps. 6 and 7). Seen thus, what Debussy "learned" from Wagner was not some sort of tonal "freedom," but the possibility of making sonority relationships an important aspect of music.

45. See Example 8.12a; also see Schumann's Piano Quartet in E♭ Major, Opus 47, iv, m. 331.

same as, or even really similar to, the *Tristan* chord. In short, *Tristan* and the *Tristan* chord are "a primary source in the history of modern music" because they are early signs of the demise of chord invertibility *à la* Rameau and, hence, of the weakening of harmonic syntax, which depends on the presence of functional substitutability.[46] Finally, it is important to recognize that, as suggested toward the end of Chapter 7, there is an inverse relationship between awareness of sonority and awareness of syntactic specificity. That is, it is precisely the functional ambiguity of the *Tristan* chord—its lack of syntactic specificity—that directs attention to its sonorous quality.[47]

Though the *Tristan* chord was certainly the most famous harmonic "invention" of Romanticism, it was by no means the only one. More or less novel harmonies and harmonic progressions were continually being devised by the composers of the period. And, as Carl Dahlhaus makes clear, ideology was important in encouraging innovation:

> The idea of originality, which imposed itself as the dominant aesthetic principle in the late 18th century, combined the demand that in 'authentic' music the composer should express the emotions of his inner self with the postulate of novelty. Alongside melodic ideas, what the 19th century valued most as 'inspirations' were chords that were surprising and yet at the same time intelligible. Such chords were felt to be expressive—the word 'expression' being used in a strong sense to refer to the representation of out-of-the-ordinary inner experience by the use of unusual means—and were expected to take their place in the historical evolution of music, an evolution that was seen as a chain of inventions and discoveries.[48]

Though the goals of originality, individuality, and expression undoubtedly stimulated the search for novel harmonic relationships, they are not reasons why Romantic composers chose the particular means that they did. For even given the constraints of tonality, there were innumerable ways of realizing these goals.[49]

Moreover, what are of interest for the historian are not single instances of some

---

46. It is also relevant to note that the total three-measure pattern is based on two schemata that are not necessarily syntax-dependent: (1) a divergent wedge, which also functions on a much larger scale as one of the organizing processes of the "Transfiguration" (see below, at Examples 8.24 and 8.28); and (2) a coordinate complementary pattern which Edward T. Cone analyzes as a phrase and its exact inversion. See his "Yet Once More, O Ye Laurels," excerpted in Bailey's edition of Wagner's *Prelude and Transfiguration from "Tristan and Isolde,"* pp. 282–83.

47. I am grateful to Jeffery Cotton for some of these observations. Both our discussions and his paper "Functional Sonority: A Reexamination of the *Tristan* Chord" helped me to formulate my views about these matters.

48. "Harmony," *The New Grove Dictionary*, ed. Stanley Sadie, 8:181.

49. Nor in analytic criticism does the "need for variety" constitute an adequate explanation of the choices made by a composer, since even within the intraopus structure of a particular work many kinds of variety are usually possible.

novel harmony or progression but, as noted earlier, those that are replicated, becoming part of the dialect of the period. For instance, measure 140 of the first movement of Beethoven's String Quartet in B♭ Major, Opus 130, begins with an unequivocal instance of an augmented triad. But it is unlikely that any historian has discussed the role of this novelty in the history of music, for it is an anomalous, isolated instance in Beethoven's *oeuvre*.[50] Many historians have, however, commented extensively on comparable harmonies in, say, Liszt's music.

As observed in Chapter 4, whether a musical relationship is considered novel is often a matter of hierarchic level. But even on the same hierarchic level the ascription of novelty may depend on interpretation. For instance, if the G♯ in the Tristan chord is analyzed as an appoggiatura, its novelty is largely a matter of degree; if the same chord is interpreted as an integral sonority-process, its novelty is, so to speak, categorical. What this suggests is that changes in degree or frequency may be symptomatic of changes in function and aesthetic/ideological values as well. Several such changes are considered in what follows.

## Changes in Frequency

### PLAGAL CADENCES.

Although plagal cadences are uncommon in Classic music,[51] they occur with considerable frequency as closing cadences in the music of the nineteenth century. They were chosen with increased frequency for both ideological and aesthetic reasons. Ideologically, they were consonant with the Romantic valuing of openness, because they create less decisive closure than authentic cadences do.[52] Aesthetically, plagal cadences were chosen because they were a way of avoiding the authentic close (V–I or i), which had come to seem an unacceptably conventional cliché. Plagal cadences, however, seldom serve to articulate internal closure.[53] Mostly they occur near the end of compositions. At times they create high-level closure; more frequently they occur *after* such closure.[54] In Chopin's Fantasie in F Minor/A♭ Major,

50. Nor have any of the analyst/critics whose discussions I have looked at even mentioned the harmony, probably because, given its context as part of a modulatory transition in a recapitulation, it is not especially striking.

51. Plagal cadences do, of course, occur in Classic sacred music—in accordance with quasi-contextual rules.

52. This seems to contradict the point made earlier that the authentic cadence is not intrinsically more closed than the plagal cadence. But the authentic cadence had come to function, during the Classic period (and before), as a strong sign of secure closure, particularly when the presence of a seventh contributed to the definition of the tonal realm.

By authentic cadences I mean progressions in which the dominant (or dominant seventh) moves to the tonic without being preceded by a tonality-defining subdominant-function harmony.

53. The plagal cadence in the lyric theme of Liszt's *Les préludes* (Example 7.23*a*) is somewhat unusual, and it employs a shift to the minor subdominant, which makes the progression sound something like a half cadence. This progression—from minor subdominant to tonic major—will be discussed shortly.

54. By high-level closure, I mean closure that establishes final and enduring tonic harmony.

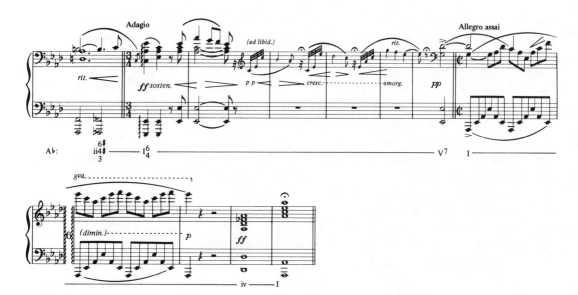

EXAMPLE 8.5.  Chopin, Fantasie in F Minor/A♭ Major, Opus 49

Opus 49 (Example 8.5), for instance, the main closure involves a progression from an augmented sixth chord (ii$^{6\sharp}_{4\sharp3}$) to I$^6_4$ (followed by a brief cadenza) to V$^7$. Resolution to the tonic follows, but it is weakened by a long appoggiatura (D♭) and partly veiled by the figuration of the coda. The final, emphatic closing gesture is plagal (iv–I).

Notice that in such cases—and they are common—the plagal progression is not a substitute for strong syntactic closure but a sign *confirming* prior closure, much as the authentic (V–I) cadence is in the Classic style. This can be related to the observation made earlier that a progression which follows strong cadential closure appears to be especially conventional.[55] This may be one reason why the confirming authentic cadence of the Classic style came to seem a blatant cliché that needed to be replaced, and why the confirming plagal cadences that replaced authentic ones gradually came to seem conventional as well.

Of the four possible subdominant-to-tonic progressions, only three function cadentially.[56] A somewhat cursory survey suggests that the familiar major-mode pla-

55. See above; the discussion of Example 7.3*b*.
56. This is because, given the constraints of tonal syntax, the progression from the subdominant major to the tonic minor (IV–i; Example 8.6*d*) does not create closure.

EXAMPLE 8.6.

EXAMPLE 8.7. Brahms, Symphony No. 1 in C Minor, Opus 68, iv

gal ("Amen") cadence is seldom used to create high-level closure. This may be because, until the tonal center has been unambiguously defined, the progression might be understood as being I–V rather than IV–I (Example 8.6a). It does serve fairly frequently as a confirming cadence, however, as the end of the last movement of Brahms's First Symphony (Example 8.7) illustrates.[57] Although it is less common, the progression from the minor subdominant to the minor tonic (Example 8.6b) is used to articulate high- as well as low-level closure. The last high-level closure in Richard Strauss's *Don Juan* occurs when, nineteen measures before the end, a long and forceful dominant preparation is broken by a long pause that is followed not by

57. For other instances, see Borodin, String Quartet in D Major, iv, mm. 665–68; Liszt, *Les préludes*, last two chords; Schumann, Piano Quintet in E♭ Major, Opus 44, i, mm. 232–38; and Tchaikovsky, *Romeo and Juliet*, mm. 515–17.

the expected tonic (or tonic substitute) but by the minor subdominant; it is this harmony that leads to the final tonic, which is prolonged till the end of the tone poem
(Example 8.8*a*).[58] The close of the first movement of Arensky's Piano Trio in D
Minor is a clear instance of low-level plagal closure in the minor mode (Example
8.8*b*).[59]

The cadence from the minor subdominant to the tonic major (Example 8.6*c*),
which is used to articulate both high- and low-level closure, is more frequently replicated than either of the other plagal progressions. Probably the most famous instance
of this cadence occurs at the end of *Tristan and Isolde* where, instead of resolving to
the tonic (or a tonic substitute), a prolonged dominant seventh chord moves to the
subdominant minor (E minor) which then resolves to the tonic (B major).[60] The last
high-level cadence in the slow movement of Tchaikovsky's Symphony No. 5 in E
Minor is also a clear instance of a plagal progression from the minor subdominant to
the major tonic (Example 8.9*a*). As with most plagal progressions, however, this
type functions much more often as a confirming cadence.[61] This is so, for instance,
in Chopin's Fantasie in F Minor/A♭ Major (Example 8.5) and the second movement
of Mendelssohn's Piano Trio in D Minor, Opus 49 (Example 8.9*b*).[62]

The use of subdominant closure at the ends of pieces may in part also result
from the interest of Romantic composers in earlier music, especially that of the Baroque. But, as argued in Chapter 5, the problem is one not primarily of origin but of
use. Why, that is, were plagal cadences chosen by Romantic composers but not by
those of the Classic period (although the cadences were just as available then)? One
reason, suggested by Ruth A. Solie (in a personal communication), is that plagal
endings are related, through the "Amen" aspects of the cadence, to the sacred. From

58. For another example of the minor mode plagal cadence, see Tchaikovsky's Symphony No. 4 in F Minor,
i, mm. 400–403, where the tonic pedal begins. The minor mode plagal cadence also serves to articulate internal
closure—for instance, at the end of Trio No. 1 in the Scherzo of Dvořák's Symphony No. 9 in E Minor ("From the
New World") and at the end of Etude No. 10 of Schumann's *Symphonic Etudes,* Opus 13.

59. I have analyzed the subdominant harmonies in both the preceding examples and the following ones as iv
(IV) chords with an added sixth rather than as ii$^6_5$ chords for two reasons: first, because the root motion by a skip
from the fourth degree of the scale (in the bass) to the tonic warrants such an analysis, especially since the ii$^6_5$ chord
normally moves by step in a cadential progression; and second, because the added sixth contributes to the sense of
cadential progression more because of the acoustic tension that it creates than because of any enhancement of syntactic relationship. Moreover, since the acoustic tension of a discord is "natural" rather than syntax-dependent,
it seems both symptomatic of the increased emphasis on sonic sensibility and consonant with the tenets of
Romanticism.

60. The similarity between the descriptions of the ends of Strauss's *Don Juan* and Wagner's *Tristan* makes
the differences especially significant; for Strauss's hero sinks slowly to earth in a quivering melodic descent, dying
darkly earthbound in the minor mode, while Wagner's heroine rises serenely to the bright heavenly bliss of the
major mode.

61. It seems possible that a general principle of style change—one calling for further study—is evident
here: namely, novelties tend to occur first on relatively low hierarchic levels and are subsequently extended to the
structuring of higher levels.

62. For other examples, see Borodin, String Quartet in D Major, ii, mm. 291–93ff.; Musorgsky, *Night
on Bald Mountain,* mm. 451–52ff. (only a touch of subdominant minor); Mendelssohn, Overture to *A Midsummer
Night's Dream* (final two measures); Schumann, Piano Quintet in E♭ Major, Opus 44, ii, mm. 189–91ff.;
Tchaikovsky, Symphony No. 5 in E Minor, iii, mm. 264–66; and Chopin, Etude in C Minor, Opus 10 No. 12
("Revolutionary"), final two measures.

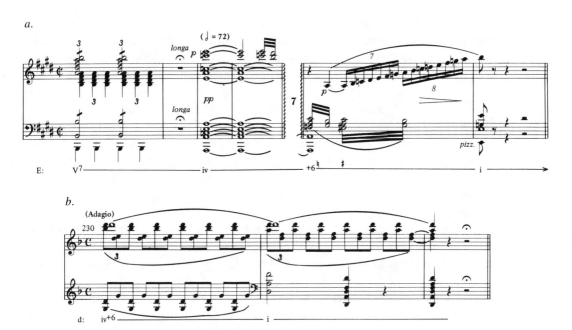

EXAMPLE 8.8.  (*a*) Strauss, *Don Juan*, Opus 20; (*b*) Arensky, Piano Trio in D Minor, Opus 32, i

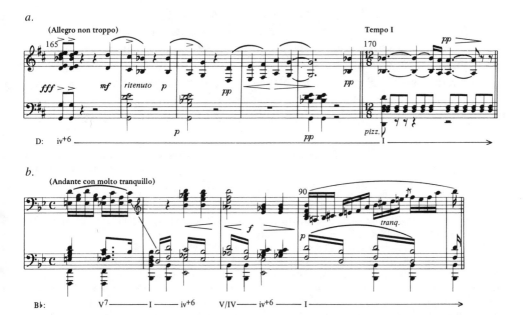

EXAMPLE 8.9.  (*a*) Tchaikovsky, Symphony No. 5 in E Minor, Opus 64, ii; (*b*) Mendelssohn, Piano Trio in D Minor, Opus 49, ii

this point of view, the choice of plagal progressions at the end of works can be related to the religious aura surrounding artists, works of art, and aesthetic experience.

Why the progression from the minor subdominant to the tonic major was the preferred version of the plagal cadence is uncertain. One reason may have been that major-mode chords are acoustically ("naturally") less tensive than minor-mode ones, which would explain why both of the plagal cadences that end on a major chord are considerably more common than the one that ends with a minor chord. From this point of view, the tendency for even minor-mode pieces to end on major chords may be symptomatic of the increased importance of secondary parameters in the creation of closure. (Put the other way around, closure in the minor mode [Example 8.6b] is necessarily more dependent upon the presence of a strong syntactic progression.)[63]

But this does not explain the prevalence of the minor subdominant-to-tonic (major) cadence. For instance, why did Chopin use this progression at the very end of the Fantasie in F Minor/A♭ Major (Example 8.5)? One reason may be that the contrast of mode makes the progression especially distinctive with the result that it can readily act as an unmistakable sign of ending.[64] The cadence is also distinctive in that it occurs only once in conventional tonal syntax and is associated with cadential articulation, though primarily as a half cadence (i–V) rather than a plagal one (iv–I). However, though its use to create final closure may seem syntactically unusual (and perhaps, partly for this reason, appealing to nineteenth-century composers), it was not unusual historically. Indeed, it occurs with moderate frequency in the work of J. S. Bach, the Baroque composer most revered by continental Romantic composers.[65] And, of course, ending a work in the minor mode with an authentic cadence to the tonic major—the so-called *tierce de Picardie*—was common in the Baroque period. In short, the sign-function of the minor-to-major plagal cadence was supported and perhaps encouraged by earlier usage.[66]

Finally, sonic quality probably played a significant part in the choice of this form of plagal cadence. That is, the major-mode tonic seems especially bright after the more somber aura of the minor subdominant. As Leonard Ratner observes, such

63. Notice, for instance, that in Strauss's *Don Juan* (Example 8.8a) a powerful dominant seventh precedes subdominant harmony, and as a result, the subdominant seems almost like an interpolation disrupting an authentic cadence.

64. In terms of the concepts of semiotics, the cadence is strongly "marked." I am grateful to Robert Hatten for calling this concept to my attention.

65. See, for instance, the end of Bach's Fugue for Organ in B Minor (BWV 579) or the close of Prelude No. 9 from Book II of the *Well-Tempered Clavier*. Handel, on the other hand, seems to use only the major-mode (IV–I) plagal progression—for instance, at the end of the "Hallelujah" chorus in *Messiah*.

66. This suggests (paradoxically, given the ideological rejection of convention) that, relative to the sign-functions of syntactic processes, surface style forms (see Narmour, *Beyond Schenkerism*, p. 164) were becoming more important. That is, as syntax was attenuated, the style forms that were used (see, for instance, Examples 7.2, 7.4, and 8.2) became more like surface signals or markers. And this conjecture seems supported by subsequent style history—specifically in the essentially nonsyntactic use of Classic closing gestures in a work such as Stravinsky's *Rake's Progress*. See Example E.2.

shifts in mode are characteristic of nineteenth-century music: "Starting with Beethoven and Schubert, nineteenth-century composers used the tonic minor in opposition to the major as an effect of chiaroscuro. This coloristic device *need not have any structural effect upon a period.*"[67] And elsewhere Ratner remarks that "the *color* value of interchange of mode is its most striking characteristic, immediately perceivable as an expressive nuance or turn."[68] Interpreted in terms developed in this study, the contrast between modes was a relationship readily perceived and understood even by novices in the audience of elite egalitarians.

DIRECT CONTRASTS OF MODE.

The parallel major and minor modes are contrasted in Classic as well as Romantic music. But both the direction and the function of modal interchange tend to be different.[69] In nineteenth-century music, shifts (typically from minor to major) serve primarily to create sonic contrast. To enhance such contrast the same melody is repeated, usually after prior closure, in the opposite mode. In the first movement of Schubert's String Quartet in A Minor, Opus 29, for instance, after the theme of the first key area reaches a half cadence in measure 22, the theme is immediately repeated in somewhat varied form in A major, returning to the minor only when the tonic is reached in measure 32. The change of mode does not affect the structure of the antecedent-consequent period; its function is essentially coloristic.[70] But the color change is not unimportant. Perhaps because the major mode has acoustic (natural) primacy, it tends to connote the presence of purity, peace, and, in some contexts, spiritual transcendence as well.[71]

In Classic music, on the other hand, not only do changes of mode usually occur in the opposite order (i.e., from major to minor), but these changes have a primarily syntactic function. For the shift to minor, either through direct change of mode (e.g., D major to D minor) or through motion to one of the minor triads of the prevailing tonality (usually the submediant), serves to begin an unstable passage—for instance, a transition or harmonic digression.[72] The last movement of Mozart's Symphony No. 38 in D Major (K. 504; "Prague") is a clear instance of this practice. Following a forceful cadence on the dominant (m. 30), the theme of the first key area begins

---

67. *Harmony: Structure and Style*, p. 263; emphasis added.

68. *Classic Music*, p. 56.

69. The iv–I plagal cadence does occur in Classic music. But as far as I can discover, it does so only in the genre of sacred music; for instance, it closes both parts of the "Offertorium" of Mozart's Requiem. What needs to be noted about this is that the same pattern may be replicated in different periods for quite different reasons.

70. For an earlier instance, see Beethoven, String Quartet in A Major, Opus 18 No. 5, i, in which the theme of the second key area begins in E minor (m. 25) and concludes with a varied repetition in E major (mm. 37–42).

71. For this point about transcendence I am again indebted to Ruth Solie.

72. I have discussed in *Emotion and Meaning in Music* why the shift to the minor mode is used to begin such passages; see pp. 226–27 and passim.

again, but in the minor mode. Instead of remaining in and returning to the tonic (as in Schubert's A-Minor String Quartet), however, Mozart's modal shift begins a modulatory transition that leads some thirty-five measures later to the theme of the second key area. The contrast of mode is unmistakable, but for the experienced listener, the contrast is understood as a sign of processive function rather than primarily one of color.[73]

COMPRESSION.

One lesson to be learned from this somewhat labored discussion is that many—indeed, perhaps most—innovations used in nineteenth-century music consisted not of the invention of new harmonies but of a change in the frequency of existing progressions (as in the use of plagal cadences) and in the use of new progressions, which often take the form of compression, either by omitting chords that customarily formed part of a progression or by combining elements from two different chords. Only these two kinds of compression, chosen because they are related to the use of plagal progressions, will be considered in this sketch.

A clear instance of compression through omission[74] occurs at the end of the first movement of Brahms's String Quartet in C Minor, Opus 51 No. 1 (Example 8.10a). In this cadence, a Neapolitan sixth chord, which normally moves through

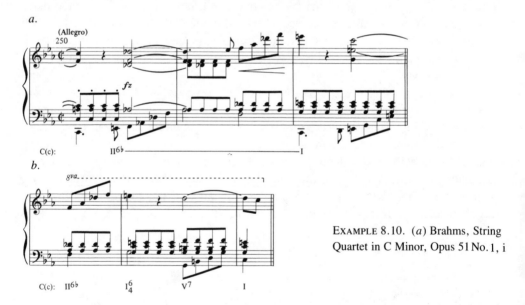

EXAMPLE 8.10. (a) Brahms, String Quartet in C Minor, Opus 51 No. 1, i

73. As is often the case, the sign-function of the shift in mode is reinforced by a striking change in orchestration from strings to woodwinds. As a result, the listener "knows" that this is not a real consequent phrase, even though it is in the minor mode. Moral: conscientious composers seldom put all their signs in one parametric basket!

74. Schoenberg describes this kind of compression as the "abbreviation of set patterns through omission of intermediate steps." See his *Theory of Harmony*, p. 359. I am grateful to Peter Hoyt for calling Schoenberg's usage to my attention.

the dominant (usually in a I$^6_4$–V progression; as in Example 8.10*b,* a "normalized" version of Brahms's music) to the tonic, is followed directly by the tonic major, creating another form of plagal progression (II$^\flat$–I). The progression is unusual not only because of the omission of dominant harmony but because it normally occurs as part of a minor-mode cadence. As a result, the brightness of the closing triad is especially conspicuous, and this brightness is enhanced by the fact that the mode-determining third is in the soprano.[75]

The final cadence of the first movement of Franck's Piano Quintet in F Minor (Example 8.11*a*) is a characteristic composite of subdominant and dominant harmonic functions. The subdominant component, an augmented sixth chord (Example 8.11*b*$^1$), normally occurring as IV$^{6\sharp}_5$ in the tonal realm of B$\flat$, is emphasized both by the preceding applied dominant (V of IV) and by the long B$\flat$ in the cello part, which moves almost directly to the tonic. At the same time, the higher strings (playing pitches present in the augmented sixth chord) strongly suggest dominant harmony, particularly in the second half of the measure when C occurs in the viola part (Example 8.11*b*$^2$). Combining subdominant and dominant functions, the composite can be interpreted as a compression of, and a substitute for, the conventional subdominant/dominant (to tonic) progression.[76] In short, convention is masked by the combining of existing elements rather than abrogated by the invention of new relationships. And compensating for weakened syntactic closure is the sense of ending provided by the resolution of strong acoustic tension, as discord resolves to concord.

EXAMPLE 8.11. Franck, Piano Quintet in F Minor, i

---

75. Even when the tonic is a major-mode triad, the presence of dominant harmony in the normal Neapolitan progression tends to mitigate the contrast in mode.

76. The presence of a tonic pedal is also a conventional element. But because it is not prepared by a strong syntactic progression, it acts largely as a style sign or marker.

EXAMPLE 8.12. (*a*) Chopin, Prelude in F♯ Minor, Opus 28 No. 8

Another kind of compression occurs when highly implicative harmonies follow one another directly, without intervening resolution. For instance, though harmonic progression by fifths is central to tonal syntax, a series of applied dominants can weaken tonal orientation, even as it intensifies the sense of ongoing process, because chromaticism heightens uniformity. This is the case in a passage from Chopin's Prelude in F♯ Minor, Opus 28 No. 8, which combines contrapuntal and harmonic relationships in a process that is at once syntactically ambiguous and forcefully continuous (Example 8.12*a*). The passage follows a four-measure theme, the final bar of which is given in the example because it illustrates a point made earlier in connection with the Prelude to *Tristan and Isolde:* namely, proportionately long nonchord tones create syntactic ambiguity. On the one hand, the relatively long A and C♯ in the second half of measure 6 suggest that the melody is moving through the F♯-minor triad;[77] on the other hand, the harmony indicates that these tones should be construed as appoggiaturas to G♯ and B.[78]

The passage that concerns us begins in measure 7. From a contrapuntal point of view, descending chromatic motion in the bass generates a series of 7–6 and 4–3 suspensions (Example 8.12*a*, staff b'). Though there is a slight break in and modification of process in the second half of measure 8, the general impression is one of great mobility with minimal formal articulation. The mobility created by voice leading is intensified by harmonic uniformity. Whether analyzed as implied motion through the circle of fifths (staff c'), such as occurs in the retransition of the slow movement of Mozart's "Jupiter" Symphony (K. 551) (Example 8.12*b*), or as a succession of augmented sixth chords (Example 8.12*a*, staff d'), local harmonic syntax forcefully propels the descending motion.

*b.*   (Andante cantabile)

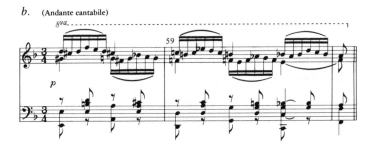

EXAMPLE 8.12. (*b*) Mozart, Symphony No. 41 in C Major (K. 551), "Jupiter," ii

77. This interpretation is supported by the fact that the long C♯s on the first two beats *are* chord tones.

78. Nor does the "*Tristan* connection" end here. As noted earlier, the first chord of measure 7 contains all the pitch (but not the interval) relationships, transposed up one semitone, of the *Tristan* chord (*T*). But the musical significance—the implicative and other relationships, both prospective and retrospective—of the two "collections" is entirely different. As the analysis on staff *a* of the example indicates, the E and the C of the half-diminished chord function as appoggiaturas to the D♯ and B, though their function is somewhat ambiguous until the chord change on the second beat of the measure. The fact that two instantiations of such a distinctive pitch set can have such disparate syntactic significance raises questions about the aesthetic relevance of set theory for the analysis of tonal music.

It is important to emphasize again that applied dominants and their "cousins" augmented sixth chords do not as a rule create cadential articulation. For though root motion is by fifths, none of the progressions involve a tritone between successive harmonies. The chords in Example 8.12, staff *d'*, were labeled IV$^{\#}_{\#}$ for the sake of convenience; they are not true subdominants. In short, though highly kinetic, such progressions, far from fostering formal closure, enhance mobility and process. And they were chosen by the composers of Romanticism because they created the openness of Becoming.

## Changes in Usage

### DECEPTIVE CADENCES.

Stylistically significant innovations may result not only from changes in frequency and from novel juxtapositions (as in compression), but from changes in the use made of familiar syntactic relationships. Consider, for instance, the use made of deceptive cadences in the eighteenth and nineteenth centuries. In the music of the Classic period deceptive cadences and irregular resolutions served for the most part to delay, and thereby to intensify, closure and formal articulation. The end of the opening section of the second movement of Haydn's String Quartet in B♭ Major, Opus 71 No. 1, is typical (Example 8.13). Following a conventional cadential gesture (mm. 17–18), comparable to that given in Example 8.2*c'*, a deceptive cadence delays closure—a delay emphasized by two fermatas. In this context—that is, coming at the end of a rounded binary theme and following an unequivocal closing gesture—the delay of the expected cadence intensifies the sense of closure created by the authentic cadence in measure 20.

EXAMPLE 8.13. Haydn, String Quartet in B♭ Major, Opus 71 No. 1, ii

In the music of Romanticism, on the other hand, instead of intensifying closure—and thereby emphasizing formal articulation—deceptive and irregular progressions more frequently serve to foster mobility and continuity, even though the harmonic progression is ostensibly the same. The striking deceptive resolution to an

EXAMPLE 8.14. Wagner, *Tristan and Isolde*, Prelude

F-major triad in measure 17 of the Prelude to *Tristan and Isolde* weakens, but does not heighten or delay, proximate closure. Rather, the F-major triad functions as a pivot chord, which at once ends one harmonic process and begins a new one that moves through its relative minor (D) to a cadence in A major (m. 24).[79] The same cadence returns in the last section of the Prelude (Example 8.14). Here, too, the resolution serves to connect parts rather than to separate them. But this time, F major/minor functions as the subdominant of C minor, moving at the end of the Prelude to the dominant of C minor, the key that begins act 1.

Such strategies foster the open, unfolding processes prized by the ideology of Romanticism. But they do not disturb foreground syntactic relationships—relationships familiar to, and understood by, the audience of elite egalitarians. Rather, as will be discussed later, they tend to obscure high-level tonal relationships that are, so to speak, "replaced" by an emphasis on melodic and motivic constancy. Melodic returns that could readily be recognized even by members of the new audience functioned as strategic substitutes for tonal returns.

COMMON-TONE MODULATION.

Changes of key through the use of a single tone common to successive chords, rather than modulation through a gradual harmonic process, occur more frequently and more strikingly in the music of the nineteenth century than in that of the eighteenth century. Such abrupt modulations are especially striking when the keys are a third apart *and* in the same mode. This is because the constraints of tonality make it un-

---

79. See Anthony Newcomb's description of the linking of tonal areas quoted below, at note 94. The mobile, noncadential character of the deceptive resolution is enhanced and confirmed by an elision in which a new motive played by the cellos begins as the preceding process ends.

likely that keys a third apart will be in the same mode.[80] To move by thirds and stay in the same mode, chromatic alteration is necessary. For instance, if one moves up a third from a C-major triad, the triad on E must be changed from minor (as it would occur in C major) to major, that is, G must be changed to G♯. This is what occurs in the themes by Liszt and Brahms given in Chapter 7 (Examples 7.23a and b).[81] In the light of one of the hypotheses being explored in this sketch, it seems possible that this strategy was chosen by nineteenth-century composers because the progression made the presence of modulation palpable even to tyros among the elite egalitarians. Looked at in another way, the Romantic valuing of motivic constancy and gradual transformation tended to mask the modulatory nature of transition passages. Striking common-tone modulations helped to compensate for such masking, making key change more salient than it might otherwise have been.

Abrupt modulation *down* a major third is more common. For instance, it occurs in the first movements of both Schubert's String Quintet in C Major, Opus 163, and Beethoven's String Quartet in B♭ Major, Opus 130. But the differences between these instances are as revealing as their similarities. In Schubert's quintet (Example 8.15a), the common-tone modulation from G major (as V of C) to E♭ major establishes a large, stable tonal area. The tension of unstable syntactic process is minimized, while the coloristic effect of tonal/modal contrast is emphasized. In Beethoven's quartet (Example 8.15b), on the other hand, a somewhat similar tonal progression—here from G♭ (= F♯) to D—initiates the unstable syntactic process of the development section.[82] As is often the case, Beethoven employs Romantic as well as Classic strategies. In the beginning of the first movement of his Piano Concerto No. 4 in G Major, Opus 58, for instance, the abrupt progression from the dominant of G major to B major does not lead to an unstable modulatory section; instead it emphasizes the contrast in color and tone between the soloist and the orchestra.[83]

The increase during the nineteenth century in the use of progressions such as

80. In the major mode the succession is I–iii–V–vii–ii–IV–vi or M–m–M–dim–m–M–m. An exception occurs in the minor mode between III and V because the triad built on the fifth of the scale is altered to assure its dominant function. The inherent ambiguity of the minor mode (see my *Emotion and Meaning in Music*, pp. 222–29) makes motion by thirds less striking than it is in the major mode.

81. A progression from C major to E major also occurs in the first movement of Beethoven's "Waldstein" Sonata, but the effect of this change of key is very different. There is no abrupt juxtaposition of tonal areas; instead, the keys are connected by a gradual modulatory process.

82. The progression down a major third—for instance, from V/vi to I (Example 8.15a)—occurs in the music of the Classic period, as in the development sections of the first movements of a number of Haydn's works (for examples, see Symphonies No. 42 in D Major, mm. 87–89; No. 43 in E♭ Major, mm. 109–13; No. 71 in E♭ Major, mm. 116–21). But in Haydn's works the progression seems to be a strategy, not for enhancing color, but for refreshing the tonic and for seeming to modulate while remaining in or close to the tonic. In most cases, Haydn avoids juxtaposing the harmonies in question by separating them with rests or an intervening solo line. His main goal was not an intensification of sonic color but syntactic play. I am grateful to Peter Hoyt for calling these examples to my attention.

83. The current tendency to view Beethoven's style as almost exclusively Classic seems mistaken to me. To understand both his stylistic development and the enormous appeal of his music to the nineteenth-century audience, it seems necessary to acknowledge the presence of important Romantic strategies in his music.

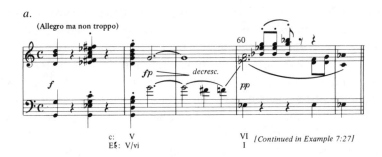

EXAMPLE 8.15.  (*a*) Schubert, String Quintet in C Major, Opus 163 (D. 956), i; (*b*) Beethoven, String Quartet in B♭ Major, Opus 130, i

those just described contributed significantly to the weakening of tonal syntax. This was so not primarily because the progressions were novel, but because they contravened harmonic motion by fifths, which is basic to tonal syntax, and because making more use of progressions that have previously been rarely chosen changed the probability relationships among *all* progressions, including those that defined tonal centers.[84] On the other hand, as already observed, the unusualness of such relationships made the fact of key change patent. Moreover, when modulation was by common tone, the basis for the tonal connection was direct and unmistakable. From this point of view, common-tone modulation is analogous to the kind of melodic connection that Schoenberg calls *linkage technique*.[85] And because both could be easily comprehended, they served the needs of the new audience.

The choice of common-tone modulation by major thirds without change of mode may also be related to the valuing of harmonic color for its own sake. The E♭-major triad that begins the second key area of Schubert's String Quintet (Example 8.15*a*) and the E-major triad that begins the second statement of the axial melody of

84. I am unable to explain the psychological bases for the power of the fifth relationship but am confident that it is not merely a matter of cultural conditioning. Rather its roots lie in the cognitive capacities and proclivities of the human mind/body. Perhaps the claims of melodic conjunction are primary after all, and the harmonic constraints of tonality took the shape they did because they provide support for such linearity. That is, the syntax of tonal harmony provides the maximum amount of vertical differentiation among successive events that is compatible with the need for conjunct melodic patterning on a particular hierarchic level.

85. See Frisch, *Brahms and the Principle of Developing Variation*, pp. 15–17 and *passim*.

Liszt's *Les préludes* (Example 7.23*a*) seem intensely bright and "majorish" because in tonal syntax it is highly probable that if motion is by thirds, a major triad will be followed by a minor one. Consequently, when a major triad follows instead, it seems transcendently radiant—particularly if the mode-defining third is in the melodic voice. Similarly, in the first movement of Schubert's Piano Trio in B♭ Major, Opus 99, the F-major theme of the second key area is approached not through its dominant, but through the dominant of D. Again the basic progression (from V to III or V/vi to I by means of a common tone) creates a striking change of character and color.[86] That Schubert went out of his way to achieve this coloristic effect seems clear, since the preceding transition had already reached and passed through the dominants of B♭, F, C, and G. And this suggests another possible reason for the choice of this strategy. Namely, the striking color of the major mode acts as a sign confirming the arrival at and stability of a new key area.[87] And the use of major as a sign of stability may, as observed earlier, be symptomatic of increased emphasis on secondary parameters—that is, on acoustic concord.

It should be evident from the preceding discussion that the choices made by a compositional community are guided by aesthetic values and, ultimately, ideological beliefs. If Schubert, for instance, chose to modulate past the dominant of F major in the transition of the first movement of the B♭-Major Trio, or to write a transition of only three measures in the first movement of the "Unfinished" Symphony, it was not because he was incapable of composing more conventional connections or because there was a general prizing of innovation, but rather because harmonic coloring, lyric expression, and so on, had become relatively more important values. Nor can such shared proclivities be explained on purely musical grounds. Indeed, the very notion of the purely musical is characteristic of formalism and acontextualism.

## The Flattening of Tonal Hierarchy

I have argued, as have many before me, that the history of nineteenth-century music was characterized by a general, and significant, weakening of tonal syntax. The phrase "weakening of tonal syntax" is, however, ambiguous. To imply, as is sometimes done, that tonal syntax was debilitated, dissolved, or destroyed in some intrinsic, irredeemable, and inevitable way is misleading. What became weakened were not, so to speak, the *principles* of tonal syntax, but the specific syntactic relationships employed by the compositional community. In other words, Romantic composers tended to choose those alternatives permitted by the rules of tonality that were syntactically relatively weak, ambiguous, out of the ordinary, or some combination

---

86. Note that in this case too the melody begins on the third of the triad.
87. The contrast with Classic practice, in which a change of mode (usually from major to minor) commonly, but not invariably, signals the beginning of instability, is obvious.

of these. But when strong syntactic relationships were chosen, their binding force remained largely undiminished. Even in a work such as Debussy's *Afternoon of a Faun,* in which syntactic relationships are for the most part so attenuated that goal-directed motion seems almost nonexistent, a subdominant/dominant-tonic progression such as that in measures 104–6 (Example 7.1) is readily recognized as cadential.

Tonal orientation became attenuated not only because Romantic composers frequently chose stylistic alternatives beyond the most common probability relationships that defined the "core" of tonal syntax,[88] but because, extrapolating from prevalent practice, composers searched for and found new possibilities—harmonic, melodic, rhythmic, and so on—compatible with the rules of the style. Perhaps the clearest instances of this kind of innovation were the many alternatives devised to avoid conventional closing patterns—for instance, through disguise, the new means of subdominant closure, or compression.[89]

As suggested earlier in this chapter, the greater number of stylistic alternatives employed in Romantic music almost automatically affected existing probability relationships. Simply stated, at any particular time in the history of some style, the total probability of all possible relationships (within and between parameters) is always equal to 100 percent. If to this number of alternatives, say, five new ones are added, the strength of the probability relationships among previously existing alternatives must be weakened in some way. But not all probability relationships need be equally affected by the proliferation of probabilities. It seems that the probability relationships at the core of the style will be less affected by proliferation than those at the periphery, and that, furthermore, even if core probabilities are slightly modified, the relative probabilities that define the tonal hierarchy on which syntax depends will remain essentially constant. Nevertheless, over the course of the nineteenth century, the tonal hierarchy defined by probability relationships became flatter and less clearly defined. This tendency toward a kind of equal probability seems to have moved from higher to lower levels—from relationships between tonal areas to those between adjacent harmonies.[90]

One set of relationships that seems to have been significantly affected by the proliferation of alternatives was that among relatively large tonal areas. Two correlative changes, both related to the increased size of musical structures, were

88. The circle of fifths relationship is the central process fostering mobility; the subdominant/dominant progression is the most forceful basis for formal articulation and closure.

89. Not all the means employed were newly devised. For instance, dynamics and orchestration had been used in eighteenth-century music to delay closure (see, for example, Haydn's Symphony No. 104 in D Major, iv, mm. 84–101). As with other strategies, the change was a matter of degree of frequency.

90. It is important to emphasize again that because hierarchies are *in principle* discontinuous, syntactic relationships change from one level to another. Thus, though our terminology and symbology tend to conflate and confound them, the probability relationships between tonal spheres (key areas) are not the same as those within a foreground harmonic progression. For instance, in the music of the nineteenth as well as the eighteenth century, key relationships of a third are considerably more probable (and common) than harmonic progression by thirds. In short, the ways in which tonal syntax was weakened, and the consequences of such weakenings, depended on the hierarchic level involved. Though necessarily beyond the scope of this study, this is an area of music theory that merits much more attention than it has thus far received.

involved.[91] First, as observed in the last part of Chapter 6, the number of parts (structural units) in musical works tended to increase. This occurred because human cognitive capacities limit the absolute duration and density of event-units. Consequently, compositions had to grow primarily by increasing the number, rather than the size, of structural units.[92] As the number of units increased, so did the number of formal sections and, because sectional articulation is facilitated by tonal differentiation, the number of key areas also tended to grow. To accommodate this growth, new key-area relationships were needed. And this accumulation led to a blurring of tonal focus.

Second, as size increased, greater and greater demands were placed on tonal memory. It seems possible that even skillful, sensitive listeners had difficulty maintaining clear tonal orientation.[93] As a result, key areas tended to be perceived as being directly related to one another in an additive succession rather than as interrelated through subservience to a common, controlling tonality. Anthony Newcomb's description of tonal relationships in Wagner's music applies, with appropriate qualifications, to much of the music of the second part of the nineteenth century: "The keys or allusions thereto in Wagner are joined like links in a chain, without there being any connection between the first and the third, other than the second. The importance rests in the local succession rather than in any relation to a single governing tonal center."[94] And according to Newcomb, tonal return plays only a minor role in creating closure. Writing of one of the cadences in *Siegfried,* he observes that "we recognize the formal closing function of the passage not by the return to D major, but by the force of the cadence itself—by its strong preparation and by the long, stable section of confirmation and the motivic peroration that follows it."[95]

Foreground harmonic relationships were also affected by proliferation as well as by changes already discussed: the weakening of the subdominant/dominant progression, emphasis on nonchord tones, and the heightening of uniformity. In general, the attempt to intensify the expressive force and kinetic mobility of individual harmonies tended to enervate larger, phrase-level relationships.[96] From this point of view, the history of tonality in the nineteenth century can be understood as a continued "foregrounding" of syntactic relationships (a droll irony given the beliefs of organicism in the essential importance of deep structures!):[97] as one moves from

---

91. The reasons for this increase had to do both with the nature of the audience and with the aesthetic/ideological values of composers (see the section "Social Circumstances, Style, and Ideology" in Chapter 6).

92. As suggested in the last part of Chapter 6, there appears to be a direct correlation between the size of a composition and the number of structural units (on any given hierarchic level) in it.

93. The decline in the efficacy of tonality as a basis for structural coherence is compensated for by the increased importance of motivic similarity as a basis for musical unity.

94. "Birth of Music," p. 52.

95. Ibid., p. 53.

96. I take it to be a fundamental characteristic of relational hierarchies that the more forceful (relatively speaking) the bonding on one level, the weaker the bonding on others. Thus very strong bonding of foreground, chord-to-chord relationships necessarily involves weakening of higher-level bonds—those of the phrase and the period.

97. It is also ironic that as large-scale tonal relationships become less palpable and, as I see it, less important, formalism seeks to make such connections central for criticism, theory, and analysis—for instance, in the music of Wagner, Mahler, and Verdi.

Wagner, through Wolf and early Schoenberg, to atonality, tonal syntax is gradually dissipated and hierarchic structures dissolved. In the ultimate Romanticism of transcendentalists such as John Cage, the "natural" acoustic qualities of individual sounds are all that remain.[98]

## FORM, IMPLICATION, AND UNITY

### Classic Scripts and Romantic Plans

Complementing the trend toward syntactically weakened harmonic and tonal relationships was an increase in the relative importance of secondary parameters in the shaping of musical process and the articulation of musical form.[99] The result was that in the domain of form, the syntactic scripts characteristic of Classic music were gradually influenced—at times even dominated—by statistical plans. Although there is in principle a categorical difference between scripts and plans, in nineteenth-century musical practice, statistical plans were always related to, though not necessarily congruent with, syntactic scripts.

Small entities—even motives and phrases—as well as large forms such as theme and variations, rondo, and so on, tended to become more planlike, reaching a statistical high point late in the patterning. But the disparity between the claims of syntactic specification and statistical generality, between scripts and plans, was particularly important and revealing in the changes that took place in both the theory and the organization of sonata-form movements. To understand these changes, it is necessary to consider briefly the nature of syntactic form and, especially, syntactic climaxes.

Eighteenth-century sonata form is a script-based schema whose parts are: (*a*) differentiated according to function (for instance, introduction, stable statement, mobile transition); (*b*) related to one another according to largely stipulated tonal areas; and (*c*) articulated into an arched hierarchy according to the degrees of closure created by the several parameters involved. A hierarchy arises out of an alternation of mobile processes and stable forms from one level of structure to another. On the lowest level of a hierarchy, individual pitches, durations, and so forth, combine processively to form motives—melodic, harmonic, rhythmic entities that are defined by

---

98. It does not seem far-fetched to suppose that a significant connection existed between the weakening of syntactic relationships and subsumptive hierarchies on the one hand, and the ideology of Romanticism, which prized the innate equality of humankind and deprecated arbitrary social distinctions, on the other. Indeed, the eighteenth-century theorist Joseph Riepel explicitly associated tonal relationships with a social hierarchy. See his *Grundregeln zur Tonordnung insgemein,* quoted in Ratner, *Classic Music,* p. 50.

Though perhaps pressing the analogy too far, I cannot resist suggesting that, beginning early in the nineteenth century and continuing into the twentieth, a kind of democratization of tonal relationships took place. This led (though not *necessarily*) to serialism and aleatory music, which explicitly exclude even local tonal dominance: all tones are, so to speak, created equal.

99. It might be thought that the increase in the relative importance of secondary parameters was a result of—a compensation for—the weakening of syntactic constraints. But this seems doubtful. The relationship was probably reciprocal, and positing causal priority does not seem either necessary or illuminating.

some degree of closure. These formal entities in turn combine with one another in a processive way, giving rise to larger formal units such as phrases. On the next level phrases join together processively, creating a new level of form, that of the period. And so on, until the highest level of structure is reached.[100]

Especially on higher structural levels, mobile, kinetic processes generally arise from a weakening of melodic, harmonic, and rhythmic shape—whether such weakening results from uniformity (as in some sort of sequence), incompleteness (of melodic or harmonic motion), or ambiguity (of harmonic or rhythmic succession). To produce convincing closure and clear articulation, the momentum of mobile motion must be broken by what I call a *reversal,*[101] in which ambiguities are resolved and unstable relationships are replaced by stable, well-shaped patterns. The process—it may be a brief moment in a phrase or a longish passage in a section—that moves from instability through reversal to stability I call a *syntactic climax.* In sonata-form movements the chief syntactic climax is the action whereby the instabilities and tensions, the ambiguities and uncertainties of the development section are resolved either directly to the stability and certainty of the recapitulation or through the clearly oriented, regularized tension of a dominant preparation.

In the first movement of Haydn's String Quartet in B♭ Major, Opus 76 No. 4, for instance, the main syntactic climax—the motion from the development section to the recapitulation—follows a succession of largely uniform processes: a quasi-chromatic, linear sequence (mm. 86–92); a circle of fifths, coupled with fourth-species counterpoint (mm. 92–95); and, following a prolongation of G minor (mm. 96–98), a succession of sixth chords (Example 8.16, mm. 98–100). This last uniformity (accompanied by a *decrescendo*) is followed by a literal reversal of the sequential motion (mm. 100–103), and this leads to tensive stability on the dominant (mm. 103–7). The whole action of the syntactic climax is completed when the dominant is resolved and the recapitulation begins (m. 108).

Two characteristics of syntactic climax are particularly pertinent for the present discussion. First, though often congruent with a statistical high point, a syntactic climax essentially involves a change in *function.* It is an action in which the tensions of instability are resolved to the relaxation of regularity. This being so, a syntactic climax can occur at a low point in the statistical/dynamic curve shaped by the secondary parameters.[102] The second characteristic—one related to the first—is that a syntactic climax can occur relatively early in a musical structure, as early as halfway in a small form and two-thirds of the way through larger ones.

The absence of a statistical climax in the Haydn string quartet discussed above

---

100. For a more detailed discussion of hierarchic structures, see my *Explaining Music,* chap. 4.

101. See my *Emotion and Meaning in Music,* p. 93 and passim.

102. It would be interesting to study the ways in which syntactic and statistical climaxes are coordinated in music from around, say, 1700 to 1900. I suspect that the relationship between them will be characteristic not only of style on different hierarchic levels, but of form and genre as well.

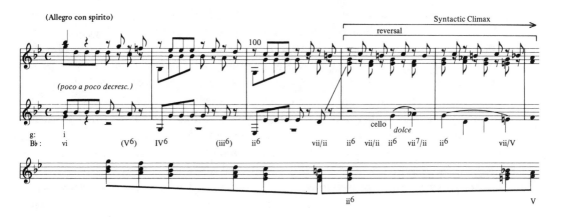

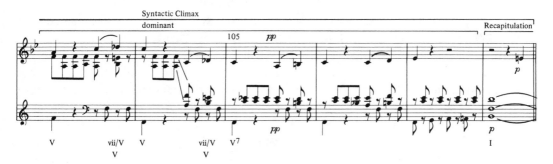

EXAMPLE 8.16. Haydn, String Quartet in B♭ Major, Opus 76 No. 4, i

(Example 8.16) is evident.[103] The temporal position of the climax relative to the overall structure of the movement depends on whether the repetition of the exposition section is counted in calculating the length of the parts. If the repetition is counted, then (as is typical in rounded binary forms such as this) the syntactic climax comes roughly two-thirds of the way through the movement; if the repetition of the exposition section is not counted, the climax comes roughly halfway through the movement.

More important for the history of form than the relative position of the climax

103. The nature of statistical climaxes was briefly described near the end of Chapter 6 in the section "Unity."

There are, of course, statistical high points in the movement, but they seem to function more as *signs* of significant syntactic change or formal function than as shaping forces in their own right. For instance, a high point occurs in measure 85, just before the beginning of the uniform processes described above; and one occurs at measure 174, signaling and forming part of a reversal at the beginning of the coda. In short, as observed in Chapter 7, not all high notes are statistical climaxes; some are signs. It is relevant to note that signs are generally more effective in scripts, where implication is quite specific, than in plans, where processes tend to be more general.

is its position in relation to the *absolute duration* of the parts—especially the parts that follow the main syntactic climax. Tension can be maintained for a considerable span of time after a syntactic climax, but the absolute duration of an abatement that follows a statistical climax cannot last very long. In a sonata-form movement, for instance, the realization of the script (e.g., the parallels between recapitulation and exposition as constraints on closure) sustains interest, as do the digressions and diversions that both syntax and script make possible. But no matter how intense and prodigal the activity of a statistical climax, the gradual dying away, the abatement, cannot endure for more than a few minutes—I should guess around four minutes is close to the maximum. The two large statistical abatements thus far discussed are considerably shorter: the abatement that ends the last movement of Tchaikovsky's Sixth Symphony lasts for about two and a half minutes (depending, of course, on the performance), while the abatement that ends the third movement of Mahler's Fourth Symphony [104] lasts for about three and one-half minutes. Particularly in the area of large forms, these differences in the exigencies of syntactic scripts as compared with statistical plans have important consequences for nineteenth-century music.

Though I cannot document the hypothesis in a sketch such as this, I suggest that the increasing importance of statistical form, coupled with the considerable growth in the size (length) of movements, leads to important changes in the structure of sonata-form movements, and more specifically to the changes in the placement of the statistical climax—that is, the place at which the secondary parameters reach their greatest degree of intensity: highest (and lowest) pitches, most frequent rate of attack, high acoustic tension (discord), loudest dynamic, most forceful sonorities, and densest textures. In the sonata forms of Haydn and Mozart, whatever statistical climax there is tends to occur before or at the syntactic climax. Moreover, as observed earlier, the high point often functions as a *sign* of syntactic structure rather than as a focal point in its own right. For Beethoven—and this is one respect in which his music often seems Romantic—statistical climax is more emphatic and more focal, and it tends to occur just before the recapitulation (as in the first movement of the Eighth Symphony) or in what is sometimes referred to as a second development (as in the coda of the first movement of the Third Symphony). In "high" Romantic symphonies the statistical climax also tends to occur late in the form, often in the coda. [105]

The Romantic preference for statistical plans—and the need for the main statistical climax to occur late in the form—accounts for Charles Rosen's observation that

---

104. See the section "Means Extended: Stretching" in Chapter 7.

105. Though opera is not a central concern of this sketch, it is perhaps worth observing that the structure of opera climaxes was, in a way, also often divided into statistical versus syntactic climaxes. Henry Raynor's description makes it clear that the enormous theatrical displays (statistical accumulation) were separate from the dramatic action of the plot. He writes that "The weakness of Scribe's libretti is that . . . his great scenes of procession and pageant *were often peripheral to the action.* . . ." (*Music and Society Since 1815*, p. 75; emphasis added.)

the generation born around 1810 preferred to place the climax, the point of extreme tension, very near the end of the work. This makes the final area of stability of the sonata uncongenial to them. What they reject, in most cases, is the sense of climax and resolution at the end of the development and the beginning of the recapitulation.[106]

As I see it, it is not so much that Romantic composers "reject" syntactic resolution, but that they especially value statistical plans and the possibilities of sublime grandeur that such plans make possible. More importantly, the valuing of plans accounts for the extended codas and so-called "second development" sections often encountered in large Romantic sonata-form movements.[107] It is not, as is sometimes suggested, a matter of "balancing" the larger development section of the form—after all, balance is a Classic, not a Romantic, value. Rather, grand codas and second developments make it possible to place the statistical climax (and in some cases the syntactic climax as well) late in the movement.[108]

Finally, discrepancies between the nature of syntactic scripts and statistical plans may help to account for the persistence of two common notions. The first is that "the sonata . . . dies; the expressive texture and structure hardened into a form. After its academic definition . . . the sonata became a cake mold into which a composer would pour his batter after mixing themes and modulations of appropriate strength."[109] Taken literally, this view is patently untenable. For molds make forms

106. *Sonata Forms,* p. 320. Kofi Agawu argues that the placement of the high point in a dynamic curve occurs about two-thirds through the piece. But he is treating relatively brief pieces or parts of pieces. See his "Structural Highpoint as Determinant," I:75.

107. James Webster writes that "the coda increased in importance; indeed the climax often comes not at the double return but in the coda. . . . This is one aspect of the 19th-century tendency to displace towards the end the weight of every form, single movements and whole cycles alike" ("Sonata Form," *The New Grove Dictionary,* ed. Stanley Sadie, 17:504).

108. During the last quarter of the eighteenth century and the first part of the nineteenth, the use of repeat signs in sonata-form movements became less and less common. First their use at the end of the second reprise was dropped and then their use at the close of exposition sections. Michael Broyles describes this shift and attributes it to the development of organic form ("Organic Form and the Binary Repeat"). And it might also be thought to be a symptom of the growing preference for plans over scripts. But the repeat of the second part of the form is dropped quite early—for instance, in Haydn's late symphonies—and other explanations are possible. One of these is that, as the essential lineaments of the script became familiar to listeners, the redundancy created by the repetition of parts of the form could be dispensed with. Another is that the fact of repetition was in some sense mechanical and explicitly conventional—an observation which, of course, supports Broyles's argument.

109. Rothstein, "The Shapes of Sounds," p. 17. In the same vein, James Webster observes that Romantic composers "often treat form in an academic manner, as a mould, not a process" ("Sonata Form," *The New Grove Dictionary,* ed. Stanley Sadie, 17:504).

What is ironic and amusing is that this view—that form is a mold—is essentially a Romantic view. Thus Liszt writes that "the artist . . . must demand emotional content in the formal container. Only when it is filled with the former does the latter have significance for him" (excerpted in Strunk, ed., *Source Readings in Music History,* p. 860). This view is in a sense related to notions about the innocence and inspiration of the composer—as though composers began writing without any schema-frame in mind. (The confusion is between molds and models!) And the depreciation of molds is related to the valuing of plans over scripts. For it seemed that because the taxonomy of a script could be stipulated (as Czerny did for sonata form) the organization was *prima facie* authoritarian and conventional rather than a unique consequence of spontaneous inspiration.

more alike. But even a casual glance at the evidence makes it clear that sonata forms by Haydn, written at roughly the same time, tend to be more alike than sonata forms by, say, Mahler—a finding that is scarcely surprising given Haydn's valuing of script and Mahler's preference for plan.[110] But careworn clichés usually conceal a kernel of truth. First, because sonata form is basically a syntactic script, it stipulates tonal and functional relationships more specifically than plans do. And, especially when plans are preferred, script constraints come to seem burdensome and perhaps even irrelevant. Second, the conflict with respect to the placement of the syntactic climax versus the statistical one makes the constraints of syntactic scripts appear artificial and arbitrary—a kind of authoritarian imposition on the free spirit of the Romantic artist.

The correlative idea that is frequently repeated is that Romantic composers were better at writing small forms than large ones. Again, the viewpoint of this study makes sense out of this notion. Because the placement of a statistical climax is constrained by the *absolute* duration of the final phase of the form (the abatement), it is difficult in large forms for the statistical and syntactic climaxes to be congruent. For instance, if the statistical climax of the third movement of Mahler's Symphony No. 4 had occurred two-thirds of the way through the movement (instead of about 90 percent), the abatement would have been more than three and one-half times longer than it actually is; that is, it would have lasted for one hundred twenty measures or about eight minutes, which is much too long! But in a small form—say sixty measures at a moderate tempo—there is no problem. The statistical climax can occur along with the syntactic climax about two-thirds of the way through the composition, leaving some twenty measures for abatement and closure.[111]

Observe, parenthetically, that the history of the *theory* of sonata form parallels the history of the form itself. That is, though theorists continue to consider the scriptlike aspects of sonata form in their accounts, these aspects tend to be combined with, and at times overshadowed by, more planlike concepts. To exaggerate only slightly, eighteenth-century theories described first-movement form in terms of stipulated tonal relationships and specified parts and subparts, as, for instance, Kollmann's account makes clear.[112] Nineteenth-century theorists, on the other hand, tended to emphasize the centrality of thematic relationships to the nature of sonata form. Such thematic relationships were pictured as following a general plan, often of a dialectical or narrative kind, in which the first theme(s) constituted a statement or thesis, the second theme(s) functioned as a contrast or antithesis, and, following thematic conflict or interaction in the development section, a resolution or synthesis took place in the recapitulation. This representation of sonata form was by no means con-

---

110. As well as Mahler's valuing of transcendence.

111. I am not unaware that many Romantic pieces, large and small, end fast and loud without any abatement. But I suspect that the dynamic curve sets the basic shape of the plan.

112. August Frederic Christopher Kollmann, *An Essay on Practical Musical Composition* (1799). For other accounts and other theorists, see Ratner, *Classic Music,* pp. 217–20 and passim.

fined to the theories of such avowed Hegelians as A. B. Marx.[113] Rather, because dialectical succession was considered to be a natural, inherent process—one consonant with such facets of Romanticism as organicism and the continuousness of Becoming—it functioned as a favorite model for the conceptualization of change in many diverse domains.

Though composers of the nineteenth century chose to rely more and more on plan-based schemata, depending less and less on script-based ones, it should be emphasized that tonal syntax almost invariably constrained and qualified statistical form and process—until the advent in the twentieth century of nontonal music. But the province of tonal syntax became more and more local rather than global. And because it shapes relationships on lower hierarchic levels, form often becomes additive. This flattening of hierarchic relationships allows for—even requires—the cumulative or emergent order typical of statistical form. The flattening of the syntactic hierarchy is a result of other changes as well. First, as we have seen, the increase in the size of movements almost necessarily results in an increase in the number of parts making up the whole. And as the number of parts increases, the centrality or preeminence of any one particular part seems diminished. Even more important, as noted earlier, the distinction between stable, thematic events and unstable, transitional passages tends to become attenuated. This is a consequence of two changes. On the one hand, thematic passages become less stable and less clearly closed; on the other hand, unstable passages generally become more thematic.

Thematic passages become less stable because goals of originality and individual expression lead to the use of extended appoggiaturas, increased chromaticism, and local harmonic intensifications, all of which heighten tension and mobility. Transitional passages become more thematic because Romantic composers chose to use motives derived from thematic passages. This usage resulted from a valuing of the expressive power of melody and a prizing of gradual transformation on the one hand, and from the rejection of what seemed conventional and impersonal "passage work" on the other. In addition, neutral figuration often found in Classic music was incongruous with the highly idiosyncratic themes favored by Romantic composers. To put the contrast as forcefully as possible: in Classic music, the neutrality and constancy of stock figuration allowed the listener to attend to the mobility of the harmonic process—the instability of syntax—while in Romantic music the inherent interest of motivic process tended to mask harmonic instability. Unsophisticated listeners could, that is, take refuge from the uncertainties of syntactic ambiguity or unpredictability by attending to comparatively well-shaped motivic patternings.[114]

---

113. For a general account of the theories and practice of sonata form during the nineteenth century, see Newman, *The Sonata Since Beethoven*, especially pt. 1, and Moyer, "Concepts of Musical Form."

114. Thematization is by no means confined to transitional passages and development sections. For the reasons mentioned above, it pervades all facets of Romantic music. For instance, accompaniment figures become "thematic," as in Chopin's "Revolutionary" Etude, Opus 10 No. 12, mm. 4ff. (the top of the figuration, C–D–E♭–D, resembles the opening motive of the work). As Rosen observes, "one of the most characteristic inventions of the 1830's . . . may be called the heterophonic accompaniment: the accompanying figuration is a fluid version of

Subsumptive hierarchies can arise only if relatively stable, formal entities on lower levels of structure can combine in processive ways to form relatively stable formal entities on a higher level. Such structuring results from the presence of clear formal relationships, the differentiation between more and less stable passages, and the articulation of closure. We have already considered why and how Romantic composers disguised formal relationships such as those characteristic of the changing-note schema, minimized the contrast between stable and unstable passages, and weakened closure both through elision and through the use of less decisive cadential progressions. Secondary parameters also served to contravene strong syntactic closure. A single instance will have to illustrate what became a fairly common strategy. In the third movement of Mahler's Ninth Symphony, a striking break in orchestration, texture, and register denies the closural force of the authentic cadential progression (Example 8.17). The unison D cannot satisfactorily resolve the preceding dominant seventh chord.

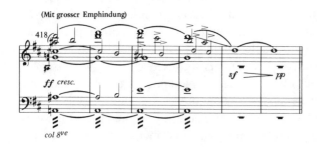

EXAMPLE 8.17. Mahler, Symphony No. 9, iii

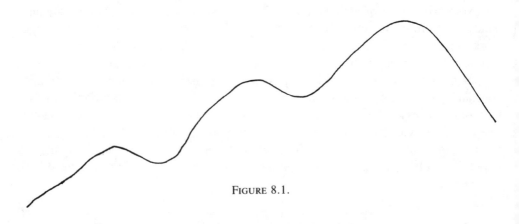

FIGURE 8.1.

the theme" (*Sonata Forms*, p. 315). It is also interesting to note that this is almost the exact opposite of Rosen's characterization of the theme/accompaniment relationship in the Classic style: "The most fruitful solution was to learn how to make themes out of formulas of conventional accompaniment. This was Haydn's discovery, and led to some of Beethoven's greatest triumphs" (ibid., p. 174).

Though processes in Romantic music are markedly open and continuous, events (such as motives and phrases) are, nevertheless, clearly articulated. This seeming paradox is possible because the ends of events are defined, not primarily by syntactic closure, but by the beginning of another pattern—very often the same event repeated sequentially. In other words, the prevalence of sequences in nineteenth-century music is partly a result of their ability to define events without dependence upon syntactic closure. Thus, clear definition of shape is reconciled with ongoing process.

Complementing and, as it were, compensating for the weakening and flattening of syntactic structure is a strengthening of statistical form. Indeed, the weaker and flatter syntactic structure is, the more readily a cumulative statistical plan can combine with it. This is so because statistical form is itself additive. Each event—each dynamic curve—in such an emergent hierarchy consists of three phases: an intensification, a climax (high point or apotheosis), and an abatement. The dynamic curves making up the larger form generally follow one another with increasing intensity. The resulting shape, described by many analysts, can be diagrammed more or less as shown in Figure 8.1.

But the constraints that govern both the individual curves and the overall curve remain constant. In short, as described in Chapter 6, emergent hierarchies, which give rise to statistical climaxes, are continuous. All of the constituent curves, and the largest, overall curve as well, have similar shapes and are shaped in similar ways.

It does not follow, however, from the compatibility of flat syntactic structures with cumulative, emergent ones that their shapes are necessarily coordinate. In nineteenth-century music statistical processes frequently transcend syntactic arrival. Such noncoordination is evident in alternative analyses of the Prelude to *Tristan and Isolde*. For instance, Hugo Leichtentritt's analysis of statistical shape places the (statistical) climax at measures 82–83, three-fourths of the way through the form, while the harmonic/tonal analyses of Alfred Lorenz and Roland Jackson place the chief return (syntactic climax?) at measures 74 and 63 respectively, two-thirds of the way and halfway through the Prelude.[115]

## An Instance of Statistical Form: Isolde's "Transfiguration"

The repertory of Romantic music is replete with instances of statistical form, and a number of these have already been considered. Only one instance will be discussed here: Isolde's "Transfiguration" (sometimes called the "Liebestod"[116]), surely one of the most famous pieces of music written in the nineteenth century. My concern is not to analyze this music, but rather to discuss features characteristic of the Romantic style in relation to the hypotheses I have developed in this sketch-history.[117]

115. These analyses are given in Bailey's edition of Wagner's *Prelude and Transfiguration from "Tristan and Isolde,"* pp. 185, 214, and 277, respectively.

116. Robert Bailey argues against the designation "Liebestod" (ibid., pp. 41–42).

117. Since much of the music of the Transfiguration is first presented at the end of the second-act duet between Tristan and Isolde, my remarks apply, with appropriate qualification, to that music as well.

The opening two-measure motive is itself highly characteristic. It combines three different modes of patterning (Example 8.18). The first patterning, which is clearest in the voice part, consists of a gap of a fourth (E♭ to A♭) followed by a chromatic fill from A♭ down to F (Example 8.18a). The second is a kind of complementary pattern in which the complement is a retrograde of the model instead of the more usual inversion (Example 8.18b). The third mode of patterning, which is emphasized by the orchestra's version of the motive, implies rising, sequential continuation (Example 8.18c). This implication is realized when the motive is repeated a minor third higher in the next two measures (Example 8.18d).[118]

The strong sense of upward striving created by this motive results not only from the fact that rising lines usually engender feelings of effort, but from the combination of the gap-fill pattern with the suggestion of sequential rise. Together, these create what I have called a *Sisyphean sequence*.[119] In such sequences, the motive rises, falls back, and then in the next statement rises again to a higher point and again falls back. Sisyphean sequences are very common in Romantic music. And it is relevant to observe that such motives are miniature statistical forms, as the diagram over Example 8.18b indicates. (This is scarcely surprising considering that emergent hierarchies are continuous.) Put in another way: Romantic music tends to be characterized by a continuous unfolding in which whole and part, seed and flower, are manifestations of a single principle. In Blake's words, one sees "a World in a Grain of Sand."

The first two measures of the Transfiguration are characteristic in other ways as well. Harmonically, they are relatively unstable, open, and ambiguous. Though the very first chord, an A♭-major triad, resolves the preceding dominant seventh chord, it is in an unstable, acoustically tensive second inversion. It moves to another mobile dominant seventh chord. Instead of resolving the dominant chord and creating closure, the next harmony (m. 2) dissolves syntactic tension: the bass fails to move and the leading tone, G (m. 1), is voided by motion to G♭. The progression (from m. 1 to m. 2) is irregular and ambiguous: is the C♭ triad a III⁶ in A♭ minor (mode switching is, as we have seen, common in the music of the nineteenth century); is it a submediant triad (VI⁶ in E♭ minor) as the following dominant chord suggests; or is it the typically Romantic progression (see above) V/vi–I⁶ in C♭ major, anticipating the main tonality (B major) of the Transfiguration? Whichever interpretation one favors (and the continuation of the sequence suggests the third), there is neither stability nor closure. Though the following B♭-major chord is acoustically stable, its function is very uncertain: it might, as mentioned above, seem part of a VI–V progression in E♭ minor, or it might be interpreted as a Neapolitan motion in B♭ major (♭II–I). But when it returns to C♭ in measure 3, the function of the B♭-major chord retrospectively seems more that of a neighbor chord (Example 8.18e).

These harmonic tensions and ambiguities are mitigated by rhythmic structure

---

118. What is remarkable about this motive is not its melodic, harmonic, or rhythmic complexity, but its enormous relational richness. In this connection, see my "Grammatical Complexity and Relational Richness."

119. See my "Exploiting Limits," pp. 188, 195.

EXAMPLE 8.18. Wagner, *Tristan and Isolde,* Act 3, Scene 3, "Transfiguration"

(Example 8.19). For though the syncopation in the vocal part (m. 2) creates modest tension, the basic rhythmic organization is quite regular. It consists of three levels of trochaic rhythms each ending on an open, mobile weak beat.[120] As a result, the form of the motive is unambiguous, even though harmonic process is not so. The presence

EXAMPLE 8.19.

120. This interpretation of the rhythmic structure of the first two measures is a radical revision of the one I gave in *Emotion and Meaning in Music,* pp. 113–15.

of a clear formal module is important because it acts as the basis for future composed *accelerandos*. (The need for well-defined modules in the structuring of cumulative, sequential forms may help to explain why, despite deviations in other parameters, the rhythmic/metric structure of Romantic music tends to be quite regular.)

Ambiguity is enhanced, however, by the uniformity of the continuous tremolo in the strings. For the background activity of a tremolo not only heightens the affective tension of a passage, but does so without any articulative patterning whatever. It is, so to speak, the ultimate statistical strategy: temporal relationships are transformed into a matter of mere amount. That is, a succession of sixteenth-notes—

, and so on—involves quasi-syntactic, metric differentiation between strong beats and weak beats on various hierarchic levels. But a real tremolo is uniform and nonhierarchic. From this point of view, the prevalence of tremolos in nineteenth-century music is yet another instance of the prevalence of statistical means.

Beginning in measure 5, the nature of the larger harmonic process becomes clear, although the process itself involves the ambiguity of uniformity. If we disregard for present purposes the intricate melodic and rhythmic relationships of the passage, the essential harmonic motion consists of a sequence of major triads rising by minor thirds and creating an extended diminished chord. This sequence is outlined in Example 8.20a, in which the triads that begin motives are written in root position.

The tension and mobility of this sequence are heightened by the increase in pace begun at measure 5,[121] where motivic and harmonic sequences occur every four beats instead of every eight. (The change of pace is signaled by a change in melodic patterning: that is, the falling fourth in the vocal part, which had occurred at the end of every two-measure module, now comes at the beginning of measure 5 [Example 8.20c].) In measure 7 the pace seems still faster when the rising fourths associated with the opening of the main motive are repeated in a stretto after only two beats instead of four. The increase in pace results both in a highly mobile countercumulative rhythmic/metric pattern (Example 8.20b) and, of course, in a more rapid rise in the main melodic line played by the orchestra (Example 8.20d). Reflecting these changes and intensifying their effect is the *crescendo* that begins with a change in orchestration in measure 5. Finally, it is relevant to observe that, even if the excitement of the undifferentiated tremolo is ignored, there tends to be an increase in the number of attacks per measure from measure 1 through measure 9, with a slight slowing in measures 4 and 6.

The end of the sequence and the impending high point (B–C–B, mm. 10–12) are signaled by a change in orchestration (m. 9) and are articulated by the dominant/

---

121. This increase in pace is clearest in the orchestra's presentation of the main motive.

EXAMPLE 8.20.

tonic cadence in G major (mm. 9–10), which reverses the diminished chord process. The last two measures of the section (mm. 10–11) begin a neighbor-note motion—B (m. 10), C (m. 11)—that is completed with the arrival of the B at the beginning of the next section. But a relationship more significant than a mere neighbor-note pattern links measures 11 and 12. Though slightly masked by passing harmonies, the progression from a second inversion A♭-major triad (m. 11) to a second inversion B-major triad (m. 12) is precisely the relationship between the first two statements of the motive: from A♭⁶₄ (m. 1) to C♭/B⁶₄ (m. 3) (Example 8.21a).[122]

EXAMPLE 8.21.

122. It is striking that had there been no reversal in measure 10—that is, had the diminished-chord process continued in a regular fashion (and always in second inversion)—then the chords in measures 11 and 12 would have been exactly as they are (Example 8.21b). For a discussion of similar strategies in the music of other composers, see my "Process and Morphology."

Several other points about these measures merit mention. First, only in measure 11 does the high point of the form occur *on* the downbeat. Second, the rate of attacks per measure slows and stabilizes in measures 9–11. Third, the syntactic and statistical climaxes are, in this case, coordinate. And finally, significant abatement and strong closure are lacking. Instead, the motivic process, which breaks off (m. 9) with the approach to the high point, begins again in measure 12 with a B-major triad (= C♭, m. 3). In terms of the "theory" of statistical form, then, a dynamic curve can be incomplete—that is, a new curve can begin before the previous one has run its course. Because the phase of abatement is missing, the larger curve of the whole is more rapidly and intensely cumulative.

Harmonic instability tends, in Romantic as well as Classic music, to be complemented by motivic constancy.[123] And because harmonic instability and ambiguity are especially prevalent and intense in Romantic music, motivic sequences are more than common. These sequences are also characteristic both because, as observed at the end of the previous section, they reconcile shape-definition with open, ongoing process and because motives in a sequence are related to one another not primarily through the conventions of syntax, but through the more "natural" recognition of similarities of contour and rhythm.

For present purposes it is not necessary to analyze the remaining curves in such detail. The next two sections begin with the main motive (mm. 12 and 29) and with the same harmony (B♮). Both develop somewhat greater intensity than the first through melodic stretching (Example 8.22a)—a strategy that Wagner uses in more lyrical passages (see Examples 8.22 and 7.44a)—and through more melodically active texture. Note that although the texture of the passage in measures 12 to 18 is basically homophonic, the accompaniment pattern within these measures is complementary (not conventional figuration) and is joined to the main thematic process (Example 8.22b).

EXAMPLE 8.22.

123. In this connection, see my *Explaining Music*, pp. 54–55. Were all parameters to change simultaneously and markedly, the result would not be heightened instability, but chaotic gibberish.

The striking "turn" motive presented in measure 19 (and subsequently) works here, as it did in the second-act duet, not only because it is consonant with the descending chromatic line latent in the original module (compare Examples 8.22c and 8.18b), but also because it is familiar to a listener acquainted with the gestural vocabulary of eighteenth- and nineteenth-century music. Though somewhat disguised by context when connected with the main motive (Example 8.22c), the stylistic provenance of the turn pattern seems clear when it becomes the basis of the sequence in measures 34–38 (Example 8.23a). It is a member of the same family of sequential gestures as one in "Eusebius" (mm. 9–12) from Schumann's *Carnaval* (Example 8.23b) and, much more remotely, the subject of Bach's C♯-Major Fugue (transposed to E♭ major in Example 8.23c for the sake of comparison) from Book I of the *Well-Tempered Clavier.* But for our purposes, the differences between these melodies are more interesting than the resemblances.

EXAMPLE 8.23. (*a*) Wagner, *Tristan and Isolde,* Act 3, Scene 3, "Transfiguration"; (*b*) Schumann, *Carnaval,* Opus 9, "Eusebius"; (*c*) Bach, Fugue in C♯ Major (BWV 848) from the *Well-Tempered Clavier,* Book I (transposed)

Bach's fugue has an almost austerely contrapuntal subject—a bi-level theme governed by implied fourth-species counterpoint (Example 8.23*d*). The turn that begins the theme serves to establish the "main" (lower) line, but it is not repeated as part of the sequential process, which is unambiguously diatonic and reaches closure on the tonic. Though there are vestiges of this contrapuntal process in Wagner's version of this schema (and with appropriate modifications in Schumann's as well), the basic generating force is harmonic—a descending chromatic progression from the B-major sixth chord in measure 34, through an augmented triad (D–F♯–A♯) on the second beat of measure 35, to an A-major sixth chord at the end of measure 35, and so on down to the E-major sixth chord in measure 38. The chromaticism and uniformity of this process are characteristic of much Romantic music. And other Romantic features are also evident, making Wagner's sequence seem more a succession of lyric motives than the single integrated structure that forms Bach's fugue subject.[124] First, the whole pattern is repeated, and its coherence draws attention to the foreground motivic organization; second, the high G♯ (m. 34), F♯ (m. 35), and so on, are brief appoggiaturas related by register, but not syntactic function, to subsequent high notes; and third, the descending triads at the end of each measure connect registers, thereby minimizing the independence of upper and lower contrapuntal lines.

Most important, neither Schumann's nor Wagner's version of this strategy is syntactically closed. Wagner's descending chromatic line is clearly part of a slight abatement, as indicated not only by the direction of the sequence, but by the dropping out of instruments (flute, clarinet, one horn, and one bassoon) and the expression marks *più piano* and *morendo*. The passage does not end with a cadence or an end-accented rhythm—or even a rest. We know that the descending sequence is over not because there is closure, but because a new section marked by a new motive, as well as a partial change of process, preempts the shaping of the music. The change of process is only partial because, though the new motive changes the direction of melodic motion from falling to rising, the chromatic descent of the bass line continues—a continuity that also contributes to the weakness of the closure of the preceding pattern.[125] The blending of one part or section with another, creating a seemingly seamless continuity, realizes one of the prime values of Romanticism. Even syntactically oriented composers such as Brahms tend to mask the articulation points between otherwise clearly defined parts.[126]

124. Note that, while the initial turn in Bach's fugue subject is an ornament giving rhythmic impetus to the ensuing pattern, Wagner and Schumann transform the turn into a *motive*.

125. Put in terms discussed earlier, there is no strong syntactic reversal, and as a result, the sections meld into one another.

126. The Romantic proclivity for masking points of structural articulation is especially evident when the type of organization is script-based or essentially formal. For instance, because the scriptlike nature of Brahms's sonata-form movements is not in doubt, the masking of traditional points of syntactic/script articulation is particularly apparent. Similarly, in order to make essentially formal plans such as theme and variations more continuous and processive, points of articulation (e.g., between variations) are usually minimized or concealed.

Though Wagner's bass line continues to descend after measure 38, its relationship to the new melodic pattern results in a change of process. Instead of a parallel sequence between melody and bass, the new process creates a divergent "wedge" pattern—that is, a schema in which the upper part ascends and the lower one descends. An abstraction of this change of process is given in Example 8.24.[127]

Divergent wedges are planlike. They stipulate no syntactic relationships and can, in fact, be completely chromatic and nontonal, as the construct given in Example 8.25 shows.[128] Their essential linearity makes them strongly implicative and goal-directed,[129] while their divergence makes them open and mobile, particularly when syntactic structuring is weak. For these reasons, the divergent wedge schema occurs more frequently in Romantic than in Classic music.

In both repertories, however, the schema tends to be the basis for unstable processive passages. For instance, a pair of miniature wedges begin the second part of the Minuetto of Mozart's Symphony No. 39 in E♭ Major (K. 543) (Example 8.26a),

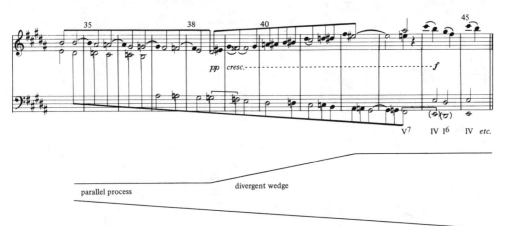

parallel process          divergent wedge

EXAMPLE 8.24.  Wagner, *Tristan and Isolde*, Act 3, Scene 3, "Transfiguration"

EXAMPLE 8.25.

127. Convergent wedge patterns are also possible, but because they tend to imply closure, they are not common in Romantic music. For a discussion of converging wedge patterns, see my *Explaining Music*, pp. 142–44, 147–48, and passim.

128. Referring to a wedge schema, Roger Sessions writes that "it is the leading of the voices—above all the outer ones—which determines the choice of chords" (*Harmonic Practice*, p. 399 [see fig. 235]). Note that this statement implies that harmony is no longer syntactic but has become a dependent parameter. For an instance from the contemporary repertory, see my Example 8.27.

129. "Linearity" may be disjunct as well as conjunct, as Example 8.26c shows.

and a divergent wedge leads to the dominant pedal in the fourth movement of Schubert's Symphony No. 9 in C Major (Example 8.26b). Similarly, Wagner's wedge passage is processive and goal-directed, leading to the provisional but tensive stabilization (on the subdominant and tonic, mm. 44–46) that precedes the surge to the main statistical climax of the Transfiguration (Example 8.24).

As they become a somewhat common strategic means, divergent wedges also migrate, becoming the basis for parts of stable thematic events.[130] Thus Beethoven's Piano Sonata in A Major, Opus 101, begins with a divergent wedge (Example 8.26c),

EXAMPLE 8.26. (a) Mozart, Symphony No. 39 in E♭ Major (K. 543), iii; (b) Schubert, Symphony No. 9 in C Major, "Great," iv; (c) Beethoven, Piano Sonata in A Major, Opus 101, i; (d) Chopin, Ballade in A♭ Major, Opus 47; (e) Brahms, Symphony No. 4 in E Minor, Opus 98, iv

130. Migration was described in Chapter 4.

as does Chopin's Ballade in A♭ Major, Opus 47 (Example 8.26*d*). The final movement of Brahms's Fourth Symphony also begins with a wedge,[131] but in this case the descending lower line is disjunct (Example 8.26*e*).[132]

Finally, it is worth pointing out that the wedge and complementary schemata are related not only in the sense that both are plans, but because the wedge combines the two parts of a complementary pattern into a single simultaneity, as in the excerpt from Schoenberg's *Verklärte Nacht* given in Example 8.27.[133]

EXAMPLE 8.27. Schoenberg, *Verklärte Nacht*, Opus 4

The final phase of intensification, leading to the statistical climax of the Transfiguration (mm. 61–64), begins with the tensive stabilization (mm. 44–46) mentioned above. The stability results from a repeated harmonic progression employing primarily the subdominant and tonic triads (Example 8.28*a*). The tension results from the openness of the harmonic progression and from the nature of the motive, its accompaniment, and its repetition. The motive (Example 8.28*a*) is given direction and impetus by strong appoggiaturas, the rising *crescendo* pattern in the second half of each measure, and the increased activity of the string accompaniment.[134] But it is

EXAMPLE 8.28. (*a*) Wagner, *Tristan and Isolde*, Act 3, Scene 3, "Transfiguration"

131. When divergent wedges are the basis of themes, their uniformity and goal-directedness makes a reversal (*R*) necessary if the parts of the structure are to be differentiated. This is the case in Examples 8.26*c, d,* and *e*.

132. It appears from this kind of wedge that the patent linearity of an upper voice can affect our understanding of the nature of a lower voice—and perhaps vice versa.

133. Though I have not done the required research, it seems likely that because they are "natural" relationships, not dependent upon syntax, complementary patterns (inversions) and wedges (simultaneous inversions) are even more common in contemporary music than in Romantic music. I have recently learned that Charles Ives used the term *wedge* for this kind of patterning, and that wedges—especially palindrome wedges—are common in his experimental compositions. See Winters, "Experimental Works of Charles Ives," chaps. 1 and 2.

134. For the accompaniment pattern, which is not given in Example 8.28 *a* and *c,* the reader is asked to consult the orchestral score.

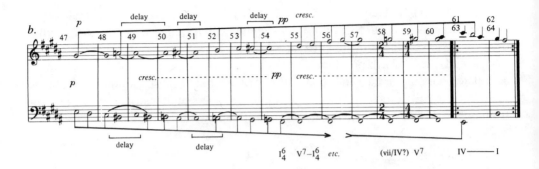

EXAMPLE 8.28. (b); (c) Wagner, *Tristan and Isolde*, Act 3, Scene 3, "Transfiguration"

truly Sisyphean; it rises (pushed by the *crescendo*) only to fall back. And repetition heightens tension by inhibiting the continuation of goal-oriented motion.[135]

The end of inhibition and the beginning of a new process are signaled by the change in motive at the end of measure 46, by a faster rate of repetition (now every half measure), by somewhat thinner orchestration, and by a change in harmony (vii instead of IV) at the beginning of measure 47. The new process is an immense divergent wedge (Example 8.28b) in which goal-directed motion is heightened both through occasional delays in the melody and the bass and through the persistent denial of accented downbeats in the rising sequence played by the first violins, horns, and so on (Example 8.28b).[136] What is important for this sketch-history is that the divergent wedge schema, as well as the gradual growth of intensity of the secondary parameters, is planlike. The music is egalitarian: only the deaf or hidebound could, I think, fail to respond to its overwhelming force and passion.

With the arrival of F♯ in the bass (m. 54), the wedge process ends, and the final surge toward the statistical climax begins. This change is signaled by a sudden *pianissimo* and the reentrance of the brass and timpani. Though the F♯ is sustained as a pedal (mm. 55–60), the melodic segment of the wedge continues bridging the two

135. For the effect of repetition on expectation and goal-directed motion, see the discussion of saturation in *Emotion and Meaning in Music*, pp. 135–38.

136. The denial of downbeats is not shown in the example.

sections as the bass had done earlier (see Example 8.24, mm. 38–42). The alternation of dominant seventh and tonic chords over the F# pedal is broken by a change in harmony to a diminished seventh (vii/IV?) that accompanies the temporary metric shift to 2/4 (m. 58). The mobility of the following measures of dominant ninth harmony is intensified by rising pitches, the return of brass instruments, and an increasing rate of attack in the basses—from half-notes to quarter-notes to eighths.

The arrival at the climax (mm. 61–64) is articulated by a strong melodic downbeat (the first in fourteen measures) on the high C# (the highest pitch in the orchestra), by the sustained high G# in the voice part,[137] by the concordant, root-position harmony, by the broadening of the melodic and harmonic motion, and by the return in partial augmentation of the motive that began the final phase of intensification (Example 8.28c). The statistical climax is characterized by relative stability in primary, as well as secondary, parameters: that is, by regularity of rhythmic, harmonic, and melodic structure, and by a clear homophonic texture. Though arrival is patent, closure is not forceful. Mainly this is a result of harmony. For instead of resolving to the tonic, the dominant ninth chords of measures 59 and 60 move to the subdominant—the harmony from which this last phase of intensification began. This lack of harmonic "progress" seems symptomatic of the change from syntactic script to statistical plan. For the enormous process of intensification has led to a new height of statistical force, but not to a change in syntactic position. The cadence of the climax, too, is only weakly closed: the chords are in root position, but the progression is plagal (IV–I).

The climax of the Transfiguration is only one among countless exemplifications of statistical form in nineteenth-century music. It is not, however, an instance of what I call an *apotheosis,* which is a high point characterized by the stability of a grand assertion of a coherent theme—often one that had previously been fragmented or partial. Such an apotheosis can be found, for instance, in the last movement of Mahler's Second Symphony, where the choral rhythmic unison is both the point of the text and the climax of the music.[138] The significance of the affirmation of an apotheosis was, I suspect, more than musical: for the elite egalitarians an apotheosis served both as a symbol and as an expression of ideological and social solidarity. But, whether apotheosis or high point, a statistical climax was, as we have seen, related to the valuing of magnitude and the sublime.

The abatement that follows the climax of the Transfiguration is typical in its generally descending melodic lines, its settling on a tonic pedal, its rhythmic regularity, its gradual *diminuendo,* and its ending *ritardando.* There is something deep

---

137. Although this pitch occurs earlier as Ab, here both its context and its length make it clear that this G# is *the* main high point. In a statistical form a number of high points usually occur before the chief climax—and some of them may be literally higher in pitch than the chief climax. But it is usually clear that they are subsidiary, sometimes because they occur too early in the form, but more commonly because they lack the kind of stability and arrival characteristic of a main climax.

138. At times the apotheosis is signified by the coming together of previously separate and disparate themes in a kind of explicit synthesis.

within our primordial affective beings that leads us to identify with such abatement processes and with statistical form as a whole, sensing in them the natural cycles of existence—the times of day, the seasons, and the course of life itself. In the case of the end of the Transfiguration, such broad metaphors are specified, so that the abatement signifies not only musical ending, but the death of Isolde, the redemption and reunion of the lovers, and continuation as eternal Becoming. Death is delineated in the dying away of sound and musical activity (the repeated use of the marking *morendo* at the end of nineteenth-century works including this one, is surely significant); redemption is connoted both by the religious overtones of the "Amen" (plagal) cadence and by the heavenly height of the sustained violins and woodwinds; reunion is expressed by the recall of the "Tristan" motive (see below). To repeat a point made earlier: because the relationships created by the secondary parameters involve incremental changes along a continuum, they establish states of relative cessation rather than of stipulative closure. And because they can only die away to nothingness, the abatement of the secondary parameters seems to symbolize the openness and continuousness of Becoming.[139]

Closure is also tenuous because the cadence (mm. 68–70) leading to the tonic pedal is plagal. And it is important to observe that the cadence is characteristic not only in its avoidance of the subdominant/dominant/tonic progression, but in its turn to the minor subdominant (m. 68)—a turn made unmistakable by its juxtaposition with the preceding major subdominant (m. 67). For this progression becomes a conventional sign of ending in music of the nineteenth century (see, for instance, Examples 8.5, 8.8, and 8.9).[140] Finally, there is the reminiscence of the "Tristan" motive (mm. 74–76). Such *reminiscences,* which are quite common in nineteenth-century music, must be distinguished from *returns* such as that which occurs at the statistical climax of the Transfiguration. For a reminiscence, unlike a return, involves the use of a motive presented earlier, but not one indigenous to the music or section being closed.[141] Because they are extraneous to the preceding processive structure, such reminiscences, understood as symbolic signs, run the risk of sentimental nostalgia.

139. The valuing of openness calls attention to the question of high-level key relationships in large-scale nineteenth-century compositions. The question has to do with the significance of beginning a movement, an act of an opera, or a whole work in one key and ending in another. Several explanations seem possible. One might be that this practice is symptomatic of the depreciation of syntactic constraints and perhaps of conventions in general. Correlatively, increased reliance on plan-based schemata may have made high-level tonal closure less important. Another interpretation might assert that closing in a different key was the result of choice, not indifference. That is, to the extent that return to a prior key enhances closure, ending in a key other than the original one represents a valuing of openness. Key changes of this sort have also been attributed to the individual composer's sense of the significance of specific tonal realms (see, for example, Grout, *History of Western Music,* p. 625). Perhaps Wagner somehow associated transcendence with the key of B major.

140. Thus the avoidance of one convention leads to the prevalence of another. Similarly, the avoidance of the conventional IV–I$^6_4$–V–I cadence gives way to the "appoggiatura-cadences" given in Examples 7.41*c*, 7.41*d*, and 8.3.

141. For another instance of reminiscence, see the last measures of the Finale of Brahms's Third Symphony. Because they are not indigenous, reminiscences may come from works by other composers. Alban Berg's quotation of the Prelude to *Tristan* at the end of the *Lyric Suite* would be an example of this.

The tenuous closure of the Transfiguration suggests that the music and dramatic action reverberate beyond the last dying sounds. And this openness reminds us of the importance of implied structure in the music of Romanticism.[142] Indeed, one of the salient characteristics of Romantic music is the richness of its implied structure.[143] If silence "frames" a composition or movement, then in Romantic music, the frame does not delimit the meaning of the work.[144] And this applies not only to the terminal part of the frame (the silence at the end of a work), but to the beginning as well. For there are compositions that begin, as it were, *in medias res*—where what is missing is the "implying" part of the musical structure. Chopin's Prelude in A Minor, Opus 28 No. 2, seems to be such a work. It presents only the abatement part of what might have been a statistical plan.

Implied structure would seem to be considerably more significant in the aesthetic effect of small forms than in that of large ones.[145] This is because in a large form, replete with intricate relationships, it is difficult to recognize what implications have not been realized; so much happens that a myriad of connections can be made between earlier and later patternings. In addition, large-scale compositions tend to seem less suggestive because, as observed earlier, statistical climaxes generally abrogate prior implicative obligations. On the other hand, in a small work, it is often quite evident what implications have not been realized. For these reasons, a large work seldom seems as *suggestive* as a small one.

The suggestiveness of unrealized implications can be related not only to openness of structure, but to the egalitarian side of Romanticism. For implied structure meant that part of the realization of a work was nonauthoritarian: it involved the imaginative participation of individuals in the audience. (This penchant for egalitarian participation may in part explain the Romantic taste for fragments and ruins, both of which allow for—indeed, call for—the imaginative involvement of the audience.) The tendency to value the unconsummated aspects of art leads in the twentieth century to conceptual art in which no actual art object is produced. Rather, what is presented is the symbolization of an idea whose realization is left entirely to the creative imagination of the audience.[146]

---

142. Implied structure is first discussed in Chapter 1 (before the final section "Commentary").

143. I am contending, not that Classic music is without implied structure, but that the power of clear syntactic realization tends to minimize and mask its presence.

144. This creates serious methodological problems for analysis and criticism. For unrealized implications are obviously more difficult to determine objectively than are the realized implications of a script. Yet these must be considered if justice is to be done to Romantic music.

145. Perhaps this is one reason why it is sometimes suggested that in the music of Romanticism small forms are usually better than large ones (see Grout, *History of Western Music,* p. 547). A more important reason for this view, however, may be the coordination of syntactic and statistical structures possible in small forms. In this connection, see above in the section "Classic Scripts and Romantic Plans."

146. It should also be noted that the valuing of implied structure produces a fundamental incongruity in the ideology of Romanticism between the prizing of artistic (and natural) necessity and that of a kind of indeterminacy. In twentieth-century music these trends continued to their "logical" ends in total serialism (necessity) on the one hand and aleatory music (indeterminacy) on the other.

## UNITY AND MOTIVIC RELATIONSHIPS

Emphasis on openness and Becoming is related to one of the central concerns of composers and theorists of the Romantic period: the unity of music. For our experience of the unity of a composition seems intimately connected with our sense of its wholeness and its completeness, and these in turn are dependent upon the strength of its closure. To the extent, then, that the closure of nineteenth-century compositions tended to be tenuous, the sense of unity was threatened as well. But lack of forceful closure was by no means the most important reason why the unity of music became a central concern of the period. Other reasons were discussed in Chapter 6. What I want to consider in what follows are primarily the theoretical problems attendant upon an account of unity through similarity. First, however, a brief discussion of the nature and bases of unity, partly recapitulating points made earlier, seems warranted.

Whatever its basis is said to be, unity is neither an objective trait like frequency or intensity, nor a specifiable relationship like an authentic cadence or a *crescendo*. Rather, it is a psychological effect—an impression of propriety, integrity, and completeness—that depends not only on the stimuli perceived, but on cultural beliefs and attitudes ingrained in listeners as standards of cognitive/conceptual satisfaction.

Because a sense of unity is the result of a concatenation of conditions, different epochs have attributed it to different aspects of music. Indeed, what any epoch takes to be the important sources of unity might serve as a touchstone for its central aesthetic/ideological concerns. For the eighteenth century, for instance, unity was a matter of coherent expression:

> The fundamental character of the subject will determine the expression, and whether it is to be grandiose or simple, gentle or strong. If joy is the theme, every musical turn of phrase, every dance step must take on a smiling colour; and although the songs and airs may vary as they follow and take over from one another, the underlying idea that is common to them all will in no way be altered. *Herein lies the unity of the work.*[147]

And, as late as 1802, Heinrich Christoph Koch writes that

> as an orator passes from the main thought by means of rhetorical figures to accessory ideas, contrasts, analyses, etc., all of which reinforce the main thought—so must the composer be guided in his treatment of his main idea, working out the harmonies, modulations, repetitions, etc. in such relationships, that he constantly maintains novelty and increase of

---

147. Charles Batteux, *Les beaux-arts réduits à un même principe* (1746), excerpted in le Huray and Day, pp. 50–51; emphasis added.

interest; and so that the episodes and accessory ideas that are especially necessary in composition do not disturb the prevailing sentiment *and hence damage the unity of the whole.*[148]

In the eighteenth century, as these quotations suggest, unity of expression is significantly dependent upon kinds of dance steps, rhetorical figures, syntactic processes, and other conventional means. As observed earlier, Classic composers use such means to represent sentiments shared by humankind. Romantic composers, on the other hand, reject convention in order to express—to present, not *re*present—their own personal and individual feelings.

The relationship between the concern with unity and the rejection of convention is perhaps clearest in the case of compositions consisting of a number of seemingly independent parts—for example, a symphony or sonata, a collection of characteristic pieces, or the like. Once the legitimacy of convention was called into question, then, as observed in Chapter 6, the relationship between diverse, and often contrasting, parts could not be taken for granted. Under the aegis of ideology, and especially of organicism, questions arose about the sources of musical unity. What made the different parts of a composition cohere to form an organic whole?

Within movements the problems were no less pressing. For the depreciation of convention made syntax per se seem a doubtful basis for coherence and gradually led to a weakening of tonal/harmonic relationships and to the domination of plans over scripts on all levels of structure. What, other than uninspired and unoriginal convention, could account for the kinds and order of parts in, say, a sonata-form movement? How could the first theme be related to subsequent events if script constraints were suspect—if they no longer could function as a viable basis for coherence and unity?[149] As functional differentiation into stable and unstable parts became attenuated and plans came to dominate scripts, hierarchic structuring was enervated. The consequences complement one another. On the one hand, the enervation of syntactic hierarchy made it difficult to comprehend diversity through subsumption. On the other hand, and at the same time, partial or weak subsumption tended to make the presence of diversity more explicit and emphatic.[150]

What was required was a mode of unity that was not dependent upon convention and learning—a unity that could in principle be understood by the more or less naïve members of the new audience, the elite egalitarians. As already observed, two strategies were especially favored: unity through statistical climax and unity through

148. *Musikalisches Lexikon,* quoted in Ratner, *Classic Music,* p. 218; emphasis added. I have quoted more than was necessary to illustrate the prevalence of the language model for music in the eighteenth century, as distinguished from the organic model prevalent in Romantic aesthetics.

149. Given the nature of the new audience for art music, doubts about relying on syntactic relationships were probably not unreasonable. Musical relationships needed to be "naturally" egalitarian.

150. It is important to recognize that diversity of expression and means was also encouraged by the ideological valuing of individuality and originality.

similarity.[151] In the first of these strategies, harmonic, melodic, and rhythmic disparities, contrasts of texture and timbre, and unrealized implications and unresolved tensions are overwhelmed and virtually obliterated by the magnitude, force, and sublimity of a statistical climax. And it scarcely needs mentioning that the unifying power of such climaxes does not depend on learned convention and syntactic sophistication.

The second strategy for achieving unity was that of pattern similarity. That this kind of unity was important in nineteenth-century thinking about music is indicated by the following quotations:

> The inner arrangement of the movements, their development, instrumentation, the manner in which they are ordered, all this works toward a single point: *but most of all it is the intimate relationship among the themes which creates this unity.*[152]

> Amongst the works of the great masters may be found innumerable pieces that are built upon a single motif. *What marvellous unity there is in the structure of these compositions!* Everything relates to the subject; nothing extraneous or inappropriate is there. Not a single link could be detached from the chain without destroying the whole.[153]

> The chief motives of the dramatic action—having become distinguishable melodic moments which fully materialize their content—now mold themselves into a continuous artistic form. The new form of dramatic music will have the unity of the symphonic movement; and this it will attain by spreading itself over the whole drama . . . So that this unity consists in a tissue of root themes pervading all the drama. . . .[154]

Still thinking about music in these terms Anton Webern writes, "To develop everything else from *one* principal idea! That's the strongest unity."[155]

Because specific instances of motivic constancy and transformation have been frequently discussed in historical and theoretical writing about music, my concern here will be primarily with the ways in which the valuing of motivic similarity is related to ideology and to other strategies chosen by Romantic composers. The first

151. Other modes, which will *not* be considered here, are: (1) unity dependent upon the presence of a coherent text or program in terms of which diversity and contrast can be comprehended; and (2) dialectic unity—that is, unity based on the notion that the tensions of diversity and contrast (the juxtapositions of thesis and antithesis) are ultimately resolved in a satisfactory synthesis.

152. E. T. A. Hoffmann writing about Beethoven's Fifth Symphony (1810), quoted in Charles Rosen, *The Classical Style*, p. 37; emphasis added.

153. Peter Lichtenthal, *Dizionario e Bibliografia della Musica* (1826), excerpted in le Huray and Day, pp. 374–75; emphasis added.

154. Richard Wagner, *Opera and Drama*, vol. 2 (1851); excerpted in Goldman and Sprinchorn, eds., *Wagner on Music and Drama*, p. 229.

155. *The Path to the New Music*, p. 35.

EXAMPLE 8.29. Haydn, String Quartet in B♭ Major, Opus 50 No. 1, i

and perhaps most important point is that the apprehension of pattern similarity is not essentially dependent upon syntactic convention.[156] In this sense, the unity arising from similarity is a "natural" relationship based on classlike similarities rather than functional differentiation.

To highlight the differences between the unity arising from functional differentiation and that created by motivic similarity, consider an instance in which the same motive acts as both the beginning and the end of a movement. Haydn's String Quartet in B♭ Major, Opus 50 No. 1, for example, begins with the motive given in Example 8.29a. As Janet M. Levy points out, because of the conventional nature of the pattern, the knowledgeable listener recognizes that it is the first half of a "misplaced" closing gesture—that its proper place is at the *end* of some passage or part, not the beginning.[157] Levy's discussion of this movement makes clear that, after a number of only partly satisfactory returns, the gesture finally serves to close the movement and thereby resolves, as it were, the disparity between position and function (Example 8.29b).

When syntactic function ceases to shape musical experience, understanding changes significantly. For syntactically unsophisticated listeners, that is, the return of the pattern (and for them it is not a closing gesture) would heighten closure. But it would do so for reasons having to do with general gestalt-like cognitive dispositions, not with learned conventions.[158]

The distinction between unity by syntactic function versus unity by motivic similarity explains why, as noted earlier, eighteenth-century composers constructed musical dice games, while nineteenth-century composers did not. For the motivic variability that results from throwing dice to "choose" measures is tolerable—that is, it works—only because the *functions* of the successive measures chosen are fixed. And it is because functional class takes precedence over pitch-pattern co-

---

156. In the last analysis, some sort of learning seems inescapably involved in the perception of similarity. For the perceptual cognition that two tones are comparable in quality or that two intervals are similar in size depends on having learned that such judgments are relevant for experience.

157. See her "Gesture, Form, and Syntax."

158. I do not want to suggest that nineteenth-century composers did not make use of conventions to shape implications. See, for instance, my discussion in *Explaining Music*, pp. 214–17, of the slow movement of Brahms's Sonata for Violin and Piano in G Major, Opus 78. On the other hand, perhaps Brahms's usage (choice) is symptomatic of his well-known classicizing proclivities.

herence that Haydn can use a pattern never before heard in a movement to close a movement, as he does in the fourth movement of Symphony No. 89 in F Major (mm. 199–211).[159]

Coherence by similarity, in contrast to coherence by function, is essentially nonhierarchic. As discussed in Chapter 2, the various versions of a motive do not per se combine to form higher-level events. This is so because the formation of a hierarchy depends on the existence of closure, which defines formal entities on any given hierarchic level. But a succession of motives, whether consecutive or not, establishes only a weak basis for closure (see below). Thus, the increasing importance of motivic unity is coordinate with the openness of statistical form. That is, the relationship between unity through hierarchic subsumption and motivic unity is reciprocal: as hierarchic coherence is weakened, its place is taken by motivic similarity. Motivic unity, statistical form, and secondary parameters, then, share an important characteristic: all tend to change incrementally—in degree rather than in kind. This suggests that the ideological connection is not only with the favoring of natural means, organic growth, and openness, but with the valuing of gradualism (whether in politics or biology) by the elite egalitarians.[160]

The growing importance of motivic unity is related to the valuing of planlike schemata in another way as well. Plans do not constrain compositional choices as scripts do. For instance, unlike a classical sonata-form movement, which is script-dominated, the statistical plan of, say, the Transfiguration stipulates neither key relationships nor functional differentiations. As a result, the number of conscious choices to be made in the composition of plan-dominated music is, as a rule, greater than in comparable script-governed music. By limiting compositional choice, motivic constancy served as a constraint compensating in part for the weakening of syntactic stipulations.

The number of compositional choices tended to increase for another reason: the Romantic valuing of individuality and originality. To the extent that composers avoided conventional means, the number of explicit choices necessarily increased.

---

159. See Levy, "Gesture, Form, and Syntax," p. 356.

160. Here I hazard some speculations that seem suspect because they are too pat, yet are suggestive enough to warrant a hearing in a note. The ancien régime was a scriptlike society in which class relationships were stipulated by constraints comparable to syntactic rules. (Consider Riepel's analogy between the tonal hierarchy and that of a farm household, cited in note 98 above.) The new social order that gradually emerged during the eighteenth century was planlike in its relationships, which were without inherited class differences. Instead of stipulated divisions, the new order was based on differences in wealth—essentially, differences in amount. It is difficult to disregard the parallels between a social order shaped by differences in monetary amounts and a music shaped by the amounts characteristic of secondary parameters, between a social order based on planlike constraints and a musical order that was comparably plan-oriented.

This calls attention to what may have been a flaw in Marx's analysis of capitalism: that is, he took capitalism to be a script-governed social order when it was in fact plan-governed. As such the social order was committed to and shaped by incremental changes in degree rather than revolutionary changes in kind. (In this connection, see note 26 in Chapter 6.)

One even more speculative observation: given the nature of a planlike order, our concern with measurement and counting is scarcely surprising. Our society is a statistical society par excellence!

Again, unity through similarity mitigated the problem of choice: once an original pattern had been chosen, motivic conservation served to reduce the number of subsequent choices.

The reference to conservation calls attention to the relationship between motivic unity and the ideological valuing of economy, mentioned in Chapter 6. Organicism, the *Ur*-metaphor of Romantic aesthetics, posited the economy of nature. It was supposed that nature's motto, like that of the elite egalitarians, was "waste not, want not!" Such thinking surely strengthened the inclination to employ motivic variation as a strategy. The economic "imperative" was also linked to notions of natural necessity and its counterpart, aesthetic inevitability. In a perfect economy nothing is wasted, everything is thought to have a reason or purpose. Similarly, each and every aesthetic relationship should be not only necessary but wholly significant.

Finally, motivic conservation was related to the valuing of emotional expression. The expressive force of secondary parameters in unusual and extreme states— very high or low pitches, exceptionally fast or slow tempos, strikingly loud or soft dynamics, and so on—were especially effective in situations of motivic constancy.[161] For instance, the pensive lyricism of the melody of the second key area in Liszt's Piano Sonata in B Minor (Example 8.30*a*) is particularly poignant because it is a close transformation of an earlier theme characterized by malevolent force (Example 8.30*b*). In short, the contrast in expression brought about by the dramatic change in register, dynamics, tempo, texture, and touch is thrown into high relief through the constancy of motivic structure.[162]

Motivic unity has been interpreted in two different ways: synchronically, as a relationship of similarity without regard to temporal ordering; and diachronically, as a process of successive development or transformation over time. Vincent d'Indy

EXAMPLE 8.30. Liszt, Piano Sonata in B Minor

161. This point was touched on near the end of Chapter 6 (see the section "Program music") in relation to Schumann's *Carnaval*.

162. At the risk of tedium, I must again emphasize that the shift from conventions of representation to "natural means of expression" was a matter of degree—of the frequency with which existing strategies were chosen. Secondary parameters played a part in eighteenth-century representation, and the nineteenth century could not dispense with convention. Witness, for instance, the similarities between the funeral marches of Chopin, Wagner, and Mahler.

seems to be making a comparable distinction when he differentiates between thematic metamorphosis and organic development:

> Thematic metamorphoses also differ, in most cases, from organic devel-
> opment . . . which consists of setting a previously stated theme in motion
> or propelling it forward . . . : in general, the same means do not suffice
> for giving a theme or a cyclic motive the ability to move through pieces
> of a different character, while still remaining recognizable. This proce-
> dure . . . is closer to variation than to development.[163]

Recently, a comparable distinction has been made by Walter Frisch who differentiates between *thematic transformation* (synchronic) and *developing variation* (diachronic), a term taken from Schoenberg's writings. Since these terms have become
common in analytic writings, I will use them rather than d'Indy's designations.[164]

In thematic transformation, the various versions of a motive, though necessarily successive in practice, are really regarded as members of a temporally unor-
dered class or set. Of course in actual musical compositions, the versions of a motive
*are* ordered, and this ordering shapes aesthetic experience. Thus in Liszt's Piano
Sonata (see Example 8.30) it makes an enormous difference that the lyric version of
the theme follows the "malevolent" version.[165] Nevertheless, as the quotations presented earlier in this section indicate, most theorists and composers who have discussed motivic unity have adopted the synchronic position;[166] that is, they have
explained how the variants of a motive or theme are related to one another—or to
some abstracted, imaginary pattern from which the variants are derived—by arguing
for their classlike conformance.[167]

The diachronic interpretation considers that motivic unity involves a process of
gradual growth, development, and variation. At times the nature of such a process is
clear and unproblematic. For instance, one of the strategies frequently replicated in
Romantic music was that of beginning a piece with a more or less inchoate pattern—
one whose structuring was psychologically and stylistically less than satisfactory.
The exemplary instance of this strategy is surely the opening of Beethoven's Ninth
Symphony. Here is John N. Burk's description:

> Themes which are gradually unfolded from mysterious murmurings in the
> orchestra—no uncommon experience nowadays—all date back to the

163. *Cours de composition musicale* (1900), quoted in Fallon, "Saint-Saëns and the *Concours*," p. 321.

164. *Brahms and the Principle of Developing Variation*, especially chaps. 1–3.

165. This motivic ordering characterizes the experience of competent listeners not only because of the relationships peculiar to this work, but because the dynamic/lyric succession is compatible with their experience of
other Romantic sonata-form movements.

166. This is also the case with contemporary theorists of motivic unity—e.g., Rudolph Reti and Hans
Keller.

167. It is not perhaps mere happenstance that the kind of cultural history developed during this period was
synchronic—a fabric of cultural relationships as manifestations of a single basic "motive." In this connection, see
the discussion of synchronic histories in Chapter 3.

opening measures of the Ninth Symphony, where Beethoven conceived the idea of building a music of indeterminate open fifths on the dominant, and accumulating a great crescendo of suspense until the theme itself is revealed in the pregnant key of D minor, proclaimed fortissimo by the whole orchestra in unison. It might be added that no one since has quite equaled the mighty effect of Beethoven's own precedent—not even Wagner, who held this particular page in mystic awe, and no doubt remembered it when he depicted the elementary serenity of the Rhine in a very similar manner at the opening of the *Ring*.[168]

Not only can change from the inchoate to the well formed be experienced, but the nature of the change can be comprehended and explained. Once the well-formed motive or theme is presented, however, the nature of subsequent development and transformation seems problematic. The problem concerns the principles that govern the process of development and transformation. It is indisputable that a succession of motivic variations often occurs in the exposition sections of sonata-form movements of the nineteenth century. The nature and order of these changes can readily be explained in relation to typical sonata-form procedures. But the theorists and critics who use the term *developing variation* seem to be making a much stronger claim, though it is seldom explicitly formulated. It is that the process of change makes sense in its own terms—that developing variation is not merely a group of techniques for motivic manipulation, but a specific and independent structural principle. However, I have been unable to find any discussion of the constraints that govern motivic *succession,* although such a discussion would appear to be a sine qua non of an adequate account of the nature of motivic development and transformation.

Let me emphasize this point with an example from the first movement of Brahms's Second Symphony. Many writers have called attention to the successive variations of the neighbor-note motive that begins this movement. As Example 8.31

EXAMPLE 8.31. Brahms, Symphony No. 2 in D Major, Opus 73, i

168. *Life and Works of Beethoven,* p. 294. Other instances of this "germinal/prestate" strategy occur from Chopin's Etude in C Minor, Opus 10 No. 12 (m. 1–8) and Schubert's Eighth Symphony (i, mm. 9–12) to Bruckner's Ninth Symphony (i, mm. 1–18).

shows, the motive recurs in varied form throughout the first key area and the transition of the exposition. The apprehension of variation involves the direct comparison of successive versions of the motive and is, in this respect, comparable to the apprehension of similarities involved in melodic stretching discussed earlier. But there is a notable and fundamental difference. In the case of a stretch melody such as the "Kiss" motive from Verdi's *Otello* (Example 7.41*a*), we can discern a *general principle* that governs the succession of patterns and are aware of the fact of phrase completion—syntactic arrival through repetition of the C♯–B at the octave above and the high-level closure of the bar form (2 + 2 + 4). Put very simply, the principle is that of increasing the size of the interval that separates the constant standard motive from the following appoggiatura. That the principle is *general* is shown by its applicability to a large number of different melodies.

In the case of motivic development and variation such as that in Brahms's Second Symphony, however, theorists and critics describe the changes from one variant to another (or relate each to an "ideal type" of the variant) and classify the variants according to the compositional technique involved (e.g., inversion, metric displacement, augmentation) but they tell us nothing about the principles governing the series as a whole—as a diachronic succession.[169] This is so despite the fact that many of these writers regularly, almost ritually, employ the language of organicism. In Schoenberg's words:

> A real composer does not compose merely one or more themes, but a whole piece. In an apple tree's blossoms, even in the bud, the whole future apple is present in all its details—they have only to mature, to grow, to become the apple, the apple tree, and its power of reproduction. Similarly, a real composer's musical conception, like the physical, is one single act, comprising the totality of the product. The form in its outline, characteristics of tempo, dynamics, moods of the main and subordinate ideas, their relation, derivation, their contrasts and deviations—all these are there at once, though in embryonic state. The ultimate formulation of the melodies, themes, rhythms and many details will subsequently develop through the generating power of the germs.[170]

169. These matters were broached in Chapter 6 in the section "Unity." All the examples of developing variation that Schoenberg gives in *Style and Idea* involve the analysis of similarity relationships (see, for instance, pp. 88 and 200). And when Walter Frisch summarizes what he understands Schoenberg to mean by "developing variation," he does not present the principles governing the temporal succession of the variants, but the ways of relating patterns in terms of similarity: "The intervals are 'developed' by such recognized procedures as inversion and combination . . . , the rhythms by such devices as augmentation and displacement" (*Brahms and the Principle of Developing Variation,* p. 9).

170. *Style and Idea,* p. 201.

Indeed, the nature of changes that are literally organic highlights the problems with the concept of developing variation.[171] For in a natural organic process, the changes—from cell to celebrity; from caterpillar to butterfly—are governed by constraints which, for each organism, define the stages of development.

If understanding of motivic relationships is to transcend the taxonomic, what is needed is a theory (however informal) that explains, rather than describes, the diachronic ordering of successive variants.[172] The failure even to recognize that the nature of motivic *succession* is a crucial problem results from an obsession with motivic constancy as the presumed basis for musical unity. This obsession has directed virtually exclusive attention to the synchronic similarities between motives and variants rather than to the diachronic processes that order successive variations. And it is impossible to create a theory of motivic development by attending solely to class similarities.

Nor is the problem entirely theoretical. The strategy of developing variation was not new; it had been an important strategy throughout the preceding centuries. What was new was its increased importance as a compositional constraint. As the repudiation of convention led to the attenuation of tonal syntax and form—as plans came more and more to dominate scripts—motivic structure was, almost by default, forced into a position of structural primacy. As late as the early twentieth century, motivic organization was a dependent parameter: in the music of composers such as Wagner and his heirs, the ordering of motives depended on the conjunction of largely foreground tonal syntax, statistical forms and processes as shaped by the exigencies of drama and text; in the music of composers such as Brahms, motivic ordering depended on conventions of tonal syntax actualized in conjunction with high-level scripts and lower-level plans involving strategies such as stretching.[173]

With the advent first of atonality and then of serialism, motivic structure (together with the organizing capabilities of the secondary parameters) had to bear the main burden of musical process and form.[174] As this occurred, the need for constraints governing the order of motives and variants became pressing. For not only

171. That the concept of developing variation is, at the very least, ambiguous is suggested by the fact that Carl Dahlhaus considers Brahms's Piano Quartet in G Minor, Opus 25, to be a clear exemplification of developing variation (*Between Romanticism and Modernism*, pp. 48–49), while Walter Frisch argues that the Piano Quartet in A Major, Opus 26, "engages with the principle of developing variation in a way that the G-Minor Quartet does not" (*Brahms and the Principle of Developing Variation*, p. 77).

172. Such a theory would constitute an invaluable contribution to the understanding of the aesthetic and the history of nineteenth-century music.

173. Here I obviously disagree with Dahlhaus's view that in the later nineteenth century "musical form . . . presented itself primarily (though by no means exclusively) as a consequence drawn from thematic ideas, not as a system of formal relations" (*Between Romanticism and Modernism*, p. 42).

174. This in part explains why serialists from Schoenberg on have been so exercised about the ideas of motivic unity and organicism. What I want to suggest here is that in this case the relationship between musical practice and cultural ideology is reciprocal. Ideology—the repudiation of convention, the prizing of natural relationships of similarity, and the valuing of innovation—led (but *not* inevitably) to the primacy of motivic relationships, and the problems attendant on such primacy led, in turn, to enhanced adherence to notions related to organicism.

does pure motivic variation lack any natural order or direction, but it is entirely open-ended (that is, a transformation can continue endlessly).[175] Schoenberg, both the advocate and victim of this development of Romanticism, was aware of the need for constraints: "It seemed at first impossible to compose pieces of complicated organization or of great length. A little later I discovered how to construct larger forms by following a text or a poem." [176] He seems in addition to have sensed the possibility of a syntax of motives. As Richard Swift has observed, Schoenberg's "comments on the opening melody of 'Der Abschied' from *Das Lied von der Erde* suggest those means by which Mahler (and Schoenberg himself) composed 'the long line': 'All the units vary greatly in shape, size and content, as if they were not motival parts of a melodic unit, *but words, each of which has a purpose of its own in the sentence.*'" [177] What Schoenberg seems to be suggesting is that the motival elements will be related to one another not primarily according to similarity, but according to function ("purpose")—as with nouns, adjectives, verbs, and so on—in the structuring of a melody or a period ("sentence").

This brings us back to the unrealized possibility mentioned near the end of Chapter 7—the possibility, that is, that the syntactification of motives might have led to the differentiation of an independent parameter whose semantic/symbolic relationships would constitute a kind of coherent motivic "language." The resulting narrative structures would involve relationships significantly different from those of "pure," abstract music that was presumably based on thematic transformation or developing variation. Unity would be a result neither of similarity relationships nor of the network of motivic association that, according to Wagner, spreads "over the whole drama, linking it all together." [178] Instead unity would arise out of a set of constraints that established the possibilities and probabilities of motivic types and orderings, whether simultaneous or successive.[179]

Discovering a basis for (a set of constraints governing) motivic succession in the absence of the conventions of tonal syntax and form was only one of a host of problems bequeathed by Romanticism and its attendant compositional strategies and proclivities. As many scholars have pointed out (and as has been suggested from time to time in the preceding chapters), many of the beliefs and attitudes, as well as the compositional problems, of the nineteenth century have persisted through the twentieth, affecting the choices of composers and the conceptions of scholars. Because our comprehension of the nature of nineteenth-century history involves an awareness of that history's consequential continuations, it is relevant to consider, if only briefly, some of the later manifestations of Romanticism.

175. Perhaps it is for this reason that the notion of "motivic exhaustion" became an important concept in music aesthetics. For it suggests that transformation is finite and that, when the end is reached, the piece has to close.

176. *Style and Idea*, p. 106.

177. "Mahler's Ninth and Cooke's Tenth," p. 166. The parentheses are in the text; the emphasis is added.

178. From *Opera and Drama*, quoted in Dahlhaus, *Richard Wagner's Music Dramas*, p. 108.

179. It was, perhaps, partly because the syntactification of motives proved to be problematic that Schoenberg turned from Wagnerian potentialities to Brahmsian possibilities. And if the future of music was to arise out of the work of Brahms, that work must surely have been *progressive*.

# Epilogue: The Persistence of Romanticism

As shared norms—conventions—became less important in constraining the choices made by nineteenth-century composers, diversity burgeoned. The result was not only an increase in the number and differentiation of dialects (Wagner versus Verdi, Brahms versus Musorgsky, Satie versus Scriabin, and so on), but a growing disparity in aesthetic/musical goals (Debussy versus Mahler). As the number of stylistic alternatives grew, the number of deliberate choices that had to be made by composers increased dramatically. The need of composers of the early twentieth century for constraints—constraints without which choice and hence composition itself is impossible—led to a kind of trial-and-error search which, too, intensified diversity.

The attenuation of syntactic relationships was, as we have seen, gradual—a trended change. As a result, the step to atonality, which occurred in a number of works composed at different times and places, could be interpreted as nothing more than the continuation of a trend. This view seemed plausible because it was consonant with ideological valuing of gradual, incremental change, and it became the basis for the doctrinaire, insider's history of the advent of the twelve-tone method. The interpretation is unabashedly (if perhaps unwittingly) Romantic, combining evolution, historical necessity, and progress. Here is Ernst Krenek's account:

> The introduction of the twelve-tone technique does not indicate a break of traditional continuity. . . . For as the transition from the area of highly weakened tonal delineation into the uncharted realm of atonality is motivated by the urge of moving onward in the direction of relentless progress, so is the establishment of secure lines of communication . . . necessitated by the same energy that propels history on its forward course.[1]

---

1. "Tradition in Perspective," p. 32. I have criticized the serialists' argument from historical necessity in *Music, the Arts, and Ideas*, pp. 263–65.

The advent of atonality may have seemed little more than a way station along the road of "traditional continuity," but the change had momentous consequences. Once the absence of a tonal center was allowed, compositional choices could no longer be thought of as departures, however distant, from the norms of tonal syntax. Conceptualization thus intensified the problems of compositional choice. What was needed was not new strategies, but new rules. One striking manifestation of this need was the deep and abiding concern of composers—especially composers of "advanced" music such as Schoenberg, Babbitt, Stockhausen, Ligeti, and Xenakis—with music theory and aesthetics.[2]

The constraints devised, and the theories developed in conjunction with them, were many and varied, and they were combined with one another in myriad ways. But all can, I think, be understood in relation to trends begun in the nineteenth century. I shall consider, albeit briefly, only the most important types of constraints.

What follows, then, is both highly selective and very general. It is selective because I will not be concerned with obvious continuations of the styles of Romanticism in the music of composers such as Strauss, Vaughan Williams, Prokofiev, and Barber, or with reversions to earlier dialects as in the music of Rochberg. Rather, I will consider less obvious manifestations of Romanticism such as are exemplified in "advanced" music and music theory, and in other realms of twentieth-century culture. The discussion will be general in the sense that it will for the most part deal with broad aesthetic/theoretical beliefs and attitudes rather than with particular compositional strategies and choices.

## Motivic Relationships

The increased importance of motivic relationships in the music of the nineteenth and early twentieth centuries, as well as the need for constraints governing the succession of motivic variants, was pointed out in Chapter 8. But a syntax of motivic succession was not realized. Instead, other strategies for limiting compositional choice were devised. Of these, the twelve-tone method was probably the most widespread and influential, perhaps partly because its constraints, though not syntactic, were explicitly formulated and hence could be readily taught, learned, and applied. Though composers of twelve-tone music invented ways of ensuring serial continuity (for instance, linking row forms through common intervals), no shared constraints governing the ordering of specific realizations of the row or of the motives derived from the row were devised.[3]

2. This concern with theory seems evidence of more than gradual change, despite assertions that reassured elite egalitarian patrons of continuity. Put the other way around: conservative composers such as Prokofiev, Strauss, Poulenc, and Barber tended to be uninterested in theory and aesthetics.

3. This account is similar to that given by O. W. Neighbour, "Schoenberg, Arnold," *The New Grove Dictionary,* ed. Stanley Sadie, 16:714.

The failure to develop such constraints explains in part why, despite the revolution in pitch organization and the "emancipation of dissonance," the forms of the Classic style not only persisted, but were often used by twelve-tone composers in a more conservative way than they had been in the music of the preceding generation of composers. For these forms—sonata form, rondo, theme and variations, dance forms, and so on—provided the constraints that enabled composers to choose appropriate melodic, rhythmic, and harmonic embodiments for their twelve-tone rows. What I am suggesting is that serial composers and others employed "borrowed" forms not solely (or even primarily) because they considered themselves to be heirs to the great tradition of European art music or because of latent neoclassical inclinations, but because they had virtually no alternative. They could not do without some way of deciding how the motivic variants that they derived from the row should be combined with or succeed one another. Seen thus, there is a significant difference between Stravinsky's use of the forms and strategies of earlier music and, say, Berg's in *Wozzeck*. For the appreciation of Stravinsky's neoclassic music entails a non-egalitarian understanding of the *play* with tradition. Berg's use of the past does not. He was proud that "there is no one in the audience who pays any attention to the various fugues, inventions, suites, sonata movements, variations and passacaglias—no one who heeds anything but the social problems of this opera which by far transcend the personal destiny of Wozzeck."[4]

The acontextualism implicit in this quotation was by no means absolute, however. To reinforce understanding, twelve-tone composers not infrequently employed general procedures and even specific gestures characteristic of tonal music as signs of formal/processive place; for the significance of a pattern depends on the listener's understanding of its function, its place in the overall form of the composition. Such a sign of place, for instance, marks the start of the development section in the first movement of Schoenberg's Third String Quartet. The sign involves a restatement (though in a different register and instrument) of the motive that begins the movement, a procedure that occurs time and time again in the music of the eighteenth and nineteenth centuries. The significance of this restatement is confirmed when, instead of functioning as an ostinato-like vamp (as it had at the beginning of the movement), the motive moves sequentially, creating an instability characteristic of development sections.

I have used twelve-tone music as a basis for discussion because it so clearly, even unequivocally, exemplifies the problems of twentieth-century Romanticism. But serial composers were by no means the only ones to be plagued by the problem of how to order motivic variants in the absence of some sort of high-level constraints. Virtually all composers who wrote motivically based music employed traditional forms to shape large-scale organization. Bartók and Hindemith may serve as examples.

4. Quoted in George Perle, "Berg, Alban (Maria Johannes)," *The New Grove Dictionary*, ed. Stanley Sadie, 2:531.

The melodic relationships employed by most twentieth-century composers tended to be those least dependent on tonal syntax. Similarity relationships—varied sequence, partial imitation, complementary structures—were the most important means for creating process and coherence. To take a brief and striking instance: the main motive of the first movement of Bartók's Fourth String Quartet is a complementary pattern, and this pattern is itself complemented by its own inversion (Example E.1).[5] In addition, the principle of complementary patterning was extended (by extrapolation) from one of simple inversion to retrograde and retrograde inversion.

EXAMPLE E.1. Bartók, String Quartet No. 4, i

## Secondary Parameters

Though the use of Classic forms solved some compositional problems, it gave rise to others. The nontonal music of the twentieth century provided no criteria for syntactic closure—for the articulation of forms and processes that had originally been based on syntactic scripts. As a result, the importance of secondary parameters in shaping musical relationships increased very significantly.

The gradual attenuation of syntactic relationships led to a peculiar situation in which *all* parameters tended to become statistical. Instead of being related to one another in terms of function, pitches were related according to similarity of class or relationships of register, and harmonies were related to one another in terms of acoustic quality—for instance, more or less discordant. With the advent of twelve-tone technique, which explicitly denied any functional relationships among pitches, melody and harmony were, in effect, relegated to the status of secondary parameters. From this point of view, attempts to serialize tone color, dynamics, and so on, were in no way incongruous or capricious.[6]

In the music of the twentieth century, perhaps even more than that of the nineteenth, the articulation of form was dependent on the use of secondary parameters, including nonsyntactic pitch relationships (higher/lower) and nonsyntactic harmony

5. Also see Example 8.27.

6. The serialization of such things as tone color and dynamics seems to have been abandoned quite quickly. It was so, one suspects, because these parameters cannot be segmented (cognitively) into discrete proportional units (see Chapter 1). The serialization of duration (which can be so segmented) proved abortive because "time's arrow" makes the comprehension of retrograde patterns problematic, while the concept of temporal inversion seems a bizarre chimera.

(concord/discord). For instance, all the important points of articulation in the first movement of Schoenberg's Third String Quartet are characterized by a marked abatement in secondary parameters: descending pitches, less discordant harmonies, simpler textures, softer dynamics, and slowing of tempo and rate of attack. In other styles secondary parameters have been used to create tone-color relationships, as Ligeti's description of his own compositions makes clear: "In these orchestral works my main goal was to build up an art form in which tone color is more important than melody, harmony, and rhythm. And melody, harmony, and rhythm have been reduced in the sense that they *do* exist, but are woven together in a heavy, dense texture." [7] The increased importance of secondary parameters is also evident in contemporary musical notation—in what is specified by the composer and what is left to the performer. To take an extreme but telling case, in graph music secondary parameters (tempo, dynamics, timbre, and texture) are for the most part specified by the composer, while the choice of particular pitches, harmonies, and rhythms is often the province of the performer.

The increase in the number and detail of performance marks in much nontonal music continues a trend begun at the end of the eighteenth century and is indicative of the increased importance of secondary parameters. The proliferation of these performance marks is symptomatic of their importance not only in the expression of feeling, but in the shaping of process and the articulation of form. At times it is possible to analyze the structure of a twentieth-century work solely on the basis of tempo designations, dynamic marks, orchestral sonorities, and changes in texture. In order for secondary parameters to shape musical form as primary parameters had previously done, the range of parametric possibilities was extended and the force of contrast heightened. [8]

The burgeoning of expression marks can also be related, through the organic model, to the valuing of economy and necessity. Since in art, as in nature, everything is related to everything else, nothing is without significance. The importance of economy (and the "necessity" that follows from it) is emphasized in Erwin Stein's essay "Musical Thought: Beethoven and Schoenberg" (1927): "If music be sounding thought rather than sounding play, everything has to make sense, nothing must be a superfluous end in itself. Economy is the overriding requirement, concentration its result. A new principle arises: everything has to be thematic, nothing decorative." [9]

7. Quoted in Christensen, "Music of Gyorgy Ligeti," p. 7.

8. Degrees of articulation are, of course, also a function of the dispositions of the several secondary parameters with respect to one another. The nature of closure (and, by the same token, of mobility) in contemporary music is a subject that very much needs scrupulous study. A typology of closural configurations, together with their relative strengths, is probably the appropriate beginning for such a study.

9. In Stein's *Orpheus in New Guises*, p. 92. The radical reduction in redundancy fostered by this attitude created formidable perceptual/cognitive problems for listeners. (In this connection, see my *Music, the Arts, and Ideas*, chap. 11.) It is an amusing happenstance of history that the same tenets of Romanticism—a current of aesthetic Puritanism ("waste not; want not")—were connected with both the "hot intensity" of much Viennese serial music and the cold austerity of much architectural modernism. In the latter case, as well as the former, the rejection of conventional constraints (e.g., Gothic revival or neoclassicism) and the valuing of nature (leave materials in their natural state; do not cover them with decoration) also played an important role.

And if every note is significant, then each is a candidate for an expression mark!

Influenced, one suspects, by scientific/mathematical models, the generation of composers that came to power after World War II felt that compositional constraints should be both comprehensive and consistent. As a result, using secondary parameters to shape script-based forms, and script-based forms as the basis for motivic development, came to seem not merely problematic, but somehow illicit—even immoral.[10] Yet the need for high-level constraints remained. And to meet this need a host of precompositional constraints were devised. To cite only one composer's work, Iannis Xenakis has used a number of mathematical models, including probability theory, set theory, Markov chains, and game theory, as a basis for precompositional constraints. Sometimes (though not always) this kind of comprehensive constraint set affected the succession of motivic variants, as well as the overall shape of the composition.

### Intraopus Norms

Any stimulus or relationship—an instrumental timbre or combination of timbres, a single pitch plus register or a pattern of pitches (whether simultaneous or successive), a pattern of durations, or most often some combination of these—that is especially prominent or becomes so by dint of repetition can act as an intraopus norm. Once established, intraopus elements function as indigenous patterns or as "sonic centers" from which other elements deviate or depart and to which they tend to return. Musical form and process arise not from the constraints of a shared dialect, but from the interaction between a temporary sonic "imprinting" and the kinds of continuing cognitive proclivities investigated by Gestalt psychology.

On a small scale, for example, direct rhythmic/metric comparison has been a strategy frequently used in twentieth-century music by composers such as Stravinsky and Bartók. As illustrated earlier (Example 7.18), this strategy involves using basically constant motivic/intervallic relationships to highlight rhythmic/metric displacement, creating a temporal tension analogous to that of melodic stretching.

On a much larger scale, many contemporary composers use intraopus sonic norms to articulate formal structures. According to Stravinsky, it is necessary

> to recognize the existence of certain poles of attraction. Diatonic tonality is only one means of orienting music toward these poles. The function of tonality is completely subordinated to the force of attraction of the pole of sonority. . . .
>
>     . . . Composing, for me, is putting into an order a certain number of these sounds according to certain interval-relationships. This activity

10. This seems the ground for Boulez's criticisms of Schoenberg. But one cannot help feeling that such "purism" is misguided, given works such as the Fourth String Quartet or Berg's Violin Concerto.

leads to a search for the center upon which the series of sounds involved in my undertaking should converge. Thus, if a center is given, I shall have to find a combination that converges upon it. If, on the other hand, an as yet unoriented combination has been found, I shall have to determine the center towards which it should lead.[11]

However, such centers are not the same as, and do not give rise to, hierarchic, syntactic relationships. Writing about such centers in Bartók's music, Leo Treitler observes: "One thing must be kept entirely clear: this C, or C–E, is in no sense a tonality. It is an arbitrarily chosen, static 'tonal center' which is not involved in any scheme for generating secondary tonal areas."[12]

Two points need to be noticed. First, a sound or a complex of sounds functions as a center not because of learned syntactic convention, but because of the innate cognitive proclivity that Gestalt psychologists have called "the principle of return." That is, the psychic satisfaction of return enables the set of sounds to function as a center—a point of stability and relative closure. Second, to function as a center, the set of sounds not only must be distinctive in some way, but must be emphasized through repetition. Thus Hindemith, for instance, argues:

The entire harmonic construction of a piece may be perceived in this way: against one tonal center chosen from among many roots others are juxtaposed which either support it or compete with it. Here, too, the tonal center that *reappears most often,* or that is particularly strongly *supported by its fourth and its fifth,* is the most important.[13]

In short, tonal centers are established through the interaction of cognitive proclivities and intraopus frequency. The trends generated by Romanticism thus eventuate in the triumph of nature over nurture, of statistics over syntax.

## Transcendentalism

Enjoyment of most styles of twentieth-century music involves the apprehension of orderly relationships, no matter how intricate or idiosyncratic they may be. But the aesthetic movement in contemporary art that I have called *transcendentalism*[14] repudiates all contrived order: intraopus norms, as well as regularities of idiom and dialect. The goal of this repudiation is the innocent perception of the peculiarity of individual sonic stimuli. Plainly, prior experience—history, learning, and even memory—is irrelevant.

11. *Poetics of Music,* pp. 37, 39.
12. "Fourth Quartet of Béla Bartók," p. 294.
13. *The Craft of Musical Composition,* p. 151; emphasis added.
14. See *Music, the Arts, and Ideas,* pp. 158–69.

Transcendentalism is also Romantic in its valuing of nature. Works of art should be understood in the way that natural phenomena presumably are: naïvely and directly, without reference to traditions and goals, schemata and classes. From this point of view, wholly random music can be understood as a way of forcing Romantic innocence and equality on contemporary audiences.

The repudiation of constraints may be possible in aesthetic theory, but it is not so in compositional practice: some means must be found for selecting sounds—or nonsounds. What the composers of transcendentalism did was to devise strategies that made particular compositional choices—choosing pitches, durations, timbres, and so on—unnecessary. In the words of John Cage:

> Those involved with the composition of experimental music find ways and means to remove themselves from the activities of the sounds they make. Some employ chance operations derived from sources as ancient as the Chinese *Book of Changes* or as modern as the tables of random numbers used also by physicists in research. Or, analogous to the Rorschach tests of psychology, the interpretation of imperfections in the paper upon which one is writing may provide a music free from one's memory and imagination.[15]

As the quotation makes clear, transcendentalism diverges from the mainstream of Romanticism in its attitude toward individualism. The increased prizing of impersonality and the decreased valuing of individual expression are partly results of cultural/ideological changes—for instance, the erosion of belief in the heroic and in the "hammerblows" of the sublime, together with a shift in which conceptual ("scientific"), systemic innovation becomes an important compositional goal. But the change in attitude is partly a consequence of a relationship mentioned earlier: namely, that individuality is always delineated in terms of a set of norms—especially conventions. If this assertion is correct, it follows that the weaker the constraints of a style are, the more difficult the delineation of individual expression becomes. And when the repudiation of constraints is absolute, as it is in some random music, individual expression is impossible.

There is, then, an inherent incompatibility between radical originality and individual expression because the latter depends on deviation from shared norms for its delineation. Therefore, to the extent that the prizing of originality leads to the abrogation of such norms, the delineation of individual expression either becomes attenuated or requires ever more radical departures from whatever norms are still prevalent. Thus, especially in those styles of twentieth-century music in which constraints have been affected by a compelling concern with originality, originality ceases to be connected with individual expression.

The special prizing of originality and the consequent radicalization of deviation

15. *Silence*, p. 10.

in the twentieth century were related to a number of facets of Romanticism. First, the belief that the arts, like other realms of culture, progressed made innovation seem desirable—even a kind of moral/historical imperative. Conservative composers were often looked upon as renegades. Second, the common conception of artistic innovation as somehow analogous to scientific discovery (exemplified in the phrase "experimental music") implied an association among categorical novelty, creativity, and value.[16] Finally, the existence of radical novelty made innovation itself an important basis for critical evaluation. For, as shared constraints—rules, strategies, and other conventional norms—became less and less important, the evaluation of relationships within compositions became increasingly problematic. What could be judged, however, was the novelty of a composition. As result, one of the chief concerns of criticism (for instance, from the 1940s through the 1960s) became the identification and often the celebration of innovation.[17]

If the concern of criticism was frequently with novelty, the concern of twentieth-century music theory has been with innate, natural universals to the virtual exclusion of any consideration of the role of learned, cultural constraints in the shaping of musical experience. The shaping power of the Schenkerian *Ursatz* is attributed to the natural relationships of the overtone series; musical coherence is, according to Reti and his followers, a result of motivic similarities that are presumably independent of prior learning—and the same basic conception underlies the formidable analyses of set theory; accounts of musical relationships in terms of preferred proportions (the golden section, the Fibonacci series, and stochastic processes) or linguistic models likewise assume that musical perception is the result of innate cognitive capacities;[18] and last, as observed above, the appreciation of sound per se, called for by transcendentalism, explicitly emphasizes the irrelevance of previous experience of any sort. If the understanding of music is essentially a matter of natural universals, then style is obviously without significance.[19]

According to such theories, then, it makes no difference when, where, or by whom a piece of music was composed.[20] Style, in this view, is but a surface habit, a transient realization of deeper, more enduring, and (hence?) more important relationships. Thus, though the swan song of Romantic love has long since been sounded, its aesthetic counterpart, acontextual formalism, continues to flourish, trumpeting *forte* through the realms of academic music theory. As Milton Babbitt

16. For a discussion of the differences between the arts and the sciences, see my essay "Concerning the Sciences."

17. An ironic outcome of this is that criticism became a matter of making class judgments—of deciding whether or not a work employed innovative techniques and the like.

18. In connection with linguistic models, see Chapter 6, note 126.

19. This is a matter not merely of theory but of practice. Style is seldom even mentioned in the studies of most contemporary theorists, since it makes virtually no difference whether one is analyzing a work by Bach or one by Brahms.

Not surprisingly, the empirical studies of psychologists have also tended to ignore the claims of style and learning, concerning themselves for the most part with supposedly unmediated responses of naïve listeners to single tones or simple tone complexes—more or less the equivalents of nonsense syllables in linguistic/memory research.

20. This being so, the intention of the composer is explicitly irrelevant.

makes clear, understanding "advanced" music does not depend on prior experience with kinds or types—with stylistic learning. Despite the use of powerful precompositional constraints, there is essentially only one level of style: that of the intra-opus relationship:

> Musical compositions of the kind under discussion possess a high degree of contextuality and autonomy. That is, the structural characteristics of a given work are less representative of a general class of characteristics than they are unique to the individual work itself. Particularly, principles of relatedness . . . are more likely to evolve in the course of the work than to be derived from generalized assumptions.[21]

I have sought to show that the constraints commonly chosen by composers of "advanced" music were consonant with important tenets of Romanticism: the repudiation of conventions, the use of *natural* formative means, and an emphasis on acontextuality. Now I want to suggest that the resulting music conforms with the spirit of Romanticism because it is *in principle* egalitarian. Given the widespread resistance to contemporary music idioms, this may seem a bizarre claim indeed. Notice, however, that egalitarianism does not require that art be understood, appreciated, and loved by every person, but only that listening competence not depend on privileged learning (whether formal or informal) of traditions, conventions, references, and the like.[22]

The rapidity of style change in the arts (encouraged by an almost obsessive concern with originality) and in culture generally has enhanced the trend toward acontextuality. Because it has become more and more difficult to keep up with successions of radical novelties, there has been a tendency to give up—to disregard past constraints and traditions. As Carl E. Schorske has observed:

> Modern architecture, modern music, modern philosophy, modern science—all these define themselves not *out* of the past, indeed scarcely *against* the past, but in independence of the past. The modern mind has been growing indifferent to history because history, conceived as a continuous nourishing tradition, has become useless to it.[23]

---

21. "Who Cares if You Listen?" p. 39. Clearly what Babbitt calls "contextuality" I have been calling "acontextuality" (because the relationships are without context on a higher stylistic level).

22. When responses to atonal music are investigated it appears that for some tasks there is no significant difference between inexperienced and experienced listeners. See Dowling and Harwood, *Music Cognition,* p. 144. Looked at from the point of view adopted in this study, the absence of learned syntactic constraints promotes egalitarianism by leveling the ranks of listeners.

The connection between egalitarianism and acontextuality is clear. An egalitarian culture will tend to favor those disciplines—mathematics, the sciences, and the like—in which the cultural insights gained through early experience are least important. And there will be a tendency for all disciplines to become as objective and rigorous—that is, mathematical and empirical—as possible, a tendency that has had a clear influence on recent theories of music.

23. *Fin-de-Siècle Vienna,* p. xvii.

To take the extreme case first, all listeners are *equal* at a performance of, say, an aleatory piece by John Cage (and I think that Cage would agree with this view), just as they *supposedly* are when "the beetle wheels his droning flight / And drowsy tinklings lull the distant folds" (Thomas Gray, "Elegy Written in a Country Churchyard").[24] But these same listeners are *not* equal when they hear a reading of Gray's poem. According to Louis Christensen, the sense-appeal of Ligeti's music is also egalitarian: "An average audience that can find immediate pleasure in the sonorities of *Atmospheres* is struck by even greater wonder at the effect of the complex vocal sound that seems to be carried within the concert hall like swirling mists."[25] And to the extent that music based on systematic precompositional constraints is autonomous, as Babbitt seems to suggest,[26] its comprehension depends on innate cognitive proclivities rather than the internalization of learned traditions and shared conventions.

The irony is, of course, that instead of leading to compositions readily understood and appreciated by the concert-going public, egalitarianism gave rise to music that became the private province of small academic coteries.[27] And this untoward outcome raises an important, even fundamental, question about humankind: Is it in our nature to be wholly natural—that is, without cultivated concepts and conventions?

Before attempting to answer this question, however, it should be emphasized that, though acontextualism is an expression of beliefs central to Romanticism, it has been actualized absolutely only in extreme formalist and unadulterated transcendentalist music. Most twentieth-century composers have employed conventions of some sort—usually, as we have seen, large-scale formal schemata. Some composers, however, have employed patently conventional patternings. Of these, Stravinsky is surely the exemplary instance.

What needs to be noticed, first of all, is that Stravinsky's use of convention is a response to the same need for stylistic constraints as Schoenberg's use of the twelve-tone method, Xenakis's use of probability theory, and Cage's use of tables of random numbers. The generality of the need is evident in the fact that it makes no difference to Stravinsky whether he borrows constraints from folk music, the high Baroque, the Classic period, or late medieval music, as long as he finds the music appealing and appropriate.[28] The concept of *borrowing* is important because it indicates that the

---

24. I say "supposedly" because there are no naïve, unmediated human experiences, whether of art or of nature. The kind of innocence called for is an impossibility, save perhaps for idiots and mystics. All human beings, always and everywhere, bring to each experience a fund of cultural learning. *Our experience of nature is just as cultural as our experience of art.*

25. "Music of Gyorgi Ligeti," p. 10.

26. See "Who Cares if You Listen?" p. 40. I have criticized Babbitt's analogy between understanding music and understanding conceptual disciplines such as mathematics, philosophy, and physics in *Music, the Arts, and Ideas,* pp. 280–82.

27. Clearly this is an overstatement. Some "advanced" music does seem to have broader audience appeal, mostly to the very young. Often this is also the audience for rock 'n' roll. Put briefly, the conditions favoring egalitarianism occur at the extremes of a spectrum that runs from the blatant emphasis of endless reiteration to the indecipherable complexity of "white noise." Minimalist music—egalitarian in its use of reiterated intraopus norms—also seems to have a growing audience.

28. Not surprisingly, the style that did *not* appeal to Stravinsky was that of German Romanticism.

constraints employed are not *imposed* on composers by the cultural context, but are *chosen* by them from a number of alternative possibilities.[29] Such borrowing enables composers to have it both ways at once: conventional constraints facilitate compositional choice, but the resulting music avoids the stigma of conventionality.

In borrowing, the "donor" style is usually regarded as a collection of discrete traits (often differentiated in terms of particular parameters) rather than as an indivisible set of interrelated constraints. For this reason, only some of the conventions of a style are, as a rule, chosen by the composer for a particular composition.[30] The chosen conventions, combined with other constraints, constitute the intraopus style of the work. In *The Rake's Progress,* for instance, Stravinsky combines constraints such as sonic centers and rhythmic/metric juxtaposition with melodic patterns, textural arrangements, and conventions of form and genre characteristic of (borrowed from) the style of Classic music.

Though borrowed patterns tend to retain their gestural significance even in the absence of the constraints that initially joined pattern and meaning together, their significance, their sign-function, becomes somehow abstract, disembodied—undergoing "a sea change / Into something rich and strange." For instance, a closing motive discussed earlier (*m* in Example 8.2) occurs a number of times in *The Rake's Progress.* Many of the features of the Classic close—emphasis on the upper sixth degree, sequential descent to the tonic, and the final $3-2-1$ motive (*m*)—are present in the last cadence of Anne's Arioso from act 2, scene 2 (Example E.2). However, not only is the motive (*m*) harmonized in a piquant way, but it is not preceded

EXAMPLE E.2. Stravinsky, *The Rake's Progress,* Act 2, Scene 2

29. From this point of view, Stravinsky's use of the constraints of serialism is not anomalous; rather, it is consistent with his lifelong habit of borrowing (beginning with his use of folk music). Such use would seem anomalous only if it were regarded (whether by Stravinsky or by historians) as being privileged in some way.

30. Clearly, the more traits (the more parametric constraints) borrowed from a single donor style, the more closely related the later and earlier styles will be. (I use the word *single* to call attention to the possibility that the constraints of a single composition may be borrowed from a number of different styles.)

(either immediately or remotely) by a tonality-defining progression. Instead, harmonic stability is a result of insistent harmonic centering.[31]

Deprived of its customary harmonic complement, the cadential motive is removed from the "real" stylistic world. Its closural meaning persists, but the gesture has become a kind of fiction.[32] Perhaps an analogy will help to make this point clear. If someone writing today closed a letter with the phrase "Your most obedient servant" (the equivalent of the gesture that ends Anne's Arioso, Example E.2), it would seem stilted and conventional. But if the same phrase closed a letter in a contemporary novel set in the eighteenth century, its conventionality would, so to speak, be transferred from the author of the novel to the fictive writer of the letter. Seen thus, borrowing and paraphrase are twentieth-century strategies for disguising convention.[33] And this strategy of disguise, employed by composers such as Mahler and Ives, has become increasingly common of late, as, for instance, in some of the music of Berio and Rochberg.

Note, however, that to the extent (and it is considerable) that the appreciation of music based on paraphrase and borrowing depends on an understanding of such conventions and their (often playful) relationship to other stylistic constraints, learning and experience are indispensable. And to the extent that learning and experience are indispensable, the music is exclusive and, in this sense, privileged. What is remarkable is that this kind of music is more accessible to most members of the concert audience than music less dependent upon learned convention—music that in theory is more egalitarian. The moral seems to be that human communication is for the most part dependent upon learning. In this sense, all competence leads to exclusiveness and, for any particular in-group, to elitism.

The answer to the question posed earlier seems clear: it is *not* in our nature to be naïvely natural, without cultivated concepts and conventions. Innate cognitive capacities and predispositions can provide only a portion of the constraints necessary for successful communication. The remaining constraints must be provided by culture—by stylistic rules and strategies, and by the classes and conventions, the syntax and schemata through which rules and strategies are realized. Without cultural constraints, memory is emasculated by the momentary; envisaging is enervated and choice crippled by confinement to the immediate. And to preclude all but immediate choice is to dehumanize the human animal. Human nature without cultural nurture is an impossibility, a grand delusion.

The overriding need of twentieth-century composers—the need for a generally accepted set of compositional constraints reconciling the claims of nature and nurture—has led to a restless, almost Faustian, search. But few lasting or fundamentally new constraints have been forthcoming. Most innovation has involved extrapolation

31. At times Stravinsky's harmonic usage is considerably more traditional than it is in Example E.2. See, for instance, the first closure of Anne's Cabaletta from act 1, scene 3, where the motive ($m$) is preceded by a clear vi–ii$^6$–V$^7$ progression.

32. In this connection, see Rabinowitz, "Fictional Music."

33. In this respect they are significantly different from earlier uses of paraphrase and borrowing.

from principles already latent (or, at times, manifest) in nineteenth-century practice. Schoenberg transforms motivic similarities into the permutational and combinatorial operations of the twelve-tone system, and these are, in turn, extended to other parameters; the Impressionist valuing of sense experience is elevated into an exclusive, almost moral, goal; and, as described in Chapter 7, Stravinsky derives a general compositional strategy from individual instances of rhythmic/metric displacement found in folk music.[34]

Such extrapolation is probably characteristic of trended changes. And it seems possible that if the extrapolation of the constraints of some parameter continues far enough, the extreme state of those constraints will eventually come into conflict with the constraints of some other parameter. For instance, extremes of frequency are constrained by the physiology of the nervous system, melodic disjunction in time by the limits of memory, and the size of orchestras and the duration of compositions by cultural priorities. Similarly, in a process comparable to the "runaway" selection model in evolution (a process in which some "trait eventually becomes extremely exaggerated, perhaps to the detriment of the bearer"[35]), when the egalitarian repudiation of learning and convention leads from disguise to denial, it conflicts with fundamental characteristics of human nature.

Though realized in different ways, through many diverse compositional strategies, the trends that I have been describing have continued for some two hundred years. They have done so because, despite astonishing changes in technology and striking scientific discoveries, the fundamental tenets of the ideology that generated and shaped the trends have persisted.[36] Two of the many reasons for such persistence seem especially pertinent here. First, once an encompassing ideology is established as a habitual way of conceiving of, organizing, and evaluating the realms of being, it tends to endure until another competing ideological network seems to account more satisfactorily for human experience. Second, the social, economic, and political concepts and values with which the ideology was initially associated have not merely continued, but have in surprising measure been successfully actualized. Lest my ordering of these reasons suggest temporal or causal priority, it needs to be emphasized that, as Jacques Barzun points out, "romanticism is a part of the great revolution which drew the intellect of Europe from a monarchical into a popular state, from the court and the fashionable capitals into the open country and the five continents, from the expectation and desire for fixity into the desire and expectation of change."[37]

The consequences of this revolution are, as Artz observes, "still being worked out."[38] In music, no stylistic stability, no classic consensus, has occurred. Though

---

34. See Example 7.18.

35. Lewin, "Is Sexual Selection a Burden?" p. 526.

36. This is not to contend that the ideology has not changed. For instance, as observed a bit earlier, emphasis on individual, personal expression was diminished in favor of a valuing of innovation and originality. But such changes have, as far as I can see, been consonant with the core beliefs of the ideology.

37. *Critical Questions*, p. 159.

38. See above, Chapter 6 at note 4.

new sets of constraints seem to follow one another, almost like fashions, none has achieved the status of cultural convention. There is perhaps a kind of poetic propriety (if not justice) in this. That is, the ideology of Romanticism becomes, as it were, writ large in cultural manifestation: in being open and Becoming—an actively fluctuating steady state, a strenuous stasis;[39] in being pluralistic—offering a plenitude of stylistic possibilities; and in being without a single, or even dominant, set of privileged compositional constraints.

Although this account of some of the characteristic style changes that occurred in art music during the nineteenth century may seem long, it remains a *sketch*-history. It is not simply that the account is incomplete, but that its primary purpose is to suggest how style change might be explained rather than merely described. In attempting to construct such an explanation, one of the things that has most impressed me is the interconnection among hypotheses about the nature of style change, musical experience, and cultural/ideological conditions. Consider the strategy of melodic stretching. To explain why it was chosen with increasing frequency by composers of the nineteenth century, it is necessary to invoke hypotheses about the nature of human cognition, prevalent musical constraints, and ideological/aesthetic goals.

Mention of aesthetic goals calls attention to a question posed early in this book: Is it possible to infer "the rules of the game" (institutional facts) simply by attending to the "play of the game" (brute facts)—the succession of stimuli?[40] I think that the answer is an unequivocal "no." There is no such thing as understanding a work of art in its own terms. Indeed, the very notion of *work of art* is cultural. The choices made by some compositional community can be understood and explained only if relationships can be discerned among the goals set by culture, the nature of human cognitive processes, and the alternatives available given some set of stylistic constraints.

Finally, a word about the validity of the account given in this sketch-history. As noted earlier, histories are interpretations, and as with all interpretations, differences are possible. Histories should be accurate, but they cannot be true in the sense that general propositions may be so. Rather, what is constructed is a network of hypotheses and observations whose several strands, woven together and reinforcing one another, form a coherent and convincing fabric of explanation.

39. See my *Music, the Arts, and Ideas*, pt. 2.

40. Though there are no absolutely brute facts because experience is invariably organized in terms of some hypothesis (the notions of "organisms" or "colored shirts" indicate the inescapability of hypotheses), it does not follow that there are no separable institutional facts—no rules of the game. As I listen to a Javanese *gamelan* or watch a game of cribbage, I will entertain hypotheses (based on my beliefs about human behavior) about the nature of the activities: that the music is to be pleasurable or symbolic, and that the game probably has a goal and will have a winner. But I may nevertheless not understand the musical relationships or the nature of the game.

Needless to say, I hope that the relationships and connections developed in my sketch-history will seem interesting and illuminating, coherent and convincing. But they do not pretend to be definitive. They are hypotheses. Some may be downright wrong, others will require refinement. All need to be tested through application to genres and repertories not considered here. It is a program of work to be done, of ideas and hypotheses to be evaluated and perhaps rejected, explored and perhaps extended. From this point of view, my sketch is not "Classically" closed, but "Romantically" open.

# BIBLIOGRAPHY OF WORKS CITED

Abraham, Gerald. *A Hundred Years of Music*. London, 1938.

Abrams, M. L. *The Mirror and the Lamp: Romantic Theory and the Critical Tradition*. London, 1953.

Ackerman, James S. "A Theory of Style." *Journal of Aesthetics and Art Criticism* 20, no. 3 (1962): 227–37.

Agawu, V. Kofi. "The Structural Highpoint as Determinant of Form in Nineteenth Century Music." 2 vols. Ph.D. diss., Stanford University, 1982.

Allanbrook, Wye Jamison. *Rhythmic Gesture in Mozart: Le Nozze di Figaro and Don Giovanni*. Chicago, 1983.

Anderson, Emily, trans. and ed. *The Letters of Mozart and His Family*. With extracts from the letters of Constanze Mozart to Johann Anton André, translated and edited by C. B. Oldman. 3 vols. London, 1938.

Arauco, Ingrid. "Bartok's *Romanian Christmas Carols*: Changes from the Folk Sources." *Journal of Musicology* 5, no. 2 (1987): 191–225.

Artz, Frederick B. *From the Renaissance to Romanticism: Trends in Style in Art, Literature, and Music, 1300–1830*. Chicago, 1962.

Ashley, Maurice. *England in the Seventeenth Century*. London, 1978.

Auden, W. H. *Forewords and Afterwords*. Selected by Edward Mendelsohn. New York, 1974.

Auspitz, Katherine. *The Radical Bourgeoisie: The* Ligue d'enseignement *and the Origins of the Third Republic 1866–1885*. Cambridge, 1982.

Austin, William W. *Music in the Twentieth Century: From Debussy to Stravinsky*. New York, 1966.

———. "Toward an Analytical Appreciation." In his edition of Claude Debussy's *"Prelude to the Afternoon of a Faun": An Authoritative Score; Mallarmé's Poem; Backgrounds and Sources; Criticism and Analysis*, 71–96. New York, 1970.

Babbitt, Milton. "Twelve-Tone Invariants as Compositional Determinants." *Musical Quarterly* 46, no. 2 (1960): 246–59.

———. "Who Cares if You Listen?" *High Fidelity Magazine* 8, no. 2 (1958): 38–40+.

Bailey, Robert, ed. Richard Wagner, *Prelude and Transfiguration from "Tristan and Isolde": Authoritative Scores; Historical Background; Sketches and Drafts; Views and Comments; Analytical Essays*. New York, 1985.

Balthazar, Scott L. "Intellectual History and Concepts of the Concerto: Some Parallels from 1750 to 1850." *Journal of the American Musicological Society* 36, no. 1 (1983): 39–72.

Bartlett, Frederic C. *Remembering: A Study in Experimental and Social Psychology*. New York, 1932. Reprint. Cambridge, 1967.

*Bartlett's Familiar Quotations*. Boston, 1968.

Barzun, Jacques. *Critical Questions: On Music and Letters, Culture and Biography, 1940–1980*. Selected, edited, and with an introduction by Bea Friedland. Chicago, 1982.

Bauer-Lechner, Natalie. *Recollections of Gustav Mahler*. Edited and annotated by Peter Franklin. Translated by Dika Newlin. London, 1980.

Bell, Clive. *Art*. London, 1949. Reprint. New York, 1958.

Benson, Lee, and Cushing Strout. "Causation and the American Civil War: Two Approaches." In *Studies in the Philosophy of History: Selected Essays from History and Theory*, edited by George H. Nadel, 74–96. New York, 1965.

Berlin, Isaiah. "The Concept of Scientific History." In *Philosophical Analysis and History*, edited by William Dray, 5–53. New York, 1966.

Berlioz, Hector. *Evenings with the Orchestra*. Translated and edited by Jacques Barzun. New York, 1956.

———. *Memoirs of Hector Berlioz*. Translated and edited by David Cairns. New York, 1969.

Berman, Laurence David. "The Evolution of Tonal Thinking in the Works of Claude Debussy." Ph.D. diss., Harvard University, 1965.

Bernal, J. D. *Science and Industry in the Nineteenth Century*. 2d ed. Bloomington, Ind., 1970.

Berry, Wallace. *Structural Functions in Music*. Englewood Cliffs, N.J. 1976.

Bevan, William. "The Welfare of Science in an Era of Change." *Science* 176 (1972): 990–96.

Black, Max. *Models and Metaphors: Studies in Language and Philosophy*. Ithaca, N.Y., 1962.

Blaukopf, Kurt, ed. and comp. *Mahler: A Documentary Study*. With contributions by Zoltan Roman. London, 1976.

Bloom, Allan. "The Education of Democratic Man: *Emile*." *Daedalus* 107, no. 3 (*Rousseau for Our Time*) (1978): 135–53.

Boulez, Pierre. "Schönberg is Dead." *The Score*, no. 6 (1952): 18–22.

Borges, Jorge Luis. *Labyrinths*. Selected and edited by Donald A. Yates and James E. Irby. New York, 1962.

Brodbeck, David Lee. "Brahms as Editor and Composer: His Two Editions of Ländler by Schubert and His First Two Cycles of Waltzes, Opera 39 and 52." Ph.D. diss., University of Pennsylvania, 1984.

Brown, Roger. "From the Viewpoint of Psychology." In *Style in Language,* edited by Thomas A. Sebeok, 378–85. Cambridge, Mass., 1960.

Browne, Richmond. "Tonal Implications of the Diatonic Set." *In Theory Only* 5, nos. 6 and 7 (double issue, 1981): 3–21.

Broyles, Michael. "Organic Form and the Binary Repeat." *The Musical Quarterly* 66, no. 3 (1980): 339–60.

Bunge, Mario. "The Metaphysics, Epistemology and Methodology of Levels." In *Hierarchical Structures,* edited by Lancelot Law Whyte, Albert G. Wilson, and Donna Wilson, 17–28. New York, 1969.

Burgers, J. M. "Causality and Anticipation." *Science* 189 (1975): 194–98.

Burk, John N. *The Life and Works of Beethoven.* New York, 1943.

Burke, Edmund. *A Philosophical Inquiry into the Origin of our Ideas of the Sublime and the Beautiful.* London, 1747.

Butler, David, and Helen Brown. "Tonal Structure versus Function: Studies of the Recognition of Harmonic Motion." *Music Perception* 2, no. 1 (1984): 6–24.

Cage, John. *Silence.* Middleton, Conn., 1961.

Cassirer, Ernst. *Rousseau, Kant, Goethe: Two Essays.* Translated by James Gotman, Paul Oskar Kristeller, and John Herman Randall, Jr. New York, 1963.

Cawelti, John G. *Adventure, Mystery, and Romance: Formula Stories as Art and Popular Culture.* Chicago, 1976.

———. *Apostles of the Self-Made Man.* Chicago, 1965.

Christensen, Louis. "Introduction to the Music of Gyorgy Ligeti." *Numus West* 2 (1972): 6–15.

Cloninger, Robert C. Review of *Cultural Transmission and Evolution* by L. L. Cavalli-Sforza and M. W. Feldman. In *Science,* Vol. 213 (1981): 858–59.

Cohen, I. Bernard. "The Newtonian Scientific Revolution and its Intellectual Significance: A Tercentenary Celebration of Isaac Newton's *Principia.*" *Bulletin of the American Academy of Arts and Sciences* 41, no. 3 (1987): 16–42.

Cohen, Morris R. *Reason and Nature.* Glencoe, Ill., 1964.

———. *The Meaning of Human History.* La Salle, Ill., 1947.

Conati, Marcello. *Interviews and Encounters with Verdi.* Translated by Richard Stokes, with a Foreword by Julian Budden. London, 1984.

Cone, Edward T. "Analysis Today." *Musical Quarterly* 6, no. 2 (1960): 172–88.

———. *Musical Form and Musical Performance.* New York, 1968.

———. "Schubert's Beethoven." *Musical Quarterly* 56, no. 4 (1970): 779–93.

———, ed. Hector Berlioz, *Fantastic Symphony: An Authentic Score; Historical Background; Analysis; Views and Comments.* New York, 1971.

Cooke, Deryck. *The Language of Music.* London, 1959.

Cooper, Grosvenor W., and Leonard B. Meyer. *The Rhythmic Structure of Music.* Chicago, 1960.

Cooper, Martin. *Beethoven: The Last Decade, 1817–1827.* With a Medical Appendix by Edward Larkin. London, 1985.

Coren, Daniel. "Inspiration and Calculation in the Genesis of Wagner's *Siegfried.*" In *Essays in Honor of Otto Albrecht: A Collection of Essays by his Colleagues and Former Students at the University of Pennsylvania,* edited by John Walter Hill, 266–87. Kassel, 1980.

Cotton, Jeffery. "Functional Sonority: A Reexamination of the *Tristan* Chord." Forthcoming.

Crocker, Richard L. *A History of Musical Style.* New York, 1966.

Culler, Jonathan. "Literary History, Allegory, and Semiology." *New Literary History* 7, no. 2 (1976): 259–70.

Czerny, Carl. *School of Practical Composition.* Translated by John Bishop. 3 vols. London, ca. 1848. Reprint. New York, 1979.

Dahlhaus, Carl. *Between Romanticism and Modernism: Four Studies in the Music of the Later Nineteenth Century.* Translated by Mary Whittall. Berkeley, 1980.

———. *Esthetics of Music.* Translated by William W. Austin. Cambridge, 1982.

———. *Richard Wagner's Music Dramas.* Translated by Mary Whittall. Cambridge, 1979.

Danto, Arthur C. *Analytic Philosophy of History.* Cambridge, 1965.

Darnton, Robert. *The Great Cat Massacre and Other Episodes in French Cultural History.* New York, 1984.

Dawkins, Richard. *The Selfish Gene.* Oxford, 1976.

Deutsch, Diana. "Tones and Numbers: Specificity of Interference in Immediate Memory." *Science* 168 (1970): 1604–5.

Dowling, W. Jay, and Dane L. Harwood. *Music Cognition.* Orlando, Fla., 1986.

Dray, William. " 'Explaining What' in History." In *Theories of History,* edited by Patrick Gardiner, 403–8. Glencoe, Ill., 1959.

———. *Philosophy of History.* Englewood Cliffs, N.J., 1964.

Dryden, John. Preface to "All for Love; or, The World Well Lost," edited by Maximillian E. Nowak, George R. Guffey, and Alan Roper. In vol. 13 of *The Works of John Dryden,* edited by Alan Roper and Vinton A. Derring, 10–19. Berkeley, 1984.

Ellis, John M. *The Theory of Literary Criticism: A Logical Analysis.* Berkeley, 1974.

Espy, Willard R. *An Almanac of Words at Play.* New York, 1953.

Fallon, Daniel. "Saint-Saëns and the *Concours de composition musicale* in Bordeaux." *Journal of the American Musicological Society* 31, no. 2 (1978): 309–25.

Featherstone, Joseph. "Rousseau and Modernity." *Daedalus* 107, no. 3 (*Rousseau for Our Time*) (1978): 167–92.

Feld, Steven. " 'Flow Like a Waterfall': The Metaphors of Kaluli Musical Theory." *Yearbook for Traditional Music* 13 (1981): 22–47.

Ferguson, Donald N. *Music as Metaphor: the Elements of Expression.* Minneapolis, 1960.

Ferguson, Eugene S. "The Mind's Eye: Nonverbal Thought in Technology." *Science* 197 (1977): 827–36.

Fisher, Stephen Carey. "Haydn's Overtures and their Adaptations as Concert Orchestral Works." Ph.D. diss., University of Pennsylvania, 1985.

Fraser, Antonia. *Mary Queen of Scots*. London, 1969.

Friedländer, Max J. *On Art and Connoisseurship*. 2d ed. Translated by Tancred Borenius. London, 1943.

Frisch, Walter. *Brahms and the Principle of Developing Variation*. Berkeley, 1984.

Frye, Northrop. *Anatomy of Criticism: Four Essays*. Princeton, 1957.

Garraty, John A., and Peter Gay, eds. *The Columbia History of the World*. New York, 1972.

Gay, Peter. *The Enlightenment: An Interpretation*. Vol. 1, *The Rise of Modern Paganism*. New York, 1966.

Gjerdingen, Robert O. *A Classic Turn of Phrase: Music and the Psychology of Convention*. Philadelphia, 1988.

Goldman, Albert, and Evert Sprinchorn, ed. *Wagner on Music and Drama: A Compendium of Richard Wagner's Prose Works*. Translated by H. Ashton Ellis. New York, 1964. Reprint. New York, 1981.

Gombrich, E. H. *Art and Illusion: A Study in the Psychology of Pictorial Representation*. New York, 1961.

———. "Criteria of Periodization in the History of European Art, III: A Comment on H. W. Janson's Article." *New Literary History* 1, no. 2 (*A Symposium on Periods*) (1970): 123–25.

———. "Style." In the *International Encyclopedia of the Social Sciences*, edited by David L. Sills, 15:352–61. New York, 1968.

Goodman, Nelson. *Languages of Art: An Approach to a Theory of Symbols*. Indianapolis, 1976.

———. "The Status of Style." *Critical Inquiry* 1, no. 4 (1975): 799–811.

Gossett, Philip. "Beethoven's Sixth Symphony: Sketches for the First Movement." *Journal of the American Musicological Society* 27, no. 2 (1974): 248–84.

———. "Gioachino Rossini and the Conventions of Composition." *Acta Musicologica* 42, fasc. 1–2 (1970): 48–58.

———. "Verdi, Ghislanzoni, and *Aida:* the Uses of Convention." *Critical Inquiry* 1, no. 1 (1974): 291–334.

Gould, Stephen Jay. *Ever Since Darwin: Reflections in Natural History*. New York, 1977.

———. *The Panda's Thumb: More Reflections in Natural History*. New York, 1980.

Grout, Donald Jay. *A History of Western Music*. 2d ed. New York, 1973.

Hanson, Norwood Russell. *Patterns of Discovery: An Inquiry into the Conceptual Foundations of Science*. Cambridge, 1958.

Heartz, Daniel. "Raaff's Last Aria: A Mozartian Idyll in the Spirit of Hasse." *Musical Quarterly* 40, no. 4 (1974): 517–43.

Hermerén, Göran. *Influence in Art and Literature*. Princeton, 1975.

Hexter, J. H. *Reappraisals in History: New Views on History and Society in Early Modern Europe*. New York, 1963.

Hiebert, Erwin N. Review of *Historical Studies in the Physical Sciences: Vol. 1,* edited by Russell McCormmach. *Science* 168 (1970): 735–36.

Hindemith, Paul. *The Craft of Musical Composition. Book 1: Theoretical Part.* Translated by Arthur Mendel. New York, 1942.

Hoijer, Harry. "The Relation of Language to Culture." In *Anthropology Today: An Encyclopedic Inventory,* edited by A. L. Kroeber, 554–73. Chicago, 1953.

Hopkins, Robert George. "Secondary Parameters and Closure in the Symphonies of Gustav Mahler." Ph.D. diss., University of Pennsylvania, 1983.

Hospers, John. "Philosophy of Art." *The New Encyclopedia Britannica,* 15th ed., 2:40–56. Chicago, 1974.

Hueffer, Francis, trans. *Correspondence of Wagner and Liszt.* Vol. 2, *1854–1861.* Rev. ed. by W. Ashton Ellis. London, 1897.

Hughes, David G. *A History of European Music: The Art Music Tradition of Western Culture.* Chapter appendixes compiled by Thomas F. Kelly. Illustrations selected by Mary R. Rasmussen. New York, 1974.

Hugo, Victor. "Preface to *Cromwell.*" Translated by George Burnham Ives. In *European Theories of the Drama,* edited by Barrett H. Clark, newly revised by Henry Popkin, 357–70. New York, 1965.

Hyman, Ray. Review of *The Processing of Information and Structure,* by Wendell R. Garner. *Science* 186 (1974): 730–31.

Jacob, François. *The Logic of Life: A History of Heredity.* Translated by Betty E. Spillman. New York, 1973.

———. *The Possible and the Actual.* New York, 1982.

Jameson, Fredric. *The Prison-House of Language: A Critical Account of Structuralism and Russian Formalism.* Princeton, 1972.

Jander, Owen. "Beethoven's 'Orpheus in Hades': The *Andante con moto* of the Fourth Piano Concerto." *19th-Century Music* 8, no. 3 (1985): 195–212.

Johnson, Douglas. "Beethoven Scholars and Beethoven's Sketches." *19th-Century Music* 2, no. 1 (1978): 3–17.

Jordan, R. Furneaux. *A Concise History of Western Architecture.* London, 1969.

Kagan, Jerome J.; Steven Reznick; and Nancy Snidman. "Biological Bases of Childhood Shyness." *Science* 240 (1988): 167–71.

Kerman, Joseph. "An die ferne Geliebte." In *Beethoven Studies,* edited by Alan Tyson, 123–57. New York, 1973.

———. *The Beethoven Quartets.* New York, 1967.

———. "Notes on Beethoven's Codas." In *Beethoven Studies 3,* edited by Alan Tyson, 141–59. London, 1982.

———. "Wagner and Wagnerism." *The New York Review of Books* 30 (22 Dec. 1983): 27.

Kindleberger, Charles P. Review of *The Great Transformation,* by Karl Polanyi. *Daedalus* 103, no. 1 (*Twentieth-Century Classics Revisited*) (1974): 45–52.

Kirby, Frank E. "Beethoven's Pastoral Symphony as a *Simfonia caracteristica.*" *Musical Quarterly* 56, no. 4 (1970): 605–23.

Kohler, Robert E. Review of *Perspectives on the Emergence of Scientific Disciplines,* edited by Gérard Lemaine et al. *Science* 199 (1978): 1196–97.

Kollmann, August Frederic Christopher. *An Essay on Practical Musical Composition.* London, 1799. Reprint. New York, 1975.

Kracauer, Siegfried. *History: The Last Things Before the First.* New York, 1969.

———. "Time and History." *History and the Concept of Time.* Special issue of *History and Theory,* suppl. 6 (1966): 65–78.

Krenek, Ernst. "Tradition in Perspective." *Perspectives of New Music* 1, no. 1 (1962): 27–38.

Kristeller, Paul Oskar. "Renaissance Platonism." In *Facets of the Renaissance,* edited by William H. Werkmeister, 103–23. New York, 1963.

Kubler, George. *The Shape of Time: Remarks on the History of Things.* New Haven, 1962.

Labrousse, C. E. "The Crisis in the French Economy at the End of the Old Regime." In *Economic Origins of the French Revolution: Poverty or Prosperity?* edited and translated by Ralph W. Greenlaw, 59–72. Boston, 1958.

La Grange, Henry-Louis de. *Mahler.* Vol. 1. New York, 1973.

Lakoff, George, and Mark Johnson. *Metaphors We Live By.* Chicago, 1980.

La Mara, ed. *Letters of Franz Liszt.* Translated by Constance Bache. London, 1894.

LaRue, Jan. *Guidelines for Style Analysis.* New York, 1970.

Le Huray, Peter, and James Day. *Music and Aesthetics in the Eighteenth and Early-Nineteenth Centuries.* Cambridge, 1981.

Lenneberg, Hans. "The Myth of the Unappreciated (Musical) Genius." *Musical Quarterly* 66, no. 2 (1980): 219–31.

Levy, Janet M. *Beethoven's Compositional Choices: The Two Versions of Op. 18, No. 1, First Movement.* Philadelphia, 1982.

———. "Covert and Casual Values in Recent Writings About Music." *Journal of Musicology* 5, no. 1 (1987): 3–27.

———. "Gesture, Form, and Syntax in Haydn's Music." In *Haydn Studies: Proceedings of the International Haydn Conference; Washington, D.C., 1975,* edited by Jens Peter Larsen, Howard Serwer, and James Webster, 355–62. New York, 1981.

———. "Texture as a Sign in Classic and Early Romantic Music." *Journal of the American Musicological Society* 35, no. 3 (1982): 482–531.

Lewin, Roger. "Is Sexual Selection a Burden?" *Science* 226 (1984): 526–27.

———. "Seeds of Change in Embryonic Development." *Science* 214 (1981): 42–44.

Liszt, Franz. *Life of Chopin.* Translated by John Broadhouse. London, n.d.

Lloyd-Jones, David. Notes to Rimsky-Korsakov's *Capriccio Espagnol.* Eulenberg No. 842.

Lord, Albert B. *The Singer of Tales.* Cambridge, Mass., 1960.

Lovejoy, Arthur O. *The Great Chain of Being: A Study of the History of an Idea.* Cambridge, Mass., 1966.

McAllester, David P. "Indian Music in the Southwest." In *Readings in Ethno-musicology,* edited by David P. McAllester, 215–26. New York, 1971.

McClary, Susan Kaye. "The Transition from Modal to Tonal Organization in the Works of Monteverdi." Ph.D. diss., Harvard University, 1976.

Malraux, André. "The Triumph of Art over History." In *The Modern Tradition: Backgrounds of Modern Literature,* edited by Richard Ellmann and Charles Feidelson, Jr., 514–22. New York, 1965.

Margenau, Henry. "Meaning and Scientific Status of Causality." In *Philosophy of Science,* edited by Arthur Danto and Sidney Morgenbesser. New York, 1964.

Mayr, Ernst. "Biological Classification: Toward a Synthesis of Opposing Methodologies." *Science* 214 (1981): 510–16.

Meyer, Leonard B. "Concerning the Sciences, the Arts—AND the Humanities." *Critical Inquiry* 1, no. 1 (1974): 163–217.

———. *Emotion and Meaning in Music.* Chicago, 1956.

———. *Explaining Music: Essays and Explorations.* Chicago, 1973.

———. "Exploiting Limits: Creation, Archetypes, and Style Change." *Daedalus* 109, no. 2 (1980): 177–205.

———. "Grammatical Simplicity and Relational Richness: The Trio of Mozart's G Minor Symphony." *Critical Inquiry* 2, no. 4 (1975): 693–761.

———. *Music, the Arts, and Ideas: Patterns and Predictions in Twentieth-Century Culture.* Chicago, 1967.

———. "Process and Morphology in the Music of Mozart." *The Journal of Musicology* 1, no. 1 (1982): 317–41.

Miles, Josephine. "Values in Language; or, Where Have *Goodness, Truth,* and *Beauty* Gone?" *Critical Inquiry* 3, no. 1 (1976): 1–13.

Miller, Dorothy C., ed. *Fifteen Americans.* New York, 1952.

Miller, George A. "The Magical Number Seven, Plus or Minus Two: Some Limits on Our Capacity for Processing Information." *Psychological Review* 63, no. 2 (1956): 81–97.

Mitchell, Donald. *Gustav Mahler: The Wunderhorn Years: Chronicle and Commentaries.* Boulder, Colo., 1976.

Mitchell, William J. "The Tristan Prelude: Techniques and Structure." In *The Music Forum,* edited by William J. Mitchell and Felix Salzer, 1:162–203. New York, 1967.

Morgan, Robert P. "On the Analysis of Recent Music." *Critical Inquiry* 4, no. 1 (1977): 33–53.

Moyer, Birgitte Plesner Vinding. "Concepts of Musical Form in the Nineteenth Century: With Special Reference to A. B. Marx and Sonata Form." Ph.D. diss., Stanford University, 1969.

Murphy, George G. S. "On Counterfactual Propositions." *History and Theory,* suppl. 9:14–38, 1969.

Nagel, Ernest. *Principles of the Theory of Probability.* In *The International Encyclopedia of Unified Science.* 1, no. 6. edited by Otto Neurath. Chicago, 1939.

Narmour, Eugene. *Beyond Schenkerism: The Need for Alternatives in Music Analysis.* Chicago, 1977.

―――. "The Melodic Structure of Tonal Music: A Theoretical Study." Ph.D. diss., University of Chicago, 1974.

Newcomb, Anthony. "The Birth of Music out of the Spirit of the Drama: An Essay in Wagnerian Formal Analysis." *19th-Century Music* 5, no. 1 (1981): 38–66.

Newman, William S. *The Sonata in the Classic Era: The Second Volume of a History of the Sonata Idea.* 2d ed. New York, 1972.

―――. *The Sonata Since Beethoven.* 3d ed. New York, 1983.

Nisbet, Robert A. *Social Change and History: Aspects of the Western Theory of Development.* New York, 1969.

Ogg, David. *Europe in the Seventeenth Century.* 8th ed. London, 1960.

Ortega y Gasset, José. "History as a System." In *Philosophy and History: Essays Presented to Ernst Cassirer,* edited by Raymond Klibansky and H. J. Paton, 283–322. Oxford, 1936. Reprint. New York, 1963.

Osgood, Charles E. "Some Effects of Motivation on Style of Encoding." In *Style in Language,* edited by Thomas A. Sebeok, 293–306. Cambridge, Mass., 1960.

Parry, C. Hubert H. "Sonata." In *Grove's Dictionary of Music and Musicians,* edited by J. A. Fuller Maitland, 4:504–35. 2d ed. London, 1908. Reprint. Philadelphia, 1926.

Piston, Walter. *Harmony.* 3d ed. New York, 1962.

Plantinga, Leon. *Schumann as Critic.* New Haven, Conn., 1967.

Platoff, John. "Music and Drama in the *Opera Buffa* Finale: Mozart and His Contemporaries in Vienna, 1781–1790." Ph.D. diss., University of Pennsylvania, 1984.

Polanyi, Michael. *Personal Knowledge: Toward a Post-Critical Philosophy.* Chicago, 1958.

Porter, Andrew. "Notes on *Le Nozze di Figaro.*" *Lincoln Center Stagebill* 13, no. 4 (1985).

Posner, Michael I., and Steven W. Keele. "On the Genesis of Abstract Ideas." *Journal of Experimental Psychology* 77, no. 3 (1968): 353–63.

Rabinowitz, Peter J. "Fictional Music: Toward a Theory of Listening," edited by Harry R. Garvin. *Bucknell Review* 26, no. 1 (*Theories of Reading, Looking, and Listening*) (1981): 193–208.

Ratner, Leonard G. "*Ars Combinatoria:* Choice and Chance in Eighteenth-Century Music." In *Studies in Eighteenth-Century Music: A Tribute to Karl Geiringer on his Seventieth Birthday,* edited by H. C. Robbins Landon and Roger Chapman, 343–63. London, 1970.

―――. *Classic Music: Expression, Form, and Style.* New York, 1980.

―――. *Harmony: Structure and Style.* New York, 1962.

Raynor, Henry. *Music and Society Since 1815.* London, 1976.

Rieff, Philip. *Freud: The Mind of the Moralist.* New York, 1959.

Roberts, John H. "Handel's Borrowings from Keiser." *Göttinger Händel-Beiträge* 2 (1986): 51–76.

———. "Handel's Borrowings from Telemann: An Inventory." *Göttinger Händel-Beiträge* 1 (1984): 147–71.

Rolf, Marie. "The Emergence of the Symbolist Aesthetic in 'En sourdine.'" Paper read at the 51st Annual Meeting of the American Musicological Society, Vancouver, 1985.

Rosen, Charles. *The Classical Style.* New York, 1971.

———. *Sonata Forms.* New York, 1980.

———. "Verdi Victorious." *New York Review of Books* 30, no. 16 (Oct. 27, 1983): 33–41.

Rosen, Charles, and Henry Zerner. "The Permanent Revolution." *New York Review of Books* 26, no. 17 (Nov. 22, 1979): 23–30.

Rosner, Burton, and Leonard B. Meyer. "Melodic Processes and the Perception of Music." In *The Psychology of Music,* edited by Diana Deutsch, 317–41. New York, 1982.

Rothfarb, Lee Allen. *Ernst Kurth as Theorist and Analyst.* Philadelphia, 1988.

Rothstein, Edward. "The Shapes of Sounds." Review of *Sonata Forms,* by Charles Rosen. *The New York Times Book Review,* 21 Dec. 1980, 17.

Rumelhart, David E. "Schemata: The Building Blocks of Cognition." In *Theoretical Issues in Reading Comprehension: Perspectives from Cognitive Psychology, Linguistics, Artificial Intelligence, and Education,* edited by Rand J. Spiro, Bertram C. Bruce, and William F. Brewer. Hillsdale, N.J., 1980.

Sadie, Stanley, ed. *The New Grove Dictionary of Music and Musicians.* 20 vols. London, 1980.

Salzer, Felix. *Structural Hearing.* 2 vols. New York, 1962.

Schank, Roger C., and Robert Abelson. *Scripts, Plans, Goals and Understanding: An Inquiry into Human Knowledge Structures.* Hillsdale, N.J., 1977.

Schapiro, Meyer. "Style." In *Anthropology Today: An Encyclopedic Inventory,* edited by A. L. Kroeber, 287–312. Chicago, 1953.

Schoenberg, Arnold. *Style and Idea.* Translated and edited by Dika Newlin. New York, 1950.

———. *Theory of Harmony.* Translated by Roy E. Carter. Berkeley, 1978.

Schorske, Carl E. *Fin-de-Siècle Vienna: Politics and Culture.* New York, 1980.

Searle, John R. *Speech Acts: An Essay in the Philosophy of Language.* Cambridge, 1969.

Sessions, Roger. *Harmonic Practice.* New York, 1951.

Shaw, George Bernard. *The Perfect Wagnerite: A Commentary on the Niblungs Ring.* 4th ed. London, 1923. Reprint. New York, 1967.

Shklar, Judith N. "Jean-Jacques Rousseau and Equality." *Daedalus* 107, no. 3 (*Rousseau for Our Time*) (1978): 13–25.

Simon, Herbert A. "The Architecture of Complexity." *Proceedings of the American Philosophical Society* 106, no. 6 (1962): 467–82.

———. "How Big is a Chunk?" *Science* 183 (1974): 482–88.

———. *Models of Thought.* New Haven, 1979.

Skinner, B. F. "Selection by Consequences." *Science* 213 (1981): 501–4.

Smith, Barbara Herrnstein. *On the Margins of Discourse: The Relation of Literature to Language*. Chicago, 1978.

Sneath, Peter H. A., and Robert R. Sokal. *Numerical Taxonomy: The Principles and Practice of Numerical Classification*. San Francisco, 1973.

Sokal, Robert R. "Classification: Purposes, Principles, Progress, Prospects." *Science* 185 (1974): 1115–1123.

Solie, Ruth A. "The Living Work: Organicism and Musical Analysis." *19th-Century Music* 4, no. 2 (1980): 147–56.

———. *Metaphor and Model in the Analysis of Melody*. Ph.D. diss., University of Chicago, 1977.

Solomon, Maynard. *Beethoven*. New York, 1977.

Stein, Deborah. "The Expansion of the Subdominant in the Late Nineteenth Century." *Journal of Music Theory* 27, no. 2 (1983): 153–80.

Stein, Erwin. "Musical Thought: Beethoven and Schoenberg." In his *Orpheus in New Guises,* 90–95. London, 1953.

Stein, Jack M. *Richard Wagner and the Synthesis of the Arts*. Rev. ed. Detroit, 1973.

Stencel, Robert; Fred Gifford; and Eleanor Morón. "Astronomy and Cosmology at Angkor Wat." *Science* 193 (1976): 281–87.

Stent, Gunther S. *The Coming of the Golden Age: A View of the End of Progress*. Garden City, N.Y., 1969.

Storr, Anthony. "Kafka's Sense of Identity." In *Paths and Labyrinths: Nine Papers Read at the Franz Kafka Symposium Held at the Institute of Germanic Studies on 20 and 21 October 1983,* edited by J. P. Sterne and J. J. White, 1–24. London, 1985.

Stravinsky, Igor. *Poetics of Music in the Form of Six Lessons*. Translated by Arthur Knodel and Ingolf Dahl. New York, 1970.

Strunk, Oliver, ed. *Source Readings in Music History: From Classical Antiquity through the Romantic Era*. New York, 1950.

Subotnick, Rose Rosengard. "The Cultural Message of Musical Semiology: Some Thoughts on Music, Language, and Criticism since the Enlightenment." *Critical Inquiry* 4, no. 4 (1978): 741–68.

Swift, Richard. "Mahler's Ninth and Cooke's Tenth." Review of Gustav Mahler, *IX. Symphonie. Partiturentwurf der ersten drei Sätze. Faksimile nach der Handschrift,* edited by Erwin Ratz, and *A Performing Edition of the Draft for the Tenth Symphony,* prepared by Deryck Cooke et al. *19th-Century Music* 2, no. 2 (1978): 165–72.

Sýkora, Václav Jan. Preface to *36 Fugues for the Piano,* by Antonín Rejcha. Translated by Margaret Bent. 3 vols. Kassel, 1973.

Thayer, Alexander Wheelock. *The Life and Works of Beethoven*. New York, 1964.

Thibaut, Anton F. J. *On Purity in Musical Art*. Translated by W. H. Gladstone. London, 1877.

Thomson, William. "Style Analysis: Or the Perils of Pigeonholes." *Journal of Music Theory* 14, no. 2 (1970): 191–208.

Treitler, Leo. "Methods, Style, Analysis." In *Report of the Eleventh Congress of the International Musicological Society, Copenhagen 1972*, edited by Henrik Glahn, Søren Sørensen, and Peter Ryom, 1:61–70. Copenhagen, 1974.

———. "Harmonic Procedure in the *Fourth Quartet* of Bela Bartók." *Journal of Music Theory* 3, no. 2 (1959): 292–98.

Trilling, Lionel. "Manners, Morals, and the Novel." *Kenyon Review* 10, no. 1 (1948): 11–27.

Walsh, W. H. *Philosophy of History: An Introduction*. New York, 1960.

Weber, William. "Learned and General Musical Taste in Eighteenth-Century France." *Past and Present*, no. 89 (1980): 55–85.

Webern, Anton. *The Path to the New Music*. Edited by Willi Reich. Translated by Leo Black. Bryn Mawr, Pa., 1963.

Webster, James. "Schubert's Sonata Form and Brahms's First Maturity." Part 1. *19th-Century Music* 2, no. 1 (1978): 18–35. Part 2. *19th-Century Music* 3, no. 1 (1979): 52–71.

Wedgwood, C. V. "The Division Hardens." In *The Reformation Crisis*, edited by Joel Hurstfield, 107–18. London, 1965. Reprint. New York, 1966.

———. "The Futile and Meaningless War." In *The Thirty Years' War: Problems of Motive, Extent, and Effect*, edited by Theodore K. Rabb, 9–19. Boston, 1964.

———. *Truth and Opinion: Historical Essays*. New York, 1960.

Weintraub, Karl. *Visions of Culture*. Chicago, 1966.

Weisskopf, Victor F. "Physics in the Twentieth Century." *Science* 168 (1970): 923–30.

Wellek, René, and Austin Warren. *Theory of Literature*. 3d ed. New York, 1970.

Westergaard, Peter. "On the Notion of Style." In *Report of the Eleventh Congress of the International Musicological Society, Copenhagen 1972*, edited by Henrik Glahn, Søren Sørensen, and Peter Ryom, 1:71–74. Copenhagen, 1974.

Westfall, Richard S. "Newton and the Fudge Factor." *Science* 179 (1973): 751–58.

White, Hayden. *Metahistory: The Historical Imagination in Nineteenth-Century Europe*. Baltimore, Md., 1973.

Wimsatt, William K., Jr., and Cleanth Brooks. *Literary Criticism: A Short History*. New York, 1962.

Winters, Thomas Dyer. "Additive and Repetitive Techniques in the Experimental Works of Charles Ives." Ph.D. diss., University of Pennsylvania, 1986.

Woodmansee, Martha. "The Interests of Disinterestedness: Karl Philipp Moritz and the Emergence of the Theory of Aesthetic Autonomy in Eighteenth-Century Germany." *Modern Language Quarterly* 45, no. 1 (1984): 22–47.

Wright, Anthony A.; Hector C. Santiago; Stephen F. Sands; Donald F. Kendrick; and Robert G. Cook. "Memory Processing of Serial Lists by Pigeons, Monkeys and People." *Science* 229 (1985): 287–89.

# INDEX

The name of a composer is indexed only if a specific composition is referred to in the text. Italics indicate that a musical example occurs on the page.

Abelson, Robert P., 245
Abraham, Gerald, 212
Abrams, Meyer L., 169n, 189, 190n, 192n, 203
Absolute music, Romantics value, 166
Ackerman, James S., 43
Acontextualism: and aesthetics, 170–83; formalism and, 170 (see also Formalism); genius and, 170–71 (see also Genius); and history, 167–70 (see also Change); represented in art, 184–87; in twentieth-century music, 339–47 passim. See also Egalitarianism; Romanticism, ideology of
Adeste Fidelis schema [Exx. 1.1b, 2.1, 2.2, 7.42]: Baroque and Classic instantiations of, 51–54; described, 51; other schemata combine with, 39n; uncommon in Romantic music, 266
Agawu, Kofi, 307n
Aleatory music, style, choice and, 34–35
Alger, Horatio, 184, 187
Allanbrook, Wye Jamison, 215n, 236n
Analogic modeling, as source of innovation, 131–33
André, Yves Marie, 191
Apotheosis, 204–5, 267–68, 323. See also Climax, statistical
Appoggiatura(s): musical process clarified by, 266, 321; prevalence in Romantic music, 264;

syntactic ambiguity of long, 281–83, 295; tension, discord and, 278
Arauco, Ingrid, 55n
Arensky, Anton, 288–289
Artz, Frederick B., 164n, 221n
Ashley, Maurice, 75n
Auden, W. H., 140
Audience: egalitarian, 171, 179, 182, 202, 205, and 210; sophistication of, 208–17. See also Egalitarianism
Auspitz, Katherine, 164n
Austin, William W., 140, 280–81
Authentication, style analysis and, 61–63
Authentic editions, Romanticism and, 193–94n
Authority, Romanticism repudiates, 165; Chap. 6 passim
Axial schema [Exx. 7.11, 7.21–23]: chosen by Romantic composers, 244; instantiations of, 242–43; mediant changing-note schema and, 241–42; prevalent in Romantic music, 241; syntax and, 242, 244–45
Axiom of constancy: choice, envisaging and, 88–90; reason for theorizing, 89

Babbitt, Milton, 345–46, 347
Bach, Johann Sebastian, 52, 53, 54, 55–56, 132, 151, 153, 273, 290, 317–18
Bailey, Robert, 282n, 311n
Balthazar, Scott L., 64n, 121n
Bartlett, Frederic C., 50n
Bartók, Béla, 55, 147, 340
Barzun, Jacques, 350
Batteux, Charles, 326n
Bauer-Lechner, Natalie, 204n
Becker, Constantin Julius, 193

Becoming: continuousness of, 199; emergent structure and, 198 (see also Emergence); historical necessity and, 200 (see also Necessity); important in Romanticism, 197, 264, 326; secondary parameters foster, 324–25; uniformity fosters, 274. See also Openness
Beethoven, Ludwig van, 17n, 22, 25, 52, 53, 55, 90n, 124–25, 127, 141, 147, 151, 154, 228–29, 230, 232, 235, 236–37, 247–248, 249, 264–65, 273, 285, 291n, 298–299, 320, 333
Bell, Clive, 188
Benson, Lee, 75, 93
Berg, Alban, 41, 324n, 339
Berlin, Isaiah, 86n, 91, 93
Berlioz, Hector, 47n, 131, 152, 181, 219, 222, 269n, 276n, 278
Berman, Laurence, 280–81
Bernal, J. D., 115, 116
Berry, Wallace, 210n
Bevan, William, 85n
Black, Max, 137
Blaukopf, Kurt, 192n
Bloom, Allan, 165
Borges, Jorge Luis, 138
Borodin, Alexander, 287n, 288n
Borrowing: and style analysis, 55–56; in twentieth-century music, 348–49
Brahms, Johannes, 127, 141, 152, 177n, 204, 243–44, 252, 254n, 262, 268, 287, 292–93, 324n, 329n, 333, 335n
Brodbeck, David Lee, 177n, 204n
Brooks, Cleanth, 163n
Brown, Helen, 275n
Brown, Roger, 61
Browne, Richmond, 275n
Broyles, Michael, 307n

Consonance/dissonance. *See* Concord/discord

Constancy. *See* Axiom of constancy

Constraints: choice and (*see* Choice); cultural, need for, 9, 157, 349; function as sets, 43–44, 141, 144; as hierarchy, 13–23 (*see also* Laws; Rules; Strategies); ideological, translated into musical, 99–100, 218–19; inferred from behavior, 12–13; interaction between, 8–9, 20–21, 112–13, 115–16; nature of, 3, 8–10; parametric autonomy of, 97–98, 114–16. *See also* Constraints, compositional; Convention; Ideology; Style

Constraints, compositional: change of (*see* Innovation); choice of (*see* Choice, compositional); devising novel, 122–34 (*see also* Innovation, sources of); exemplary works disseminate, 151; expression depends on, 344; external, 111–22, 152–60; function as sets, 45, 141–42, 150; goals implicit in, 36, 100–101, 136; hierarchy of, 13–23, 32–33; ideology translated into, 99–100, 155–56, 218–19; knowledge of, 10, 12, 351; learned, 10; natural, valued, 168, 171, 173–77, 189; need for, 212, 337–39; plans versus scripts as, 245–57, 303–11; prevalence of, 23–30 (*see also* Dialect; Idiom; Intraopus style); replication of, 139–42, 150–52 (*see also* Replication); in Romantic music (*see* Romanticism, music of); rules and, 17–19 (*see also* Rules); strategies and, 20–23 (*see also* Strategies); transmission of, 120–22; in twentieth-century music, 337–38, 342, 346–51; variable over time and place, 49. *See also* Form, statistical; Form, syntactic; Motivic relationships; Syntax (tonal)

Convention: absence of syntax emphasizes, 278; human need for, 249; individuality and originality depend on, 219–20; and parody, 222; repudiation of, and unity, 201, 327; Romanticism repudiates, 164–67, 176, 184–85, 219–20; Stravinsky's use of, 347f. *See also* Constraints; Convention disguised

Convention disguised: through di-

vergence, 226–41 (*see also* Changing-note schema, mediant version; Changing-note schema, tonic version); through emergence, 223–26; through fiction, 169; in twentieth-century music, 349

Cooke, Deryck, 210n.

Cooper, Grosvenor W., 278n

Cooper, Martin, 90n

Coren, Daniel, 180n, 181

Cotton, Jeffery, 284n

Counterfactuals, 74–75, 86

Covert causalism, 143, 148

Creativity, choosing important for, 142. (*See also* Innovation; Originality

Criticism: style and, 31–32, 34–35; of twentieth-century music, 345. *See also* Evaluation; Formalism

Crocker, Richard L., 44n, 79n

Culler, Jonathan, 166n

Culture: analysis of, 9; changes in, and parametric differentiation, 116–19; and style analysis, 45; and style change, 112–16, 119–22

Czerny, Carl, 202, 203

Dahlhaus, Carl, 45n, 133, 185–88, 192n, 271, 282–84, 335n, 336n

Danto, Arthur C., 72

Darnton, Robert, 169n

David, Jacques Louis, 169n

Dawkins, Richard, 44

Debussy, Claude, 223–24, 269–70, 273–74, 280–81

Deceptive cadences: Classic vs. Romantic use of 296–97; in Wagner, 46–47. *See also* Modulation

"Deep" structure: organicism emphasizes, 194–95; in twentieth-century thought, 195

Deutsch, Diana, 232n

Developing variation: constraints governing, problematic, 332–36; organicism and, 334–35; syntactification and, 336, 338

Dialect (musical): nature of, 23; strategies and, 23–24

Dialectic, music as, 134, 203, 308–9

Dice games, musical: 193; syntactic function and, 329

Disguise through divergence, 226–41. *See also* Changing-note schema, mediant version; Changing-note schema, tonic version

Disguise through emergence, 223–26, 232; Romanticism values, 198–99, 225

Displacement: and migration, 124; as mode of innovation, 124–25

Donizetti, Gaetano, 276, 277–78

Dowling, W. Jay, 346n

Dray, William, 82n, 86–87

Dryden, John, 176

Dvořák, Antonin, 227n, 288n

Economy: Romanticism values, 194, 331; in twentieth-century music, 341–42

Egalitarianism: acontextualism and, 167–88 passim; audience of, 171, 179, 182, 205, 210; and avant garde music, 347; in belief, not behavior, 183; central to Romanticism, 182; children and, 174–75; and desire for distinction, 183; and formalism, 188; genius and, 170–75; gradual change valued in, 168, 171–72, 330; hierarchies rejected in, 178–80; history and, 170; implied structure and, 325; represented in art, 183–87; and Romantic love, 186–87; statistical Climax symptom of, 204–5, 206, 322–25, 330. *See also* Romanticism, ideology of

Ellis, John M., 36, 87n

Emergence: disguise through, 223–26, 232; Romanticism values, 198–99, 225

Emotions: represented, vs. feelings expressed, 221; social nature of, 221. *See also* Expression; Feeling

Enlightenment, character of, 165

Envisaging, choice depends on, 89–90

Espy, Willard R., 58

Evaluation: aleatory music and, 34; and implied structure, 33; style and, 32–36

Exemplary works: culture identifies, 151; disseminate innovation, 151

Explanation, historical: causal, 78–79, 82; hypotheses required for, 69, 77–79; in music, 98–101; noncausal, 80, 82–84, 96–97; nontemporal, 79–83; temporal, 83–86. *See also* Historical accounts; History of music/style; Implication

Expression, dependent on convention, 213–14, 220, 257, 259–60. *See also* Convention; Individuality

# INDEX OF MUSICAL EXAMPLES

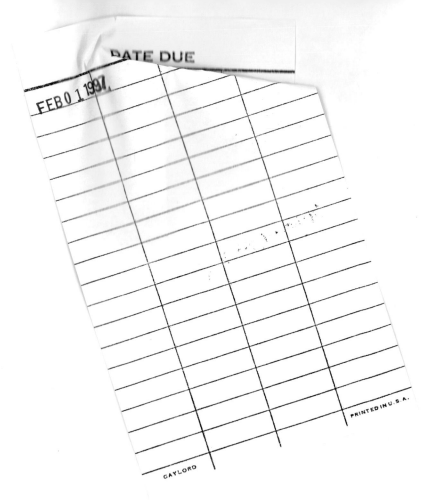

DATE DUE

FEB 0 1 1997

PRINTED IN U.S.A.

GAYLORD